A Guide's Guide to Philadelphia

By Julie P. Curson

CURSON HOUSE, INC.
Philadelphia

Note·

Things happen fast in Philadelphia, so there might be some changes since this book came out. Inflation is also a factor. Federal and municipal budget cuts have caused many temporary (and, unfortunately, some permanent) limits on staff and facilities resulting in changes of hours an attraction is open. If you're going to a particular place, call ahead to be sure it will be open.

An **asterisk** (*) indicates that the same place or event appears elsewhere in the book with more details. You'll find that place in the **Index**.

For Harry A. Pontz

And for my friends who gave me
their support and encouragement
to finish this fifth edition.

ISBN 0-913694-05-3
Library of Congress Catalogue Card Number: 86-071145
Printed in the United States of America
First Edition, First Printing — March 1973
First Edition, Second Printing — July 1973
Second Edition — January 1975
Third Edition — February 1978
Fourth Edition — March 1982
Fifth Edition — September 1986

Typography by rci Services, Inc.
Illustrations by Wally Neibart.
Front cover photograph by Joseph Nettis.
Back cover photograph by Shelly Roseman.
Maps by SANCHEZ.

Contents

Maps

INTRODUCTION

The past decade has given Philadelphia many reasons to celebrate. The nation's bicentennial was celebrated here in 1976. The city's tricentennial was celebrated in 1982. And now we celebrate the bicentennial of the Constitution of the United States.

Each of these occasions has been just cause for a new edition of *A Guide's Guide to Philadelphia*.

But a special occasion is just one reason to write a guidebook. For Philadelphia, there are many, many reasons. So here's my fifth edition.

Philadelphia is a city of history worth knowing and exploring.

Philadelphia is a city with great culture. There are probably more major museums and cultural organizations here than anywhere in the country.

Philadelphia is a city with a major league team for every major sport, and Philadelphians are highly supportive and vocal fans. It's a city with ethnic diversity, a melting pot for a multitude of nationalities.

Philadelphia is a city with three flowing waterways and a major port. It's a city with the largest municipally maintained park in the world.

And it's a city with a promising future.

Redevelopment moves at a rapid pace. Old neighborhoods are reborn. Dilapidated buildings are being converted to dramatic new uses. New buildings are changing the city's skyline.

Creative new restaurants prosper along with the tried and true, and Philadelphia has justifiably gained a national reputation as a "restaurant city." Over 200 restaurants are described in Chapter 18.

This fifth edition of *A Guide's Guide to Philadelphia* brings you up-to-date on everything that's happening in Philadelphia. It tells you about attractions and events for everyone, the young and the old, families and groups, tourists and natives. The comments are mine, and I tried to be honest and objective.

If something is overlooked, or if you have any comments, please write to me. Address all correspondence to: Julie P. Curson, 250 South 18th Street, Philadelphia, Pennsylvania 19103.

Have fun!

Julie P. Curson

Capsule Summary Code

Every attraction in this book has a capsule summary of information that you need to know. This is what you should look for.

NAME OF ATTRACTION
Address with Philadelphia ZIP code
Telephone (area code 215, unless noted otherwise)

Hours: Opening and closing times for you to visit on your own and with no specially planned guided tour. The amount of time you should allow for a visit (not including time you might have to wait).

Tours: Regularly scheduled or specially arranged guided tours for individuals or groups; the group procedures, restrictions and method of reservations. How long will your tour be? In some cases, Philadelphia Public School teachers can make special arrangements, and this will be indicated here. In some instances, it's necessary to write or call in advance, even though you're not requesting or getting a specially planned guided tour.

Cost: How much is the admission? To get group rates, sometimes it's necessary to call ahead, and it's always better if one person pays for the entire group. Sometimes it's required. Information about membership plans.

Lunch: This information is provided when facilities are available.

SEPTA: These are the routes that go closest to the attraction. If you're not sure how to get there, call SEPTA at 574-7800.

Other: Gift shops, programs and special events are listed here. Also any unusual suggestions or requests.

E & H: This is information especially for the elderly or handicapped. It includes wheelchair accessibility, indication of steps and excessive walking, or anything else that might hinder or help you to plan and take the tour. Special facilities for the blind and deaf are included where available. More information is in Chapter 16.

Chapter 1.
Transportation and Tours.

Philadelphia

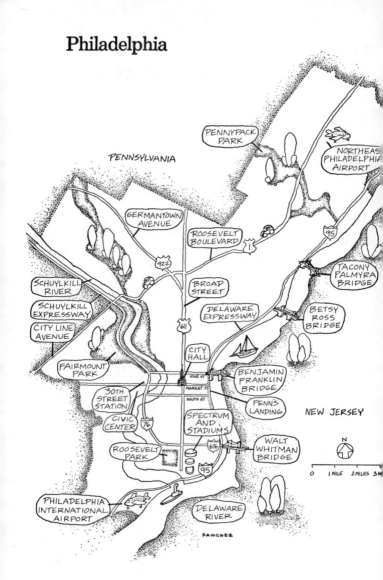

Philadelphia is on the move—and you can move with it, under it, around it and through it.

This chapter tells you how you can sit back, relax and enjoy the sights while someone else does the driving.

At the end of the chapter, you'll read about tour and guide companies that plan a tour for you, and perhaps even escort you if you provide the transportation.

Tourist Information

PHILADELPHIA VISITORS CENTER
The Philadelphia Convention and Visitors Bureau
1525 John F. Kennedy Boulevard—19102
568-6599 or 800-523-2004

Hours: Daily except Christmas, 9 to 5.
SEPTA: Buses 2, 12, 17, 27, 32, 33, 38, 44, 45, Market-Frankford Subway-Elevated or subway-surface trolleys; SEPTA commuter trains to Suburban Station. The Fairmount Park Trolley-Bus also orginates here.
E & H: There are 8 steps at the entrance, as well as a long ramp.

The Philadelphia Visitors Center is the place to go for information about what there is to see and do in Philadelphia.

You can go there for brochures about Philadelphia, listings of hotels, restaurants and current events, or to have questions answered. Aside from information, there's a possibility that you can get free tickets to some of the events that are being held.

If you can't get to the Visitors Center, call the **Philly Fun Phone,** 568-7255, for a recorded message on what's happening in Philadelphia today.

11

Local Transportation

SEPTA
200 W. Wyoming Avenue—19140
574-7800

That's the Southeastern Pennsylvania Transportation Authority, Philadelphia's public transportation system, which operates more than 150 bus, trolley and rail routes.

SEPTA routes going to points of interest are listed throughout this book. But you can also call SEPTA for specific directions. Be ready to tell them where you are and where you want to go.

The SEPTA system includes nearly 2,500 buses, articulated buses, conventional trolleys, star-spangled trolleys, trackless trolleys, highspeed trains, subway trains and an elevated train that goes over and under the city. SEPTA also controls the extensive railroad commuter system. You'll learn more about some of these vehicles later in this chapter.

A SEPTA **Information Center** is at 841 Chestnut Street in center city. It's open on weekdays from 8:30 A.M. to 4:30 P.M. Schedules are available, and senior citizens and handicapped riders can get SEPTA identification cards which enable them to ride at special fares.

A SEPTA **Customer Service and Sales Office** is in the underground concourse at 15th and Market Streets in center city (at the bottom of the twin escalators). Agents are on duty Monday to Friday from 7 A.M. to 6 P.M. They can answer your questions, provide schedules and brochures and sell you tokens or a TransPass.

Most of the SEPTA fares in Philadelphia are $1.25, and exact change is required. A transfer is 25¢ extra. Senior citizens can ride free of charge during the day or for 60¢ during peak hours (6 to 9 A.M. and 3:30 to 6:30 P.M.). Three children under 42 inches can ride free if they're with a fare-paying rider. SEPTA information for the handicapped is in Chapter 16.

If you're planning to ride SEPTA often, their $15 weekly or $55 monthly Transpass is a good idea.

You can also use a token in place of exact fare. SEPTA tokens are $1, and they're available at several subway-elevated stations and at SEPTA depots. Call SEPTA for the exact locations, or stop at the SEPTA Sales Office at 15th and Market Streets.

All SEPTA bus and trolley stops are clearly marked

along their routes. Look for the SEPTA transit stop signs attached to poles at mid-block or street corner locations.

An interesting and inexpensive way to see Philadelphia is to ride from one end of the city to the other. The route 32 bus goes from Broad and Spruce Streets, around City Hall, up the Parkway, through Strawberry Mansion, East Falls and Roxborough to Andorra, at the city limits. You'll go from the center city business district to scenic residential sections in one hour. This 15-mile trip costs $1.25, and the buses run frequently.

We can boast that the nation's longest trolley route is right here in Philadelphia. You can ride the Route 23 trolley from 11th and Bigler Streets in South Philadelphia through center city, North Philadelphia, Germantown, Mt. Airy and on to Chestnut Hill via Germantown Avenue. The 25-mile round-trip takes over two hours and costs $1.25 each way. You'll see some of Philadelphia's richest, poorest, newest and oldest sections.

Charter bus rates are available by calling SEPTA at 471-2880.

The downtown **Route 76 MidCity Loop Bus** is a unique way to get around center city. The fare is only 60¢, and buses run every five minutes from 9 A.M. to 4:30 P.M. on weekdays, and every 10 minutes at other times and on Saturday. (But never on Sunday.)

Philadelphia is really an easy city to find your way around in, and the Route 76 MidCity Loop Bus makes it even easier.

Route 76 travels between 6th and Market Streets and 18th and Chestnut Streets. It goes in both directions on the Chestnut Street Transitway. From west on Chestnut at 18th, it heads north on 18th to Kennedy, then west to 19th, south on 19th and then east on Chestnut. From 5th and Chestnut, it goes north on 5th and loops around the Liberty Bell Pavilion at Market before returning to Chestnut Street from 6th.

SEPTA's new **Airport High Speed Line** provides non-stop train service between the four domestic air terminals at Philadelphia International Airport and all three center city rail stations: 30th Street Station, Suburban Station at 16th and John F. Kennedy Boulevard, and Market East—just north of Market between 10th and 12th. Trains run every half-hour, every day from 6 A.M. to midnight. The ride takes less than 30 minutes from Market East to Terminal E at the airport. The one-way fare is $4.50 for adults and $2.25 for children under 12.

Plane Rides and Airport Tours

Philadelphia International Airport is in the southwest section of the city, less than a half-hour drive from center city. Flight information is available by calling 492–3181.

Airlines serve Philadelphia International Airport with flights to every major American city and several foreign capitals. Commuter flights connect Philadelphia with nearby cities. You can depart from Northeast Philadelphia Airport and connect with another flight at Philadelphia International or Washington National Airport.

All major airlines have ticket offices in center city, as well as at Philadelphia International Airport.

PHILADELPHIA INTERNATIONAL AIRPORT
Industrial Highway west of Island Road—19153

Tours: Call 492–3158 at least 2 weeks in advance to schedule groups of 10 to 40, grades 3 to 6, for weekdays from September to June at 10 A.M. Allow 90 minutes. One adult must accompany every 10 youngsters. Scouts and other groups can sometimes be scheduled at other times.

Cost: Free.

Lunch: Some 20 food and beverage concessions serve everything from haute cuisine to ice cream. Some have seating; others are stand-up.

SEPTA: Buses M, U, 37; Airport High Speed Line.

E & H: Wheelchair access for entire tour. There's a lot of walking.

Your tour of the Philadelphia International Airport starts with a 12–minute slide show on the history of aviation and airport operations.

Then you'll take a walk through the terminal to see the ticketing and check-in procedures, a concourse and the baggage claim area. A stop at a security check-point emphasizes the importance of airport security.

And, finally, you'll take a mini-tour of the airfield and learn about landing and take-off procedures and what it takes to get a plane ready for departure.

NORTHEAST PHILADELPHIA AIRPORT
Ashton Road and Grant Avenue—19114
673-4400

Tours: Groups of no more than 50 are scheduled from
April to September, weekdays except holidays, at 10
A.M. Allow one hour. Call a week in advance. Visitors
must be at least 4 years old.
Cost: Free
SEPTA: Bus 20 to Grant Avenue and Academy Road.
E & H: Wheelchair access.

Tours of the Northeast Philadelphia Airport begin when
one of the knowledgeable Airport guards meets you at the
Main Terminal Building.

You won't board any of the Allegheny Commuter,
Wings Airways or private planes, but you'll see them take
off and land from your position on the field walkway.
You'll visit the airfield firehouse, and you'll look over to
the 76-foot-high control tower in the center of the field.
This is the city's first freestanding structure of its type.

FLEET HELICOPTER TOURFLIGHT
Delaware Avenue and Poplar Street
(next to Riverfront Dinner Theater)
282-4100

Tours: Weekends, 1 to 4, by reservation only, weather permitting. Up to 4 passengers per ride. Allow 12 to 14
minutes flight time.
Cost: $29.50 per person, payable in advance when making
reservation. Group rates for 18 or more.

Lift off from Fleet's riverfront heliport for a panoramic
view of Philadelphia. Your route covers 25 to 30 miles. On
a clear day you can see up to 50 miles. Get an aerial look at
the center city skyline, Fairmount Park, Boat House Row,
the zoo, the sports complex, Naval Base, Penn's Landing
and more.

Don't forget your camera!

MARLIN AVIATION
Northeast Philadelphia Airport
Delaware Aviation Building
698-3137

Tours: Daily, 8 to 5, weather permitting. First come, first served, but call ahead to be sure a plane and a pilot are available.
Cost: $1 per minute. There's a 3 passenger limit, and a small child will be permitted to ride on an adult's lap.

If you have a special plan in mind, talk to your pilot before you take off. Otherwise, a popular flight plan takes you on an aerial "U" tour from the Northeast, across Roosevelt Boulevard and over to the Betsy Ross Bridge. You'll wave to William Penn in center city, swoop down over New Jersey and then head up the Delaware River back to the airport.

STERLING HELICOPTER
Penn's Landing Heliport, Pier 36 South
Delaware Avenue and Catharine Street
271-2510

Hours: Weekends, 1 to 5. Closed some holidays.
Tours: No reservations necessary, but you can call ahead to be sure. Copters seat either 3 or 4 passengers and the pilot.
Cost: $20 per passenger. $40 minimum for larger copter (seats 4); $20 minimum for smaller (seats 3). Discounts available for children (they must be with an adult).

On weekdays, Sterling Helicopter provides flight training and aerial services for companies like KYW-TV, Sunoco Traffic Update–Shadow Traffic Network, the Associated Press, The Philadelphia Inquirer and the Daily News.

But on weekends, you can go in the same helicopters for an exciting aerial tour of center city Philadelphia.

From one-thousand feet at speeds of 100 miles per hour, the view is breathtaking and the picture-taking possibilities are endless. You'll lift off from the pier and swoop across the Delaware to Camden before crossing over the Ben Franklin Bridge. From there it's a bird's-eye view of Independence Mall, center city, the Art Museum, Boat House Row and Fairmount Park. Then you'll head south over the University of Pennsylvania, across the Schuylkill, over Rittenhouse Square and eastward toward Washington Square and Penn's Landing.

The trip takes about eight minutes. The chances are good that you'll want to do it again.

SWALLOW AVIATION
Northeast Philadelphia Airport
Delaware Aviation Building
698-9925

Tours: Daylight or evening hours. Call at least a day ahead to schedule 40-minute "champagne flight" or sightseeing trip.

Cost: $95 for single engine plane (seats 3 adults) or $155 for twin engine plane (seats 5 adults) "champagne flight." Sightseeing trips vary with route and aircraft.

When Swallow Aviation's single and twin engine planes and their pilots aren't scheduled for flying lessons or charter service, they're available for sightseeing. You can plan an aerial tour of Philadelphia by day, or you can see the city's lights by night. Celebrate a special occasion with Swallow Aviation's "champagne flight."

Train Rides and Station Tours

Philadelphia has one of the most comprehensive railroad commuter networks in the country. And it's the most important intermediate stop on AMTRAK's busy New York–Washington corridor.

The Penn Central and Reading railroads were taken over by ConRail in 1976. ConRail currently runs the commuter trains under contract to the Southeastern Pennsylvania Transportation Authority. Most of the commuter lines run into attractive suburban areas, and they use modern air-conditioned electric trains. For train information, call **SEPTA** at 574-7800.

A handsome, new commuter tunnel, opened late in 1984, connects the old Penn Central and Reading lines from 12th to 16th Streets. The sparkling new Market East Station, below ground (just north of Market Street between 10th and 12th) replaces the old Reading Terminal Station. Don't miss the 880-foot-long ceramic mural expanding the length of the Market East platform. Its 62 colors on 250,000 tiles suggest the great outdoors. See if it reminds you of trees, grass, streams, shrubbery and a beautiful blue sky.

AMTRAK runs the heavy inter-city traffic from Wash-

17

ington through Philadelphia to New York, Boston, Chicago and other points, as well as the Harrisburg commuter trains. More than half of the trains to Washington and New York are the famous Metroliners, which run at speeds up to 110 miles an hour. Other trains offer sleek new Amfleet service. Board the **AMTRAK** trains at 30th Street Station. For information, call 824-1600.

Hearing handicapped persons with access to a teletypewriter should call 800-562-6960 in Pennsylvania or 800-523-6590 in the rest of the United States.

AMTRAK tickets can be purchased at Suburban Station, 16th and Kennedy Boulevard; at 30th Street Station, at the AMTRAK Rail Travel Center at 1708 Kennedy Boulevard (weekdays only), or from a travel agent.

Can you think of anything more exciting than taking youngsters on their first visit to a train station? And then a round-trip ride on a silverliner commuter train to one of Philadelphia's lush suburbs? You probably remember your first train ride.

Philadelphia's early railroad executives built their grand homes in the western suburbs along the tracks of their "main line" to Paoli. Today, the Main Line has some of America's most beautiful estates. They're in Overbrook, Merion, Narberth, Wynnewood, Ardmore, Haverford, Bryn Mawr and Paoli. Localites remember the names of these communities along the route of the Paoli Local with the help of this expression: "Old Maids Never Wed And Have Babies. Period."

In addition to taking train rides, you can go on a fascinating tour of 30th Street Station.

30TH STREET STATION
30th and Market Streets—19104
895-7121 (Passenger Service Office)

Hours: You could visit on your own anytime, day or night. Groups can be scheduled Monday to Saturday, except holidays, 10 to 3, and contingent on the station schedule.

Tours: For groups of 10 to 20, at least 1st grade. Allow 20 minutes to an hour. Call at least one week ahead.

Cost: Free.
SEPTA: Buses 9, 30, 31, 45; subway-surface trolleys 10, 11, 13, 34, 36; Market-Frankford Subway-Elevated; or any of the commuter trains to or from Suburban Station.
E & H: People in wheelchairs are able to tour the station's main floor.

30th Street Station is the main railroad station in Philadelphia. It's a monumental structure that was built with opulence in the early 1930s and added to the National Register of Historic Places in 1978.

Every day hundreds of passenger and freight trains pass through Philadelphia to New York, Boston, Washington and points beyond.

An equal number of commuter cars ride the rails to Philadelphia's scenic suburbs.

What else is there to see in the station besides trains? The ticketing and baggage operations. After everyone in your group is "trained," you'll be given a memento.

PATCO HIGH SPEED LINE
Port Authority Transit Corp.
922-4600

We recommend this computer-operated train ride, even though it takes you out of Philadelphia and into New Jersey. Or, you can take it for a quick ride from 8th and Market Streets to 16th and Locust Streets.

The man who controls the computer sits in the front car. Don't hesitate to ask him how the train works.

These air-conditioned high-speed trains travel at speeds up to 75 miles per hour. The 14½-mile route takes only 23 minutes.

Trains leave every 10 minutes or less from any of four underground stops in Philadelphia: Locust Street at 16th, 13th, or 10th, or 8th and Market Streets. You'll be underground until you get to the Benjamin Franklin Bridge. And wait till you see the view from there!

The view from the bridge alone is worth the fare ($1.60 one way for the entire trip, or 75¢ from Philadelphia to Camden, $1.40 to Collingswood). Nine stops are made in New Jersey, as far as Lindenwold.

Special fares can be arranged for senior citizens and handicapped riders during off-peak hours. Call PATCO for details.

ZOO MONORAIL*
34th Street and Girard Avenue
386-4201

Hours: Daily from April to November, 9:30 to 4:30 weekdays, till 5 weekends; weather-permitting, weekends in
March.
Cost: Weekdays: adults, $2.50; children under 12, $2.
Weekends and holidays: 50¢ more. Group rates for 15 or
more: 50¢ less.
E & H: People in wheelchairs should board at the south
end near the Wolf Woods where there's a ramp entrance. You'll have to transfer to the monorail seat.

This is another one-of-a-kind transportation in Philadelphia. This monorail has canopied, open-air cars that circle
the 42-acre zoo.

The 18-minute ride is a nifty way to orient yourself to
everything that the Philadelphia Zoo has to offer.

Another **Monorail** travels above the 8th floor **Toyland
at John Wanamaker** Department Store, 13th and Market
Streets. The "spaceship" monorail, "Lunar Explorer," is
operational from Thanksgiving to Christmas.

Boat Rides

R & S HARBOR TOURS
Penn's Landing Boat Basin
Delaware and Lombard Street—19147
928-0972

Tours: May to November, daily, 10 to 5 on the hour; also
Friday to Sunday, 2-hour sunset cruise at 7:30.
Reservations are necessary in advance for groups of 10
or more. Call ahead to be sure the boat is sailing. Write
or call for information, charter parties or reservations.
(Pier 9 North, Delaware and Race Streets, Phila., Pa.
19106)
Cost: 1-hour: adults, $3; children 12 and under, $2. 2-hour:
adults, $5; children, $3. Groups of 10 or more should
call or write a month ahead for reservations and group
rates.
Lunch: Sodas and light snacks are sold aboard, or you can
brown bag it.
SEPTA: Bus 5 or 40 to 2nd and Lombard. Parking is
available at dock.
E & H: There's wheelchair access to the top deck.

All aboard the 100-passenger "Rainbow" for a delightful, narrated sightseeing cruise of the Delaware River!

A 50-minute cruise heads south on the river as far as the Walt Whitman Bridge before turning around and heading back north to the Ben Franklin Bridge. The two-hour trip goes all the way to the Philadelphia Naval Base.

You'll see scenic Penn's Landing and ships from around the world. And you'll see why we boast that the Port of Philadelphia is the world's largest freshwater port.

SPIRIT OF PHILADELPHIA
Penn's Landing Boat Basin
Delaware Avenue and Spruce Street—19106
923-1419; groups of 20 or more, 923-4993

Tours: For brunch, lunch, dinner and dancing in the moonlight. Reservations required for most cruises.
Cost: Varies with the cruise.
E & H: Wheelchair access on boarding deck only, and the wheelchair cannot be used on the gangplank.

The 600-passenger "Spirit of Philadelphia" cruises the Port of Philadelphia while providing live entertainment, dancing, food and drinks. It has both open and closed decks, and since it's really a restaurant, you can read more about it in Chapter 18.

Bus Tours and Terminals

There are two bus terminals in center city Philadelphia. **Greyhound** (568-4800) routes depart from 17th and Market Streets. **Continental Trailways** (569-3100) buses depart from 13th and Arch Streets, as well as the **Transport of New Jersey** (569-3100 or 569-3752) buses that connect with nearby New Jersey communities and beach resorts.

GRAY LINE TOURS
569-3666

Every important city in the world offers sightseeing bus tours, and Philadelphia is no exception. So take a Gray Line Bus Tour of Philadelphia and let your driver do the talking.

An assortment of tours with varying schedules and prices are offered. The tours depart from the Philadelphia Centre Hotel, 18th Street and Kennedy Boulevard. Meet your guide in the hotel lobby. Pickups can also be arranged from other center city hotels and motels.

Tour 1 is the most popular: 3 hours in Historic Philadelphia with stops at Independence Hall*, the Betsy Ross House* and Christ Church*.

Tour 2 is the Cultural Tour. This includes stops at the Philadelphia Museum of Art* and one or two of the Fairmount Park Houses*. It's 2½ hours.

The price of Tour 1 is $7.75. Tour 2 is $9.25, but you can take a six-hour Grand Combination (Tour 3) for $15. Children 12 and under pay $4, $6.25, or $7.50 for the combination.

Gray Line also runs tours to Longwood Gardens, Valley Forge, Gettysburg, the Pennsylvania Dutch Country and Hershey, Pa.

Departure schedules and more details are available by calling Gray Line. If you have a group of 30 or more, call 568-6111 for Charter information.

SEPTA BUS RAMBLES
574-7800

Take a ramble and join a fun-filled day trip to the popular attractions around Philadelphia. The Rambles leave from 16th and Kennedy Boulevard, 69th and Market Streets or Frankford and Bridge Streets.

There's at least one excursion each weekend to distant points like New Hope, the Amish Country, Valley Forge Park, Washington Crossing, Brandywine Battlefield, Longwood Gardens, St. Peter's Village, Crystal Cave, Gettysburg, Hershey (Chocolate City), Peddler's Village and summer Folk Festivals around Pennsylvania.

Call SEPTA for information, or pick up a seasonal "Rambles" brochure from SEPTA* or at the Visitors Center.

Trolley Rides

SEPTA's fleet of trolleys, which is the largest in the nation, covers a good portion of Philadelphia with 10 routes.

SEPTA also has three suburban trolley routes. All three are fun to ride, and they originate at 69th Street Terminal in Upper Darby, just west of the city. Just hop the Market–Frankford Subway–Elevated and ride to the end of the line at 69th and Market Streets.

The Norristown High-Speed Line, which runs frequent service on its 13.5 mile line through the picturesque Main Line suburbs, is America's original high speed line and the last interurban trolley line in the country.

The Media trolley line is also interesting to see. It runs 8.5 miles west to Media, the county seat of Delaware County*. The line takes you through pretty suburban areas and winds up trundling down the middle of Media's main street.

The third line runs 5.3 miles to Sharon Hill.

Call 574-7800 or 574-7777 for fares, schedules and maps for each route.

You can take an old-fashioned trolley ride on the **PENN'S LANDING TROLLEY** and, at the same time, see Philadelphia's waterfront, Queen Village, Society Hill and Old City from a beautifully restored, turn-of-the-century trolley car.

The round-trip excursion along Delaware Avenue between the Benjamin Franklin Bridge and Fitzwater Street takes 25 minutes. You can board at Dock Street or Spruce Street after you buy a ticket from the platform dispatcher, or at the U.S.S. Olympia office.

The fare is $1 for adults and 50¢ for children under 12. Call 627-0807 for group rates and charter information. Penn's Landing trolleys run from 11 A.M. to dusk, Thursday to Sunday, from Memorial Day to Labor Day, and weekends only from Easter to Memorial Day and Labor Day to early December.

Trolley–Bus Rides

You've read about tours by trolley. You've read about tours by bus. Now you can go on a trolley-bus tour. What's a trolley-bus? I'll explain.

Between 1896 and 1946, Philadelphians were taken to Fairmount Park in open-air trolleys. The **Fairmount Park Trolley-Bus** is a replica of these trolleys. They have 31 seats, open-air sections, leather strap-hangers, clanging bells and colorful red and green exteriors. They're replicas of their predecessors, except they don't need trolley tracks.

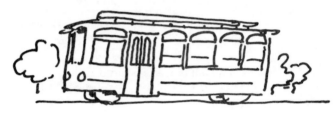

The trolleys weave through the park Wednesday to Sunday from late April through November. A trolley departs from the Philadelphia Visitors Center at 16th Street and Kennedy Boulevard every 20 minutes between 10:00 A.M. and 4:20 P.M., or from the Visitor Center* at 3rd and Chestnut Streets every 20 minutes from 11 A.M. to 2:30 P.M. You can board at any stop along the route, and take as many round-trips as you wish. A round-trip takes 90 minutes.

You can lengthen the ride by making stops at any of the restored Fairmount Park Houses, Memorial Hall, the Zoo, the Japanese Exhibition House, the Philadelphia Museum of Art or any other Parkway cultural institution along the way. (Read about these attractions later in the book.) There are 20 stops in all. Just use your all-day ticket to board the next trolley that comes along.

It's a one-fare ride for the day with off-and-on privileges as you go: adults, $3; senior citizens, $1; students 13 to 21 with I.D., $2; children under 12, free. Be sure to show your ticket for discounts to the houses, museums and other attractions you choose to visit along the route.

Your driver-guide will tell you about the history of Fairmount Park* and the sites you'll see.

These Fairmount Park Trolleys are also used for a "Germantown Tour" and "Town and Country" tours to Society Hill and center city before heading into Fairmount Park. Call 568–6599 or 879–4044 for the schedule.

Right before Christmas, the trolleys take shoppers up and down Chestnut Street in center city. You'll hear them coming as they pipe holiday music into the December air. The trolleys are a natural for the holidays. They're red and green.

You can charter a Fairmount Park Trolley for evening and off-season rides, and anytime you want to have a special time in Philadelphia. Call 879–4044 for rates, details and any other information.

Clang, clang, clang goes the trolley.

Carriage Rides

Horse-drawn carriage rides were revived in Philadelphia for the Bicentennial. Tourists and Philadelphians alike love the carriages. They love to clip-clop around the cobblestone streets of Old Philadelphia just as the colonists did 200 years ago.

You have a choice of companies and a variety of carriages to make your tour. All have driver-guides (sometimes in colonial garb) to narrate your trip. Don't worry about the horses; they only go out when the weather permits.

These companies are licensed by the Pennsylvania Public Utility Commission. Their rates are controlled and supposed to be equal. They offer a 20-minute ride ($10 for up to 4 people), a 40-minute ride ($20 for up to 4 people), or larger carriages that take adults ($2.50) and children ($1.25) in groups for shorter rides. The rate is double for longer rides. Day or evening taxi service is provided by reservation. The cost is approximately $20 an hour for a one-horse carriage. Get a horse!

Ben Franklin Carriages has a fleet of one-horse surreys with fringe on top. Five adults can comfortably ride in one.

Philadelphia Carriage Co. faithfully restored 15 antique carriages. Their largest accommodates eight riders.

Their standard pick-up points are Independence Hall and Head House Square (2nd and Pine or Lombard Streets). A reserved carriage will pick you up anywhere in center city.

'76 Carriage Company (923–8516) has one- and two-horse carriages to take you on round-trip tours from Independence Hall or Head House. Also look for them outside the Hershey Hotel on South Broad Street.

Their smaller antique wagons carry up to four adults. The large two-horse carriages are replicas of old police wagons, and they can hold as many as 20 adults. They can also be reserved in advance for groups.

Tours are given daily from 9:30 to 5:30, and till midnight on Friday and Saturday from Head House.

Ups and Downs

CITY HALL TOWER*
Broad and Market Streets (enter at northeast corner)
686–4546

Hours: Weekdays, 9 to 4:30. Closed some holidays.
Tours: No tours, and reservations are not necessary. It's first come, first served. Children under 12 must be with an adult.
Cost: Free
E & H: No wheelchair access.

You're used to traveling back and forth. Now travel up and down.

At City Hall, the glass-front elevator goes up the 548-foot William Penn Tower in one-and-a-half minutes.

Before taking the ride, take a look at the exhibits on William Penn and the construction of City Hall.

On the way up you'll see the various levels, the workings of the 23-foot wide clock, and the 604 steps that circle the elevator shaft. (No, you can't use the stairs. If you want to exercise, you'll have to jog along Kelly Drive.)

You may have been on bigger elevators than this one. But have you seen any that are as exciting?

More Ins and Outs of Getting Around Philadelphia

Additional information can be obtained by consulting the Yellow Pages or your travel agent.

All major **rent-a-car** companies are located in center city, at suburban hotels and at Philadelphia International Airport.

There are limousine services available from the airport to Philadelphia, Wilmington, Atlantic City and Fort Dix. You'll see drivers or "hot line" telephones at the airport terminal. Limousines also go from the airport to center city, the Dunfey on City Line and Northeast Philadelphia hotels.

Limousines are also available for hire. (The companies are listed in the Yellow Pages.) If you're a movie star, or would like to pretend you're a movie star, rent a limo for a day and have the driver show you Philadelphia.

Radio **taxicab** service is available in all areas of Philadelphia. Yellow Cab, United, Crescent, Society Hill, Quaker City and Victory are the most common.

How Else Can You Tour?

Several small, private companies provide a variety of tours of Philadelphia and its suburbs. In most cases, you'll have to provide your own transportation.

They're listed here, objectively, in alphabetical order, with a brief description of their individual services. Call or write to them for more details.

ABC Bus & Walking Tours 2929 Gelena Road, Phila., Pa. 19152 (677–2495). Choose from six planned tours of Historic Philadelphia, the Italian Market or Valley Forge, or intineraries that are customized for your group. Multilingual. Reservations only.

About Town Tours 105–A Lombard Street, Phila., Pa. 19147 (925–8687). Specialized intineraries for groups and V.I.P.s, especially conventions and foreign business people. Multilingual. Reservations only.

Access Philadelphia 250 S. 18th Street, Phila., Pa. 19103 (732–7139). Business people and their families who are relocating to Philadelphia can benefit from the services provided by Access Philadelphia. All facets of living in Philadelphia are considered. It'll certainly make your move easier.

Asher Tours 5547 Germantown Avenue, Suite 202, Phila., Pa. 19144 (849–3790). Half- or full-day custom bus tours of historic and contemporary Germantown. Reservations only. See Chapter 3 for more details.

At Your Service 302 Old Lancaster Road, Devon, Pa. 19333 (296–2828). Half- or full-day custom tours of Old or Contemporary Philadelphia. For large or small groups. Multilingual. Reservations only.

AudioWalk & Tour Norman Rockwell Museum, 6th and Walnut Streets, Phila., Pa. 19106 (information, 925–1234; reservations, 925–4567). You can tour eight blocks of historic Philadelphia at your own pace with your own rented cassette and player and accompanying map. The tour lasts 80 minutes and your rental is for three hours.

Black History Strolls and Tours 339 S. 2nd Street, Phila., Pa. 19106 (923–4136). Walking tours of Old Philadelphia and bus tours with emphasis on black history, business, religion, education, the arts. Day or night life. Multilingual. Reservations only.

C & C Associates, Tours and Special Events. 110 East 64th Avenue, Phila., Pa. 19120 (924-7693 or 924-0160). Customized tours for large and small groups of Old Philadelphia and surrounding attractions. Multilingual. Reservations only.

Centipede, Inc. 1315 Walnut Street, Phila., Pa. 19107 (735–3123). Scheduled walking tours and warm-weather evening **Candlelight Strolls*** of Old Philadelphia with colonial-costumed guides. Call for schedule and reservations. Bus tours, group and convention planning by reservation. Multilingual.

Culture Tour 3605 Sipler Lane, Huntingdon Valley, Pa. 19006 (947–8991). Personalized half- or full-day tours for large or small groups to area museums and historic sites. Multilingual. Reservations only.

Foundation for Architecture Tours One Penn Center at Suburban Station, Suite 1560, Phila., Pa. 19103 (569-3187). Reservations are suggested for individuals who want to join any of the Foundation's scheduled architectural walks. They cover the City Hall area, Old City, the University of Pennsylvania campus, or the neighborhoods of Spruce Hill, Rittenhouse Square and Washington Square. The organization is devoted to promoting Philadelphia to natives and visitors as a museum of architecture. Most tours cost $3 or $5. Members of the non-profit Foundation get a discount along with other benefits including events that are planned mornings, afternoons, evenings and weekends throughout the year.

Friends of Independence National Historical Park 313 Walnut Street, Phila., Pa. 19106 (597-7919). 90-minute guided walking tours of the National Park depart daily from July 1 to Labor Day, except July 4th, from the Visitor Center, 3rd and Chestnut Streets. Rain or shine; first come, first served. Free. Call for the schedule.

Hospitality PhiladelphiaStyle 1346 Chestnut Street, 8th floor, Phila., Pa. 19107 (545-1234). Personalized itineraries for out-of-town civic and cultural groups are the specialty of this non-profit corporation. They'll take you to the forefront and behind-the-scenes of your favorite interest.

House of Lloyd Tours 1700 Walnut Street, Phila., Pa. 19103 (732-8880). Custom tours and cultural planning service for large or small groups according to particular interest. Reservations only.

Lively Arts Group 3900 Ford Road, Phila., Pa. 19131 (877-7788). Special interest tours to nearby cultural and historical attractions. Reservations only. Offers seminars and special events for nominal membership.

Philadelphia Open House P.O. Box 40166, Phila., Pa. 19106 (928-1188). Turn to May in the Calendar of Annuals Events and read about this unique opportunity to participate in unusual tours of Philadelphia.

Julie Curson (that's me!) I plan tours, and I take groups on tours of Philadelphia. Reservations only. Call me at 732-7111. Or write to me at 250 S. 18th Street, Phila., Pa. 19103.

Chapter 2.
Independence National Historical Park.

Historic Philadelphia

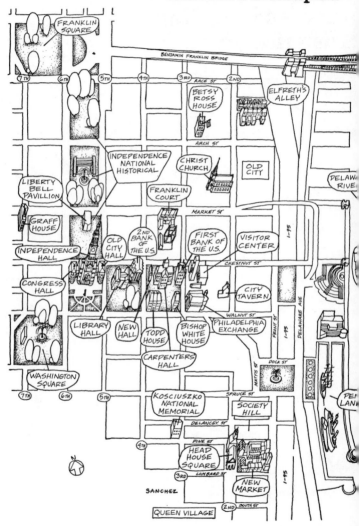

William Penn is the tallest man in Philadelphia. His 37-foot-tall statue is perched on top of the 500-foot City Hall Tower, gazing down over the city he founded in 1682.

Penn's father was owed a debt by King Charles II of England. In return for the debt, the younger Penn accepted land in America. He came here to establish a colony based on religious freedom so people could live together and worship as they pleased, including Penn's fellow Quakers who had been persecuted in England.

Penn modestly named the new colony Pennsylvania, meaning "Penn's Woods."

He selected this area as the capital of the new colony, naming it with the Greek word Philadelphia meaning "City of Brotherly Love."

In Penn's time Philadelphia was only two square miles between the Delaware and Schuylkill Rivers and Vine and South Streets.

Thomas Holme, Philadelphia's original city planner, laid out the new city in a simple grid system which still survives today. Five parks were created. Centre Square is now the location of City Hall. The other four park squares are now called Rittenhouse, Logan, Franklin and Washington.

From 1699 to 1701, Penn lived in a slate roof house at 2nd and Sansom Streets. In 1773 the City Tavern was built across the street. (There's more about that later in this chapter.) Penn's house was demolished in 1867, but the site is now Welcome Park, named for the ship Penn sailed to America, and for your welcome to Independence National Historical Park.

Welcome Park's paving is a clever, scaled design of Penn's grid pattern for his city. Trees grow at symmetric sites marking the four park squares.

Informative wall panels and quotes underfoot tell you about Penn, his life and his Quaker beliefs. You'll feel welcome indeed at this outdoor museum that's unlike any other museum.

Now, back to early Philadelphia.

Philadelphia's early settlers were Dutch, Irish, Swedish, German, Welsh and English. They were merchants, brewers, carpenters, bricklayers and tradesmen. These people wanted peace, opportunity and freedom of worship. (Many of the churches where Philadelphia's settlers worshipped are still in existence. You'll read about them in Chapter 5.)

This center of religious freedom was also to become the center of freedom for our country.

33

When delegates from the colonies chose a site to gather, Philadelphia seemed to be the logical place. Aside from providing inspiration for change, Philadelphia was the largest English speaking city outside of London. And it was in the center of everything. (Philadelphians like to think it still is.)

The First Continental Congress met in Philadelphia in 1774 at the small Carpenters' Hall near 4th and Chestnut Streets. They planned to make their rights as colonists known to Great Britain, but their grievances persisted. So a Second Continental Congress convened in May of 1775, meeting two blocks west in what was then known as the State House of Pennsylvania.

Today this same structure, known as Independence Hall, is faithfully restored. The Declaration of Independence was adopted here on July 4, 1776, marking the creation of our country.

Eleven years later, in 1787, a Constitution was drawn up and signed by delegates of each of the 13 states. Now, 200 years later, Philadelphia and the nation celebrate the Constitution's bicentennial.

Philadelphia was the nation's capital from 1790 through 1800, and during this time the Congress of the United States met in the new County Court House building at 6th and Chestnut Streets. It was in this building that the first 10 amendments were added to the Constitution. And it was here that George Washington and John Adams took their Presidential oaths of office.

Most of the historic buildings relating to the Revolutionary War period have been restored to their original grandeur by the National Park Service and are now part of Independence National Historical Park. Spend two days touring the area, and you'll remember it for the rest of your life.

The best way to learn American history is to make the City of Philadelphia your classroom. Philadelphia has more buildings relating to American history than any other city in the country.

Independence Hall was proclaimed a National Historic Site in 1943. In 1948, Independence Square and its surrounding blocks were designated by the Federal Government as Independence National Historical Park. Millions of dollars were pumped into the restoration of Independence Mall and the neighboring historic structures, and more that 200 dilapidated warehouses and lofts were demolished.

Today this area is known as "America's most historic

square mile." It's also Philadelphia's greatest attraction.

A three-block colonial mall was built as a fitting approach to Independence Hall's classic design. The mall includes the Edwin O. Lewis Fountain and Quadrangle, where the 13 original colonies are symbolized by 13 jets in the fountain, a double row of 13 brick archways and 13 flagpoles that fly their flags over Arch Street. (In Philadelphia we consider 13 a lucky number.)

When you stroll through this historic area you'll be tracing the footsteps of George Washington, John Adams, Benjamin Franklin and the other great men who made America free.

Independence Park is a compact area. It's easy to get around on foot, it has plenty of benches to rest on, and numerous restaurants to refresh yourself in. there's **no admission charge** to any of the buildings and **reservations aren't necessary.**

Visiting hours are from **9 to 5 daily,** unless otherwise noted. Only Independence Hall and the Liberty Bell Pavilion are open (from 11 to 4) on Christmas and New Year's. The most popular attractions are open later during the summer months. Call 597-8974 to ask about the ones you're interested in.

National Park Service guides or attendants are stationed at every historic building.

SEPTA routes traveling in the area include the D, 38, 42, 44, 50 and Route 76 Loop buses directly to Independence Hall. The Market–Frankford Subway–Elevated and bus routes 12, 17 and 33 go to 5th and Market Streets. The PATCO High-Speed Line stops at 8th and Market Streets.

Unless otherwise noted, wheelchair access is difficult at many of the park buildings because their original 18th and 19th century architecture includes entrance steps and interior stairways.

If you're not in Philadelphia and need additional information, write to the Superintendent of Independence National Historical Park, 313 Walnut Street, Phila., Pa. 19106.

Try to start your tour with a trip to the Visitor Center, which provides an excellent orientation to the entire area.

VISITOR CENTER
3rd and Chestnut Streets
597–8974 or 597–8975

Hours: Daily, 9 to 5; till 6 in summer. Allow at least 45 minutes.
Other: A gift shop sells National Park and other publications, "historic" documents, slides and mementos.
E & H: Complete wheelchair access. Outside the Center's front-entrance there are 3 bronze engraved street models of the National Park attractions with all information in braille.
Reminder: This is where you pick up tickets to tour the Bishop White House and Todd House. It's also where to pick up a summertime schedule of special activities taking place outdoors in the park.
Note: If you can't get to the Visitor Center, or if you'd like to "Pre-Visit" the National Park, then see "Tours to Go" in Chapter 13.

The National Park Service encourages you to start your visit to the park in its enormous new Visitor Center. (This is not to be confused with the Philadelphia Visitors Center described in Chapter 1.) The wall maps, exhibits, brochures and staff will help you with your orientation.

A computer exhibit at the Visitor Center (opening in 1987) offers a highlight of National Park exhibits across the nation celebrating the Constitution's 200th birthday. What better place for a show like this than the city where the Constitution was born. A variety of computer games and puzzles will graphically tell you the history of this great document.

The Visitor Center also houses two 300-seat theaters so there's always room to see John Huston's 28 minute film, "Independence." The shows are every half-hour from 9:00 till closing in the summer months. The rest of the year, it's every 30 or 45 minutes from 9:30 to 4:30. The giant wall clock will tell you how many minutes there are till the next feature.

"Independence" takes you back to Philadelphia in the years 1774 to 1796. It shows you the history that took place in the area that surrounds the Visitor Center. You'll recognize the set.

The Visitor Center also houses an environmental artwork by Red Grooms. "Cornucopia" was commissioned by the Institute of Contemporary Art* in 1982 to celebrate Philadelphia's tricentennial. It's a monumental combination of painting and sculpture that whimsically depicts "Washington Crossing the Delaware," numerous other local landmarks, historical events, current events and personalities.

The **Bicentennial Bell,** the British Government's Bicentennial gift to the people of the United States, is hung in the Visitor Center's 130-foot Bell Tower. The bell was cast at Whitechapel Bell Foundry in London, where the actual Liberty Bell was cast in 1752. Queen Elizabeth came here to dedicate the bell on July 6, 1976. Her speech is inscribed on a large bronze plaque that also has a sculpture of the Queen. It's adjacent to the Bell Tower.

This bell's inscription reads, "Let Freedom Ring." As America's ceremonial bell, it rings on special occasions and daily at 11 A.M. and 3 P.M. If you hear the bell, pretend they're ringing it just for you.

INDEPENDENCE HALL
Chestnut Street between 5th and 6th
627-1776

Hours: Daily, 9 to 5; till 8 in summer. Allow 30 minutes inside the Hall.

Tours: All tours of Independence Hall are guided tours, and they originate from the East Wing. No reservations, except for Philadelphia Public School teachers, who should call the Museum Education Department at the Board of Education, 299-7778, for tour arrangements.

Lunch: Weather permitting, picnic in Independence Square or Independence Mall. Several cafeterias and lots of hot dog vendors are in the area. A dozen or more informal and assorted eateries are on the third level of The Bourse*, across from Independence Mall on 5th Street.

Other: The West Wing is a Park Information Center with maps, brochures and some souvenirs and books available.

E & H: A Park Service attendant will put a ramp over the 3 steps at the rear entrance facing Independence Square. The Assembly Room and Supreme Court Chamber are easily accessible.

Independence Hall, America's most meaningful landmark, opened in 1732 as a State House for the Colony of Pennsylvania. The State Assembly first occupied the building in 1735.

In 1775 the Second Continental Congress moved in with delegates from all 13 colonies. They adopted the Declaration of Independence here on July 4, 1776. In 1787 the Constitution of the United States was drafted and approved here.

Independence Hall is faithfully restored to be exactly as it was in 1776 when history was being made.

Come see where America started.

Picture the delegates from the Colonies locked in the Assembly Room during the long, hot summers of 1775 and 1776, all working towards one goal: Freedom.

Imagine the Assembly Room again, from May 15 to September 17, 1787, when the delegates (this time from the original States) again debated behind locked doors till they agreed on a Constitution.

Admire the silver inkstand used by the delegates to sign the Declaration and the Constitution.

Look at the chair that Ben Franklin referred to when he said, "...I have the happiness to know that it is a rising and not a setting sun." Listen as your guide relates its symbolism.

Think of young Tom Jefferson dancing upstairs in the 100-foot Long Room, where many gala social events were held. Today you might hear a live harpsichord concert, reminiscent of the colonial period.

Try to picture our country's first judges dressed in wigs and black robes presiding over the early Pennsylvania and Federal Courts.

Step into **Independence Square**, the four-acre block that includes Independence Hall. Look at the west wall of Independence Hall and see the **"Great Clock."** It's an exact replica of the 1776 timepiece.

Study the 56 antique-design gas lamps that represent the 56 signers of the Declaration.

Try to picture yourself as an anxious citizen on July 8, 1776, hearing a public reading of the Declaration of Independence for the very first time.

LIBERTY BELL PAVILION
Independence Mall
Market Street between 5th and 6th

Hours: Daily 9 to 5; till 8 in summer. The bell is on view 24 hours a day.
E & H: Wheelchair access.

The Bicentennial began in Philadelphia when America's symbol of democracy, the Liberty Bell, was moved from Independence Hall to its new home at midnight on January 1, 1976.

The 2,080-pound bell continues to hang from its original yoke. It was ordered in 1751 to commemorate the anniversary of William Penn's 1701 Charter of Privileges for the people of Pennsylvania. It was to hang in the tower of the State House of Pennsylvania.

Touch the Liberty Bell and listen to its inspiring message. Read its Biblical inscription and feel its famous crack. Take a picture of it. A National Park guide will tell you about the bell's history and answer your questions.

You can't visit Philadelphia without seeing the Liberty Bell. It would be like shopping in New York and not visiting Bloomingdale's.

If you can't get to the bell during the day, visit it at night. The bell is floodlit and visible through the modern, glass-walled structure. Even when the building is closed, you can still hear the bell's story (in English or any of several foreign languages) by pushing one of the outdoor audio-buttons.

While Independence Hall and the Liberty Bell Pavilion are the park's favorite attractions, there are a number of other important sites you can visit. Go on your own or with a daytime walking tour or an evening **Candlelight Stroll***. Colonial-costumed Centipede and Friends of Independence National Historical Park guides lead these tours as described at the end of Chapter 1.

You can get specific information on these and other tours from the National Park Visitor Center (597–8974) or the city's Visitors Center (568–6599).

BISHOP WHITE HOUSE
309 Walnut Street

Hours: Daily, by scheduled tour only.
Tours: 10 tickets are allotted per tour, and you must get them at the Visitor Center at 3rd and Chestnut Streets.

The Bishop White House, built in 1786, is restored and furnished with original and period pieces. A large assortment of cooking utensils surrounds the hearth. The kitchen table is set for the youngsters, while the dining room is rich and formal. The "outhouse" is in the house, which was quite unusual for the time.

The second floor library was faithfully recreated from an oil painting by one of the Bishop's grandchildren. The painting is on display in the library.

Bishop William White was the first Protestant Episcopal Bishop of Pennsylvania, Chaplain to the Continental Congress, Rector of Christ Church and Rector of St. Peter's Church. The Bishop lived and greeted his parishoners here till his death in 1836.

CARPENTERS' HALL
320 Chestnut Street
925-0167

Hours: Daily, except Monday, 10 to 4. Closed Easter, Thanksgiving, Christmas, New Year's. Allow 15 minutes.
Tours: Groups of 10 or more are requested to call ahead.
Other: A small gift shop sells books and mementos of the era and the trade.

The Carpenters' Company of Philadelphia was founded as a guild in 1724 to teach architecture to carpenters and to help their families in times of need. Their guild hall was built in 1770.

In 1774 Carpenters' Hall was the meeting place for the First Continental Congress. An exhibit with original furnishings describes this historic event.

The hall was used as a storehouse and hospital when the British occupied Philadelphia during the Revolutionary War. The First Bank of the United States opened for business here in 1791, with the Second Bank following in 1816. Carpenters' Hall is still owned and maintained by the Carpenters' Company. Its members meet here four times a year.

You'll see furnishings, documents and tools that were used to build America. And you'll see a magnificent model

of the building under construction, along with a description of the materials and methods that were used in 1770.

CITY TAVERN
2nd and Walnut Streets
923-6059

Hours: See Chapter 18 for dining information.

City Tavern was reconstructed for the Bicentennial at
the site of the tavern where Ben Franklin, John Adams
and other delegates to the First Continental Congress
gathered to "pop a few" after work, have dinner and talk
about the situation in the colonies.
Adams was prompted to call this "the most genteel tavern in all America."
The original City Tavern was built in 1773. Delegates to
the Congress first met here on September 5, 1774. (Who
says you can't mix business and pleasure?)
Most of the well-known people of 18th century Philadelphia frequented City Tavern for food, drink and social
events. It was only for the social events that women were
to be seen here.
Several rare 18th century maps and documents are
hung in the tavern. The furnishings, staff dress and menu
are authentic from the colonial period.

CONGRESS HALL
6th and Chestnut Streets

Construction began in 1787 on what was originally in-
tended to be the county court house. The building was
completed in 1789, and shortly thereafter the United
States Congress took it over until 1800.
Philadelphia, as you know, was capital of the United
States between 1790 and 1800. Take a few minutes to see
the House Chamber where John Adams was sworn in as
President. Then go upstairs to see the Senate Chamber
where George Washington took the oath of office for his
second term.
The Mint, the Bank of the United States and the
Department of the Navy were founded in this very building. Congress Hall was used as a court house during the
19th century.
A note for political science fans: The two houses of Con
gress are called "upper" and "lower" because of this
building. The House Chamber was on the lower floor, and
the Senate Chamber was on the upper floor.

41

FIRST BANK OF THE UNITED STATES
116 South 3rd Street

The First Bank of the United States was built between 1795 and 1797, after it received a 20 year charter from Congress in 1791. Stephen Girard bought the building when the charter expired and used it as a private bank until 1831.

This is probably the oldest surviving bank building in America. It was also the Treasury Department's first home.

A sparkling restoration provides an ideal setting for summertime theatrical presentations and occasional exhibitions. The interior is early 20th century, while the outside is as it was in 1797. The Visitor Center (across the street) will have current information for you.

FRANKLIN COURT
314–322 Market Street, and beyond into Court
Also reached from Chestnut Street by walkway adjacent to the Philadelphia Maritime Museum.
597–2760 or 597–2761

Hours: Daily, 9 to 5; till 6 in summer. Allow at least one hour.
E & H: Market Street buildings and underground museum are wheelchair accessible from the Court.

Welcome to Independence National Historical Park's fabulous new attraction. The Franklin Court complex blends reconstructed historic homes with a grassy courtyard and an underground museum.

The Department of the Interior wanted to rebuild Ben Franklin's home but they couldn't find any drawings or plans. Since the Department won't recreate an historic home if they can't be sure of its accuracy in every detail, they put up a "ghost" frame on the plot where Franklin's home stood.

Three of the five Market Street homes were designed and originally built by Ben in 1786.

Today they house **Franklin's Tenant House,** a museum with 18th century "Fragments of Franklin Court" archaeological discoveries recovered from the site, the **Aurora Print Shop** which was once operated by Franklin's grandson, a **Postal Museum** and a "200-year-old" branch of the U.S. Postal Service.

The **B. Free Franklin Post Office** (597–8987) at 314–316 Market Street is the only U.S. Post Office where employees wear colonial garb and hand-cancel every piece of outgoing mail with the distinctive signature of "B. Free Franklin." When Franklin was postmaster, he used the middle name "Free" because he wanted a country that was free from England's rule. If you're a philatilist, this is the place to catch up with the latest commemorative issues.

Walk through the archway to **Franklin Court** and marvel at the frame where Franklin's home stood. Ben lived here with his wife and two children when he served in the Continental Congress and Constitutional Convention. He died here in 1790.

Glass-covered pits show archaeological remains such as 18th century privy sites. Engraved stones give informative bits and pieces of correspondence between Franklin and his wife, Deborah.

Now descend to the **underground museum.** The gallery includes original and exact reproductions of Franklin memorabilia. Walk through the neon-lit hall of mirrors that reflects Ben Franklin, a man of "Unlimited Dimension."

Next is something everyone loves: the Franklin Exchange. Pick up a phone and dial any of 47 famous Americans and Europeans to hear what they have to say about Franklin.

Be sure to see "Franklin on the World Stage." A doll-size cast of Ben and the rest of the characters portray meaningful moments of American history. You'll be with Ben before the British House of Commons in 1766, at the Court of Versailles in France in 1778 and before the Constitutional Convention in Philadelphia in 1787. Performances are continuous. The three acts run for a total of 13 minutes.

By all means, don't leave without seeing the film "Portrait of a Family." It stars the late Howard daSilva as Ben, and it's terrific. The movie is shown every half-hour from 9:30 to 4:30 (except at 1 P.M.). When museum hours are extended in the summer, the last showing is a half-hour before closing.

GRAFF HOUSE
7th and Market Streets

This is a reconstruction of the boarding house where the 33-year-old delegate from Virginia, Thomas Jefferson, lived in the summer of 1776 when he attended the Second Continental Congress.

The original house was built by Jacob Graff, a brick-layer, in 1775. It was demolished in 1883.

Enter through the garden on 7th Street and view the first floor exhibits on the Declaration of Independence. You'll see a seven-minute film about Thomas Jefferson called "The Extraordinary Citizen." The informal theater seats 40.

Jefferson rented the second floor of the Graff House. His bedroom and the front parlor are furnished from the period.

If you saw the movie "1776" you remember the agony Jefferson went through putting his thoughts on parchment. His words became the Declaration of Independence.

There's also a brief sound-and-light show celebrating the Fourth of July.

KOSCIUSZKO NATIONAL MEMORIAL
3rd and Pine Streets

Thaddeus Kosciuszko, a Polish engineer, lived in this restored 18th century corner house from November, 1797, to May, 1798.

This is a fitting national memorial to a man who left his homeland to join our Revolutionary forces. Kosciuszko put his engineering skills to work at designing defenses. His plans for Saratoga are said to have brought about the turning point in the war for the United States.

A portrait gallery, a chronology of Kosciuszko's life and Polish and American tributes are on display downstairs.

The second floor room where Kosciuszko lived is furnished from the period. Many of his personal possessions are there. Tapes in English and Polish describe these belongings.

An informal theater seats 50 viewers for a six-minute film about Kosciuszko.

LIBRARY HALL
105 South 5th Street, across from Independence Square
627-0706

Hours: Weekdays, 9 to 5. Closed holidays. Call ahead.
Note: Library Hall is open only to serious scholars.

Library Hall was originally built in 1790 for the Library Company of Philadelphia. It was recently rebuilt as the library for the American Philosophical Society*.

Among the treasures here are Benjamin Franklin's will, a copy of the Declaration of Independence in Thomas Jefferson's hand, William Penn's 1701 Charter of Privileges, books, manuscripts and an outstanding portrait gallery.

NEW HALL
(Marine Corps Memorial Museum)
Chestnut Street east of 4th

New Hall was originally built in 1790 by the Carpenters' Company and was used as a War Department Office.

It was rebuilt in the 1960s as a United States Marine Corps history museum.

It only takes a few minutes to see the exhibits on two floors portraying Marines in the Revolution from 1775 to 1783. The story is told with dioramas, paintings and a Memorial Room.

OLD CITY HALL
5th and Chestnut Streets

This Congress Hall look-alike was built in 1790 as the first permanent home for Philadelphia's city government. But instead, the United States Supreme Court used it from 1791 to 1800. Philadelphia's municipal offices and courts were here in the 1800s.

Old City Hall is now alive with multi-media exhibits. The first floor shows you how the U.S. Supreme Court spent its 10 years there.

The second floor brings you back to the Philadelphia of 1774 to 1800. You'll stroll down an 18th century brick street, you'll visit a circus, and you'll see the occupations, crafts, schools and day-to-day activities of the period.

PEMBERTON HOUSE
(Army-Navy Museum)
Chestnut Street east of 4th

The Army–Navy Museum is housed in a replica of the 18th century home of Quaker merchant Joseph Pemberton.

As with New Hall, it only takes a few minutes to go through the three floors of exhibits. Since they're so close, you should combine visits.

The Pemberton House has a fascinating collection of Army and Navy artifacts that include model ships, flags and old military weapons.

Ask to see a 12-minute film called "A Force of Citizens." It's about the gathering of defenses for the United States following formation of the Colonial Army.

Be careful not to get seasick when you cross the simulated gun deck of an early 19th century frigate. And don't be surprised if you hear the waves.

PHILADELPHIA EXCHANGE
3rd and Walnut streets

Note: The building is closed to the public, but its exterior restoration is open to admiration.

This Classical Revival building, designed by famous Philadelphia architect William Strickland, was built in the 1830s. It housed the Philadelphia Stock Exchange* for many years.

Remember: An **asterisk(*)** indicates that the same place or event appears elsewhere in the book with more details. Look in the Index for additional pages.

PHILOSOPHICAL HALL
(Independence Square)
5th and Chestnut Streets

Note: The Hall is open only to the Philosophical Society's scholarly members.

The American Philosophical Society was founded in 1743 by Benjamin Franklin. (How did he find the time to found so many things?) Franklin served as its president from 1769 till his death. It continues to be a learned society that gives research grants and publishes scholarly books.

The Society built this handsome home between 1785 and 1789. Its library is directly across 5th Street in Library Hall*.

SECOND BANK OF THE UNITED STATES
420 Chestnut Street

From September 17, 1986 through 1987, the Second Bank of the United States houses an exhibition called "Miracle at Philadelphia." This is the focal point for the celebration of the Constitution's 200th birthday. Among the exhibit's highlights are four drafts of the Constitution, along with priceless documents and artifacts gathered from the Library of Congress, the Historical Society of Pennsylvania, the Library Company and the American Philosophical Society.

The building itself is another fine example, both on the interior and exterior, of Greek Revival architecture by William Strickland. The bank was built in the early 1820s. Restoration was completed in the early 1970s.

Note: Tickets will be necessary for this special exhibition. Admission will be for an allotted number of visitors each half-hour. Individuals and small groups can pick up tickets at the I.N.H.P. Visitor Center on the day of their visit. Groups of ten or more can call ahead to the Visitor Center for reservations or write for tickets to the "Miracle at Philadelphia" Exhibit, 313 Walnut Street, Phila., Pa. 19106.

In 1988, the Second Bank returns to its role as a portrait gallery of local history from 1740 to 1840. Among the 185 works are 85 paintings by Charles Willson Peale, the man whose idea it was in 1781 to honor America's leaders in such a gallery.

You'll see the Marquis de Lafayette in oils by Thomas Sully, Stephen Decatur by Gilbert Stuart, a life-size wood sculpture of George Washington by William Rush and portraits of General Horatio Gates by James Sharples and Charles Willson Peale.

Other portraits are of prominent military and civic leaders, ambassadors and diplomats of the period.

If you've never seen a physiognotrace, this is a chance to see a reproduction of this 19th century wizardry. You might even be able to have *your* silhouette made by it.

Summer Treat: The Friends of Independence National Historical Park serve 18th-century-style cold refreshments in their Tea Garden. It's in the shaded walkway next to the Second Bank. See Chapter 18 for details.

TODD HOUSE
4th and Walnut Streets

Hours: Daily, by scheduled tour only.
Tours: 10 tickets are allotted per tour, and you must get them in advance at the Visitor Center at 3rd and Chestnut Streets.

The four-story Todd House is a typical, comfortable 18th century middle-class Quaker home. It was built in 1775 and later restored to resemble the period between 1791 and 1793 when Dolly Payne Todd lived here with her first husband, John.

John Todd was an attorney, and his law office/library occupies the room overlooking the busy intersection. Among the furnishings is the forerunner of today's office copier—a machine that made multiple copies of correspondence. How did it work? You'll have to visit the house!

You'll also see the dining parlor, a fully equipped kitchen, a company parlor and two bedrooms. The furnishings are 18th century English and American.

John Todd died in the 1793 yellow fever epidemic, and Dolly later married a man who became the fourth President of the United States.

Every First Lady's name is memorable, but this First Lady's name had a delicious ring to it. Dolly Madison.

EDGAR ALLAN POE
NATIONAL HISTORIC SITE
530 North 7th Street—19123
597-8780

Hours: Daily, 9 to 5. Allow 30 minutes, more if you're a
   Poe fan.
Tours: Groups of 10 or more should call ahead. Exhibits
   are self-explanatory. National Park Service guides take
   you through the house. Every year, special tours and
   events commemorate the birth of Poe around the third
   week of January.
Cost: Free
Lunch: You can picnic on the grounds, but no refreshments are available or permitted inside.
SEPTA: Buses 43, 47.
Other: A small shop sells an assortment of Poe books.
E & H: There are 2 steps at the entrance to the visitor center and to the house. Only the first floor is accessible to
   wheelchairs. Steps in the house are steep and narrow.

Several homes and museums along the East Coast
honor the memory of Edgar Allan Poe, but this home is
the one that was singled out by Congress as "most
fitting" for a National Historic Site.

The complex has been maintained by the National Park
Service since 1980 and is a short ride from Independence
National Historical Park. It includes the three-story 19th
century brick house facing Spring Garden Street, two
adjoining buildings and a small park.

Poe, his wife and his mother-in-law rented the house in
1843 and 1844. Regrettably, there are no traces of the
family, but this time is thought to have been the happiest
and most prolific of Poe's anguished life.

Walk through the house and let your imagination take
over. See if you can feel what inspired Poe to write "The
Tell-Tale Heart," "The Black Cat" and "The Gold Bug"
while living here. An eight-minute audio-visual presentation offers some clues, and exhibits give some insight into
his mysterious life and the literary era.

Many more of Philadelphia's historic attractions are maintained by the U.S. Department of the Interior and are considered part of Independence National Historical Park. They are, however, run by their individual historical societies or religious affiliates. Among these are Christ Church and Christ Church Burial Ground, the Free Quaker Meeting House, Gloria Dei Church, Mikveh Israel Cemetery, St. George's Church, Old St. Joseph's Church and, in Germantown, the Deshler–Morris House. They're all described in later chapters and you can find them all in the Index.

Some of the **restaurants** that are convenient to the Independence National Historical Park are described in Chapter 18.

Chapter 3.
Neighborhoods.

Philadelphia is a city of neighborhoods. There are at least a hundred of them.

In Philadelphia, people closely identify with their neighborhoods. You can tell that when you see celebrities on The Tonight Show with Johnny Carson: They always tell what section of Philadelphia they're from.

Many neighborhoods bear names that were derived from the earliest settlers in that area.

The Lenni Lenape Indians are responsible for names like **Passyunk**, meaning "in the valley"; **Wyalusing**, from "old man's place"; **Poquessing**, from "place of mice"; or **Manayunk**, meaning "our place of drinking."

Other neighborhoods derive their names from an activity that was prominent at the site. **Fishtown** was a popular place for fishing along the Delaware River in the 18th and 19th centuries.

Roxborough was referred to in the late 1600s as a place where foxes burrowed in the rocks. **Fox Chase** is what you guessed it is.

Many neighborhoods took their names from people's estates. **Holmesburg** was the section where William Penn's surveyor and friend, Thomas Holme, settled in 1682.

Logan was the estate of Penn's secretary, James Logan. **Wynnefield** is where Penn's physician, Dr. Thomas Wynne, decided to build his home. (If your ancestors were friendly with William Penn, there would be a neighborhood named after your family.)

Some neighborhoods are known for their ethnic character. (More about that in Chapter 12.) **South Philadelphia** is the southern section of the city between the Delaware and Schuylkill Rivers. This neighborhood has a large Italian population. In fact, it's Philadelphia's largest foreign-born population segment.

South Philadelphia is famous for its bakeries, bocce, the Italian Market* and many Italian **restaurants.** (See Chapter 18 for more on these restaurants.) In recent years, "Rocky" has made South Philadelphia even more famous.

Chinatown is a community within center city Philadelphia. It's in the area of 8th to 11th on Race Street. At least a quarter of the 4,000 or more Chinese who make their homes in Philadelphia live in this section. Their origins here date back to 1870 when Philadelphia's first Chinese laundry opened at 9th and Race Streets.

The greatest attraction in Chinatown is the more than three dozen fine restaurants and the numerous shops that carry food delicacies, gifts and imported goodies. A magnificent Chinese Gate spans 10th Street, just north of Arch. It was dedicated in 1985. Read more about Chinatown in Chapter 12.

Eastwick is one of Philadelphia's newer neighborhoods, brought about by 20th century planning.

Eastwick is approximately four square miles of southwest Philadelphia. It's bounded roughly by 58th Street south of Tinicum National Environmental Center* and Philadelphia International Airport west to Dicks Avenue and Cobbs Creek where it abuts Delaware County.

Eastwick was conceived in 1954 by the late, great Greek city planner Constantinos Doxiadis. It's supposed to be the largest urban renewal project in this country.

Work began in the early 1960s to build Eastwick. To date it is a neighborhood with thousands of new homes, schools, shopping centers and recreation facilities.

Franklin Town is a 50-acre, privately developed city within center city Philadelphia. It's bounded by Spring Garden, Race and Vine Streets between 16th and 21st Streets.

Franklin Town began in the 1970s. So far there are highrise apartment buildings, the Wyndham Franklin Plaza Hotel*, Community College of Philadelphia*, restored homes, new homes and plans for additional housing and office development.

And so it goes.

The original two-square mile City of Philadelphia that was founded by William Penn in 1682 was incorporated under Penn's Proprietary Charter of 1701. Then, for over a hundred years, dozens of little independent towns sprouted up in Philadelphia County.

In 1854, the City was consolidated with its surrounding towns and the City and the County became one and the same. The boundaries were the same 130 square miles of Philadelphia we know today.

This chapter is about a few of the neighborhoods that have played significant roles in the history of Philadelphia and the United States. Several other neighborhoods are mentioned throughout the book as the locations of various attractions.

Germantown

In 1683, William Penn deeded an area of land six miles northwest of Philadelphia to a group of German settlers. Francis Daniel Pastorius led the first group of 13 families to what we now call Germantown. They were anxious to pursue Penn's dream of a "Holy Experiment." To prove their spirit, they built one of the first industrial towns in America.

In 1691, Germantown was made a borough within the County of Philadelphia.

Germantown was on the main route from Philadelphia to Reading, Bethlehem and points west. The road was heavily traveled by traders, Indians and settlers. In the 1760s, the stagecoach started its route through Germantown to Wilkes-Barre, Buffalo and Niagara Falls.

By the mid-18th century, Germantown was an established community with many schools and churches. America's first paper mill was built in Germantown in 1707. A Market Square was built in 1703 for food merchants. A firehouse, a jail and stocks were also built. The Square is still a picturesque site at Germantown Avenue and School House Lane.

Various trades and professions of Germantown homeowners were represented along the Germantown road.

Weavers, carpenters, shopkeepers, tanners and doctors lived side-by-side. Long gardens occupied the lots behind their homes. Many of the homes were large and gracious, set back on considerable plots of land.

We're sure you've heard about the Battle of Germantown.

During the Revolutionary War, most of Germantown was occupied by the British. Battle scars still remain in some of the homes that became troop headquarters and fighting grounds. The successful American advance was halted on October 4, 1777, by soldiers who occupied Cliveden*, a mansion that proudly stands at 6401 Germantown Avenue.

The yellow fever epidemic that struck Philadelphia in 1793 was a boon to Germantown. Many of the city's residents escaped to this suburban town where prosperous Philadelphians built their summer retreats.

In fact, Germantown was temporarily the nation's capital in 1793 while President George Washington stayed at the Deshler–Morris House*.

Many historic buildings still stand along the old Germantown Road—now called Germantown Avenue.

In 1969, the U.S. Department of the Interior designated Germantown Avenue a Registered Historic Road. The three mile stretch from Loudoun to Cliveden is particularly historic.

You should try to spend at least one afternoon in Germantown to go on an unusual tour of its colonial homes and landmarks.

You can visit Germantown on your own, or with a group. **Tours of Historic Germantown** for groups of 12 or more, with you providing the transportation, can be arranged by writing one month in advance to Tours of Historic Germantown, 6401 Germantown Ave., Phila., Pa. 19144. Or you can call 848-1777. Group luncheons at Cliveden and Stenton can be arranged the same way. You'll be reading about those attractions.

You can also **Experience Historic Germantown** on a private bus tour arranged by the Association of Historic Germantown Houses and the C.A. Asher Candy Company*. Different tours enable you to focus on different historic houses, museums and businesses in the area. For information, call Asher Tours, 849-3790.

The Germantown Historical Society in conjunction with Philadelphia Open House* sponsors two Germantown Open House Tours in May. Colonial homes and gardens are open to the public with special bus transportation along Germantown Avenue for a Sunday candlelight tour and a Wednesday afternoon tour. Call the Germantown Historical Society (844-0514) or Philadelphia Open House (928-1188) for the exact dates and ticket information.

SEPTA: If you're going to Germantown on your own, trains run from center city to stations on or near Germantown Avenue. Trolley 23 goes up and down Germantown on the nation's longest trolley line. It originates at 10th and Bigler Streets in South Philadelphia, then heads north along 11th Street through center city making the 12.8-mile one-way trip to Germantown Avenue and Bethlehem Pike.

Note: Flat shoes are requested to prevent damage to the floors of the colonial homes.

E & H: The gardens and first floors of most homes are wheelchair accessible. Call ahead to be sure, though. At Stenton, for example, arrange to have a ramp placed at the step leading to the house. The barn entrance is at ground level.

Germantown

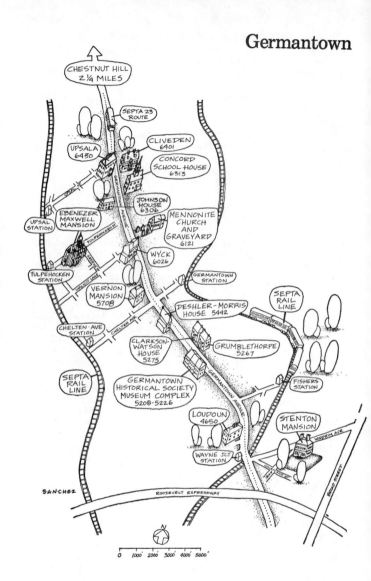

CHESTNUT HILL
2¼ MILES

SEPTA 23
ROUTE

UPSALA
6430

CLIVEDEN
6401

CONCORD
SCHOOL HOUSE
6313

UPSAL
STATION

EBENEZER
MAXWELL
MANSION

JOHNSON
HOUSE
6306

MENNONITE
CHURCH
AND
GRAVEYARD
6121

TULPEHOCKEN
STATION

WYCK
6026

GERMANTOWN
STATION

VERNON
MANSION
5708

DESHLER-MORRIS
HOUSE 5442

SEPTA
RAIL
LINE

CHELTEN-AVE
STATION

CLARKSON-
WATSON
HOUSE
5275

GRUMBLETHORPE
5267

SEPTA
RAIL
LINE

GERMANTOWN
HISTORICAL SOCIETY
MUSEUM COMPLEX
5208-5226

FISHERS
STATION

LOUDOUN
4650

STENTON
MANSION

WAYNE JCT
STATION

WINDRIM AVE

S·A·N·C·H·E·Z

ROOSEVELT EXPRESSWAY

BROAD STREET

N

0   1000'   2000'   3000'   4000'   5000'

The following sites are listed in order as if you were going north on Germantown Avenue.

STENTON MANSION
18th and Windrim Streets
329–7312

Hours: Tuesday to Saturday, 1 to 4. Closed January. Special arrangements can be made for group tours at other times. Allow at least one hour.

Tours: Groups of no more than 40, at least 3rd grade, can be scheduled by calling a few weeks in advance.

Cost: Adults, $2; senior citizens and students 14 and older, $1; children under 14 and school classes accompanied by their teachers, free.

SEPTA: Trackless Trolley 75.

Other: A gift shop in the spinning room wing of the kitchen offers charming items (embroidery, needlepoint, note paper and the like) that reflect Stenton's lifestyle.

Stenton was designed and built from 1723 to 1730 by James Logan, a young chap who came to Pennsylvania as William Penn's secretary. At that time it was a 500-acre summer residence. Today there are only five acres.

The house complements the man who built it. Logan was a scholar, a statesman and a businessman. He served the Penn family for 50 years. He was an adviser to Benjamin Franklin, and he also served as Chief Justice of Pennsylvania.

Among Stenton's spacious rooms was the finest library in the Commonwealth. The children's room has pint-size furnishings, an original cradle and dolls. There's also a fully furnished three-story built-in doll house.

Stenton is still flanked by the original weaving shed and barn. The barn was recently restored and now houses colonial farm tools and charts explaining how Stenton's gardens and crops were planted.

LOUDOUN
4650 Germantown Avenue
842-2877

Hours: Sunday, 1 to 4. Closed mid-December through April. Special arrangements can be made for group tours at other times. Allow about one hour.
Tours: Call at least a week ahead for groups of no more than 40.
Cost: Adults, $1.50; children, 75¢.
Lunch: Groups of 12 or more can make special arrangements for a prepared salad luncheon to be served. Call a few weeks ahead to schedule in conjunction with group tour. If you bring your own lunch, you're welcome to use Loudoun's grounds, but please don't leave any trash.

The stately Loudoun mansion is high above Germantown Avenue. It was built in 1801 by Thomas Armat, and later owned by the Logan family. The Greek portico was added in 1830. Loudoun was willed to the city in 1939 by Maria Dickinson Logan. Some visitors say that her ghost is still in the house.

Furnishings are exhibited on three floors, including the basement kitchen. Most of the items are from the 18th century and belonged to the Armat, Dickinson and Logan families. There's also a recently restored underground spring house that dates to the mid-1700s.

Continuing north on Germantown Avenue, at 4821 is the **MEHL HOUSE.** This dates back to 1744. Generations of the Mehl family occupied the home until the early 1900s. It's privately owned, but it's open to the public every year for the Germantown Open House Tour in May.

The Germantown Theatre Guild and Philadelphia Theater Caravan* performs in what was originally the Mehl's carriage house.

Several of Germantown's early settlers are buried in the **LOWER BURIAL GROUND** at 4900 Germantown Avenue (at Logan Street). Gravestones date back to 1708.

The **GERMANTOWN HISTORICAL SOCIETY MU-SEUM COMPLEX** (844–0514) extends from 5208 to 5226 Germantown Avenue. Its six buildings date from as early as 1740. Four of the buildings are open to the public.

Hours: Tuesday, Thursday, 10 to 4; Sunday, 1 to 5. Closed Christmas, New Year's, July 4, Memorial Day and Labor Day weekends. Special arrangements can be made for group tours at other times.

Cost: Adults, $1.50; groups of 10 or more, by appointment only, $1, unless noted otherwise. Pay an admission to see one of the houses, and you're welcome at all of them.

Tours: Small groups can schedule in advance for 1- to 2-hour tours, with 2 adults accompanying youngsters.

BAYNTON HOUSE
5208 Germantown Avenue

Baynton House contains the library of the Germantown Historical Society. You'll discover interesting manuscripts, old newspapers and family records of generations of Germantown residents.

You're welcome to use the references at the library, but they can't be taken out of the House.

COYNINGHAM-HACKER HOUSE
Germantown Historical Society Museum
5214 Germantown Avenue

Tours: The fire law limits groups to no more than 15 because of the original 18th century floor, stairway and woodwork. Allow 3 weeks notice for tours at times other than regular hours.

Welcome to the Germantown Historical Society's orientation center where you'll get an overview of the neighborhood's colorful history. This 18th century Federal-style home gives you an idea of how folks used to live in Germantown.

The rooms are furnished with items from the 17th, 18th and 19th centuries. At the time of the colonial settlement, life was austere. By the next century the rooms were more lavish. And by the 1800s, the homes became cluttered with Victoriana.

You'll see three centuries of period furniture, china, silver, quilts and tools. Sleighs, fire-fighting and farm equipment are in the Von Trott Museum Annex.

HOWELL HOUSE
5218 Germantown Avenue

Howell House is one more colonial Germantown home that survives on this block. It's now a charming little museum of quilts, samplers, needlework and toys.

The **ENDT HOUSE** (5222 Germantown Avenue) and the **BECHTEL HOUSE** (5226 Germantown Avenue) complete the complex.

GRUMBLETHORPE
5267 Germantown Avenue
843-4820

Hours: Saturday, 1 to 4; special arrangements can be made for group tours at other times. Allow 45 minutes.
Tours: Call 2 weeks in advance for groups of more than 20, at least 4th grade level.
Cost: Adults, $2; students and children under 12, $1.

John Wister, a wealthy merchant, was the first Philadelphian to build a summer home in Germantown: Grumblethorpe. (How did he ever come up with a name like that?) This home, which dates back to 1744, is a fine example of simple colonial architecture.

The building materials were completely local. The stone for the walls came from Wister's woodlands. Wister was a noted horticulturalist, and his garden is still maintained.

Grumblethorpe's furnishings are from the middle 1700s. The summer kitchen has barely changed since its original use. The cupboards are full of unusual old things. If you're interested in privies, Grumblethorpe's has been recently restored.

During the Revolution, Grumblethorpe was converted into soldier's quarters by the British. In fact, a bloodstain from British General Agnew's wound still shows up on the front parlor floor.

CLARKSON-WATSON HOUSE
5275 Germantown Avenue

Hours: Tuesday, Thursday, 10 to 4; Sunday, 1 to 5.

The costume museum of the **Germantown Historical Society** is housed here. You'll see a large collection of local costumes and finery dating from 1750 to 1950.

This is where Thomas Jefferson spent the summer of 1793 to avoid the yellow fever epidemic that raged in

Philadelphia. Everybody talks about where Washington slept, but nobody talks about where Jefferson slept.

You can't miss the **TRINITY LUTHERAN CHURCH** and its imposing tower across the street at 5300 Germantown Avenue. The church, built in 1865, is noteworthy for its Tiffany stained glass windows.

The oldest part of its corner Church House dates back to 1723. The first metal type to be cast in America was made in the cellar here in 1772. A colonial printer, Christopher Sauer, lived here and printed the first American Bible in the German language.

DESHLER–MORRIS HOUSE
5442 Germantown Avenue
596-1748

Hours: April to December, Tuesday to Sunday, 1 to 4. Closed January to March and major holidays. Special arrangements can be made for group tours at other times. Allow 45 minutes.

Tours: Groups of up to 50 can be scheduled by calling at least 2 weeks in advance. Any group of 8 or more must call in advance for reservations, whether or not you want a guided tour.

Cost: 50¢.

We think of the White House in Washington, D.C. as our President's official residence. But did you know the "White House" was once in Germantown? Well, it was.

In 1793, when the yellow fever epidemic struck Philadelphia, President Washington and his wife moved to what is now the Deshler–Morris House. Cabinet meetings and official dinners took place that November in the Deshler–Morris front parlor.

The Washingtons enjoyed the house so much that they returned for six weeks the following summer along with Mrs. Washington's two grandchildren.

The other famous resident at Deshler–Morris was Sir William Howe. He made the home the headquarters for his British command after the Battle of Germantown in 1777. David Deshler, a shipping merchant, built the house in 1772. It was later owned by the Morris family between 1834 and 1948, when it was bequeathed to the Federal government. It now belongs to Independence National Historical Park*.

Eleven rooms of Deshler–Morris have been expertly restored and furnished. You'll see period and original pieces, beautiful woodwork, Pennsylvania marble and Delft fireplaces, Oriental rugs, a room filled with toys and an 18th century kitchen complete with a walk-in fireplace.

The garden is lush with flowers, shrubs and trees, some of which date back to Washington's time.

Imagine how royally the colonial notables were entertained in this White House. Yes, this is one place where Washington actually slept.

The historic **BRINGHURST HOUSE** is next to the Deshler–Morris House at 5448 Germantown Avenue. It belongs to Independence National Historical Park*, but isn't open to the public.

If you look across the street, you'll see the **GERMANTOWN MARKET SQUARE** and the **FROMBERGER HOUSE**. The Federal government rented this house in 1793 and used it as the Bank of the United States. It's now the Germantown Insurance Company.

VERNON MANSION
5708 Germantown Avenue

Vernon Mansion's facade is in typical early 19th century Federal style with marble steps balanced by iron railings and large fluted Doric columns. The house dates back to 1803.

In 1812, John Wister (the grandson of the Grumblethorpe John Wister) bought the mansion and named it Vernon. Wister was a botanist, and some of the rare shrubs and trees he planted still grow in the large public park that surrounds the house.

A statue of John Wister is out front. He's dressed in plain Quaker clothes and the hat he always wore in public.

There's also a monument bearing the statues of Francis Daniel Pastorius and the 13 families who were the original settlers of Germantown.

Vernon Mansion is closed to the public.

WYCK
6026 Germantown Avenue
848-1690

Hours: April to December, Tuesday, Thursday, Saturday,
1 to 4. Special arrangements can be made for group
tours at other times. Allow one hour.
Tours: Groups of up to 40 can be scheduled by calling a
few weeks ahead.
Cost: Adults, $2; senior citizens and students, $1; children
under 12, 50¢.

One section of Wyck dates from around 1700, making it
the oldest home in Germantown. In fact, the earliest section of Wyck was built seven decades before its neighbor
Cliveden, and almost a century before George Washington became President.

Architect William Strickland designed alterations to
Wyck in 1824 giving it the subtle touch of Greek Revival
style that remains unchanged today.

For 283 years Wyck was owned and occupied by nine
generations of one family. Many of their heirlooms and
furnishings can be seen in six rooms on the first floor.

In colonial times Wyck was surrounded by 20 acres of
woods and farmland. Today it's on two-and-a-half acres
along with an original smokehouse and ice and carriage
houses. Wyck is most pleasant in warm weather when its
formal rose garden is in bloom, the woods are green and
the vegetable garden is sprouting.

If you'd like to visit what is one of the oldest homes in
this country that has been occupied by the same family
(and also where Revolutionary soldiers were hospitalized
in 1777, and where the Marquis de Lafayette was formally
honored at a reception in 1825), then you've come to the
right place!

MENNONITE CHURCH AND GRAVEYARD
6121 Germantown Avenue
843-0943

Hours: Tuesday to Saturday, 10 to 12 and 1 to 4. Special
arrangements can be made for group tours at other
times. Allow at least 30 minutes.
Tours: Call or write at least a week in advance for groups
of no more than 50. Arrangements can also be made for
a slide show on Germantown's Mennonite history and
to visit other Mennonite sites in the area.
Cost: Free, but donations are accepted.

Other: A gift shop offers books about Mennonite and Germantown history, along with handmade arts and crafts.

The Germantown Mennonites, or German Quakers, were the first Mennonites to establish themselves in the colonies. In 1708 they built a log cabin to worship on this very site. The present stone meetinghouse replaced the log cabin in 1770. Its tiny chapel looks as it did in the 1800s. The basement with its drinking well has been restored to its 1770 appearance.

The church museum has memorabilia of Mennonite and Germantown history. A library* is available for reference on the same subjects.

A small graveyard fills the church's front yard. Its oldest stones date from the 1730s, and most of them belong to early settlers of Germantown.

EBENEZER MAXWELL MANSION
200 W. Tulpehocken Street (at Greene Street)
438–1861

Hours: April to December, Wednesday, Friday and Saturday, 11 to 4; Sunday, 1 to 5. Group tours can be scheduled in advance at other times. Allow one hour.
Tours: Groups of up to 40 should call at least 2 weeks ahead. A variety of programs including 8 of Germantown's historic homes are available for school groups.
Cost: Adults, $2; senior citizens, students and children, $1.
SEPTA: Bus H, or SEPTA train to Tulpehocken Station.

Go two blocks west of Germantown Avenue at Tulpehocken Street (6200 block) for a look at 19th century Philadelphia. You've come to Philadelphia's only house-museum of the Victorian period.

Ebenezer Maxwell had his Norman Gothic-style suburban villa built in 1859. Only one other family occupied it since the Maxwells, and little has changed since the original construction. Odd-shaped high windows, a gingerbread slate roof and three-story tower dominate the exterior.

Large, sunlit and functional family rooms are gradually being restored and furnished from the period. Chunky Rococco Revival-style pieces dominate the library, parlor and bedrooms. Magnificent examples of Victorian stenciling can be seen on the upstairs walls and ceilings.

When you visit the Ebenezer Maxwell Mansion, keep in mind that this was a prestigious suburban section of

Philadelphia when the Maxwells lived here. The man of the house was among the first center city merchants to commute daily on the Reading Company's new line to town.

The garden surrounding the house has proper Victorian landscaping. A guide to the plantings is available.

Does the Ebenezer Maxwell Mansion remind you of the mansion in the Charles Addams cartoons?

Well it should. Because this is what inspired him.

JOHNSON HOUSE
6306 Germantown Avenue
438-9366

Hours: By appointment only, Tuesday to Saturday, 10 to 4. Special arrangements can be made for group tours at other times. Allow at least one hour.
Tours: Call 843-0943 or write at least 2 weeks in advance for groups of no more than 50.
Cost: Adults, $1.50; children, 75¢.

The Johnson House, owned by the Mennonite Church and Graveyard Corporation, is typical of the homes built for well-to-do Germantown families in the 1760s.

The Johnson House became the scene of major fights during the Battle of Germantown. If you want proof, look, or rather hunt, for the bullet holes and cannon ball scars.

The house had a unique function before the Civil War. It was the underground railroad station. Slaves were temporarily camped here when they were smuggled north from the Southern states.

Today, Johnson House is furnished and looks as it did in colonial days.

CONCORD SCHOOL HOUSE
6313 Germantown Avenue

Hours: April through October, Tuesday, 10 to 1; Thursday, 1 to 4.

Tours: Arrangements for a visit must be made in advance by calling Kirk and Nice, 438-6328. They keep the School House key.

Cost: Adults, 50¢; children, 25¢.

You know that schools weren't always the sleek and modern buildings that they are today. Now you can go back into history to see where children spent their school days at the time of our independence.

The Concord School House is a tiny one-room school built in 1775. The original school bell is housed in the belfry. The original books and desks are in the schoolroom.

A plot plan on the wall identifies the occupants of the **UPPER GERMANTOWN BURYING GROUND.** Peek out the window and see the graves of many early Germantown settlers and Revolutionary War victims.

CLIVEDEN
6401 Germantown Avenue
848-1777

Hours: April through December, Tuesday to Saturday, 10 to 4; Sunday, 1 to 4. Closed holidays. Allow at least one hour.

Tours: Call a few weeks in advance to schedule for up to one busload, and no more than one school class at a time. Tours led according to youngsters' age levels. Special 90-minute programs can be scheduled for school groups.

Cost: Adults, $2; senior citizens, $1.50; students and children, $1. Groups of 20 or more, $1.50.

Other: A gift shop features reproductions of 18th century decorative arts, games, books on Philadelphia and colonial cooking, items of the National Trust and antiques and handmade crafts on consignment.

Note: Start your visit in the restored 18th century barn. It's now a reception center and small museum.

This historically important house was built in the 1760s by jurist Benjamin Chew. The Chew family owned and occupied the mansion until 1972. Now it's open to the public, and it's one of a select group of houses that is owned and maintained by the National Trust for Historic

Preservation.

Before you go inside, walk around the six-acre block for an outside look at what was once Germantown's most elaborate 18th century home. Cliveden was also built as a summer home. The stables, coach house, cook and wash houses are still in the yard. They're built with the same solid masonry as the Georgian style house.

The British were so impressed with Cliveden's sturdy construction that they made it a fort during the Battle of Germantown. The home took quite a beating, but it managed to withstand the attacks led by George Washington himself. Musket fire and cannonball marks are still visible in walls and ceilings. Many of the marble statues in the garden are scarred by bullets.

Cliveden's elegant furnishings reflect the outstanding taste of each generation that resided here. Many pieces are signed by important 18th century craftsmen.

UPSALA
6430 Germantown Avenue
247-6113

Hours: April through December, Tuesday and Thursday, 1 to 4. Special arrangements can be made for group tours at other times. Allow at least 45 minutes.

Tours: Call one week ahead to schedule groups of no more than 25, at least elementary school age. Two adults must accompany youngsters.

Cost: $2; children under 12, $1. Groups of 20 or more, $1.50.

Upsala was built in 1798 on the site the Continental troops camped on during the Battle of Germantown.

The Upsala facade is similar to the Vernon Mansion, in that it's the classic Federal style. You'll recognize the similarities of the stone front with Doric columns and marble steps.

The wood in Upsala is from the neighborhood. The mantlepieces, floors, stairs and doors are all original. And the structure hasn't been altered since it was built. Seven of Upsala's rooms are filled with period furnishings.

If you continue along Germantown Avenue, you'll pass more 18th century homes, churches and school buildings (including some that haven't been listed here).

The 6500 block has three more interesting homes. **BARDSLEY HOUSE**, at No. 6500, was originally one room deep. As you'll see, there have been many additions to the white stucco frame. The house was named for its owner, John Bardsley, who achieved a fair amount of fame in the 1870s importing English sparrows to eat the caterpillars that plagued neighborhood plants.

The **BILLMEYER HOUSE**, at No. 6504, and the double house across the street at No. 6505–07, also date back to the late 1700s.

On the next block, at No. 6613, is the original building of the **CHURCH OF THE BRETHREN**. It was built in 1770 by the first group of Dunkards that gathered in Pennsylvania. (Their name comes from the unusual way in which members are immersed at baptism.)

The **SCHOOL**, at No. 6609, was built in 1740 by **ST. MICHAEL'S LUTHERAN CHURCH**. Founded in 1717, the Church now occupies its third building on the site. Services are still held in German on Sunday mornings, followed by a version in English.

Continue north along Germantown Avenue and you'll come to another Philadelphia neighborhood, **Chestnut Hill**. This is the highest point in Philadelphia and was once abundant with chestnut trees.

Chestnut Hill is one of Philadelphia's finest residential sections. It's famous for its exclusive shops. The galleries, restaurants, farmers markets, boutiques and stores of Chestnut Hill are among the most charming in the country. Some of the **restaurants** convenient to Germantown and Chestnut Hill are described in Chapter 18.

Old City

Old City is in the shadow of the Ben Franklin Bridge, from Vine Street to Chestnut and from the Delaware River to 5th Street. This was the heart of William Penn's Philadelphia.

Elfreth's Alley*, the nation's oldest continuously occupied residential street, is here. So are several of the 18th century churches (see Chapter 5). Here, too, are Fireman's Hall* and the Betsy Ross House*.

In recent years, Old City was a commercial area for industry and wholesale distributors. Their structures are excellent examples of late 18th and early 19th century architecture. No fewer than 60 examples of cast iron building facades remain, mostly from the 1850s.

Since the late 1960s, many of these commercial loft buildings have been rehabilitated to provide expansive, well-lit living and working areas for artists and architects. They also have retail spaces on the street level.

Some examples of apartment conversions are Little Boys Way at 209 Cuthbert Street (once a sewing notions factory), St. Charles Court at 3rd and Arch Streets (formerly a hostelry for the Arch Street Friends), The Sugar Refinery at 225 Christ Church Walkway (built in 1782 and once the country's largest sugar refinery), The Wireworks at 301 Race Street (built at the turn-of-the-century for a factory that made insulated electric wire), The Chocolate Works at 231 N. 3rd Street (comprising five buildings from the early 20th century that housed the Wilbur Chocolate Company), and the Hoopskirt Factory at 309 Arch Street (built in 1875, and you can guess what they made there until 1894).

What Soho has been to New York City, Old City has become to Philadelphia.

Other city art galleries have opened Old City extensions. The Clay Studio* at 49 N. 2nd Street provides work and exhibition space for craftspeople. Drama groups and small theaters have assembled a la Greenwich Village. The Painted Bride Art Center* moved to Old City from South Street in 1981.

You'll want to stroll through Old City to see its historic attractions and its recent changes and additions.

SEPTA routes to the area include any of the Market Street bus or subway lines to 2nd Street, Bus 5 running north on 3rd Street or south on 2nd Street and Bus 50 running north on 5th Street and south on 4th Street.

As the population comes to a neighborhood, so do restaurants. Several of Old City's eating and drinking places
are described in Chapter 18.

Queen Village

This neighborhood is in the oldest part of Philadelphia.
It was settled by the Swedes prior to 1640. It was originally called Wiccaco. Then it was named Southwark, for
its English counterpart south of London. The newest
name, Queen Village, honors Swedish Queen Christina's
role in promoting the area's original settlement.

Queen Village is directly south of Head House Square in
Society Hill. Its borders are Front to 6th Street and Lombard to Washington Avenue.

Queen Village was a separate neighborhood that
became part of Philadelphia when the City and County
were consolidated in 1854.

Queen Village has many of Philadelphia's oldest houses,
and they, too, are being restored. The Shippen family
developed Kenilworth Street between Front and 2nd
Streets in the 1740s. The neighboring homes belonged to
sea captains, mariners, riggers and ropemakers who worked hard to make Philadelphia a major 18th century sea-
port.

New houses, as well, have sprouted in Queen Village.
Striking individual townhomes and contemporary
clusters are throughout the neighborhood.

If you want to see some interesting homes, look on
Monroe, Pemberton, Fitzwater, Catharine and Queen
Streets. Also look at the Court at Old Swedes develop-
ment facing the Delaware River at Queen Street.

America's first naval yards were on the Delaware at the
foot of Federal Street. They're long gone, but at one time
frigates were outfitted and repaired in Southwark. The
waterfront activity made this a bustling neighborhood.

The historic sites in Queen Village include Old Swedes'
Church (Gloria Dei)*. This is the oldest church in Pennsylvania.

The famous **SHOT TOWER** at Front and Carpenter
Streets was built in 1808 to manufacture shotgun ammunition. It remained an arsenal for 100 years, and was the
first arsenal in the country.

By today's standards, the manufacturing process was
relatively simple. Lead was dropped from the top of the

175-foot tower through screens with different size holes. The hot lead fell into cold water vats and then hardened into bullets. Some of the bullets are still on display at Old Swedes' Church. Shot Tower is now a recreation center.

A colorful part of the neighborhood is **SOUTH STREET** from 2nd to 7th, and extending a block north and south to Lombard and Bainbridge Streets.

Old, dilapidated stores from another era were bought or leased by young people who converted them into craft houses, book stores, second-hand shops, leather shops, restaurants, cafe theaters, antique shops and coffee shops.

South Street was once one of Philadelphia's most popular shopping streets. Today it's similar to Greenwich Village in New York. Older Philadelphians are shocked to find that this longtime run-down area has become strong and viable again.

Colorful street maps are posted on some store fronts and street corners to make your strolling easier.

You can comfortably spend a few hours dining and browsing here. Most of the shops and restaurants are open daily from late morning till late in the evening. South Street is especially lively on weekends and for cabaret and nightlife.

The South Street area is a mecca for good, imaginative **restaurants**. Read about several of them in Chapter 18.

Society Hill

Directly south of Independence National Historical Park lies a neighborhood known as Society Hill. It's loosely bounded by Walnut and Lombard Streets and Front and 7th Streets.

Society Hill got its name because it was land that William Penn granted to a stock company called the Society of Free Traders. Their goal was to promote trade in Pennsylvania. The Delaware waterfront at Front and Pine Streets was a hill. And that's why it's called Society Hill.

For many years, Society Hill was a meeting place and parade ground. The hill gradually disappeared over the years, but the name remained. (In the 1960s it became an "in" place for prominent Philadelphians to live.) Churches rose in the neighborhood, along with a market place and a community center.

Today a great deal of Society Hill looks as it did in colonial times. It's one of the nation's finest examples of urban renewal, and it's virtually impossible to buy a home here for less than $150,000.

The blight of the Industrial Revolution has rapidly disappeared. The major force for renewal came in June, 1959, when the antiquated Dock Street Markets were closed. (A modern Food Distribution Center* opened simultaneously at its sprawling new site in South Philadelphia.) The three Society Hill Towers luxury apartment buildings were completed in 1964.

Over 900 homes from the 18th and 19th centuries have been restored and rebuilt with loving care to resemble their original condition. Even the new homes in Society Hill have been designed to look colonial or to blend with their surroundings.

Many of the new homes are built in clusters around a common courtyard. Delancey Mews is at 2nd and Delancey Streets; Addison Court is at 6th and Pine Streets; Bingham Court is at 4th Street and St. Joseph's Walk; Lawrence Court is tucked between 4th and 5th Streets and Spruce and Pine.

Colonial style brick walkways weave through Society Hill. You can stroll on the major streets or these walkways to see historic homes, recent courtyard developments, colonial churches and small parks. (My father built the one between 3rd and 4th Streets on Delancey.)

Some of the Society Hill homes are open to the public. You can visit Hill Physick Keith House*, Powel House*, "A Man Full of Trouble Tavern"* and the former Abercrombie mansion that's now the Perelman Antique Toy Museum*.

Stop at Head House Square* and NewMarket*. Admire the shops and numerous restaurants. See the 18th century-style street lights, cobblestone streets, narrow alleys and brick sidewalks. Have an ice cream cone or some jelly beans.

Guided tours can be arranged with some of the guide services listed in Chapter 1. We're partial to the carriage rides or Fairmount Park Trolley-Bus* tours.

SEPTA routes to 2nd and Pine Streets are buses 5, 40 or 90. Route 50 buses go north on 5th Street and south on 4th. Buses D and 42 originate their westbound routes from 2nd and Dock Streets.

HEAD HOUSE
2nd and Pine Streets

This little red brick structure was built at the northern end of the colonial 2nd Street marketplace in 1804. Fire-fighting equipment was kept behind the large green double-doors that face Pine Street. An early 18th century man-drawn fire wagon is still here. The 2nd floor was used as a meeting place and community center.

2ND STREET MARKET
2nd Street from Pine to Lombard

This open-air market in the center of 2nd Street between Pine and Lombard was originally built in 1745 and known as "New Market."

The stall dividers have been reconstructed so you can picture how Ben Franklin, George Washington, Thomas Jefferson and the rest of the fellows went to buy their provisions. Incidentally, Ben Franklin never pulled rank to get to the front of the line. He waited in line at the supermarket, just like you and I.

The market area of **Head House**, as it's called today, is the focal point of Society Hill.

Both sides of 2nd Street from Pine to Lombard are now lined with delightful shops, cafes, restaurants and intriguing sights. Some of the shops are restored, while others are recently built.

The activity continues to bustle at Head House during the summer. Visitors come by car, carriage, bicycle, stroller and foot to dine, shop, browse and have fun.

Local artists, craftsmen and entertainers come to the marketplace for 10 weekends from late June till early September. The **Crafts Market** hours are noon to midnight on Saturdays and noon to 6 on Sundays. Workshops for adults and children are on Sundays from 1 to 3.

A word to the wise: parking can be difficult. Try the four-level garage at 2nd and Lombard Streets.

NEWMARKET
Pine to Lombard, Front to 2nd Streets
627-7500

Today's NewMarket encompasses an entire block on the east side of Head House Square. It's a multi-level commercial complex of specialty shops, offices, the Market at NewMarket and restaurants. It beautifully combines the old and new with colorful canopies, massive wood sculpture, stacked glass cubes and a see-through elevator.

NewMarket took 18th century homes on the 2nd Street side and combined them with an ultra-modern glass facade on the Front Street side.

A year was dedicated to archaeological exploration of the block before the restoration began. The thousands of items that were found indicate that a marketplace and homes were on the site in the 18th century. Period restorations show Georgian, Federal and Victorian architectural styles.

You can dine internationally at NewMarket and Head House Square. **Restaurants,** from informal to elegant and indoor to outdoor, are described in Chapter 18.

For handicapped persons, a steep ramp at the Front Street entrance makes wheelchair access easiest. It's also a short distance from the underground parking garage entrance on Front Street.

Note: Don't pass NewMarket. You have to see it.

University City

University City gets its name from the many educational facilities within its boundaries, from the Schuylkill River west to 44th Street and from the river north to Powelton Avenue.

This neighborhood's history can be traced to five years before William Penn appeared on the scene. In 1677 William Warner, an Englishman who's said to have been Philadelphia's only Puritan, purchased from the Indians 1,500 acres in the area. Warner called his estate Blockley.

Today 300 acres of that huge estate remain as Woodlands Cemetery. A handsome Federal-style mansion, built in 1788 and called "Woodlands," is preserved beyond the cemetery's gates at 40th Street and Baltimore Avenue.

Settlement grew in the area, especially after bridges were built to span the Schuylkill. Private estates covered entire blocks and summer villages sprang up in clusters. By the mid-19th century, Philadelphia's western suburbs prospered. University City was incorporated into the City in 1854.

Hundreds of homes and no less than 50 churches remain from that period and from subsequent decades. Over the years, however, much of University City's grand suburban residential atmosphere has been altered by the growth of great institutions including the Veterans Hospital and the Civic Center complex.

The University of Pennsylvania moved in 1872 from the center of Philadelphia to a campus that hasn't stopped growing in University City. A few blocks east, Drexel University (formerly known as Drexel Institute of Technology) was founded in 1890. The Philadelphia College of Pharmacy and Science moved in 1928 to its campus bordering the Woodlands Cemetery.

University City Science Center was founded in 1965 with the backing of 28 Philadelphia area colleges and universities. Its research and office buildings on 16 acres along nine blocks of Market Street make Philadelphia an internationally recognized "think tank" on just about any scientific subject.

The World Forum for Science and Human Affairs will further expand the Center's capability and attract multilingual and international meetings. A huge auditorium, conference rooms, seminar halls, restaurants, retail shops, recreation facilities and a 300-room hotel will be the newest addition to the University City Science Center along the north side of Market Street from 36th to 38th Streets.

This combination of private and institutional wealth and resources has blessed University City with a variety of outstanding architecture. Many of the neighborhood's historic mansions have been adapted by the University of Pennsylvania for educational use. Blocks of unusual single homes, twins and rowhouses exist throughout the western section of University City on Locust, Spruce and Pine Streets, Larchwood and Osage Avenues, St. Mark's Square and Woodland Terrace. Powelton Village is seeing a rebirth northwest of the Drexel campus.

The Penn campus (I'm partial to my alma mater) has been a magnet for great architects. There is a unique blending of buildings designed by Frank Furness, Cope and Stewardson, Eero Saarinen, Louis Kahn and Mitchell and Giurgola, to name a few.

Drexel University's original and main building is the home of the Drexel Museum Collection* at 32nd and

Chestnut Streets. It was designed by the Wilson Brothers, finished in 1892, and is still spectacular. And it would be remiss not to mention the contemporary architecture of Children's Hospital on 34th Street and the International House*.

A good time to explore University City is on the Philadelphia Open House* tour held the first Sunday afternoon in May.

You can call the West Philadelphia Partnership for information about the "University City Guide" they publish along with the West Philadelphia Chamber of Commerce. The University City Historical Society (387–3019) and the University City Arts League (382–7811) also sponsor ongoing programs in the community.

Several SEPTA routes traverse University City. They include the Market–Frankford Subway–Elevated; buses D, 30, 31, 40, 42; trolleys 10, 11, 13, 34, 36; and the commuter trains to 30th Street Station.

Some of the **restaurants** in University City are described in Chapter 18. There are also several campus-favorite sandwich shops, fast food establishments and cheerful cafeterias in the University Museum, hospitals and university facilities. Most of the people in University City are from the academic world and are very friendly, so feel free to ask them what's nearby.

You can see from this brief description and throughout this book that University City offers all kinds of cultural events, recreational facilities, hotels, office complexes, world-renowned medical centers, residential communities and campus environments. It's no wonder that the people of University City call their neighborhood Philadelphia's "Other City."

Chapter 4.
Museums and Historic Sites.

It's only natural that the city where the country was founded would be rich in historic attractions. You've read about the sites of Independence National Historical Park.

Now examine the dozens of museums, 18th century homes, taverns, a colonial street and a Revolutionary fort. Some concentrate on a specific theme such as shoes or toys, some dwell on a particular period in history, some are devoted to a prominent person and some are more general in their appeal. But you'll surely want to visit at least a few.

In some cases, art and artifacts overlap with objects and places of antiquity. So some of the attractions described in this chapter might be equally appropriate for the section on Art Museums in Chapter 9, and vice versa.

"A MAN FULL OF TROUBLE TAVERN"
127 Spruce Street—19106
922-1759

Hours: By appointment only, daily, from 10 A.M. Candlelight tours can be scheduled from 7 to 9 P.M. Allow at least 30 minutes.

Tours: Call the tavern or 743-4225 between 9 to 10 A.M. and 4 to 5 P.M. at least one week in advance.

Cost: Adults, $1; children 10 to 16, 50¢; under 10, scout groups, Philadelphia school groups and servicemen in uniform, free.

Lunch: No facilities.

SEPTA: Buses 5, 40, 42, 90.

E & H: No wheelchair access.

"A Man Full of Trouble" is the only remaining 18th century tavern in Philadelphia. It's a Society Hill landmark that dates back to 1759.

The Knauer Foundation restored the tavern with period furnishings that include Delftware, pewter and finds from nearby excavations.

As in most colonial dwellings, the kitchen is in the basement. The first floor was formerly used by guests for food and drink. The bedrooms and a sitting room are on the second floor.

AFRO-AMERICAN HISTORICAL AND CULTURAL MUSEUM
7th and Arch Streets—19106
574-3670

Hours: Tuesday to Saturday, 10 to 5; Sunday, 12 to 6. Closed holidays. Allow at least one hour.

Tours: All exhibits are self-explanatory. Groups of 20 or more should call a week ahead to schedule visits and special rates. Philadelphia Public School teachers call the Museum Education Department at the Board of Education, 299-7778, for study programs and to arrange visits.

Cost: Adults, $1.50; senior citizens, handicapped and children under 12, 75¢. Groups of 20 or more: adults, $1; senior citizens, handicapped and children, 50¢. One person must pay for everyone. Membership (Student, $5; Individual, $10; Family, $25) entitles you to free admission, shop discounts, a newsletter and invitations to special events.

SEPTA: Bus 48, Market Street routes or a short walk from Independence Hall.

Other: A gift shop sells African artifacts, jewelry, books and clothing. Cultural programs are scheduled in the museum's auditorium. Call to find out what's planned.

E & H: Complete wheelchair access.

This is the largest museum of its kind in the world. It's also the first of its kind in the United States, opened in 1976 during America's Bicentennial celebration.

The Black History Museum's five levels of galleries are used for changing exhibits to portray the Afro-American experience in Pennsylvania and the country.

The "Wall of Respect" is a permanent exhibition of 30 notable blacks in American history. Among them are Daniel Hale Williams, physician and surgeon who performed the first heart surgery; Benjamin Banneker, surveyor who helped design Washington, D.C.; Phyllis Wheatley, poetess in the era of the American Revolution; and Thurgood Marshall, the first black justice to serve on the U.S. Supreme Court.

Don't leave the area without observing the museum's two outdoor sculptures. "Nesaika" is an African deity, and the 13 "Whispering Bells" honor a black patriot, Crispus Attucks, who was the first casualty of the Revolutionary War. (See the section of Chapter 9 on Street Art.)

AMERICAN-SWEDISH
HISTORICAL MUSEUM
1900 Pattison Avenue—19145
389-1776

Hours: Tuesday to Friday, 10 to 4; Saturday, 12 to 4.
Closed holidays. Allow one hour.
Tours: Call 2 weeks in advance to schedule groups of 10 to
40, at least 4th grade level.
Cost: Adults, $1.50; senior citizens, students, $1; children
under 12 with an adult, free; school groups with
reservations, free. Memberships are available.
Lunch: No indoor facilities, but in nice weather you can
picnic in the surrounding park.
SEPTA: Buses 17, C, G; Broad Street Subway to Pat-
tison.
Other: Festivals are celebrated in April, June and
December (see Chapter 19). A small gift shop sells
Swedish crafts, knick-knacks, stationery, jewelry and
books.
E & H: No wheelchair access.

The American-Swedish Historical Museum resembles a
17th century Swedish manor house which is very much at
home in Philadelphia's Franklin D. Roosevelt Park.
Its 14 rooms have artifacts from early Swedish settle-
ments along the Delaware River. (The museum's site was
part of New Sweden in the 1600s.) The displays honor
Swedish and American-Swedish contributions to the cultural, economic, social and technological development of
the United States.
Part of the museum's ongoing Bicentennial exhibit,
"200 Years of Friendship: Sweden and America
1776-1976," occupies the John Hanson Room. The exhibit was dedicated by His Majesty Carl XVI Gustaf
King of Sweden when he visited the museum on April 6,
1976.
The John Erikson Room contains its namesake's contributions to science. The Jenny Lind Music Room has
memorabilia from her American concert tour from 1848 to
1851.
The Pioneer and Arts and Crafts Rooms are enchanting
for youngsters. One simulates an 18th century Dalarna
farmhouse. The other contains jewelry, ceramics and a collection of 28 Swedish costumed dolls—all handmade in
Sweden and dressed in authentic peasant costumes.

ATWATER KENT MUSEUM
15 South 7th Street—19106
922-3031 or 686-3630

Hours: Tuesday to Saturday, 9:30 to 4:45. Closed holidays. Allow 45 minutes.
Tours: You're on your own.
Cost: Free.
SEPTA: Buses D, 42, 76, Market Street routes.
E & H: There is a ramp at the rear entrance, off the Liberty Walkway. Once inside, all floors can be reached by elevator. All of the restrooms are accessible to wheelchairs; a parking lot is next door.

The Atwater Kent Museum is a wonderful place to learn about Philadelphia's early growth and progress.

The main gallery portrays Philadelphia from 1680 to 1880: from William Penn to the Centennial celebration. There are objects from every aspect of life in Philadelphia: weapons, model ships, model railroads, model houses, model streets, clothing, furniture, books, dolls, musical instruments, silverware, crafts and cockroach traps. (As I said, it has *every* aspect.)

"The City Beneath Us" is a changing exhibit of archaeological finds that have been unearthed in Philadelphia.

A small room shows "Philadelphia in Two Dimensions: The City's History through Maps." The city's growth over 300 years is shown in 29 different ways. While you're tracking the city's geographic changes, you can study the art of map-making from hand-drawn engravings to computerized satellite surveys.

Two other small rooms show the development of Philadelphia's municipal services. The water and gas utilities are in one exhibit and the police and fire departments are in another. Be sure to see the 1890 Rogues Gallery with its old mug shots of local anarchists and horse thieves.

You won't want to miss a marvelous display on the second floor of antique toys and dolls native to this area.

BELLAIRE MANOR

20th Street and Pattison Avenue—19145
664-8456

Hours: By reservation only, daily, 10 to 4. Allow one hour.
Tours: Guides in colonial costume will escort you, no more than 10 in a group and 2 groups per hour. Children must be with an adult. Call 2 weeks ahead.
Cost: Adults, $1; children under 12, 50¢. Group rates arranged in advance.
Lunch: No food is allowed in the house, but you can picnic in the park. Refreshments are available nearby at the golfhouse.
SEPTA: Bus 17, C, G.
E & H: There's one step at the entrance to each building. Arrangements can be made in advance for a ramp to be put down.

Built in 1714, Bellaire Manor is the oldest of the Fairmount Park houses and one of the oldest houses in Philadelphia. It's tucked away in Franklin D. Roosevelt Park, a section of Fairmount Park in the southern part of the city.

A visit to Bellaire takes in a description of its early Georgian architectural style, and the colonial lifestyle of the area's early Swedish settlers. You'll see five rooms that are furnished with period pieces and reproductions representing two centuries of occupants at the property.

The bake house is also restored, functionally furnished, in use and part of the tour. If something smells real good, it might be fresh bread in the kiln or hot soup in the cauldron.

An authentic colonial herb garden is behind the bake house. I know you're familiar with parsley, sage, rosemary and thyme. But you might also recognize aloes, hyssop and lamb's leg.

BENJAMIN FRANKLIN BUST

Arch Street east of 4th

Don't miss, or rather you can't miss, the bigger-than-life bust of Benjamin Franklin while you're walking through historic Philadelphia. Ben overlooks Arch Street and the Arch Street Friends' Meeting House*, only a block away from Franklin's grave in the Christ Church Burial Ground*.

Franklin came to Philadelphia in 1723 when he was 17. His contributions to Philadelphia, the colonies and later the United States and the world are renowned.

As a statesman, Franklin was United States emissary to France during the Revolution. He wrote the "Franklin Almanack" and published a daily newspaper, "The Pennsylvania Gazette."

As a civic leader, he started the colonies' first fire insurance company, the first circulating library and the first hospital. As an inventor, he experimented with electricity. (You remember the kite and key story.)

Franklin was an extraordinary man. When he decided he needed bifocals, he invented them.

You'll learn more about Franklin's wit and genius when you visit Franklin Court* and the Benjamin Franklin National Memorial at the Franklin Institute*.

Back to the bust. This 16-foot-high statue was made out of 80,000 copper pennies. They symbolize one of Franklin's most famous sayings: "A Penny Saved is a Penny Earned." Most of the coins were donated by Philadelphia school children and youngsters of employees of the Philadelphia Fire Department.

BETSY ROSS HOUSE
239 Arch Street—19106
627-5343

Hours: November through April, daily, 9 to 5; till 6 from May through October. Closed Thanksgiving, Christmas, New Year's. Allow 20 minutes.

Tours: You're on your own. No reservations taken.

Cost: Free.

SEPTA: Buses, 5, 48, or Market Street routes.

Other: There's a large souvenir shop. An annual celebration is held on **Flag Day, June 14.**

E & H: Wheelchair access to the adjacent park only. The house has 4 floors.

You'll know you're at the right house when you see a 13-star flag waving outside. The flag is a copy of the original "Old Glory" with 13 stars in a circle on a blue field.

You'll enter through Atwater Kent Park, a neo-colonial retreat with brick and wrought iron, rhododendrons, azaleas, English ivy, magnolia and hawthorne trees.

The remains of Betsy Ross and her third husband, John Claypoole, were re-buried here in 1975.

This tiny two-and-a-half story red brick structure was

83

built in the early 1700s as the Ross family's home. We think it's the place where upholsterer and flagmaker Betsy Ross, at George Washington's request, stitched together the first American flag.

Five rooms are handsomely decorated with period and original furnishings. Life-sized models depict Betsy Ross' busy life as a seamstress, musket ball maker for the Continental Army, homemaker, wife and mother of seven daughters.

Notice how small the house is.

It's a good thing we only had 13 states then, instead of 50. Betsy would have needed more space.

CIGNA CORPORATION MUSEUM
1600 Arch Street—19103
241-4894

Hours: Weekdays, 9 to 5. Closed some holidays. Allow one hour at the ground floor exhibits.
Tours: You're on your own with no reservations necessary to see ground floor exhibits. Inquire about guided group tours of the gallery museum.
Cost: Free.
SEPTA: Buses 2, 27, 32, 76, Kennedy Boulevard or Market Street routes.
E & H: There are 3 low steps at the main entrance on 16th Street, or a ramp at the Arch Street entrance of the new building. Everything else enables complete wheelchair access.

This is the world headquarters of America's first stock and marine insurance company. It was founded in 1792 at Independence Hall and was one of the first companies to underwrite fire insurance. You can see a fascinating collection of marine and fire artifacts that commemorate CIGNA's historic as well as innovative past.

The ground level public exhibits include fire fighting memorabilia ranging from hats, buckets and brigade equipment to antique fire apparatus stationed on a realistic brick and cobblestone street. The full-size pieces are visible at all hours through the glass walls of CIGNA's contemporary building addition at 17th and Arch Streets.

The museum upstairs has a wonderful collection of model ships, model fire engines, firemarks, old insurance documents, portraits, maritime art and lithographs, engravings and water-colors of 19th century Philadelphia. The gallery museum can be seen by appointment only.

CIVIL WAR MUSEUM AND LIBRARY
1805 Pine Street—19103
735-8196

Hours: Weekdays, 10 to 4; weekends, by appointment only. Closed holidays. Allow 45 minutes or more.

Tours: Individuals and groups will be guided on arrival. Groups of no more than 35, at least 10 years old, can be scheduled. Children must be with an adult, and groups are requested to call ahead.

Cost: $2. Organized groups, school classes, veterans and servicemen, free.

SEPTA: Buses 2, 17, 90.

E & H: No wheelchair access. There are 4 floors of exhibits.

The Military Order of the Loyal Legion maintains this museum as a showplace for its Civil War mementos. The Legion was founded by three Philadelphia Union Army officers on April 15, 1865, the day President Abraham Lincoln died. Their intent was to perpetuate Lincoln's ideals.

The Legion now has 21 State Commanderies, and Pennsylvania's operates this museum. Hundreds of war items as well as an extensive library fill the four-story townhouse.

The only known collection of military escutcheons lines the entrance hallway. These hand-painted insignias were made popular by local artists after the Civil War. Each painting contains symbols and words detailing a soldier's entire military history.

One room is devoted to Ulysses S. Grant. His full dress uniform and personal items are encased. His portraits, photographs and correspondence cover the walls.

One section of the Lincoln Room recalls the President's assassination with newspaper front pages, mourning handkerchiefs, funeral badges and a walking stick retrieved from his box at Ford's Theater on April 14, 1865.

Other exhibits in the museum include soldiers' field gear, saddles, uniforms, flags, medals, Confederate money, artillery and Civil War weapons.

If you're a Lincoln buff, or a Civil War buff, you're required to see this museum.

Remember: An asterisk(*) indicates that the same place or event appears elsewhere in the book with more details. Look in the Index for additional pages.

ELFRETH'S ALLEY
Between Arch and Race, Front and 2nd Streets
574-0560 (Museum)

Hours: Elfreth's Alley is a public thoroughfare. The museum is open daily, 10 to 4. Call ahead to be sure, since it's manned by volunteers. Closed Thanksgiving and Christmas through New Year's. Special arrangements can be made in advance for groups to visit at other times.

Tours: You're on your own, except on **Elfreth's Alley Day** (see below).

Cost: Free.

SEPTA: Bus 5, 48, or a short walk from any Market Street route.

Other: Souvenir postcards, jewelry and mementos of the Alley are sold at the museum.

E & H: No wheelchair access to the museum, but the street itself is brick and cobblestone and wide enough for a car.

Elfreth's Alley is a charming little street hidden among modern-day warehouses and wholesale stores. It's lined with 33 houses that date back to the early 1700s. It's the oldest continuously occupied residential street in America. And it's a National Historic Landmark.

The people who lived along Elfreth's Alley were tradesmen. Jeremiah Elfreth, the street's namesake, was a blacksmith. See if you can tell the difference between these colonial homes in Old City* and the elegant residences of Society Hill.

No. 126, Mantua Makers House, is the **ELFRETH'S ALLEY MUSEUM.** The two downstairs rooms have period furnishings. At the second floor photo gallery you can view pictures of the interiors of many of the alley's preserved homes. A colonial herb garden is in the backyard.

Elfreth's Alley Day is celebrated on the first Sunday in June when residents of the street don colonial dress and hold open house for the public. Hours are 12 to 5. It costs $5 for adults, $3 for senior citizens, and children 12 and under tour free but must be with an adult.

FIREMAN'S HALL

2nd and Quarry Streets (between Arch and Race)—19106
923-1438

Hours: Tuesday to Saturday, 9 to 5. Closed holidays.
Allow 45 minutes.
Tours: You're on your own. Firemen are on duty to answer
questions. Groups of 20 or more are requested to call
ahead, and guided tours can sometimes be scheduled.
Cost: Free.
SEPTA: Bus 5, 48, or a short walk from any Market
Street route.
E & H: Complete wheelchair access.

In addition to all of his scientific and diplomatic
achievements, Ben Franklin also organized the nation's
first fire company: the Union Fire Company, founded in
1736.
Several rival volunteer groups followed until 1871,
when all of the companies finally merged and became the
professional Philadelphia Fire Department. This was
another nation's first that happened in Philadelphia.

Fireman's Hall is a splendid restoration of an 1876 firehouse that belonged to Engine Company 8. A modern
wing with multi-media exhibits was added in 1976.
Together they provide a memorable tribute to the Philadelphia Fire Department and fire fighting history
Engine Company 8 is the direct descendent of the Union
Fire Company. The first exhibits you'll see here explain
the early volunteer companies, the role played by insurance companies and the early methods of fire fighting.
Two floors of exhibits include all kinds of apparatus
from leather buckets to hand-drawn, horse-drawn and
motor-driven vehicles, some of which you can climb on.
Clever historical displays feature firemarks, uniforms,
helmet frontispieces, hand tools, hose sections, ladders,
scale model fire engines and a "jump" net. A "dateline" of
the development of fire fighting advancements winds
through the museum.
Walk into the chief's office and firemen's quarters and

see furnishings of the day, listen to typical firehouse banter and grasp the authentic brass pole that would whisk firemen to the floor below. Step up to the wheelhouse and direct a fireboat along the waterfront.

You'll want to observe the original "Joker System" as it receives and records fire alarms. At the same time, you'll hear any alarms that might be sounded in the city during your visit.

This is an easy way to learn about the importance of home safety and fire prevention. Pay attention to these exhibits so the local firemen won't have to visit you!

FIRST TROOP,
PHILADELPHIA CITY CAVALRY
"First City Troop" Armory
23rd and Ranstead Streets—19103
564-1488

Hours: Weekdays, by appointment only. Allow 45 minutes.
Tours: Groups of no more than 15, at least 4th grade level, are scheduled by calling a few days in advance.
Cost: Free.
SEPTA: Buses D, 42, Market Street routes.
E & H: There's one step at entrance. Call ahead for assistance and to use elevator to get to museum on 2nd floor.

You always thought the first 13-stripe flag was the American flag. Right? Here's the place where you'll be told you were wrong.

The "First City Troop" was founded on November 18, 1774. Their flag had 13 stars and stripes. The original "Old Glory" will be shown to you during your tour. Was Betsy Ross guilty of plagiarism? Or was it coincidence?

The "First City Troop" is the oldest continually active military company in the United States. The members parade through center city three times a year—on horseback—on their anniversary in November, the anniversary of George Washington's death in December and George Washington's birthday in February.

The armory's museum also includes a collection of militaria and important art by Eakins, Peale, Rembrandt and Pennington. The uniforms worn by members of the troop from the time of the Revolution through the Vietnam War are on exhibit. If you'd like to know more about the troop's history, call for a tour. If you want to see a parade, call for an exact schedule.

HENRY GEORGE BIRTHPLACE
413 South 10th Street—19147
922-4278

Hours: Weekdays, 1 to 4. Closed holidays. Allow 20 minutes.
Tours: Visit on your own, or no more than 10 can be scheduled at once (larger groups will be divided). Groups should call or write at least a week in advance.
Cost: 50¢. Group rates can be arranged in advance.
SEPTA: Buses 40, 47; trolley 23.
E & H: No wheelchair access.

This unpretentious townhouse is where Henry George was born in 1839. George was a well-known 19th century American economist and social philosopher. The house is now a museum, a library and the Philadelphia branch of the Henry George School of Social Science.

Henry George spent his youth in Philadelphia, headed to California in search of gold, worked there as a journalist, and finally returned East and settled in New York City. It was while George lived in California that he developed his economic theories, culminating in 1879 with the publication of "Progress and Poverty." His writing is the text and basis for the Henry George School.

George advocated a single tax. He theorized that all men have an equal right to work, but the land on which they work can vary in value. Therefore, he said, it is the land that should be taxed, and not the men or the industry working on the land.

George spent his last 20 years as a lecturer on economics, returning several times to speak in Philadelphia. He was the mayoral candidate in New York City twice, losing the first time in 1886 and dying six weeks before the election in 1897.

Visit the Henry George Birthplace if you'd like to find out about his economic philosophy.

HILL PHYSICK KEITH HOUSE
321 South 4th Street—19106
925—7866

Hours: Tuesday to Saturday, 10 to 4; Sunday, 1 to 4.
Closed holidays. Allow 30 minutes.
Tours: Scheduled in advance for large groups that are
divided into smaller groups of no more than 20. Children must be accompanied by an adult. Call at least a
week in advance if you're coming with a group of 10 or
more, to schedule group tours and to arrange group
rates.
Cost: Adults, $2; students, $1; children under 10, 50¢.
Groups of 10 or more adults, $1.25.
SEPTA: Buses 50, 90, Chestnut or Walnut Street routes
to 4th Street.
Other: An annual plant sale takes place one weekend in
late April. If you have a green thumb, call for details.
E & H: No wheelchair access. There are 6 steps at the entrance and 2 floors to visit.

Dr. Philip Syng Physick owned this 22-room house from
1790 till his death in 1837. Dr. Physick was one of the first
doctors to practice at Pennsylvania Hospital*. In fact,
he's referred to as the father of American surgery. Among
his famous patients was Chief Justice John Marshall.
This three-story single home with surrounding gardens
was built in 1786. It's an outstanding example of architecture and furnishings of the Federal period.
You can visit the drawing room, study, dining room,
bedroom and a small room that contains many of Dr.
Physick's instruments. In addition to the elegant furnishings, there are artwork, china and silver collections.

THE HISTORICAL SOCIETY
OF PENNSYLVANIA*
1300 Locust Street—19107
732-6200

Hours: Tuesday to Friday, 9 to 5; Saturday, 10 to 3.
Closed holidays. Allow one hour.
Tours: Scheduled for groups of 10 to 35, at least 4th grade.
Call in advance to the Education Department to sched-
ule a group tour.
Cost: Museum and exhibits free.
SEPTA: Buses D, 42, 90 or Broad Street routes.
Other: A museum shop sells stationery, historical books
and prints.

E & H: There are 6 steps at the main entrance. Complete wheelchair access by calling ahead to use the 13th Street ramped entrance. Elevator to 2nd floor for library and research facilities.

The Historical Society of Pennsylvania was founded in 1824 for the purpose of "elucidating the history of the state." It still performs that function, as well as expanding its focus to include the 13 original colonies and their surrounding states. The research facilities, collections and exhibitions here are unparalleled.

The Society's storehouse is divided among manuscripts, newspapers, art and artifacts.

The manuscript collection, alone, is among the greatest depositories of its type in the world. It has over 14 million items. A few of the highlights are the Penn family archives, President Washington's and Buchanan's papers and a wealth of information on Pennsylvania's most important colonial families.

There are materials on black history in America, a printer's proof of the Declaration and the first draft of the Constitution of the United States.

The Society's newspaper collection is equally impressive. Every era of printing technology that has been used in this country is represented. There are 8,000 bound volumes of newspapers along with hundreds of rolls of microfilm. Individuals using the Society's Reading Rooms (see Chapter 11) have access to many of these materials.

The Society is also the repository for the Genealogical Society of Pennsylvania, but there's more about that, too, in Chapter 11.

There are over 800 oil paintings from the 18th and 19th centuries, including works by the Peale family, Edward Savage, Gilbert Stuart, Thomas Sully, Benjamin West and Joseph Wright. The Society's mammoth collection of prints and drawings of Philadelphia scenes is regularly used to illustrate magazines and books.

The society also has fine furnishings and silver items that belonged to William Penn, George Washington and Thomas Jefferson. It has William Penn's beaded wampum belt which was given to him by the Delaware Indians to symbolize their 1682 treaty.

The shows in the Historical Society's grand exhibition space change several times a year so you can see many of their prized possessions. A special guided tour of the Society varies according to the group's interest and frequently includes going into the storage areas.

JOHN WANAMAKER MEMORIAL MUSEUM
John Wanamaker Department Store
13th and Market Streets, 8th floor—19101
422-2737

Hours: Monday to Saturday, 12 to 3. Allow 30 minutes.
Tours: You're on your own; exhibits are self-explanatory.
Cost: Free.
SEPTA: Any Market or Chestnut Street route.
E & H: Wheelchair access.

John Wanamaker founded the nation's first department store at this location in 1876. It was expanded with the present building in 1911. Mr. Wanamaker's office was on the 8th floor.

John Wanamaker was the pioneer in retailing. His office remains behind glass now, untouched since the day he died at the age of 84 in 1922. His Bible, books, bowler hat, walking sticks, clock collection, art work, family photographs, a portable fan, typewriter, knick-knacks and desk-top china cats are just where he left them. It's a wonder he could think so brilliantly amidst his hundreds of favorite possessions!

A museum adjacent to Mr. Wanamaker's office is a must for anyone interested in retailing, advertising and nostalgia. There are portraits and photographs of John Wanamaker, his family, his homes, his stores, their early delivery wagons and window displays.

There are samplings of early store merchandise like silk stockings and high button shoes. There's a head-measuring contraption to make sure your John Wanamaker hat fitted properly, and a gawky machine that validated your sales slip. There are exhibits that tell you about John Wanamaker's notable contributions to Philadelphia and to the nation.

The engraved silver trowels used at the Wanamaker store groundbreaking on June 12, 1909, are displayed, and there's an enormous photograph of President William Howard Taft dedicating the store on December 30, 1911. It's estimated that 30,000 citizens were present for the occasion in the marble Grand Court. A bronze star still marks the spot where the President stood.

Take time to read some of John Wanamaker's "Messages from the Founder." They're as relevant and witty today as when he wrote them.

THE MUTUAL ASSURANCE COMPANY
240 South 4th Street—19106
925-0609

Hours: Weekdays, except holidays. Call ahead to schedule your visit. Allow 30 minutes.
Tours: Groups of up to 10 will be accommodated with guided tours. Enter through the Locust Street garden.
Cost: Free.
SEPTA: Buses D, 42, 50, 90.
E & H: No wheelchair access. Exhibits are on the 2nd and 3rd floors.

There are several reasons to visit The Mutual Assurance Company, also known as The Green Tree. The tree symbolizes a principle on which the company was founded in 1784. Prior to that time, no company would risk issuing fire insurance to property owners who had trees in front of their buildings. The Mutual Assurance Company would.

In 1801 they became the first company to issue perpetual insurance whereby a building could have a policy maintained forever. One Mutual Assurance policy is still in force since 1810.

You'll recognize the "green tree" firemark on several historic homes in the area. If you don't know the significance of a firemark, you haven't been to Fireman's Hall*.

The Company offices have occupied these adjoining historic homes since 1912. The Shippen–Wistar mansion was built in 1750 and the Cadwalader mansion dates from the 1820s. Both are impeccably restored and have interesting histories. Notice the plaque outside commemorating President George Washington's visit in 1787.

The company's furnishings are as elegant as their home. The board rooms and dining room are lined with an impressive portrait collection of board chairmen. Artists include the best of their day: William Merritt ˙Chase, Thomas Eakins, Bass Otis, Rembrandt Peale, Philip Pearlstein and Franklin Watkins.

A museum includes tools and trappings of colonial fire fighting, a firemarks collection, helmets, early insurance policies, company advertisements, a model of an 1854 handpump fire engine and antique silver, china and crystal that belonged to various members of the board.

**NEW YEAR'S SHOOTERS
AND MUMMERS MUSEUM**
Two Street and Washington Avenue—19147
336-3050

Hours: Tuesday to Saturday, 9:30 to 5; Sunday, 12 to 5.
May to mid-October, till 10:30 on Tuesday nights (concerts are at 8: see Chapter 10). Open Monday legal holidays. Closed Thanksgiving, Christmas, New Year's.
Allow at least one hour.
Tours: Groups of 20 or more should call at least 2 weeks
ahead for special rates and for a mummer or volunteer
to guide you through.
Cost: Adults, $1.50; children under 12, students and
senior citizens, 75¢. Group rates for 20 or more: adults,
75¢; senior citizens, 50¢. Membership (Student, $5; Individual, $10; Family, $25) enables free admission,
newsletters, shop discount and other privileges.
SEPTA: Buses 5, 50, 64.
Other: A gift shop sells Mummerabilia.
E & H: Complete wheelchair access.

Finally, the Mummers have been immortalized in their
own museum.

Mummers, in case you didn't know, evolved from the
pre-16th century word "mum" meaning to be silent.
(Mum's the word.) In an old English custom, villagers in
costume enacted pantomimes at Christmas like "Old
Father Christmas" and "St. George and the Dragon." The
early settlers brought these customs to the colonies.

Long before the Civil War, these settlers held open
houses at New Year's. They called on friends and neighbors in costume. On January 1, 1876, individual groups
paraded to Independence Hall and then to other parts of
the city. The custom grew. In January, 1901, Philadelphia's City Council formally recognized 42 Mummers
clubs and gave them permission to parade for cash prizes.

Nearly every child in Philadelphia looks forward to seeing the colorful Mummers "cake walk" up Broad Street
on New Year's Day to the tune of "Oh, Dem Golden Slippers."

Now you can enjoy "Mummermania" all year long at
the Mummers Museum.

You've probably wanted to know about Mummers, but
didn't know who to ask. Now you can find out how many
clubs there are, how many men participate in a club, how
you can join, how themes are chosen, how costumes are
made, what they weigh and what they cost.

You'll relive Mummers history, you'll take part in a parade and you'll learn how to strut and properly hold an umbrella. By pushing a few buttons, you can compose the string-band music of accordions, banjos, saxophones and bell lyres.

Nobody leaves without knowing "what's 2.55 miles long, 69 feet wide, 12 feet high and covered with feathers"? And nobody leaves without humming "Oh, Dem Golden Slippers."

OLD FORT MIFFLIN
Fort Mifflin Road near International Airport,
on the Delaware River
365–5194

Hours: Weekends, 12 to 5, or by reservation at other times by calling at least a week ahead to 686–3630. Closed mid-December to early March. Allow 30 minutes to tour inside the Fort, and 30 minutes to see the surrounding grounds.

Tours: You're on your own. Frequently on Sundays, members of the Old Fort Mifflin Historical Society don their colonial uniforms and re-enact military life at the 18th century camp.

Cost: Adults, 50¢; children under 12, 25¢. Group rates for 20 or more.

Lunch: There are sodas for sale and picnic areas.

SEPTA: Airport Bus M from Broad Street and Snyder Avenue to foot of Penrose Bridge, and then a long walk. Go by car via the Overseas Terminal Road and follow signs to the Fort. There's plenty of free car and bus parking space.

Other: A small gift shop sells flags, books and assorted mementos of colonial history.

E & H: The grounds are all wheelchair accessible, but it would be difficult to negotiate some of the old buildings.

The British started to build Fort Mifflin in 1772. It was completed in 1776 by the Revolutionary forces under the direction of Benjamin Franklin.

The story goes that Fort Mifflin's 400 brave soldiers attacked the British ship "Augusta" and the gunboat "Merlin" in 1777. This small band boldly resisted over 2,000 British troops and 250 ships that sailed up the Delaware. The Fort was finally conquered after days of constant battering by British warships. About 250 Revolutionary soldiers died in the battle.

In 1797 the Fort was rebuilt. In the 1860s it was converted into a prison for Civil War military deserters, bounty jumpers and political prisoners. The 49-acre site was used to store ammunition as recently as the Korean War.

Today you can visit scenic Old Fort Mifflin. You can picture the hardships and the eventual defeat of its colonial soldiers. You can see why it's been named a National Historic Landmark.

See the authentic and exact reproduction cannons and carriages of the war, the Arsenal, Officers' Quarters, Soldiers' Barracks housing an exhibit "Defense of the Delaware," Blacksmith Shop and museum displaying artifacts and mementos of the Fort's two centuries.

Just outside the Fort sits what is thought to be Philadelphia's oldest house, built in the 1660s by a Swedish settler. It was hit by American cannon fire during the siege of Fort Mifflin and thus called **Cannonball Farmhouse.**

PENNSYLVANIA HOSPITAL
8th and Spruce Streets—19107
829-3971 (Public Relations)

Hours: The Pine Building is open weekdays, 9 to 5, and you can browse on your own. Closed holidays. Allow at least one hour.

Tours: By reservation only, weekdays, 9 to 5. Call at least one week ahead to schedule groups of no more than 35, at least 7th grade level, and with 2 adults accompanying students.

Cost: Free.

SEPTA: Buses 47, 90.

E & H: There's wheelchair access to everything but the 3rd floor amphitheater. Call ahead to make arrangements. Some steps are involved.

Pennsylvania Hospital was founded by Benjamin Franklin and Dr. Thomas Bond in 1751. It's the oldest hospital in the country. Its original building, the Pine Building, is one of the finest remaining examples of colonial architecture. The interior recently underwent a major (and magnificent) restoration.

Visitors learn all about the hospital's history. You'll walk through the Great Court and see a 19th century portrait gallery of great men associated with Pennsylvania Hospital. You'll examine early American medical instruments, art objects and the rare book library.

You'll also see the country's first surgical amphitheater. (You've seen amphitheaters similar to this one in the movies.) The round amphitheater with its domed skylight was built in the hospital's Central Pavilion in 1804. It was last used in 1868, and it's the only amphitheater of its type left in the country. As many as 150 students bought tickets to sit on the edge of their seats in the three tiers of galleries and observe operations which could only be performed on bright sunny days.

Also, look in the Gallery Pavilion for Benjamin West's famous painting of "Christ Healing the Sick in the Temple."

The **HISTORY OF NURSING MUSEUM** is also in the Pennsylvania Hospital, and you'll see this as part of the tour.

Exhibits include class books, photographs, pins, uniforms, caps, correspondence and assorted memorabilia from the area's nursing schools. An early hospital wing has been reconstructed.

Note: The hospital's medical facilities are not included on this tour.

Pennsylvania Hospital offers another unique public service called **TEL–MED**. You can call 829-5500 and request to hear any of 300 taped one- to five-minute messages about health and your body.

Among the subjects covered are aging, diet, first aid, home health care, mental health, smoking, drug abuse and alcohol problems. There are messages on everything from hiccups to hay fever and sports tips to face lifts. All are in easy-to-understand language and some are available in Spanish.

TEL–MED operates 24 hours a day, every day of the week. When you call TEL–MED, you'll be told how to select the tape that interests you. If you don't already have the TEL–MED brochure listing all of its messages, you'll be told how to get it.

TEL–MED is a medical information service of Pennsylvania Hospital, funded by Blue Cross of Greater Philadelphia, aimed at keeping you healthy. It is not a substitute for your personal physician, diagnosis or treatment.

PERELMAN ANTIQUE TOY MUSEUM
270 South 2nd Street—19106
922-1070

Hours: Daily, 9:30 to 5. Closed Thanksgiving, Christmas, New Year's. Allow one hour.
Tours: You're on your own, but groups of 25 or more are requested to call ahead.
Cost: Adults, $1.50; senior citizens, $1.25; children under 14, 75¢. Groups of 25 or more: adults, $1; children, 55¢.
SEPTA: Buses 5, 42.
E & H: All 3 floors are accessible by elevator. Call ahead for arrangements to use side door with only one step.

Leon Perelman must have the largest collection of early American tin and cast iron toys in the world, and he was kind enough to make them available for public view.

Mr. Perelman wanted me to be sure to tell you that he's still adding toys to his collection. Recent acquisitions that aren't in the permanent exhibits are in the entrance foyer where he has changing shows.

Over 2,000 toys are on display on three floors. If you're wild about banks, you'll find more than 200 still and mechanical ones like "Jumbo," the elephant who tosses pennies into his slotted back when you twist his tail. If you're a cartoon fan, look for the old Toonerville Trolley and Popeye riding his motorcycle.

There are games, dolls, a rare collection of cap pistols, fire engines and stage coaches; and we could go on and on.

More than two centuries ago, the museum was James Abercrombie's Society Hill manse. Mr. Perelman takes great pride in his fun-filled restoration.

PHILADELPHIA CONTRIBUTIONSHIP FOR THE INSURANCE OF HOUSES FROM LOSS BY FIRE
212 South 4th Street—19106
627-1752

Hours: Weekdays, 10 to 3. Closed holidays. Allow 20 minutes.
Tours: You're on your own. Call ahead if you're planning to come with a large group or want to see the upstairs.
Cost: Free.
SEPTA: Buses D, 42, 50, 90.
E & H: There are 6 steps at the entrance, or arrange in advance to enter through the garden where there's one step.

You might have noticed the "Hand-in-Hand" firemarks nailed on the front of historic properties in Philadelphia. The clasp of four crossed hands symbolizes strength, and the firemark on the building indicates that property is insured by the oldest fire insurance company in America.

Ben Franklin helped found the Philadelphia Contributionship in 1752, and he signed the parchment scroll of policyholders that's carefully displayed under glass in the company's museum.

Philadelphia Contributionship's handsome Greek Revival-style headquarters were designed and built by Thomas U. Walter in 1836.

A small, charming museum includes fire fighting and insurance memorabilia, firemarks, speaking horns, the original company seal, beautiful old furnishings and "Franklinobilia." That's a word I just invented to describe exhibits of all the things he thought of first.

If you arrange in advance for a guided tour, you'll also get to see the upstairs board rooms and dining room.

PHILADELPHIA MARITIME MUSEUM
321 Chestnut Street—19106
925-5439

Hours: Monday to Saturday, 10 to 5; Sunday, 1 to 5. Closed Thanksgiving, Christmas, New Year's. Allow one hour.

Tours: Groups of no more than 30 can be scheduled for guided tours by calling the Education Department at least a week in advance. A variety of programs includes tours for special education, gifted and handicapped groups.

Cost: Adults, $1; children 12 and under, 50¢. Groups of 10 or more adults, 75¢; children, 35¢. Membership entitles you to free admission, films, newsletters, research assistance and more.

SEPTA: Buses D, 42, 50, 76.

Other: A small gift shop features books, graphics, games and maritime objects that you're not likely to find elsewhere.

E & H: Complete wheelchair access.

There's no shore in sight and you're lost at sea. How will you find your way to land? And how does a boat float? These are just a few of the questions that will be answered when you visit the Philadelphia Maritime Museum.

Those of you who are curious about the Port of Philadelphia are "ordered" to visit the Maritime Museum and see three floors of contemporary and tastefully designed exhibits relating to the sea and maritime life.

The displays include historical items such as charts, prints, scrimshaw, whaling harpoons, navigation instruments, flags and naval weapons. Scale models of hundreds of ships from around the world fill one entire wall.

Another wall is devoted to a cutaway view of the "Philadelphia," a frigate that set to sea in 1800. Charming illustrations depict the activities on each deck.

An entire gallery tells about "The Titanic and Her Era." View dozens of objects that survived her doomed maiden voyage of April 14, 1912.

What you don't see on exhibit here can be seen in the Philadelphia Maritime Museum's "visible storage." Practically every painting, model, artifact and navigation tool the museum owns can be seen through glass. It's a fascinating look at what's behind the scenes in a museum.

The Philadelphia Maritime Museum also maintains a library for serious researchers and a Workshop on the Water*, at Penn's Landing boat basin.

There isn't a better way to learn about ships, the seas, and the Port of Philadelphia.

Ship ahoy!

POWEL HOUSE
244 South 3rd Street—19106
627-0364

Hours: Tuesday to Saturday, 10 to 4; Sunday, 1 to 4. Open till 5 from mid-June to Labor Day. Closed Easter, Thanksgiving, Christmas, New Year's. Allow 45 minutes, and arrive at least 30 minutes before closing time.

Tours: All visitors are accompanied by a guide. Groups of 10 to 50, at least junior high school level, are scheduled by calling 2 weeks ahead.

Cost: Adults, $2; senior citizens and students with ID, $1; children under 12 with an adult, 50¢. Groups of 10 or more adults, $1.25.

SEPTA: Buses 5, 90, or Walnut Street routes.

E & H: No wheelchair access. There are 5 steps at the entrance and 2 floors to visit.

Samuel Powel was the Mayor of Philadelphia before, during and after the Revolution. His Society Hill home, built in 1765, was certainly appropriate for a man of his position. The exterior facade is typical Georgian style.

Pretend you're one of Mayor and Mrs. Powel's most honored guests as you visit the lavish dining room, the drawing room and the elegant ballroom with its magnificent crystal fixtures and damask fabrics. This is one place where George Washington actually danced.

Would you like to see what it's like to live in Society Hill splendor? Then rent the Powel House for an evening for a party or a catered dinner.

RYERSS MUSEUM
Cottman and Central Avenues—19111
745-3061

Hours: By reservation only, Sunday, 1 to 4; Wednesday to Saturday, by appointment only. Allow one hour.
Tours: Call at least one week in advance to schedule a guided tour for groups of 5 to 15.
Cost: Free
Lunch: There's a pavilion, tables and benches in Burholme Park if you want to picnic.
SEPTA: Buses N, Y. There's plenty of free parking.
E & H: There's a ramp at the entrance. Exhibits are on 2 floors, and there's an elevator.

The Ryerss' family mansion was built in 1859 to resemble an English country estate. A tower built in 1890 enabled its residents to see center city Philadelphia—a distance of 10 miles. The museum wing was added in 1920. In 1976, the Ryerss Museum was placed in the National Register of Historic Places. It was completely restored in 1980.

This Victorian home has a number of fascinating collections. There are period clothing, Oriental arts including many ivory pieces, a case of footwear from around the world, old children's playthings and even suits of armor.

The dining room and parlor are restored and furnished with period pieces including an unusual "square" piano.

The Ryerss Museum and Library (see Chapter 11) is in the Burholme Park section of Fairmount Park in the Northeast. The building and grounds belong to the City of Philadelphia.

SHOE MUSEUM
Pennsylvania College of Podiatric Medicine*
8th and Race Streets (enter on 8th)—19107
629-0300 Ext. 219 (Public Relations)

Hours: Weekdays, 9 to 4. Closed holidays. Allow 45 minutes.

Tours: Exhibits are self-explanatory. Arrangements must be made in advance to visit 6th floor. Groups of no more than 25, at least 4th grade level, should call 2 weeks ahead. You can combine your visit with a scheduled tour of the College (see Chapter 13).

Cost: Free.

SEPTA: Buses 47, 61.

E & H: Wheelchair access.

Put your best foot forward, step into the College's spacious lobby and surround yourself with "Footwear Through the Ages."

Nearly 500 pairs of footwear are in the collection which, for the most part, is on the College's sixth floor.

There are burial sandals from Egypt, two-heeled shoes from Morocco and Japan, slippers from China, Eskimo snowshoes, Dutch wooden shoes, Indian boots and more.

As Ed Sullivan used to say, "It's a really big shoe." And speaking of celebrities, Joe Frazier's boxing shoes are there, Billie Jean King's tennis shoes are there, Bernie Parent's skates are there, and Dr. Baruch Blumberg and the late John B. Kelly, Jr.'s jogging shoes are there.

If you're a celebrity, send them your shoes.

Chapter 5.
Churches and Religious Sites.

How many times have you heard people talk about the churches they went out of their way to see in Europe? Well, Philadelphia has many historic churches that should be visited. In fact, Philadelphia probably has more churches of historic significance than any other city in America.

Philadelphia's churches aren't as old as the European variety, but many of them are very old by American standards—founded by the first Philadelphians and worshipped in by the founders of our nation.

Philadelphia was the birthplace of religious freedom. It was here that William Penn brought to reality his dream of a "Holy Experiment," a place completely free from religious persecution. And so you can visit here the first Quaker meeting house in America, the first synagogue, the first Methodist church and many other firsts.

Religion was a very important part of life in Colonial Philadelphia. Most of the 18th century churches remain active and have their own congregations right up to the present day. Many of them are fascinating to visit.

Old Philadelphia Churches

Thirteen churches of colonial origin have formed the Old Philadelphia Churches Historic Association. They include seven Protestant churches, four Roman Catholic churches, one Quaker meeting house and one synagogue. They're all interesting, and most are within walking distance of Independence Hall.

A descriptive sign on the sidewalk outside of each church gives more of its history and background.

ARCH STREET MEETING HOUSE
4th and Arch Streets—19106
241-7199

Hours: Monday to Saturday, 10 to 4, except Thursday, 11 to 4. Weekly Meetings are Sunday at 10:30 and Thursday at 10.

William Penn donated this plot to the Society of Friends in 1693. By 1804 there were enough members to require the construction of a meeting house as you see it today.

Many Quakers in England chose to go to prison rather

than worship according to the dictates of the Church of England. William Penn, himself, was confined in England for insisting on the Quakers' rights to hold their own worship service.

You know the rest of the story. Pennsylvania was Penn's "Holy Experiment," where everybody could worship in freedom. If you want to brush up on the story, there's a 15 minute slide show here on "The Life of William Penn."

The Arch Street Meeting House is still used regularly by the Quakers. The Philadelphia Yearly Meeting is held here every spring.

Take a look at the original hand-hewn benches and see the simplicity of the interior. The Exhibit Room has clothing, Bibles and examples of Quaker life. Don't miss the gigantic "dollhouse" of a typical Quaker home during the Revolutionary period.

CHRIST CHURCH
2nd and Market Streets—19106
922-1695

Hours: Monday to Saturday, 9 to 5; Sunday, 12 to 4. Allow 15 minutes. Visitors are welcome at services daily at 9 and 11 and Wednesday at noon.

Christ Church, founded in 1659, is the birthplace of the Protestant Episcopal Church in the United States. A clause in Penn's Charter of 1681 from King Charles II provided that as soon as 20 residents of the Colony requested a minister, one would be sent by the Bishop of London.

The font in which William Penn was baptized in 1644 was sent to Philadelphia in 1697. It's the larger of Christ Church's two baptismal fonts.

Fifteen signers of the Declaration attended Christ Church. You can sit in George Washington's, Robert Morris', Benjamin Franklin's and Betsy Ross' pews. Be sure to look at the colorful Patriots' Window depicting them at worship.

The present Christ Church structure was built between 1724 and 1754.

Bishop William White was appointed rector of Christ Church in 1779. He was consecrated Bishop in 1789. You can visit the Bishop White House* a few blocks away on Walnut Street.

CHRIST CHURCH BURIAL GROUND
5th and Arch Streets (enter on 5th Street)

Hours: April 1 to October 1, daily, 9 to 4:30. Closed the rest of the year except by special appointment.

If you come here when the Burial Ground gates are closed, walk to the corner of 5th and Arch Streets so you can see four graves: Benjamin Franklin's, his wife Deborah's, and their children's. A bronze plaque outlines Franklin's illustrious life.

Local tradition says that fame and fortune will come to you if you toss a Franklin penny on Ben's grave. (We try it once a month. If you buy another copy of this book for a friend, we'll know that the tradition works.)

Seven other signers of the Declaration are also buried in the churchyard or in the Christ Church graveyard. Christ Church and its Burial Ground are part of Independence National Historical Park*.

GLORIA DEI CHURCH (Old Swedes')
Swanson (below Front) and Christian Streets—19147
389-1513

Hours: Daily, 9 to 5.
Tours: You're on your own, but call ahead if you're bringing a group.
SEPTA: Bus 64.
Other: The Guild House is a small gift shop, open Saturday from 12 to 2, with items imported from Sweden.

Organized in 1642, Gloria Dei is the oldest church in Pennsylvania. It's probably the oldest building in Philadelphia. Their congregation worshipped in a log cabin before the present building was completed in 1700.

Gloria Dei is also known as **Old Swedes' Church**. It was designated a National Historic Site in 1942. Old Swedes' was admitted to the Episcopal Diocese of Pennsylvania in 1845. It is also part of Independence National Historical Park*.

Gloria Dei has a Parish Hall, an old Caretaker's House, a Rectory, an 18th century Guild House and a graveyard—all around a pleasant grassy courtyard.

The church has barely changed over the centuries.

It has to be the only church with model ships suspended from the ceiling. They're the "Key of Kalmar" and "Flying Griffin," the ships that brought the first Swedish settlers to America.

Old Swedes' is filled with relics and religious artifacts.

106

The font and altar carvings date from 1642. Queen Christiana's 1608 Bible is in the sacristy, and there are mementos of Jenny Lind, who sang at Old Swedes' in 1851. Also, look at the samples from the nearby Shot Tower* which are exhibited in the vestry.

An **Annual Colonial Fair** is held at Gloria Dei the first weekend in June. The **Lucia Fest** is in December. See Chapter 19 for details.

HISTORIC ST. GEORGE'S METHODIST CHURCH
235 North 4th Street—19106
925-7788

Hours: Daily, 10 to 4. Visitors are welcome at Sunday services at 11 A.M.

Tours: Volunteer guides are always on duty. Groups of 10 or more should call ahead. Allow up to an hour.

Other: A gift shop has items relating to St. George's and a selection of non-religious merchandise.

The original Philadelphia Methodists who organized here in 1767 bought this building from a German Reformed Congregation. Historic St. George's is the oldest continuously used Methodist Church in the world. The only break in its activities occurred during the British occupation of Philadelphia, when it was used as a riding school for cavalry.

Francis Asbury preached his first sermon at St. George's in October, 1771. He was sent to America by John Wesley, Methodism's English founder, to enlarge the church in the colonies. The church looks almost the same today as it did when Asbury preached there.

A **Methodist Historical Center** adjoins the church. Your guide will take you to the museum where exhibits relate the story of Methodism and the church. Historic St. George's is also part of Independence National Historical Park*.

As far as we know, this is the only church that ever influenced the location of a bridge. The plans for the construction of the Benjamin Franklin Bridge had to be altered to prevent the demolition of Historic St. George's.

Remember: An asterisk(*) indicates that the same place or event appears elsewhere in the book with more details. Look in the Index for additional pages.

HOLY TRINITY
ROMAN CATHOLIC CHURCH
6th and Spruce Streets—19106
923-7930

Hours: For Mass only, Sunday at noon. From May to September the church remains open till 4 P.M.

Holy Trinity was the first Catholic church in the United States founded especially for German- and French-speaking Catholics. Germans accounted for a large portion of the local 18th century Catholic population.

Holy Trinity's present building was constructed in 1788, the third Roman Catholic church in Philadelphia. Few alterations have been made to the original structure, so you'll see it almost exactly as did those who attended its first Mass in 1789.

The church's exterior is one of Philadelphia's best examples of Flemish bold, the alternating red and black brickwork style.

Holy Trinity is administered by Old St. Mary's Roman Catholic Church*.

MIKVEH ISRAEL SYNAGOGUE
44 North 4th Street—19106
Independence Mall East
922-5446

Hours: Visitors are welcome at services Saturday at 9:30 A.M., and in conjunction with tours of the National Museum of American Jewish History*.
Tours: Groups of 20 to 100 should call 10 days ahead to schedule. Allow 30 minutes.

Colonial merchant Nathan Levy brought the Jewish community of Philadelphia together in 1740 to found Mikveh Israel Synagogue. Today it's the oldest synagogue in Philadelphia and the second oldest in the U.S.

Mikveh Israel became a rallying point for all American Jews during the Revolution as they fled from British-occupied cities. Among its early congregants were Haym Salomon and the Gratz family.

Although most of the members today are of Ashkenazic (Middle and Eastern European) background, Mikveh Israel still maintains its Sephardic (Spanish and Portuguese) traditions. Men and women are seated in separate sections.

Mikveh Israel was originally at 3rd and Cherry Streets. It recently moved to its new home on 4th Street, sharing a modern brick structure with the National Museum of American Jewish History*. Tours of the museum also include a visit to the synagogue.

MOTHER BETHEL A.M.E. CHURCH
419 Richard Allen Avenue
(formerly South 6th Street)—19147
925-0616

Hours: By reservation only, Tuesday, Wednesday, Thursday, 10 to 3. Visitors are welcome at 10:45 A.M. Sunday services which are followed by a tour at 1 P.M.
Tours: Call at least a week ahead to schedule groups of no more than 100. Allow 30 to 45 minutes.

In 1782, at the age of 22, Richard Allen bought his freedom from slavery to a Germantown family. Five years later he led 40 black worshippers from St. George's Methodist Church to become a "Free African Society." They founded a new church, Mother Bethel African Methodist Episcopal, which is today the "mother church" for an international denomination numbering five million. Allen bought the present church site in 1794.

Mother Bethel was one of the first institutions established by blacks in America. The church stands on the oldest property continuously owned by blacks in America. It's now a National Historic Landmark.

In 1816, Richard Allen was the nation's first Negro to be named a Bishop. He died in 1831, and you can see his tomb and his wife's in the church basement. (The basement was a station on the underground railroad prior to the Civil War.)

A tour of Mother Bethel also includes a description of the magnificent stained glass windows.

OLD FIRST REFORMED CHURCH
4th and Race Streets—19106
922-4566

Hours: Weekdays, 9 to 3; Saturday, 9 to noon; Sunday, following worship at 11 to which visitors are welcome.
Other: The third Friday of each month, from 11 to 7, a Festival at Old First ties in with the season to present foods, crafts, festivities and perhaps an ethnic celebration closest to the date. The Church also provides accommodations for youth hostelers during July and August (see Chapter 20).

The First Reformed Church was organized in 1727 by

German refugees seeking religious freedom in Philadelphia. Three different houses of worship have since been built at the present site.

The current church dates from 1837. It combines the designs and original materials from the two earlier churches. As the neighborhood became commercial, the location was abandoned in 1887, and the building became a paint warehouse. In 1967 the congregants returned to the original Old City* site.

The building has been beautifully restored, and the furnishings are either originals or exact duplications of the originals.

You have to see the churchyard the last two weeks of December. The nativity scene has props in a natural setting with live animals. It's a work of art. Old First Reformed deserves an award for its imagination and creativity. The least it warrants is 30 seconds on the evening news.

"OLD PINE" PRESBYTERIAN CHURCH
4th and Pine Streets—19106
925-8051

Hours: Weekdays, 9 to 5; call ahead to be sure. Visitors are welcome at Sunday services at 10:30. A coffee hour follows.

Built in the late 1760s, this is the only remaining colonial Presbyterian building in Philadelphia. The lot was donated to the First Presbyterian Church in 1764 by William Penn's sons, Thomas and Richard Penn.

John Adams attended church here while in the Continental Congress. Later, during the British occupation of Philadelphia, the church was used as a hospital and then as a cavalry stable. Many prominent colonists are buried in "Old Pine's" churchyard.

OLD ST. AUGUSTINE'S
ROMAN CATHOLIC CHURCH
243 N. Lawrence Street—19106
(North 4th Street below Vine)
627-1838

Hours: The half-hour before each Mass. Daily Mass is weekdays at 7:30 and noon; Saturday at 8 A.M. and 5:15 P.M.; Sunday at 12:30 A.M., 8 and 11 A.M.

Old St. Augustine's was founded in 1796 as a place of

worship for the German and Irish Catholic residents of Philadelphia's northern section. Commodore John Barry, George Washington and Stephen Girard were among the contributors to its first building fund.

When it was completed in 1801, Old St. Augustine's was the largest church in Philadelphia, and the fourth Catholic church in Philadelphia.

The original structure was destroyed by fire in May, 1844, after three days of anti-Catholic street rioting.

The new building was designed by Napoleon LeBrun, who was also the architect for the Academy of Music* and the Cathedral Basilica of SS. Peter and Paul*. Old St. Augustine's was rebuilt on the original site in 1847.

This was the original "mother house" of the Augustinian Fathers in the United States. It was also the site in 1811 of what is now Villanova University, the oldest Catholic institution of higher learning in the country.

OLD ST. JOSEPH'S CHURCH
Willings Alley near 4th and Walnut Streets—19106
923-1733

Hours: Visitors are welcome daily, 6:30 to 6. Mass is daily at 6:30, 7:30, 8, 12:05; and 5:05; also at 6 on Saturday; Sunday at 6, 7:30, 9, 10, 11, 12:15 and 5:30.

This is the oldest Roman Catholic Church in Philadelphia, and Mass has been celebrated here for more than 200 years.

Religious freedom in America was born at Old St. Joseph's. From 1733 to 1763, Old St. Joseph's was the only Roman Catholic Church in the city. In fact, Catholic worship wasn't permitted in the colonies or in England except at Old St. Joseph's.

The present building is the third one for the church. It dates back to 1838 and is part of Independence National Historical Park*.

OLD ST. MARY'S CHURCH
252 South 4th Street—19106
923-7930

Hours: Daily, 7 A.M. to sunset. Mass is Saturday at 5 P.M.; Sunday at 9 and 10:30 A.M.

Old St. Mary's was established in 1763 as the Roman Catholic Church expanded in Philadelphia. It's Philadelphia's second oldest Catholic church, and was the main Catholic church during the Revolution.

Members of the Continental Congress attended Mass here on July 4, 1779, to celebrate the third anniversary of the Declaration.

John Barry, General Stephen Moylan and other noted colonists are buried in the graveyard.

ST. PETER'S CHURCH
3rd and Pine Streets—19106
925-5968

Hours: Tuesday to Saturday, 9 to 4. Visitors are welcome at Holy Communion on Sunday at 8:30 and 10:30 A.M.

St. Peter's was established in 1753 as a new "South end" chapel for Christ Church, the mother church at 2nd and Market Streets.

St. Peter's looks the same today as it did when it was built in 1760 on land that was given by Thomas and Richard Penn. George and Martha Washington attended St. Peter's during 1781 and 1782. So did Mayor Samuel Powel and his family. They occupied Pew 41.

Some of the many patriots buried in the churchyard include naval hero Stephen Decatur, artist Charles Willson Peale and John Nixon, who first read the Declaration of Independence to the people.

More Churches and Sites of Religious Interest

Philadelphia's religious heritage of the 18th century has been preserved and enriched in the 19th and 20th centuries.

There are additional churches of the 18th century and several of later origin that are also noteworthy for their religious beliefs or their architecture.

Several historical societies and museums have taken the historic documents from the religious edifices and have made them available to the public through exhibitions and library collections.

Many of these collections could also be appropriately included in Chapter 12 on International Philadelphia. Their ethnic appeal is obvious.

William Penn would have liked that.

BETH SHALOM SYNAGOGUE
Old York and Foxcroft Roads
Elkins Park, Pa. 19117
887-1342

Tours: By appointment only, Monday to Wednesday, 11 to 3; Sunday, 10 to 2. Allow 45 minutes. Groups will be scheduled by writing ahead to the chairman of tours. Others must call ahead.
SEPTA: Bus 55.

Frank Lloyd Wright designed only one synagogue in his lifetime, and this is it. Built in 1959, the unusual Beth Shalom Synagogue was Wright's last major completed work.

The structure rises from a hexagonal base. Its asymmetrical dome juts 110 feet into the air, and from inside the sanctuary you can look through the dome.

Your guide will explain the architect's symbolism of the opaque dome, the steel beams and the fountain pool.

BRYN ATHYN CATHEDRAL
Route 232 (2nd Street Pike) and Papermill Road
Bryn Athyn, Pa. 19009
947-0266

Hours: Monday to Saturday, 9 to 12 and 2 to 5. Visitors are welcome at services Sunday at 11 A.M.
Tours: Groups of 10 to 50 can be scheduled for guided tours, except Sunday, by calling a few weeks ahead.
Cost: Free.
E & H: There's one step at the entrance.

If you're interested in Gothic architecture, it's worth a trip 15 miles north of center city Philadelphia to see one of the area's architectural and scenic wonders.

Construction of Bryn Athyn Cathedral was begun in 1914, in the style of medieval craft guilds. You'll be given an explanation of this, along with descriptions of the stained glass windows and the overall design. The Swedenborgian faith will be described for those who are interested.

Just to give you an idea of the Cathedral's size, the entire population of Bryn Athyn can gather inside.

And while you're in the neighborhood, you really should combine your visit to the Cathedral with a tour of **Glencairn** (see Chapter 17).

CATHEDRAL OF
IMMACULATE CONCEPTION
816 N. Franklin Street—19123
922-2222

Hours: Open for services only. Divine Liturgy is Sunday
at 8:30, 10 and noon; Saturday at 5:30 P.M.
Tours: Scheduled weekdays for groups of up to 100. Call
ahead and allow 30 minutes.
SEPTA: Bus 47.

If you've been to the William Penn Tower*, you may
have noticed a glowing golden dome as you looked to the
northeast. It belongs to the largest Ukrainian Catholic
cathedral in the world—the Cathedral of the Immaculate
Conception of the Blessed Virgin Mary.

This is also the "mother church" of all Ukrainian
churches in America. In Philadelphia alone there is a
closely-knit community of about 45,000 Ukrainians in the
northern part of the city. Pope John Paul II came here to
visit the church and its parishioners on October 4, 1979.

The tour here includes the church, the chancery office,
the school annex and a look at several other Ukrainian
establishments within the block.

If you would like to see and learn more about the Ukrai-
nian culture and folk art, visit the **UKRAINIAN HERI-
TAGE STUDIES CENTER.** It's located on the Manor
Junior College campus at Fox Chase Road and Forrest
Avenue in Jenkintown, Pa. Call 885-2360 for details.

CATHEDRAL BASILICA OF
SS. PETER AND PAUL
18th and Race Streets—19103
(enter through Chapel on north side)
561-1313

Hours: Daily, 9 to 3:30. Visitors welcome at daily Mass in
Chapel at 7:15, 8 A.M., 12:05 and 12:35 P.M. Sunday
Mass is at 8, 9:30, 11, 12:15 and 5.

The imposing Roman-style church facing Logan Circle
on the Benjamin Franklin Parkway is the head church of
the Philadelphia Archdiocese. Almost 2,000 worshippers
can be seated here at once. There are over 300 Roman
Catholic churches in Philadelphia.

Construction of SS. Peter and Paul was begun in 1846,
and it was completed and dedicated in 1864.

The Cathedral of SS. Peter and Paul was designated a

Basilica in 1976 following its major role in the 41st International Eucharistic Congress which brought over a million Catholics to Philadelphia in an eight-day period.

Six of Philadelphia's last nine bishops and archbishops are buried beneath the altar of SS. Peter and Paul.

CATHOLIC HISTORICAL SOCIETY
263 South 4th Street (headquarters)—19106
925-5752

Hours: Weekdays, by appointment only.

Society Hill's Catholic Historical Society maintains one of the country's largest collections of books relating to Catholicism. The Society receives more than 5,000 newspapers and periodicals pertaining to their faith.

Most of the collection is housed in the Society's museum and library at the St. Charles Seminary in Overbrook.

If you're involved in research into Catholic history, call the archivist in the library at the Seminary (839-3760) to find out if the information you want is available.

CHAPEL OF THE FOUR CHAPLAINS
1855 N. Broad Street—19122
235-3020 or 236-6394

Hours: Weekdays, 9 to 4. Closed holidays. Allow 20 minutes. Visitors welcome to Sunday Vespers at 4.
Tours: Call a week ahead to schedule groups of up to 300.
SEPTA: Bus C, or Broad Street Subway to Columbia and a short walk north.
E & H: No wheelchair access.

This unique interfaith chapel is a lasting memorial to four Army chaplains who lost their lives in World War II. The chapel is located in the lower level of Baptist Temple, which was built in 1889.

The four honored chaplains are George L. Fox and Clark V. Poling, Protestants; John P. Washington, Roman Catholic; and Alexander D. Goode, Jewish. They were stationed aboard the troopship "Dorchester" when it was torpedoed by a German submarine on February 3, 1943.

The chaplains gave their life jackets to four soldiers, linked arms, prayed and went down with the ship.

President Harry S. Truman dedicated the chapel on February 3, 1951. The Presidential Seal that hung from the pulpit is among the mementos exhibited in an adjoining museum. There are also models and photographs of the sunken ship, photographs of the chaplains, some of their belongings, a postal exhibit of the 3¢ commemorative stamp that honors them, flags and tributes.

The chapel itself has a revolving altar to accommodate the Protestant, Catholic and Jewish faiths. A mural on one wall depicts the sinking of the "Dorchester" and the four chaplains' heroic action.

FREE QUAKER MEETING HOUSE
Independence Mall
5th and Arch Streets—19106
923-6777

Hours: Memorial Day to Labor Day, daily except Monday, 10 to 4; Sunday, 12 to 4. Allow 20 minutes.
Tours: You're on your own, but guides are present to answer questions.
E & H: There are 4 steps at the entrance limiting wheelchair access.

The Free Quaker sect was founded in 1781 by a group of 200 "Fighting Quakers." These Quakers were disowned by the peace-loving Society of Friends because they supported the Revolution. Thus they needed their own place of worship and built this brick meeting house in 1783.

The Free Quakers met here till 1834. By then the Revolution was long over, the Quakers were reunited and the Free Quaker members had dwindled to a handful.

In later years, a second floor was added to the interior and the building served as a library and a school and for commercial use.

When Independence Mall was created in the early 1960s, the Free Quaker Meeting House was moved a short distance to its present site and completely restored. Almost two centuries of alterations were removed so the building now looks as it originally did in 1783. It's no longer used for worship but is a museum and part of Independence National Historical Park*. The simple wooden benches are back, as well as the three-sided balcony.

The Junior League of Philadelphia has its offices on the lower floor, and its members serve as guides. A continuous five-minute slide show provides historical background on William Penn, the Society of Friends and the dissenting Free Quakers.

Remember: An asterisk(*) indicates that the same place or event appears elsewhere in the book with more details. Look in the Index for additional pages.

JEWISH IDENTITY CENTER
1400 Englewood Street—19111
745-0984

Hours: Tuesday, Wednesday and Friday, 10:30 to 2:30. Other hours by appointment. Closed Federal and Jewish holidays. Allow one hour.
Tours: Call a week ahead to schedule no more than 25.
Cost: A donation is requested.
SEPTA: Buses Y, 59.

At this modest storefront location in Northeast Philadelphia is a carefully culled collection of memorabilia, photographs and printed material relating to the Holocaust.

Founded by the late Jacob Riz, a survivor of a World War II Soviet labor camp, the Center aims to educate visitors in this brutal period in world history.

Films about the Holocaust are available for viewing at the Center, and a non-circulating library is available for research on the Holocaust, Israel and Jewish-related subjects.

MIKVEH ISRAEL CEMETERY
Spruce Street between 8th and 9th
922-5446

Hours: You'll get a good view anytime by looking through the entrance gates.
Tours: Special arrangements can be made to open the gates by calling in advance.

The Mikveh Israel Cemetery was founded in 1738, two years before Mikveh Israel Synagogue*.

Nathan Levy originally acquired the ground from William Penn in 1738. He wanted it to be his family burial plot. The Levy family expanded the cemetery and donated it to the synagogue in 1766 so members of the Jewish community could be buried together.

Among the distinguished American Jews buried here are Nathan Levy (his ship "Myrtilla" carried the Liberty Bell to Philadelphia) and members of his family, Haym Salomon (patriot and financier of the Revolution) and Michael Gratz (who helped expand the U.S. into the West).

Rebecca Gratz's stone has an interesting story behind it. Sir Walter Scott is said to have modeled his Rebecca in the novel "Ivanhoe" after Rebecca Gratz.

Mikveh Israel Cemetery is maintained by Mikveh Israel

Synagogue. It's part of Independence National Historical Park*.

NATIONAL MUSEUM
OF AMERICAN JEWISH HISTORY
Independence Mall East
55 North 5th Street—19106
923-3811

Hours: Monday to Thursday, 10 to 5; Sunday, 12 to 5; Friday, by appointment only. Closed holidays and Jewish Holy Days. Allow 30 minutes.

Tours: Exhibits are self-explanatory, and docents are always available to answer questions. Large groups should call a week ahead to schedule tour of exhibits and adjoining Mikveh Israel Synagogue*.

Cost: Adults, $1.75; students and senior citizens, $1.50; children, $1.25; under 5, free. Discounts are available to groups planning a tour. Membership enables free admission, special programs and other privileges.

Other: A museum shop offers one-of-a-kind artwork, ceremonial objects, jewelry and unusual mementos.

E & H: Complete wheelchair access.

The National Museum of American Jewish History, adjoining Mikveh Israel Synagogue*, opened in 1976. It's dedicated to telling the story of Jewish participation in the growth and development of America.

A permanent gallery, "The American Jewish Experience: From 1654 to the Present," is divided into periods showing how events affected the social, political, economic and cultural life of Jews in the nation. And vice versa.

Two smaller galleries have changing exhibits. There's also a reconstruction of the Gratz family's sitting room as it looked in 1845.

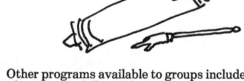

Other programs available to groups include films shown at the museum followed by discussion and a tour, a speakers bureau, and "Walking Tours of Old Jewish Philadelphia." Call for details if you know a group that might enjoy any of these.

PHILADELPHIA JEWISH ARCHIVES CENTER
At Balch Institute
18 South 7th Street—19106
925-8090

Hours: Weekdays, 9 to 5. Closed Federal and Jewish holidays.

The Philadelphia Jewish Archives Center is an educational institute for the collection and preservation of the public and private records of the Philadelphia area Jewish community. Established in 1972, it is a service of the Federation of Jewish Agencies.

Material is donated to the Center by Philadelphia area organizations, institutions and individuals. Among its records are those of the Jewish Publication Society, Association for Jewish Children, Hebrew Sunday School Society and Hebrew Immigrant Aid Society. A small non-circulating library and a photograph collection are also available to researchers.

Most of the archives here date from the mid-19th century, with a few items from earlier periods.

PHILADELPHIA MUSEUM OF JUDAICA
615 N. Broad Street at Mt. Vernon—19123
627-6747

Hours: Weekdays, 10 to 4; Sunday, 10 to 12. Closed Jewish Holy Days.
Tours: Exhibits are self-explanatory. Call in advance to arrange a guided tour.
SEPTA: Bus C; Broad Street Subway to Spring Garden Street and walk 2 blocks north.
E & H: There are 6 steps at the entrance.

Founded in 1795, Congregation Rodeph Shalom (Reform) is the oldest Ashkenazic synagogue in the Western hemisphere. It also houses and operates the Philadelphia Museum of Judaica.

The museum has a permanent collection of Jewish ceremonial art, artifacts and historical documents dating from 2000 B.C. to today. Three times a year there are major photography, sculpture, lithograph or painting exhibitions related to Judaism.

When you visit the museum, look at the synagogue's sanctuary and notice the architecture. This 1927 building is considered to be one of the country's outstanding examples of Byzantine design.

PRESBYTERIAN HISTORICAL SOCIETY
425 Lombard Street—19147
627-1852

Hours: Weekdays, 9 to 5. Closed holidays.
Tours: Call a few weeks ahead to schedule groups of up to 50, at least 7th grade level. Children must be accompanied by adults. Allow 30 minutes.

This is a non-circulating archives and research center in an impressive colonial structure. The resources on American and foreign Presbyterian and Reformed Church life are extensive.

There's a permanent artifacts display and changing exhibitions. Many fine oil paintings and sculptures relating to the Presbyterian Church are shown, along with a 15-minute film about the Historical Society.

Six larger-than-life statues dominate the exterior of the building; they're famous Presbyterians done by Alexander Stirling Calder.

ST. PAUL'S CHURCH
225 South 3rd Street—19106
351-1400

Hours: Weekdays, 9 to 4:45.

This 18th century church is now the headquarters of the Episcopal Community Services of the Diocese of Pennsylvania.

The 10-pew chapel still retains its colonial atmosphere. An old churchyard has the graves of the Edwin Forrest family. Forrest was a local 19th century actor who willed a fortune to members of his profession. (The Forrest Theater* is named after him.)

If you're just walking by, look for the 18th century iron grill entrance gates. They're considered to be among Philadelphia's finest examples of this work.

You can walk by the church and impress your companion by saying, "This is the church where Stephen Girard got married."

ST. PETER'S ROMAN CATHOLIC CHURCH
5th Street and Girard Avenue—19123
627-3080 or 627-2386

Hours: Daily, 7:30 to 6. Mass is Monday to Saturday at 7:30, 12:15 and 5:30; Sunday at 7:30, 9:30, 11 (in Spanish), 12:30 and 3:30. A special Shrine Mass is Sunday at

3 and 7:30.

Hours at St. John Neumann Museum: Weekdays, 10 to 4; Saturday, 10 to 5; Sunday, 1 to 5.

Tours: Call in advance to schedule groups daily, except Monday. Visit includes a tour of the Shrine, Mass (if requested), blessing with the relic and a talk on Saint John Neumann.

SEPTA: Bus 50; trolley 15.

Other: A film on the life of Saint John Neumann is shown Sunday at 2, and other times by request. A gift shop is open daily.

St. Peter's has gained international prominence for its **Saint John Neumann Shrine** at 1019 North 5th Street.

Blessed John Neumann was the fourth Bishop of Philadelphia from 1852 till his death at age 49 in 1860. He was a founder of America's first parochial school system which was here in Philadelphia. He is the first American male to be canonized a saint (June 19, 1977) by the Catholic Church.

Saint John Neumann's remains are visible in a glass-sided crypt beneath the church's altar table. Artifacts of his life, including a rosary, chalice, copies of sermons and a will, are exhibited. Twenty-six stained glass windows tell the story of his life. Pope John Paul II visited the Shrine on October 4, 1979.

TEMPLE JUDEA MUSEUM
OF KENESETH ISRAEL
Old York and Township Line Roads
Elkins Park, Pa. 19117
887-8700

Hours: Monday to Wednesday, 1 to 4; before and after Friday services at 8:30 P.M. Group tours at other times by appointment. Closed Federal and Jewish holidays. Allow an hour or more.

Tours: Call at least one week ahead to schedule no more than 40 adults or school children.

SEPTA: Bus 55.

E & H: Complete wheelchair access.

When Temple Judea merged with Keneseth Israel in 1982 a museum was established to exhibit the Judaica collections of both synagogues. The ark of the former Temple Judea is a permanent feature of the displays, along with antique and contemporary ceremonial and art objects.

Exhibits, which change every few months, focus on

religious holidays, festivals and life-cycle events.

A tour can also include a visit to the sanctuary with a detailed description of magnificent stained glass windows by Jacob Landau.

Center City Places of Worship

If you're visiting Philadelphia, or looking for a change of pace, the following places of worship are within walking distance of the various center city hotels. Call ahead for their specific schedules of services.

Arch Street Presbyterian Church 1724 Arch Street, 563-3763. "The Church of Penn Center." Built in 1855, its grand interior is done in Greek Revival style.

Arch Street United Methodist Church Broad and Arch Streets, 568-6250. "The City's Central Church" has daily and Sunday worship, Sunday organ recitals, community dinners and other events. Tours follow Sunday morning service.

Central Philadelphia Monthly Meeting 15th and Cherry Streets, 241-7260. The 1856 Meeting House of classic architecture has been joined with a contemporary three-story brick and glass structure to form the Friends Center Complex. Included are the offices of eight Quaker organizations, a library and book store.

Fifth Church of Christian Science 1915 Pine Street, 545-2899.

First Baptist Church 17th and Sansom Streets, 563-3853. Built in 1898 in Byzantine and Romanesque styles to resemble the Church of St. Sophia in Constantinople. A frequent site for concerts and community events. Open for "prayer and quietness," weekdays 11:30 to 1:30.

First Presbyterian Church 21st and Walnut Streets, 567-0532. The "Mother Church" of American Presbyterianism; established in 1698. Sunday, Wednesday and Thursday services.

First Unitarian Church 2125 Chestnut Street, 563-3980. Built in 1885 (their fourth home) after being established in 1796 as the first "Unitarian" American church.

Holy Communion Lutheran Church Chestnut Street west of 21st, 567-3668.

Holy Trinity Episcopal Church 1904 Walnut Street, 567-1267.

Philadelphia Ethical Society 1906 Rittenhouse Square, 735-3456. Sunday morning meeting of Ethical Culture Movement stresses ethics and good living over theology.

St. Clement's Episcopal Church 2000 Cherry Street, 563-1876. Completed in 1859 with later additions of the present high altar, wrought iron gates and stained glass windows. Tours are available by appointment.

St. George's Greek Orthodox Cathedral 256 South 8th Street, 627-4389.

St. John's Catholic Church 21 South 13th Street, 563-4145.

St. Luke and the Epiphany Episcopal Church 330 South 13th Street, 732-1918. Built in 1840, and the site of a pre-Civil War conference between Northern and Southern members of the Episcopal Church to preserve its unity.

St. Mark's Episcopal Church 1625 Locust Street, 735-1416. Built in the 1850s, and "The Church of the English Actors Union."

St. Patrick's Roman Catholic Church 242 South 20th Street, 735-9900.

Society Hill Synagogue (Conservative–Reconstructionist) 418 Spruce Street, 922-6590. An early 19th century historical landmark designed by Thomas U. Walter as a Baptist Church. Bought by a Rumanian Jewish congregation at the turn of this century; its early 20th century qualities have been preserved.

Temple Beth Zion–Beth Israel (Conservative) 18th and Spruce Streets, 735-5148. Formerly a 19th century, Gothic-style church, and transformed into a synagogue in 1954. Daily morning and evening services.

Tenth Presbyterian Church 1700 Spruce Street, 735-7688.

Vilna Congregation (Sons of Abraham Synagogue) 509 Pine Street, 592-9433. Daily and Saturday morning services.

YM-YWHA (Conservative) 401 S. Broad Street, 545-4400. Services Friday evening and Saturday morning, holidays and festivals from September to May.

Chapter 6.
The Waterfront.

The English explorer, Henry Hudson, discovered a river in 1609, and the next year it was named in honor of Virginia's first governor, Baron Thomas de la Waare. Today it's the Delaware River.

William Penn quickly saw the strategic importance that both the Delaware and Schuylkill Rivers could play in his dream of a "Holy Experiment," and when he laid out the plan for Philadelphia in 1682 the two rivers became the east and west boundaries of the city. The Schuylkill remained the western border until 1854, when the Borough of West Philadelphia was merged into the city.

Its situation on the Delaware River today enables Philadelphia to boast of the largest fresh water port in the world, and the second busiest port in the nation. It's the largest petroleum port on the East Coast, and a major center for grain, ore, iron ore and coal. Ships from all over the world can be seen on the Delaware, and it's a rare day when you don't spot a large freighter on the move. (You'll want to watch the ships from Penn's Landing.)

Four bridges span the Delaware River to connect Philadelphia with New Jersey.

The **Tacony–Palmyra Bridge** (opened in 1929) links Northeast Philadelphia with Burlington County, and it costs only 25 cents to drive across. It's a drawbridge, so be prepared to wait if there's a ship approaching.

The **Betsy Ross Bridge** (opened in 1976) connects the Bridesburg section of the city with Pennsauken, New Jersey. The **Walt Whitman Bridge** (opened in 1957) links South Philadelphia and Gloucester City.

The most interesting of the four spans is the **Benjamin Franklin Bridge**. It runs from center city Philadelphia to Camden. When it was built in 1926, it was the largest single-span structure in the world, boasting of 8,291 feet from portal to portal. You can drive across the bridge for 90 cents or you can ride a PATCO* train for 75 cents. But the most interesting way to cross is on foot or by bicycle. There's a 10-foot wide walkway along the bridge's south side, which is open to hikers and cyclists from 7 A.M. until 6 P.M. The view is fabulous, the picture-taking possibilities are excellent, and—best of all—it's free. Call the Delaware River Port Authority (925–8780) to make sure it's open on the day you want to cross.

Remember: An **asterisk(*)** indicates that the same place or event appears elsewhere in the book with more details. Look in the Index for additional pages.

Penn's Landing

Penn's Landing is Philadelphia's newest pride, joy, and attraction. William Penn would certainly never recognize the sleek marina and riverside esplanades as the same place along the Delaware where he landed his small ship "Welcome" more than 300 years ago.

Dozens of ugly, run-down piers were demolished to make way for marinas, walkways, overlooks, a sculpture garden and parks. You can drive to Penn's Landing, arrive at the marina by boat, or you can handily walk from the adjacent Society Hill, Old City and Queen Village neighborhoods.

Penn's Landing currently extends from Market Street south to Lombard Street and covers 37 acres.

The construction of Penn's Landing began in 1967, and there's more work to be done. Additional recreation space, apartments, townhouses, restaurants, hotel and office buildings are underway or on the drawing board.

The Penn's Landing development has spurred growth beyond its boundaries. What were once commercial piers just north of the Penn's Landing site are now luxury residential properties. The Philadelphia Marine Center incorporates 15 acres of water and piers 12 to 19 north to include a 300-slip marina, boat show, sales and service centers.

Penn's Landing itself has become an ideal site for special events and celebrations. Queen Elizabeth docked her royal yacht "Britannia" at Penn's Landing when she paid a visit to Philadelphia. Many of the world's "Tall Ships" paid a courtesy call when they participated in the Bicentennial's Operation Sail and to celebrate Philadelphia's 300th birthday in 1982. They returned again to commemorate "Freedom Sail International" in July of 1986.

Displays along the Penn's Landing esplanade will familiarize you with the port's history and her traffic. Look for the enormous murals at the Market, Chestnut and Walnut "Malls" depicting the Philadelphia waterfront in 1702, 1753 and 1876.

The three-and-a-half acre Great Plaza at Chestnut Street provides a tiered, terraced amphitheater facing the river. Designs in the pavement show the Delaware and a compass pointing overseas to Philadelphia's sister cities*.

Graphs, charts and drawings near the river's edge explain the city's topography and the river's channel and depths. Colorful panels point out the ships you might see along the Delaware, their flags and funnel insignias.

A highlight of your trip to Penn's Landing should be a visit to a few of the ships permanently moored there.

E & H: Gangplanks and stairs make wheelchair access to the ships impossible. It's best to view the ships and the river from the flat esplanades of Penn's Landing.

SEPTA buses to Penn's Landing include the D to the foot of Chestnut Street, 5 and 42 to Front and Walnut or Locust Streets, or the 17, 33 or 48 to Front and Market Streets.

GAZELA OF PHILADELPHIA ex Gazela Primeiro
923-9030

Hours: Labor Day to Memorial Day, weekends, noon to 5; school groups at other times by appointment. Memorial Day to Labor Day, daily, 10 to 6.

Cost: 50¢.

Tours: Call at least 2 weeks ahead to schedule groups of up to 80.

The Gazela of Philadelphia is a 177-foot square-rigged sailing ship built in 1883. She's the last of a Portuguese fleet that fished for cod off Newfoundland as recently as 1969.

The Gazela sailed to Philadelphia in 1971 under auspices of the Philadelphia Maritime Museum. Penn's Landing Corporation owns her now, and she's lovingly maintained and operated by the Philadelphia Ship Preservation Guild.

She was the oldest of the 18 "Tall Ships" from around the world to participate in OpSail on July 4, 1976 in New York City. In 1984, she participated in the "Return of the Tall Ships" in Quebec, Canada. She again returned to New York harbor to celebrate the Statue of Liberty Centennial on July 4, 1986, and immediately following that event, the Gazela of Philadelphia led the flotilla of "Tall Ships" to Penn's Landing for "Freedom Sail International." Today, she's a permanent working exhibit and sail training vessel in Penn's Landing. The Gazela can fly 13 sails from her three masts.

Come aboard and relive the bygone days at sea. Listen for the sound of the crew singing sea chanties. Imagine the pounding of waves and the spray of the briny deep. Marvel at the spartan living accommodations where sailors longed for the comforts of home. And view the hold where freshly caught fish were kept.

Note: You can tell the Gazela has an ambitious sailing schedule. You might want to call ahead to be sure she's in port.

U.S.S. OLYMPIA
922-1898

Hours: Daily, 10 to 4:30 in winter; 10 to 6 from Memorial Day till late September. Closed Christmas, New Year's.
Tours: Call a week ahead if you're bringing a group of 25 or more.
Cost: A combined rate for the Olympia and the Becuna: adults, $2.50; senior citizens, $1.50; children under 12, $1.25. Special rates are arranged in advance for groups of 15 or more: adults, $2; children, $1.
Others: Souvenirs and refreshments are sold on board. Flat shoes are best for touring the historic ships.

Admiral Dewey's famous flagship at the Battle of Manila Bay in 1898 has been restored as a floating museum. This is the ship where Dewey gave the famous order: "You may fire when you are ready, Gridley."

The Olympia is the last survivor of the Spanish-American War. She served in World War I and ceremoniously brought the Unknown Soldier back from France in 1921 to be buried in Arlington Cemetery. The Olympia took her final cruise in June, 1976, from Pier 11 North in Philadelphia to her present berth at Penn's Landing.

Most of the Olympia's 16 cabins have been restored, and you can tour the entire ship from topsides to berth deck. The ship's restoration includes many exhibits relating to the Spanish-American War, including old naval weapons, uniforms and assorted mementos from the ship's crew.

U.S.S. BECUNA
922-1898

Hours and Tours: Same as Olympia.
Cost: A combined admission rate with the Olympia.

What's that big black thing next to the U.S.S. Olympia? It's the World War II submarine, U.S.S. Becuna.

The Becuna was commissioned in 1944 and saw action in the South Pacific. She was transferred to the Atlantic fleet in 1949, finished active service as a training vessel and conducted more than 10,000 dives before they decommissioned her in 1969.

WORKSHOP ON THE WATER
925-5439 or 925-7589

Hours: Early May through first week of October, Wednesday to Sunday, 9:30 to 4:30.

Cost: Adults, 50¢; senior citizens and children under 12, free.

Other: An annual regatta, usually the first Saturday of October, recreates boating of bygone eras along the Delaware. Call for specifics.

Did you ever wonder what kind of boats our forefathers were accustomed to seeing along the Delaware? Well, here's your chance to find out.

The 110- by 30-foot covered barge, which is permanently moored in Penn's Landing, is the Philadelphia Maritime Museum's* Workshop on the Water.

At one end of the barge are restored historic small sailing craft with names like "sneak box," "sturgeon skiff" and "Delaware Ducker." They range from approximately 12 feet to 23 feet.

This is an ongoing workshop. At the other end of the barge you're likely to see in current construction another example of the traditional small craft. Participants in workshop activities study sailmaking, toolmaking, painting and all of the skills of boat building. If you'd like to participate, call for a schedule and details.

Just a short walk towards Chestnut Street and north of these historic ships, the **MOSHULU** sits anchored in the Delaware. The largest all-steel sailing ship still afloat is now permanently converted into a restaurant (see Chapter 18), and it's in Philadelphia.

The four-masted Moshulu is almost 400 feet long and as high as a 10-story building. The rigging is intact, and there are assorted samples of sailing gear on board.

The Moshulu has a wonderful history. She was built in Scotland for a German company in 1904 and spent the early part of her life hauling coal, coke, nitrate and lumber around the world. We won't tell you the whole story. It might spoil your visit.

After you've toured the ships, come ashore. There's a lot more to see at Penn's Landing.

A two-acre **WORLD SCULPTURE GARDEN** surrounds a gigantic sundial that was installed to commemorate Penn's Landing in 1682. If you ever wanted to guess the time in this ancient way, this is your chance to try it, unless you come on a cloudy day.

William Penn returned again late in 1982, this time to stay. He's cast in bronze by sculptor Carl Lindborg and looks as he did at age 38 when he arrived in 1682.

The stone sculptures include a 16th century sacred bull from India, a pair of five-foot pre-Columbian spheres from Costa Rica, a pair of late 17th century Korean tombstones, an Etruscan sarcophagus from Italy and an "inukshuk" (or sign post) from Canada. The late 19th century 20-foot totem pole watching over the garden is also from Canada.

The **PORT OF HISTORY MUSEUM** at Walnut Street is a City of Philadelphia showplace for exhibits that change regularly. They're from the city's varied collections and borrowed shows. It's also a popular locale for celebrations and special events.

The museum's hours are Wednesday to Sunday, 10 A.M. to 4:30 P.M. It's closed holidays. Admission is $2 for adults, $1 for children 5 to 12, free for children under 5. Call ahead to 925-3802 for a preview of what's happening.

What else is there at Penn's Landing?

You already know about Spirit of Philadelphia* and R & S Harbor Tours* of the Port of Philadelphia, and the Penn's Landing Trolley* that travels Delaware Avenue (refer back to Chapter 1), but there are festivities throughout the summer.

The Penn's Landing Corporation sponsors "Down by the Riverside," nearly a hundred concerts and special events taking place from May through September. See the local newspapers or call 923-4992 (and see Chapter 10) for their schedule.

Fireworks light up the sky around July 4th. Check the papers for the time and date. Foreign and U.S. Navy vessels frequently drop anchor at Penn's Landing and invite the public on board. Call 923-4992 to find out who's going to be here.

By now you've got the point. Penn's Landing is an exciting place to visit.

You can easily come to Penn's Landing by car or chartered bus because there's plenty of space for parking. It's $3 to park a car for the day, or $5 for an over-size vehicle. You can come by bicycle because there are places to park and lock your bike. You can also come by SEPTA as described at the beginning of this chapter.

If you own a boat, come by boat. The docks are open between Memorial Day and Labor Day. Call the Penn's Landing Marina at 923-9129 for information. The docks are available on a first come, first served basis and there's a daily fee.

Come to Penn's Landing for a leisurely lunch or dinner in the floating **restaurant** on the Moshulu. Enjoy the sparkling new Chart House on the waterfront at Lombard Street. Or watch the waterfront while dining at the Riverfront, its dinner theater or a restaurant at NewMarket or one along Front Street (see Chapter 18). Or have a picnic in the sculpture garden or any of the comfortable seating areas.

A reminder for the **elderly and handicapped:** All of the open, level stretches of Penn's Landing are easily accessible to wheelchairs. Unfortunately, it won't be possible to board the historic ships.

Philadelphia's Other Waterfronts

Philadelphia has two waterways in addition to the Delaware: the Schuylkill and the Wissahickon. (If you're not a native Philadelphian, don't try to pronounce them.) Both rivers flow through Fairmount Park. Both are described in more detail in Chapter 8.

Penn's Landing (on the Delaware) is Philadelphia's newest waterfront attraction, but the Schuylkill and the Wissahickon offer a variety of recreational activities. You'll be reading about these pastimes in Chapter 14.

Chapter 7.
Science and Nature.

ACADEMY OF NATURAL SCIENCES
19th Street and Benjamin Franklin Parkway—19103
299-1000

Hours: Weekdays, 10 to 4; weekends and holidays, 10 to 5. Closed Thanksgiving, Christmas, New Year's. Allow at least 2 hours.
Tours: Groups and school classes can schedule any of the Academy's 25 natural history lessons (most of them including live animals) for a weekday. Call 299-1060 for reservations.
Cost: Adults, $3.50; students 13 to 18 or with college ID, senior citizens and military personnel, $3.25; children 3 to 12, $3; under 3, free. Group rates for 10 or more: adults, $2.50; students and children, $2.25. Membership (Individual, $25; Family, $35) provides free admission, newsletters, library privileges, a magazine subscription and discounts for classes, field trips and the Museum Shop.
Lunch: The Eatery has machines for beverages, sandwiches and desserts. Or you can brown bag it. Reservations are necessary on weekdays for groups. Call 299-1060.
SEPTA: Buses 32, 33, 38 or Market Street routes to 19th Street.
Other: The Museum Shop is a fun gift place for children and adults seeking the unusual. It's filled with ecology kits, educational books, jewelry, mineral specimens, fossils and rare shells.
E & H: The Parkway entrance has 7 steps, but the 19th Street entrance enables complete wheelchair access.

When you visit the Academy, you'll get a feeling of what it's like to be in the animal worlds of Africa, Asia and North America, because you'll see animals that are native to those lands. And you'll see them in their natural settings. Thirty-five groupings of stuffed animals from around the world are on display.

There are wonderful exhibits of birds, fishes, decoys, Egyptian mummies, insects, gems and crystals, endangered species and species from the past. A distinguished show comes to the Hall of Changing Exhibits on the Academy's first floor every few months.

The Academy was founded in 1812, and it's the oldest natural history museum in America.

A total renovation of the Academy has recently taken place, and Dinosaur Hall was unveiled in 1986. You'll meet the likes of a 15-feet tall, 40-feet long tyrannosaurus rex and a dozen other awesome creatures that roamed the earth long before man appeared. When did dinosaurs live? How long did they last? How fast did they grow? What made them become extinct? These are just a few of the questions you'll answer on a computer for dinosaur data and other ingenious exhibits. You'll sit in a footprint, dig a fossil, stop in the dinosaur weigh station and see "Magnificent Monsters," shown every 20 minutes in an informal theater. Discovering Dinosaurs is a fabulous, world-class, one-of-a-kind exhibit. Don't miss it!

The Academy's animal room has 90 "critters" to choose from for the half-hour live animal Eco Show. It's presented in the auditorium several times each weekend. Check your listing of "Today's Specials" on arrival at the Academy. If you can't get to the Academy to see the show, look into "Eco Show on the Road" (see Chapter 13 on "Tours to Go").

There's also a popular film presentation, "Dinosaurs," and several mini-shows each weekend on changing topics. Check the program schedule when you get there.

Right within the Academy is a mini-museum for children called **OUTSIDE IN**. There's more about that in Chapter 15.

Saturday classes for children and weeknight classes for adults are presented during the school year, and classes for children are presented weekdays in the summer. Call 299–1060 for details. The Academy's library is described later in this book.

Bird-watchers will be especially interested in a hot-line provided by the Academy and the **Delaware Valley Ornithological Club**. Call 567–**BIRD** to keep up with the latest in local, unusual sightings.

You shouldn't miss the Academy.

Naturally.

BARTRAM'S HOUSE AND GARDEN
54th Street and Lindbergh Boulevard—19143
729-5281

Hours: The house is open May through October, Tuesday to Sunday, 10 to 4; November through April, Tuesday to Friday, 10 to 4. Allow 30 minutes. The garden is part of Fairmount Park and is open dawn to dusk.

Tours: A staff member is always available to answer questions. Guided tours of the house and garden can be arranged for groups of 10 or more by calling the John Bartram Association several weeks ahead. A self-guided tour of the grounds is available for 75¢. Ask about adult tours that can include a slide show, the house, the garden, and tea and goodies in the 18th century kitchen. Children's tours can focus on botany or colonial life and crafts such as apple pressing, butter churning, candle making or maple sugaring.

Cost: Adults, $2; children 6 to 18, $1; under 6, free. Group rates available when scheduling in advance for 10 or more. The garden is free.

Lunch: A picnic pavilion, ball field and a playground are on the surrounding grounds. Gourmet box lunches can be ordered in advance for groups of 10 or more.

SEPTA: Bus 52, trolley 36.

Other: A museum shop sells books, pottery and tinware reproductions, and items related to the 18th century lifestyle.

E & H: First floor of house and entire grounds are wheelchair accessible.

Visit America's oldest botanical garden.

Only 44 acres of John Bartram's 280-acre farm remain, but what's left is a garden oasis along the Schuylkill River in the industrial areas of Southwest Philadelphia. This is a small but significant portion of the sprawling Fairmount Park* system.

Romp around the grounds and look at the collection of trees and shrubs by this Quaker farmer who became King George III's Royal Botanist. There's an ancient ginkgo, oaks, pawpaws, persimmons, magnolias, Franklinias, and a yellowwood tree. Many specimens are labeled.

Bartram built his house between 1728 and 1731, and an addition in 1770. The house, now a National Historical Landmark, has recently been restored and filled with lovely antiques and 18th century furnishings.

Look outside over the window of Bartram's study for an inscription carved by John Bartram, himself, in 1770. He made certain that his religious philosophy was inscribed in stone for longevity.

CYCLORAMA OF LIFE
Lankenau Hospital
Lancaster Avenue west of City Line Avenue—19151
645-2207

Hours: Weekdays, 9 to 5. Closed holidays. Allow 45 minutes.
Tours: You're on your own. Groups of 5 or more should call ahead, and a maximum of 25 can visit together. All visitors should be able to read.
Cost: Free.
SEPTA: Buses 105, G.
E & H: The museum is on Lankenau's ground floor inside the main entrance that is reached by a ramp.

Cyclorama of Life is a self-explanatory health museum. Audio-visual displays and participation experiments take you through the processes of life from its beginning to old age. Along the way are stops to learn about smoking, alcohol, sex, drugs and their various effects.

Play "Drug Roulette" and see if you would escape the harmful effects of drugs. Listen to "Pandora," the transparent woman, tell you about her anatomy.

DAVID RITTENHOUSE
LABORATORY OBSERVATORY
209 South 33rd Street—19104
(enter from 33rd Street, south of Walnut Street)
898-8176 (weekdays, 9 to 5)

Hours: Monday and Thursday nights: Mid-September through March, 7:30 to 9; April through mid-August, 9 to 10:30.
Tours: No more than 20 can visit at once. Groups of 10 or more must call at least a week ahead. Children must be with an adult.
Cost: Free.
SEPTA: Buses 30, 42, D.
Other: Dress comfortably. You'll be standing during the entire visit.
E & H: No wheelchair access. After taking elevator to 4th floor, there are 2 flights of steps.

The Departments of Astronomy and Astrophysics at the University of Pennsylvania provide a close-up look at the heavens for serious star gazers. Be sure to come on a cloudless night.

Various phases of the moon, constellations, star clusters, nebulae and other planets are often visible, depending on the time of the year, through the enormous eight-inch refractor telescope.

A University faculty member will be on hand to read heaven's timetable and answer your questions.

FRANKLIN INSTITUTE
20th Street and Benjamin Franklin Parkway—19103
564-3375 (recorded information) or 448-1200

Hours: Monday to Saturday, 10 to 5; Sunday, 12 to 5. Closed July 4, Labor Day, Thanksgiving, December 24, Christmas and New Year's. Allow at least 2 hours; better yet, a whole day. And plan to come again.

Tours: Reservations are necessary for school groups interested in special lessons and demonstrations planned according to grade level. Call 448-1201. Philadelphia Public School teachers should call Museum Education at Board of Education, 299-7778, for special arrangements.

Cost: Adults $4; children 4 to 12, $3; senior citizens, $2.50; under 4, free. Half-price admission if you arrive after 4 P.M. School groups and other groups of at least 20, $2.50. Individual and family memberships provide free admission to the Museum and Planetarium, guest tickets, discounts in The Museum Store and workshops, publications, special travel ventures and family programs. Student membership ($10 for ages 8 to 25) includes free admission to the Museum and Planetarium.

Lunch: A huge Food Stop (seating 300) fast food cafeteria is on the ground level. A lunchroom can be reserved (448-1201) weekdays by school groups of 10 or more and other groups of 15 or more.

SEPTA: Buses 32, 33, 38, 44, 48. There's parking on weekends at the Museum's 21st Street lot.

Other: The Museum Store is filled with scientific toys, books, kites, jewelry, T-shirts, star maps and various innovative wonders.

E & H: The receiving entrance on 21st Street near the Boeing 707 is level, and a guard is on hand to open the door and assist you. Call 448-1201 (weekdays) in advance. There are 4 low steps at the Winter Street entrance to the museum and Fels Planetarium. Elevators stop at all floors, but certain display areas are separated by steps. Rest rooms and the Food Stop are wheelchair accessible.

The Institute is a "touch me" place, and their exhibits invite you to push buttons, pull levers, spin wires and slide weights.

It's a fabulous way to learn about hard-to-explain things like the principles of science, technology, time, perception, measurements, meteors, aviation, communications and atomic energy. Learning is fun when you walk through a giant heart, play on the world's largest pin-ball machine, "engineer" a train or "fly" a plane. The "Franklin Flyer" is a simulated airplane that lifts 10 feet off the ground three times each day. And who's the pilot? You are!

Pick up your "Schedule of Events" when you get there. Then, set out on an adventure of scientific exploration.

You're certain to be captivated by the Institute's demonstrations of liquid air, computers, weather reporting, the forces of light, static electricity, ships and waves.

Shipbuilding on the Delaware is where you can design a duck or set sail on your own while you learn about local shipbuilding from William Penn's time to the mid-20th century.

Help build a mountain in The Changing Earth as you discover the forces that shape our planet.

Do optics interest you? Then make hand shadows, freeze your shadow, learn to focus and refract.

Electricity comes alive with Franklin's electrical experiments weekdays at 11:30 and 2:30 and weekends at 12:30 and 2.

The Hall of Aviation leads you through the history of flight from man's dreams of flying gods and magic carpets to the reality of jets and supersonic transport.

Who wouldn't love the Science Arcade where 10 video games painlessly teach you science while you play. (Tokens are 25¢ or 5 for $1.)

The outdoor Science Park, which is open Memorial Day to Halloween, features more "touch me" and "do-it" exhibits. You can explore a recycled house, tell time with a sundial or walk around an authentic lunar module.

Then you can take off in "Big Ben," a real Boeing 707 British Airways jetliner that landed in the Science Park. You can board it at the Hall of Aviation. Inspect the cockpit, see the galley and visit the seating compartment.

The **BENJAMIN FRANKLIN NATIONAL MEMORIAL** is a tribute to this great man with an illustrious lifetime. A four-part exhibit of personal possessions and science artifacts called "Ben Franklin: Ideas and Images" surrounds the enormous Franklin sculpture. It's the largest collection of "Frankliniana" anywhere. This area is free to the public (if you enter from 20th Street), but children have to be with an adult.

Science and Computer Workshops, which are programmed for pre-schoolers through adults, meet weekdays and weekends throughout the year. The groups are small and everyone has a chance to build or experiment with Apple IIe computers, rocks, minerals, model airplanes and amateur radio...just to name a few things. There's a fee for these workshops. For information, call 448-1286.

The Franklin Institute also schedules special evening programs throughout the year. Call 448-1254 for information about these.

FELS PLANETARIUM
In the Franklin Institute
20th Street and Benjamin Franklin Parkway
564-3375 (for current schedule)

Hours: Weekdays at 12:30, 2; Saturday at 12, 2, 3, 4; Sunday at 2, 3, 4. Shows for school groups only are weekday mornings. Live constellation show is at 1 P.M. Children's Show is Saturday at 10:30 A.M. (see Chapter 15).
Tours: Reservations are necessary on weekdays for groups of 10 or more. Call 448-1201.
Cost: Weekends, $1.50; weekdays, $1; school shows, 50¢; all in addition to Franklin Institute admission. (Children under 4 are not permitted at the regularly scheduled shows.)
E & H: The Planetarium is level with the floor, and spectators may remain in wheelchairs.

The Fels Planetarium is the way you can travel into the Universe to learn about the sun, the stars and the heavens. Shows about the constellations and patterns in the sky change every few months, and they're relevant to the current season. Call 563-1363 for a Sky Report.

In addition to the shows listed above, a live constellation show is presented for backyard astronomers on Saturdays and Sundays at 1 P.M. The live program changes as the sky changes, so you'll be able to look up and recognize the stars.

MEDICAL SITES

If you need medical care, Philadelphia is the best place to be. We can qualify as the medical capital of the world.

You can tour Pennsylvania Hospital, the nation's oldest; Pennsylvania College of Podiatric Medicine, one of the nation's five podiatry schools; or Scheie Eye Institute, specializing in eye care.

You can tour Smith Kline & French, where pharmaceuticals are developed and manufactured. You can also tour another vital health care service, the American Red Cross. All of these tours are described later in Chapter 13.

Philadelphia is a major medical research and dissemination center. Numerous journals and texts originate here from the world's largest medical publishing houses.

A great many of our country's physicians get their education at one of Philadelphia's six medical schools: Hahnemann, Medical College of Pennsylvania, Philadelphia College of Osteopathy, Temple University, Thomas Jefferson University and the University of Pennsylvania (the nation's first medical school).

Attractions with medical significance are detailed in this chapter and elsewhere in this book. Several others welcome individuals or small groups who are interested in careers in medicine and allied professions.

These tours are designed for adults, but they might be of interest to youngsters. If you're visiting here for a short period of time, it's a good idea to write ahead and plan a special tour.

AMERICAN COLLEGE OF PHYSICIANS 4200 Pine Street, 19104 (243-1200). The administrative headquarters are housed in a handsome West Philadelphia mansion, along with the editorial offices of "Annals of Internal Medicine." Tours for medical professionals must be scheduled in advance by contacting the Office of Public Information.

FRIENDS HOSPITAL Roosevelt Boulevard and Adams Avenue, 19124 (831-4772). The nation's oldest private psychiatric hospital was founded in 1813 and is in Northeast Philadelphia. Tours are for medical professional people only; write three to four weeks in advance. The magnificent 99-acre grounds are open to the public during three weekends in April and May (see Chapter 19) for the Friends Hospital Garden Days.

HAHNEMANN ARCHIVES AND HISTORY OF MEDICINE ROOM 245 N. 15th Street, 19102 (448-7811). This country's first homeopathic medical college was founded in 1848 by Samuel Hahnemann. It continued with homeopathic and related elective courses till 1959. Today, Hahnemann excels as a university and hospital pioneering in heart study and treatment, cancer research, renal care, hypertension and mental health. The Lucy F. Cooke Room exhibits memorabilia of world-renowned doctors affiliated with Hahnemann, hospital and school archives, and reference collections on homeopathy and the history of medicine. A slide program presents "Firsts and Foremosts of Hahnemann." Hours are by appointment, weekdays, 9 to 5.

HISTORICAL DENTAL MUSEUM OF TEMPLE UNIVERSITY SCHOOL OF DENTISTRY 3223 N. Broad Street, 19140 (221-2889). Anyone is welcome to tour the museum weekdays from 11 to 3. Stop by at Room 460. The museum has undergone renovation, so call ahead to make sure it's completed, and the exhibits are up.

PHILADELPHIA COLLEGE OF PHARMACY AND SCIENCE 43rd and Kingsessing Avenue, 19104 (596-8967). The library and the relics of an old apothecary shop may be visited by appointment. If you're interested, ask to see the wonderful collection of antique apothecary jars.

PHILADELPHIA COUNTY MEDICAL SOCIETY 2100 Spring Garden Street, 19130 (563-5343). There are no tours here, but this is where you should call or write for a schedule of lectures, meetings or special medical events that take place in Philadelphia. The Philadelphia County Medical Society also publishes "Philadelphia Medicine."

TEMPLE UNIVERSITY SCHOOL OF PHARMACY'S KENDIG MEMORIAL MUSEUM 3307 N. Broad Street, 19140 (221-4990). See all of the equipment a druggist needed to dispense medicine before pills were mass produced. Weekday tours for small groups by appointment.

UNIVERSITY OF PENNSYLVANIA SCHOOL OF DENTAL MEDICINE 40th and Spruce Streets, 19104 (898-8943). If you're interested in dentistry, call for tour information.

UNIVERSITY OF PENNSYLVANIA SCHOOL OF MEDICINE, HISTORY OF MEDICINE MUSEUM Medical Laboratories Building, School of Medicine, 2nd floor, Hamilton Walk west of 36th Street, 19104 (898-7588). This permanent exhibit of medical records, instruments and equipment offers highlights in the history of the oldest medical school in the country. (It was founded in 1765.) And, it's the place to see Thomas Eakins' famous painting of "The Agnew Clinic." There are also changing exhibits taken from the school's noteworthy collection of medical memorabilia. Hours are weekdays, 9 to 5. You're on your own, but call ahead if a group visit is planned.

MORRIS ARBORETUM
101 Hillcrest Avenue (entrance)
9414 Meadowbrook Avenue (office and classes)—19118
247-5777

Hours: Daily 10 to 5; except November to March, 10 to 4; June to August, Thursday till 8. Closed Christmas, New Year's, and if the weather is very bad.
Tours: For the public on Saturday and Sunday at 2. For groups of 10 to 15 per guide, at least kindergarten age, scheduled at least 3 weeks in advance. If under 14 years old, one adult must accompany every group of 10. Call 242-3399 to schedule.
Cost: Adults, $2; children under 14 and senior citizens, $1. Group rates can be arranged when scheduling tour. Individual and family memberships entitle you to free admission and discount to classes.
Lunch: No food is allowed on the grounds. Ask for directions to picnic grounds at Harper's Meadow in Fairmount Park. It's a half-mile walk from the Arboretum.
SEPTA: Bus L, or a short walk from either Chestnut Hill train station.
E & H: The main roads are paved.

This 175-acre estate in Chestnut Hill is administered by the University of Pennsylvania. It's a veritable outdoor museum of trees, plants and wildlife as well as an entry in the National Register of Historic Places.

There are 3,500 varieties of exotic shrubs, native shrubs and trees. There are conifers, hollies, azaleas, magnolias, dogwoods, witchhazels (that's right!), an oak row, ivies and a medicinal garden. The scenic Wissahickon flows through the magnificent estate.

The spring and fall flowerings and the summer rose garden are all beautiful. The stately evergreens and tropical fern house can be seen in winter.

Small animals roam the grounds, but don't pet them.

There's an ongoing program of lectures and courses in gardening, botany and horticulture. Brochures on special programs are available on request.

If you have a green thumb, try to be here for the Plant Festival Sale on Mother's Day weekend, or the Holly and Green Sale, a weekend before Christmas.

MUTTER MUSEUM
College of Physicians
19 South 22nd Street—19103
561-6050 Ext. 41

Hours: Tuesday to Friday, 10 to 4. Closed some holidays. Allow 45 minutes. Children under 14 must be accompanied by an adult.

Tours: Scheduled for groups of 10 to 30. Allow 30 to 90 minutes. Call 3 weeks in advance for reservations. Specialized tours are offered for groups interested in art and antiques.

Cost: Free. Donations are accepted to offset museum expenses.

SEPTA: Buses 7, 12, 42, D, or any Market Street route.

E & H: There are 8 steps at the building's main entrance. Call ahead to arrange access to a street-level, rear entrance. Once inside, everything is wheelchair accessible.

The Mutter Museum, housed in a grand Greek Revival style 1909 building, would interest students who are intrigued with medicine and its related fields. The museum's specialties are pathology, anatomy and medical history exhibits, primarily from the 19th century. A 15-minute slide show presents an overview of the College of Physicians and its Museum collections.

You'll be face-to-face with over 300 skulls and two dozen skeletons, including a 7'6" giant. You'll examine medical kits, X-ray equipment, walking sticks, hearing aids, thermometers, spectacles and stethoscopes, the likes of which you've never seen.

Be sure to see Chevalier Jackson's collection of items he removed from his patients: pins and needles and buttons and lockets. The cancerous tumor that was removed from President Grover Cleveland's mouth in 1893 is also on display.

If you've ever wondered what an upstate Pennsylvania doctor's office might have looked like in the early 20th century, here's your chance to find out. A desk, examining-surgery chair, treatment facilities, telephone and office equipment are here, awaiting your visit.

A formal medicinal herb garden (open weekdays 9 to 5) is maintained in the yard. At least 60 varieties of plants are labeled with their common and botanical names and their uses for healing.

Longer tours for adult groups include a walk through the College of Physicians*. Founded in 1787, this is the oldest independent and private medical society in the country. Its library is described in Chapter 11.

There are many oil paintings, sculptures and art objects associated with the medical field, and there are interesting collections of memorabilia relating to Madame Curie, Louis Pasteur, Joseph Lister, Benjamin Rush and other noteworthy members of the profession.

PENNSYLVANIA HORTICULTURAL SOCIETY
325 Walnut Street—19106
625-8250

Hours: Weekdays, 9 to 5, except June through August, 8:30 to 4:30. Also open one weekend in December for a special holiday exhibition.
Tours: Call ahead if more than 30 are coming together to the Society or its gardens. A program on "Indoor Gardening in the Classroom" is available for Philadelphia Public School teachers. A large selection of horticultural films is available for classroom use on a rental basis.
Cost: Free. Inquire about membership in the Society.
SEPTA: Buses 5, 42, 50.
Other: A small shop sells some nifty planters, stationery, books and appropriate gift items.
E & H: There are 2 low steps at the entrance. An elevator can be taken to 2nd floor library.

You'll find an imaginative nature exhibit at the Horticultural Society at any given time. It might be unusual flowers, a bonsai exhibit or a maritime show with seascapes, herbarium specimens and seaweed designs. The show changes each month.

The Society also provides expert advice to people who want to plant their own vegetable or flower gardens. If you're lucky enough to have a city garden, ask about entering it in the Society's annual contest.

Almost a hundred activities including plant clinics, demonstrations and garden visits are planned for members. The most ambitious project is the famous Philadelphia Flower Show which is held each March at the Civic Center (see Chapter 19).

By all means, don't miss the typical 18th century garden that's adjacent to the Society's headquarters. Its unusual trees, shrubs and flowers are representative of those that grew in Philadelphia before the year 1800.

The Pennsylvania Horticultural Society plays a major role in the greening of Philadelphia with its "Philadelphia Green" project. Plants and gardening information are provided free of charge to organized urban residents so they can improve their environment.

Individuals can read up on gardening and receive plant care advice from the Society's 14,000-volume library*, or by calling the **Horticulture Hot Line** at 922–8043 on weekdays, except Wednesday, from 9 A.M. to noon.

For additional **GARDENING TIPS**, the Penn State University Cooperative Extension Service in cooperation with the U.S. Department of Agriculture helps city dwellers make vacant lots into mini-farms. Thousands of Philadelphians have harvested vegetables in their new gardens since the **Urban Gardening Program** began in 1977. You can call the **Garden Phone, 276–5183**, on weekdays from 8:30 to 4:30 for answers about growing, cooking and preserving home-grown fruits and vegetables.

Yes, you, too, can be a "gentleperson" farmer.

PENNYPACK ENVIRONMENTAL CENTER
Verree Road south of Bloomfield Avenue—19115
671-0440

Hours: The park is open dawn to dusk. The Center is usually open daily, 9 to 5. Call ahead to be sure, or orient yourself with maps that are posted outdoors.
Tours: School groups of 10 to 50 can be scheduled for 90-minute indoor or outdoor nature programs on weekday mornings or afternoons. Call at least a week in advance. Read below about other programs.
Cost: Free.
SEPTA: Bus W.
Other: A small shop sells books, field guides, bird feeders, bug boxes, jewelry and novelty nature items.
E & H: There are some paved bike paths, but otherwise no special facilities.

The Environmental Center in the heart of Pennypack Park* features indoor nature exhibits that complement this natural setting. Explore the park on your own and feast your eyes on dozens of varieties of birds, waterlife, deer, small game, trees and exotic wildflowers.

Stop by the "bird blind," a protected area where any of 15 species might be sighted feeding themselves from fall to early spring. Or, join a nature program that might include the study of bugs, birds, insects, the creek, the stream, nests, plants, wildflowers, tracks and signs of wildlife along the trails. Peaceful activity is the theme among nature's inhabitants of Pennypack Park.

Two, three or four programs happen each month and you can get the schedule up to two months ahead. Also, special crafts, nature workshops and programs can be scheduled in advance for weekdays throughout the year for groups of 15 or more.

PHILADELPHIA'S PARKS

(Just to name a few.)

The world's largest municipal park is right here in Philadelphia. We think **FAIRMOUNT PARK** is so important that the next chapter is devoted to it.

Park land exists in every section of Philadelphia. Some sections of Fairmount Park, however, stand on their own as significant, large green chunks of Philadelphia.

PENNYPACK PARK spreads out over 1,300 acres in Northeast Philadelphia from Tacony State Road north to Pine Road, and on both sides of Pennypack Creek. Pennypack, named by the Lenape Indians, means "without much current."

The creek's banks are surrounded by unusual trees and wild flowers. It's a haven for small animals and birds. It's a place to rest from the tension of day-to-day activities. There are picnic areas, recreational facilities, bridle paths, walking trails, a 150-acre bird sanctuary and the Pennypack Environmental Center*.

FRANKLIN D. ROOSEVELT PARK is 365 acres in South Philadelphia across from the sports complex at Pattison Avenue, from Broad to 24th Streets.

It's the site of the American–Swedish Historical Museum*, Bellaire Manor* and numerous recreation facilities. You can swim or play golf, bocce and tennis. Or you can participate in track and field events. You can also attend the cultural events which are scheduled throughout the summer.

147

COBBS CREEK PARK is the biggest green portion of West Philadelphia. It is almost 800 acres with a 150-acre creek flowing across the city limits into Delaware County. Pennsylvania's first grist mill was built along this creek in 1643.

Aside from its densely wooded areas, Cobbs Creek Park is well equipped with recreational facilities for all kinds of ball sports, summer camping, golf, ice skating, horseback riding and supervised playgrounds.

FRANKLIN, LOGAN, RITTENHOUSE and **WASHINGTON**, the four green squares of center city Philadelphia, are ideal play and picnic areas. They all have drinking fountains and seating areas. They're perfect settings for shows, having your picture taken after you get married, exhibits and special events that are scheduled throughout the year. All four of the squares were named in 1981 to the National Register of Historic Places*. Each of the squares has its own history and character.

Franklin Square* (Northeast) greets the visitor approaching Philadelphia from the Benjamin Franklin Bridge. Its early history includes service as a colonial burial ground, ammunitions storage base during the Revolution and later as a cattle marketplace.

Today Franklin Square houses a permanent 14-foot high memorial to Philadelphia police and firefighters who lost their lives in service.

Logan Square* (Northwest) sits midway on the Benjamin Franklin Parkway surrounded by grand cultural, municipal, religious and hotel dwellings. When the Parkway was built in the 1920s, Logan Square became a circle to ease the traffic flow, but we still call it a "square." You'll notice the resemblance to the Champs Elysees and the Place de la Concorde. Philadelphia's versions were designed by a Frenchman, Jacques Greber.

Logan Square is distinguished by its Swann Fountain, designed by sculptor Alexander Stirling Calder to depict Philadelphia's three major waterways. This is a perfect setting for picnics or splashing after a visit to the Parkway attractions.

Directly across from Logan Circle, and facing the Cathedral Basilica of SS. Peter and Paul*, is **Sister Cities Plaza**. Flags and concrete markers signify Philadelphia's Sister City relationships with Florence, Italy, and Tel Aviv, Israel. Philadelphia is also the Sister City of Tianjin, China, and Inchon, South Korea.

On the Cathedral's south side, between Race Street and the Benjamin Franklin Parkway, is another grassy plot called **Torun Triangle**. It commemorates Philadelphia's Sister City relationship with Torun, Poland, which was the birthplace of astronomer Nicolaus Copernicus. A sundial monument to Copernicus is on the Triangle.

Rittenhouse Square* (Southwest) is surrounded by fashionable brownstone houses, high-rise apartment buildings and hotels. It's the stage for an annual clothesline art exhibition, flower show, and concerts presented evenings during the summer (see Chapter 19).

Washington Square* (Southeast) in the 18th century was known as Potter's Field, the first public burial ground for the poor. Hundreds of Continental soldiers and British prisoners of the Revolutionary War were also buried here.

Today Washington Square is distinguished as the site of the Tomb of the Unknown Soldier of the American Revolution. An eternal flame burns at the memorial, watched over by a statue of George Washington.

By now you get the idea: Philadelphia is a city of parks. They're all over. Enjoy them.

AWBURY ARBORETUM is a 55-acre park in Germantown. But it's not a part of Fairmount Park. Aside from offering recreation facilities, the arboretum's rolling lawns and beautiful vistas filled with trees, plants, shrubs and wildlife are always a nice oasis to enjoy nature. An observatory enables you to watch birds during their spring and fall migrations. Awbury's entrance is at Washington Lane, just north of Chew Avenue. Call 843-5592 for additional information.

SCHUYLKILL VALLEY NATURE CENTER
8480 Hagy's Mill Road (Upper Roxborough)—19128
482-7300

Hours: Monday to Saturday, 8:30 to 5; Sunday, 1 to 5. Closed holidays, and Sundays in August.
Tours: Scheduled in advance for groups of 20 or more and led by a staff of teacher-naturalists. Cassette players are available for visitors going on their own along 2 of the trails. Reservations are necessary for groups. An outstanding study program is available for all grade levels which is coordinated with follow-up materials. Call for a schedule, and call to arrange a classroom theme.
Cost: Adults, $2; children under 12, $1. Groups of 10 or

149

more by reservation, $1. Special rates for school groups; ask when making reservations. Individual and family memberships enable unlimited free visits, special programs, gift shop discounts, newsletters, library borrowing and guest privileges.

Lunch: No food is sold, but picnicking is allowed in specified areas.

SEPTA: It's a long walk from the bus 61 stop at Ridge and Port Royal Avenues. There's plenty of free parking.

Others: There's a shop selling natural history items, and it's a good idea to bring your camera.

E & H: Widener Trail is paved perfectly smooth, making it accessible for anyone in a wheelchair or requiring a level path. It also has special high curbs to guide the blind. Complete wheelchair access in the Discovery Museum.

This magnificent 360-acre sanctuary is made up of woodlands, fields, thickets, ponds and six miles of trails. You'll see birds, wild animals, plants and trees in a natural setting—untouched by the city.

The hands-on nature, natural history and ecology exhibits in the Discovery Museum correspond to what you'll see on your own, if you go in a study group, or if you go on a self-guided tour with your family or friends.

Special walk and talk nature programs are presented on Saturdays and Sundays. They're usually at 2 P.M., but it's wise to check in advance and then plan your visit with this in mind.

Adult and children's workshops are offered each spring and fall on appropriate subjects like weather and nature photography. They usually run for four to six weeks. Call for specifics.

If you're an educator in the Philadelphia area, Schuylkill Valley's Teaching Resource Center provides help and loans materials for developing your own teaching program. Some 400 volumes are available to choose from. Ten times as many volumes are in the Center's library. Read about it in Chapter 11.

TINICUM NATIONAL ENVIRONMENTAL CENTER
86th Street and Lindbergh Boulevard—19153
365-3118

Hours: Main entrance is open daily, 8 A.M. till sunset. Visitor Center: daily, 8:30 to 4.

Tours: Guided nature walks are weekend mornings at 9. Call ahead for the topic. Groups can schedule at other times by calling at least 2 weeks ahead. Children should be accompanied by adults. Go on your own with a copy of the self-guided nature walk "Boardwalk Loop" that covers ⅔ of a mile in 45 minutes.

Cost: Free.

Lunch: There are benches around, but no food is sold and no cook-outs are allowed.

SEPTA: Buses U and 37 go to 84th and Lindbergh. When driving, call for directions before heading out to Tinicum.

Other: Wear comfortable shoes, and bring binoculars if you can.

E & H: About 2 miles of dike roads are well-graveled. Pick up a pass at the Visitor Center that allows a car to be driven along the roads from 8 to 4.

Tinicum is a 1,200-acre preserve situated along Darby Creek. It's just a few miles from City Hall and a stone's throw from the Philadelphia International Airport. Forget about concrete sidewalks and skyscrapers and jet airplanes for a few moments, because Tinicum shows you what Philadelphia was like before man's arrival.

The name Tinicum comes from the Indian word meaning "islands of the marsh." It refers to the time when marshes extended to the islands in the Delaware River.

Tinicum is a native habitat for marsh plants and thousands of birds—especially water fowl. Depending upon the season, you might see ducks, geese, heron, egrets, gallinules, muskrats, weasels, rabbits, turtles and snakes.

You can follow the lengthy nature trail on foot or by bike. You can launch a canoe, if you have one, into Darby Creek. And you can fish if you have a Pennsylvania Fishing License. (See Chapter 14.)

The best time for bird-watching is in the spring and fall when the birds are en route to or from the South. Call 567-BIRD for recent sightings. Since 1965, over 280 bird species have been sighted at Tinicum.

Nature charts and bird identification aids are available. There's an observation platform where your binoculars will come in handy, and there's a "photography blind" where up to 10 visitors can surreptitiously set up equipment or quietly view the flora and fauna.

Tinicum is administered by the U.S. Fish and Wildlife Service.

A note for Philadelphia and Delaware County educators: Ask about Tinicum's accredited 15-hour courses in environmental education.

WAGNER FREE INSTITUTE OF SCIENCE
17th Street and Montgomery Avenue—19121
763-6529

Hours: Tuesday to Friday, 10 to 4; Sunday, noon to 3. Closed holidays. Allow 30 minutes. (Before going on a hot summer day, consider that there's no air-conditioning.)

Tours: Teachers of grades kindergarten to 7 can schedule in advance for a class lesson weekday mornings from September to June; 15 to 60 students. Otherwise reservations are not necessary.

Cost: Museum, free; Discovery Room, 35¢

Lunch: A room is available, by reservation, for groups brown-bagging it.

SEPTA: Buses 2, 3.

Other: A museum store sells moderately priced toys, games and objects related to natural science. A series of evening lecture courses is offered to adults at Northeast Philadelphia and center city branches of the Free Library. Programs include ecology, geology, physical science, computers, diet and nutrition. Certificates are awarded upon completion.

E & H: No wheelchair access. There are 6 steps outside, exhibits are on 2nd floor and there is no elevator.

This will remind you of how museums used to be. It's one enormous exhibition hall, vintage 1865, neatly crammed with displays of over 21,000 specimens.

The exhibits span the gamut of the animal kingdom from protozoa to man; from the tiniest bug to a dinosaur's hip. (Now, that's hip.) There are worms, insects, corals, fishes, birds, minerals, mollusks, fossils, skulls, skeletons and you name it from every branch of natural science.

The Discovery Room is a mini-museum that was created just for kids. Youngsters can touch, smell, rub and have fun learning about natural science.

Wagner Free Institute's library is described later in Chapter 11.

WISTAR INSTITUTE MUSEUM
36th and Spruce Streets—19104
898-3708

Hours: Weekdays, 10 to 4. Closed holidays.
Tours: Groups of 12 or more should call for reservations a few days in advance. A 30-minute taped cassette tour can be requested on arrival. Children under 12 must be with an adult.
Cost: Free.
SEPTA: Buses 30, 40, 42; trolleys 11, 13, 34, 36.
E & H: There are 13 steps at the entrance on 36th Street. Arrangements can be made in advance to use a ground level entrance on Spruce Street.

This is another worthwhile museum for high school students who are interested in careers in medicine. It isn't a museum for the squeamish. There are exhibits on the human body, anatomy and biology. (The Wistar Institute is a world-renowned biomedical research facility.)

You'll see collections of skulls and skeletons. The first showcase explains the evolution of skulls from fish to man, a development that took 300 million years. Another exhibit shows the evolution of posture from a dog on all fours to a semi-erect monkey to man.

The museum's most historical displays are the "anatomical specimens of demonstration dissections" used by Doctors Casper Wistar and William Horner for studying and teaching in the 19th century. There's also a graphic explanation of the "Wistar strain" of rats.

Other exhibits and graphs compare the growth of boys and girls from birth to 20 years. Man's racial heredity and family-line inheritances are also charted. It shows why some of us are tall, why some of us are short, why some of us have brown, blonde or red hair.

153

ZOOLOGICAL GARDENS (Philadelphia Zoo)
34th Street and Girard Avenue—19104
(in Fairmount Park)
387-6400 (recording) or 243-1100

Hours: Daily, 9:30 to 5. During warmer months, the zoo is open till 6 P.M. Closed Thanksgiving, December 24, Christmas, December 31, New Year's. Come for a whole day, any day, any weather!

Tours: Scheduled daily at 10 or 11:15 A.M., and additional times on weekends, for groups of 10 or more. Allow one hour. An adult must accompany each group of 10 children. To schedule a tour, call 243-1100 Ext. 317 at least 2 weeks in advance. Philadelphia Public School teachers should call the Museum Education Department at the Board of Education, 299-7778, for special arrangements.

Cost: Adults, $4; senior citizens and children 2 to 11, $3; under 2, free. Groups of 15 or more: adults, $3; senior citizens and students 12 to 18, $2.50; children, $2. Groups can buy for 50¢ less, at least 2 weeks in advance (call 243-1100 Ext. 224), a combination ticket that includes admission, the jungle bird walk and children's zoo. Free on Mondays (except holidays) November through February. Membership (Individual, $30; Family, $35) provides free admission (and to other zoos also), guest tickets, a magazine subscription, newsletter, shop discount, Members Day events and special events.

Lunch: There are picnic groves with tables, and many refreshment stands. The Impala Cafe seats nearly 200 indoors and outdoors by the impala fountain.

SEPTA: Bus 38, trolley 15. There's plenty of free parking.

Other: Strollers are for rent; film and souvenirs are sold. The Zoo Shop, near the 34th Street entrance, is a unique boutique for sophisticated animal-related items.

E & H: Wheelchairs are for rent. Everything at the zoo is accessible, including rest rooms. Printed descriptive material is available for the deaf; inquire at Education Department. Special tours are scheduled for groups of hearing impaired or physically disabled visitors. Van tours can be scheduled for groups that arrive in their own vehicle. Call 243-1100 Ext. 317.

America's oldest zoo is a fun place to spend a day. Parents have been known to keep returning long after their children have grown.

The Philadelphia Zoo is an all-weather attraction with

10 heated (or air-conditioned) buildings. The residents are particularly fond of winter visitors. In fact, they're known to make a bigger fuss when their audience is smaller!

Every effort has been made to keep the animals in their natural settings. The 42-acre zoo houses over 1,800 mammals, birds, reptiles and rare species from throughout the world.

The most ambitious project in the zoo's history opened to rave reviews in 1986. The World of Primates puts visitors in the same natural one-acre landscape and jungle habitat as its permanent occupants—families of lemurs, gibbons, gorillas, monkeys and orangutangs. A state-of-the-art orientation center awaits you in the restored 1907 Kangaroo House.

Things really swing in The World of Primates—and in the TreeHouse. But animals don't live here! It's the visitors who climb, crawl, crouch and swing as they activate "gizzmos" with their "magic rings" to discover what it's like to be an animal. It's a wonderful rebirth for the 1874 Gothic-style Antelope House. Admission to the Tree-House is $1, and groups will certainly want to make reservations in advance.

The African Plains exhibits let ostriches, cranes, geese, antelope, giraffes, zebras and their friends wander together as they would in the wilds of their homelands. The human eye will find it hard to detect that the massive rocks, caves and 40-foot baobab tree are synthetic.

Birds fly freely in the Bird House as they do in the tropics. It's well worth the extra 35¢ admission to do the jungle bird walk. The Bear Country always ranks among the zoo's most popular people lures.

The Reptile House has an electronic rain forest thunder shower to make the snakes feel cozy. The rain storms are weekdays at 11, 12 and 1; weekends, on the hour. There's an exciting new fish exhibit here, too. Several aquariums have the varied species that are likely to be swimming in the nearby Schuylkill River.

Visit at meal time. Schedules are posted so you can watch when the lions and tigers, small cats, elephants, birds, penguins, reptiles and mammals are fed. But remember, please don't feed any of the animals yourself.

Look behind the glass walls of the zoo's nursery (near the apes' outdoor home) for babies receiving special care. Abandoned and rejected little animals in need of special care are hand-raised, weighed, doctored, fed baby food and treated as if they were human.

There's a zoo inside the zoo—a **CHILDREN'S ZOO***, where youngsters can get to know the little animals on a first-name basis. The animals can be touched, petted and fed. A zookeeper gives demonstrations throughout the day. There are daily animal shows, sea lion demonstrations, cow milking, sheep dog demonstrations and pony rides (additional fee) from April to November. There's an additional 50¢ charge to enter the Children's Zoo (except in the winter). The little zoo closes a half-hour earlier than the big zoo.

The **MONORAIL SAFARI*** is an 18-minute, mile-long aerial trip high above the tree tops. You'll hear descriptions about the buildings, the grounds and the animal collections. The monorail runs every day (weather permitting) from April to November. The charge on weekdays is $2.50 for adults and $2 for children under 12. On weekends and holidays it's 50¢ more. Groups of 15 or more pay 50¢ less. Call 386-4201 for more information.

Chapter 8.
Fairmount Park.

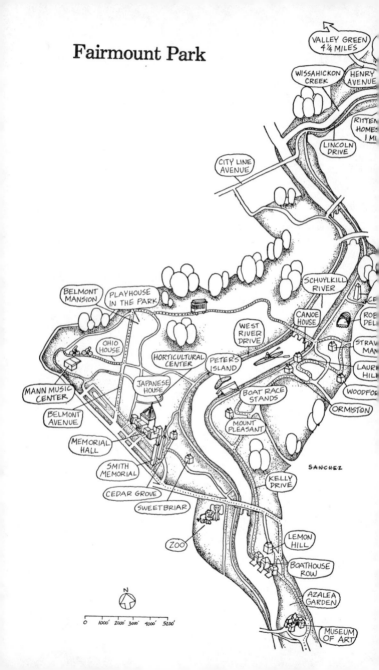

Fairmount Park is the largest and grandest landscaped park within a city anywhere in the world.

It owes its inspiration to William Penn.

Legend has it, that shortly after Penn arrived in Philadelphia, he went to the top of a hill overlooking the Schuylkill (a dutch word meaning "hidden stream") to admire the view, and exclaimed, "What a beautiful faire mount this is." Penn's public relations advisor was with him at the time, and said, "Bill, that's a terrific name. We'll call this place Faire Mount. The people will love it." And thus it was shown as "Faire Mount" on Thomas Holme's 1682 Plan for Philadelphia.

We already know that Penn envisioned a "greene countrie towne" with gardens, parks and open spaces.

But could Penn or his advisors possibly have imagined that by the 20th century Fairmount Park would grow to over 8,700 acres, with more than three million trees and stretching into every part of the city? Could Penn have envisioned that Fairmount Park would have 200 acres of waterways, with at least as many buildings? That it would be a "people's park," with 100 miles of nature trails, paved bikeways and bridle paths? And that it would be the site of hundreds of historic, cultural and recreational facilities?

The Fairmount area west of the city was a popular place for Philadelphia gentlemen to build their summer mansions. The first official City interest in the area happened in 1812 when the City of Philadelphia bought five acres near the hilly site where Penn had first surveyed the area. Construction began there immediately for what became the **Fairmount Water Works** surrounded by landscaped gardens. This was the first steam-pumping station of its kind in America, and it provided Philadelphians with pure drinking water from the Schuylkill.

The pumping technique was gradually replaced by paddle wheels and water turbines, but the water works continued to function until 1911. The water itself was raised to an enormous reservoir on the "faire mount."

The original four water works buildings and pumping station still overlook the Schuylkill River. They were designed by Frederick Graff in charming Greek Revival style, and were recently cited by the American Society of Civil Engineers as a national historic landmark in the development of American engineering.

From 1911 until 1962 the water works buildings housed the Philadelphia Aquarium with its thousands of species of fish, reptiles and invertebrates. Today the 19th century "faire mount" reservoir is the site of the Philadelphia Museum of Art*.

The water works buildings to the west of the museum are undergoing major restoration, spearheaded by the Fairmount Park Commission, Philadelphia Water Department and the Junior League of Philadelphia.

Tours of the **Fairmount Water Works** are offered April to November, Wednesday to Sunday, from 10 to 4. Allow 20 to 30 minutes. Call 236-5465 for information and reservations if you have a group of 15 or more. (You'll read in Chapter 13 how you can tour Philadelphia's 20th century water treatment plants and pollution control facilities.)

Be sure to take in the spectacular view of the Art Museum, Boat House Row outlined in lights and the water works—especially at night—from across the river on the West River Drive or the Schuylkill Expressway.

The water works is a popular area for fishing in the Schuylkill, for strolling on a pleasant day or for renting a bicycle*.

The Schuylkill's scenic riversides lured early Philadelphians to build their country estates there. Several of these mansions survived the Revolution and others were built later.

By the mid-1850s civic and community leaders in Philadelphia were devoting a great deal of effort to acquiring those houses and park land to preserve it for the City. Their first purchase was Lemon Hill* in 1844, setting the course for Fairmount Park as we know it today.

More than 60 Fairmount Park buildings are historically certified and appear in the National Register of Historic Places. Several of the mansions stand majestically awaiting your visit.

Fairmount Park itself became a reality in 1855 when the Philadelphia City Council acted to make Lemon Hill part of a Fairmount Park for the use and enjoyment of the city's residents. The City formally received authority in 1867 from the General Assembly of Pennsylvania to buy more land for the park. Shortly thereafter a Fairmount Park Commission was established by the City to maintain and protect the park.

The park flourished and grew on both sides of the Schuylkill as more land was acquired by gift or purchase. From a five-acre tract in 1812, Fairmount Park has grown to more than 8,700 acres.

Sections of the park are scattered throughout the City, but the major tract of 4,000 acres stretches northwest along both sides of the Schuylkill from Penn's original "faire mount."

It was on 236 acres of this tract in West Philadelphia that the City hosted the huge international exposition to mark the country's Centennial* in 1876. Over 200 buildings went up on the fairgrounds. You can see a scale model exhibit in Memorial Hall*, the only major building that remains from the celebration. The Philadelphia Zoo* was also opened in time for the Centennial, and was the first zoo in America.

Peter's Island, in the middle of the Schuylkill River, has been a wildlife preserve since 1969. Over a thousand geese, swans, ducks and red-crested poachers now make the island their home. The land is off limits to people, but the geese frequently swim across the river, and you can see them on the west bank near Montgomery Drive.

They say Fairmount Park's **Azalea Garden*** qualifies Philadelphia as the azalea capital of the world. Over 2,000 azalea bushes blossom each spring along Kelly Drive behind the Art Museum.

A short distance further along Kelly Drive, and just beyond the boat houses, look for the **Ellen Phillips Samuel Memorial Sculpture Garden*** and the **Glendinning Rock Garden**.

More than 200 statues are scattered throughout the park. If you have a group that's touring Philadelphia by bus, the Philadelphia Museum of Art will schedule a trained guide to escort you on a 90-minute **Sculpture Tour of Fairmount Park**. Arrangements must be made at least a month in advance by calling 787-5449. You'll pick up your guide at the Art Museum and then return her there after the tour.

The major attractions in this part of Fairmount Park can be reached by private car. But a most delightful, convenient, charming and inexpensive way to tour the park is on the Fairmount Park Trolley–Bus*.

More rustic sections of Fairmount Park are found along the **Wissahickon and Pennypack Creeks**. Wild flowers, trees and small animals are plentiful in these areas.

"Wissahickon" is the Indian word for "catfish creek." The creek stretches six-and-a-half miles from the Schuylkill to beyond the City's northwest boundary, and it's completely off limits to automobiles.

The **Valley Green** section of Fairmount Park is along the upper Wissahickon Creek. This is near the area that was settled by Francis Daniel Pastorius* and the German settlers. Valley Green is a miniature version of Colorado, with massive trees, rocky cliffs, boulders and steep paths.

Forbidden Drive is a popular five-and-a-half mile stretch along the Wissahickon. It has been designated by the U.S. Department of the Interior as a National Recreation Trail. It's great for hiking and horseback riding. There are marked paths for bikers, horsemen, joggers and nature walkers.

There's also a Perrier Parcourse Fitness Circuit along Forbidden Drive for people wanting to test their physical stamina and agility. It has 18 exercise stations along one-and-a-half miles. Another Perrier Parcourse is along the West River Drive near Montgomery Avenue. A half-mile exercise course is in Tacony Creek Park near Adams Avenue and Crescentville Road in the Far Northeast.

The Valley Green Inn is a quaint historic restaurant that has been open since 1850 (see Chapter 18). It sits beside the flowing creek that was once used by mills to make cornmeal, linseed oil, flour and paper. (William Rittenhouse's paper mill was the first of its kind in America, and its site is part of The Rittenhouse Homestead* that has been restored nearby along the Wissahickon.)

Valley Green can be reached by winding dirt roads and bridle paths, by car or, on special occasions, by the Fairmount Park Trolley–Bus. It's a pleasant gathering point to relax, hike, meditate and feed the ducks. You can fish for trout in the springtime, skate on the creek in winter and enjoy a pleasant meal in the old Valley Green Inn.

A rustic covered bridge spans the Wissahickon at Thomas Mill Road, north of Valley Green. The bridge is 97 feet long and 14 feet wide. It's the only covered bridge within a large American city. Bring your camera!

Did I make the point that Fairmount Park is brimming with history, art and horticulture? If I didn't, where have I gone wrong?

You can play baseball, football, cricket, tennis or golf. You can swim, hike, bike ride, ice skate, toboggan, go boating, attend concerts, watch shows and even go to a summer camp in Fairmount Park. You can dine at Valley Green Inn. All of these activities are described later in this book.

Other Fairmount Park attractions you should know about are the American–Swedish Historical Museum, John Bartram's House and Garden, Boat House Row, Bellaire, Chamounix, the Japanese Exhibition House, Mann Music Center, Pennypack Environmental Center, Playhouse in the Park, the police stables, Robin Hood Dell East, Ryerss Museum and Library and, of course, the spectacular Philadelphia Zoo. They're explained in other chapters; check the Index.

MEMORIAL HALL
N. Concourse Drive, near 42nd Street
and Parkside Avenue—(West Park)—19131
686-2176

Hours: By reservation only, daily, 8:30 to 5.
Tours: Try to call at least 2 weeks ahead to schedule group visit.
Cost: Free.
SEPTA: Bus 38.
E & H: There are several steps at the entrance, or there is a ramped entrance on the north side. The Centennial exhibit is in the basement.

Memorial Hall was built in 1875 to serve as an international art gallery and to remain as a tribute to the nation's 100th birthday celebration. President Ulysses S. Grant officially opened the Centennial in its 150-foot high "Great Hall" on May 10, 1876. It's the only major building that remains from the Centennial. You can hold your own celebration in Memorial Hall. It's available to rent for private parties.

Memorial Hall has been designated a National Historic Landmark. Its interior has been meticulously restored, and its Victorian ornamentation is carefully preserved. Today it houses the Fairmount Park Commission's administrative offices, police headquarters and recreation facilities. The Commission's office also serves as a **Fairmount Park Information Center.** You can stop by (enter at the building's west side) for information and brochures on cultural events and activities in Fairmount Park.

Memorial Hall's basement has an amazing exhibit. It's

163

an enormous 20- by 40-foot scale model of the Centennial fairgrounds that shows all 249 buildings, roads and landscaping of the 1876 celebration site. A sound-and-light narrative will tell you about the events of the first world's fair ever held in America.

A short walk down the road from Memorial Hall, at Lansdowne Drive, is the twin-towered **SMITH CIVIL WAR MEMORIAL ARCH**. It was built in 1896 with statuary honoring heroes of the Civil War.

Sit at one end of the curved stone bench and have a friend go 50 feet away to the bench's other end. Now whisper a message into the corner of the bench and your friend will hear you. That's why it's called the "whispering benches." How does it work? I would tell you, but I'm sworn to secrecy.

OHIO HOUSE is also nearby at Belmont Avenue and States Drive. The Ohio State Exhibition Building of the Centennial is the only other building, besides Memorial Hall, that still remains from the 1876 exposition.

Ohio House was restored in the mid-1970s. The architectural style is Victorian Gothic. It's constructed with stones from dozens of Ohio quarries, each of which is engraved with the quarry's name.

FAIRMOUNT PARK HOUSES
787–5449

The original estates of several prominent 18th century Philadelphians were completely restored in the mid-1970s and are beautifully furnished with authentic antiques. These are among the more than 20 historic homes that remain in Fairmount Park.

Each house reflects the personality and interests of its former owner. They range from simple brick row house style to elaborate mansions. All were summer homes for country living away from the hot city, and they take you back to a time when Philadelphia was the second largest city in the British Empire. Can you imagine that?

Hours: Wednesday to Sunday, 10 to 5.
Tours: There are 3 ways to visit the houses:
1. You can visit individually with private transportation and a good map of Fairmount Park.
2. You can arrange in advance to take a private tour (from one to 350 people) on the date of your choice with trained guides from the Art Museum. You'll visit one to three houses taking up to two-and-a-half hours.

Charges vary with the size and the type of group. Call for details. You provide the transportation.

3. You can ride the Fairmount Park Trolley–Bus* with on-and-off privileges all day and visit whichever houses you choose, along with other sites on the 10-minute route. Admission charges are discounted when you show your trolley-bus ticket.

Cost: To visit houses individually: adults, $1; children under 12, 50¢. To visit houses while riding the trolley-bus: adults, 80¢; children, 40¢.

Lunch: Bring a picnic lunch and choose a nice quiet spot.

E & H: No wheelchair access. There are steps leading to all of the houses and a considerable number of stairs within all of them.

CEDAR GROVE (787-5449), a Quaker farmhouse, was moved to West Fairmount Park in 1927 from its original 1748 construction site in Frankford.

You can see five generations of furnishings from an early Quaker family. William and Mary, Queen Anne, Chippendale, Hepplewhite and Sheraton styles are well represented.

There's an 18th century herb garden, and there are rumors of a lady ghost living on the second floor. You can tell me if it's true.

LAUREL HILL (235-1776 or 627-1770), named for the clusters of laurel bushes on its surrounding East Fairmount Park hillside, has an original Georgian style center section dating back to 1760. An 1800 addition in the Federal style has an unusual octagonal room.

The mansion is often called Randolph after the family that occupied it from 1828 to 1869. Dr. Philip Syng Physick gave it to his daughter Sally when she married Dr. Jacob Randolph.

LEMON HILL (232–4337) was built in 1800 by Henry Pratt, who bought the 350-acre farm estate of Robert Morris. Pratt replaced Morris' 1770 farmhouse, "The Hills," with Lemon Hill as you see it today overlooking the Schuylkill. Pratt renamed his new home for the lemon trees that flourished in his gardens.

Lemon Hill has three floors, each with an oval salon. This architectual design exists in only three other buildings in the East; a clubhouse in Boston, the Thomas Jefferson Rotunda at the University of Virginia and the White House in Washington. (You're now one of the few people who know this.) Lemon Hill's furnishings are magnificent examples of the Federal style.

MOUNT PLEASANT (787–5449) was built by John MacPherson, a wealthy Scottish sea captain, in 1761. It's an important example of elegant, symmetrical Georgian architecture that was more common to buildings in Virginia than Pennsylvania. The front door and the back door are identical, so don't be confused.

The furnishings include the finest examples of Chippendale, along with antique pewter, china and porcelain.

An educational "touch-it" exhibit for children demonstrates colonial skills such as soap-making and weaving flax into fabric. You'll get a good idea of how 18th century life centered around the hearth.

Benedict Arnold purchased the house as a wedding present for his bride, Peggy Shippen, in 1779. But the following year, the Arnolds suddenly decided to take up residence in England.

STRAWBERRY MANSION (228–8364), the largest mansion in Fairmount Park, has a mixture of late 18th and 19th century furnishings that reflect its various owners' tastes. You'll see Federal, Regency and Empire styles.

Antique toys fill the attic. The Empire parlor has a fine collection of Tucker porcelain, the first true porcelain made in America. An elegant music room brings to mind beautiful colonial receptions.

SWEETBRIAR (222–1333) looks exactly as it did when it was built in 1797. This was one of the first riverside houses designed to be lived in all year.

Sweetbriar and its decor reflect the fine taste of the original owner, Samuel Breck, who came to Philadelphia from Boston after the Revolution to escape heavy taxes.

This is a classic example of Federal style architecture.

Don't miss the floor-to-ceiling windows in the two gracious parlors overlooking the Schuylkill River. They'll give you an idea of the kind of windows Presidents look out of from the Oval Office.

WOODFORD (229–6115) was built as a one-story country residence in 1734 by Judge William Coleman, a patriot and friend of Benjamin Franklin.

The beautiful second floor Palladian windows were added two decades later by the new owners, a Loyalist family who frequently entertained the Tories here.

Again, there are outstanding examples of colonial furnishings. There's also an enormous Pennsylvania Dutch kitchen and delightful children's toys and games.

ORMISTON (763–2222) is undergoing restoration and maintenance thanks to the Royal Heritage Society of Delaware Valley, a non-profit organization founded in 1982 to preserve British heritage and memorabilia in Pennsylvania.

The Georgian-style brick house was built near Mount Pleasant in 1798 by Edward Burd, a lawyer who married the daughter of Chief Justice Edward Shippen. Burd named his country estate "after the name of his Grandfather's Seat near Edinburgh." Burd died in 1833, but the house remained in his family till 1869.

The furnishings are sparse in this spacious three-story mansion, but an exhibit each summer focuses on some aspect of Philadelphia's ties with England. The basement bake oven and open fireplace still work, and Ormiston is a popular site for private teas and receptions.

You can rent it for a party, visit on your own, or stop by along the Fairmount Park Trolley–Bus route. Ormiston is open from May 15 to September 15, Wednesday to Sunday, from 10 to 4.

HORTICULTURAL CENTER
North Horticultural Drive, east of Belmont Avenue
(West Park)
686-0096 or 686-0097

Hours: May to September: Wednesday to Sunday, 9 to 3; October to April: weekdays, 9 to 3; weekends, 9 to 12. Allow at least one hour to see the Center and the arboretum.

Tours: You're on your own, but groups of 10 or more should call a week in advance.

Cost: $1 donation is requested.

Lunch: Groups can schedule in advance to use picnic facilities or the conference room.

Other: There's parking at the entrance, or come by Fairmount Park Trolley-Bus.

E & H: Complete wheelchair access. Use any of the level entrances into the greenhouses.

Fairmount Park's Horticultural Center is on the grounds of the Centennial's Horticulture Hall, which stood until 1955. It's the showcase of a 22-acre arboretum that includes the Japanese Exhibition House* and magnificent Asian and North American trees that were planted during the Centennial in 1876.

If you love plants and flowers, you'll love the greenhouses here. Thousands of annuals and perennials are continually sprouting, waiting for transplanting to city parks, parkways, offices and museums.

One of the greenhouses is used for exhibition. Permanent planting beds and seasonal floral displays surround a lovely indoor fountain with sculpted cherubs dating back to 1876.

If you're looking for someplace to put your green thumb to good use, ask about volunteer programs at the Horticultural Center.

LAUREL HILL CEMETERY
3822 Ridge Avenue—19123
228-8200

Tours: Stop by on your own during the day (park on Ridge Avenue) or join a tour sponsored occasionally by The Friends of Laurel Hill or as part of Fairmount Park happenings. 60- to 90-minute tours for 5 to 50 adults can be scheduled at least 3 weeks in advance by calling the Executive Vice-President of The Friends of Laurel Hill: 242-9437.
Cost: $1 per person for Friends guided tours.
Other: Be sure to wear flat, comfortable shoes.

Laurel Hill Cemetery adjoins East Fairmount Park and overlooks the Schuylkill River from above Kelly Drive. It spans 95 acres on both sides of Nicetown Lane. It was planned in 1836 by John Notman, making it the first architect-designed cemetery in America.

The park and garden landscaping were integral to the design. At least one specimen of every rare tree that could grow in the local climate was included. Many of them still remain.

Laurel Hill is noted for its magnificent mausoleums, monuments and sculpture. Works by Joseph A. Bailly, Alexander Milne Calder, Alexander Stirling Calder, John Notman, William Strickland and Thomas U. Walter, representing several architectural styles, are throughout the grounds.

Many prominent Philadelphians, including signers of the Declaration, authors, artists and merchants, are and continue to be buried here.

The cemetery is listed in the National Register of Historic Places.

THE RITTENHOUSE HOMESTEAD
207 Lincoln Drive—19144
(just south of Wissahickon Avenue)
843-0943

Hours: April through October: Saturday, 10 to 4; Sunday, 2 to 4. Other times by appointment.
Tours: A guide is available to answer questions and provide historic background.
Cost: Adults, 50¢; children under 12, free.
Lunch: Picnic and play areas are directly across the road.

The Rittenhouse Homestead is a quaint part of historic Germantown nestled along the Wissahickon Creek, just a

169

short distance from other historic homes along Germantown Avenue (see Chapter 3). This was the site of America's first paper mill, built in 1690.

William Rittenhouse, the first Mennonite minister in America, built his home here in 1707. Nicholas, the Minister's son, enlarged the house in 1713. Then, in 1732, it was the birthplace of David Rittenhouse.

David Rittenhouse grew up to be a patriot of the Revolution as well as a noted scientist and astronomer. Rittenhouse Square* and the Rittenhouse Observatory* were named for him.

A visit to the Homestead offers a glimpse into the lifestyle of our colonial ancestors and the Mennonite life. View the downstairs of the little stone house with its period furnishings. A smaller outbuilding is said to have the largest hearth in Pennsylvania.

Chapter 9.
The Visual Arts.

If it's culture you want, you've come to the right city.

Philadelphia's museums, galleries, film centers, dance troupes, theater companies, orchestras and musical groups have international reputations. So if you think the next two chapters on "The Visual Arts" and "The Performing Arts" are really big, it's only because Philadelphia has really big things to offer in the arts.

Additional programs for children are described later in Chapter 15.

This chapter deals with things you'll look at which, for the most part, are permanently in place. They include art, films, and sculpture that you'll come across as you wander around Philadelphia.

Art Museums and Galleries. A Few Art Classes to Join.

AIA GALLERY
17th and Sansom Streets—19103
569-3186

Hours: Weekdays, 10 to 5 (unless in use for a meeting). Allow 20 to 30 minutes, depending on the show.
Cost: Free.
SEPTA: Any Chestnut or Walnut Street route to 17th.
Other: Take time to browse in the Architects Book Information Center that sells architecture and design-related publications, posters, toys and unusual gift items.
E & H: The gallery is one floor below the book center and reached by stairs.

You'll reach the creative AIA Gallery by going through AIA's imaginative book center. For those who don't know, AIA is the American Institute of Architects.

The gallery is a bright room used to show projects by architects or works related to architecture. The exhibits change every month.

You can stop in or call ahead to find out what's being exhibited. While you're there, ask about joining the local architects each year when they plan a fun-filled educational week of traditional and offbeat events. It's called Architect's Week and it's usually held in late May or early June.

AIA's local Foundation for Architecture has a year-round schedule of City events and tours (see Chapter 1).

ART IN CITY HALL
Broad and Market Streets—19107
686-1776

Hours: Weekdays, 9 to 5. Closed holidays.
Tours: You're on your own, or combine with a tour of City Hall described in Chapter 13.
Cost: Free.
SEPTA: Buses 12, 17, 27, 32, 33, 38, 44, 45, 76, C; subway-surface trolleys 10, 11, 13, 34, 36; either subway route.
E & H: Complete wheelchair access. Enter at east arch and take elevator at northeast corner.

A new function came to City Hall in 1985—a gallery to showcase Philadelphia artists. The exhibitions run for approximately two months. Each show is curated by a local gallery director with works chosen by a jury of local gallery directors and art professionals.

The works range from traditional to avant garde in a variety of mediums, and they center on a theme related to Philadelphia.

So next time you're in City Hall*, stop by the second floor, outside the Mayor's Office, and the fourth floor, outside City Council Chambers, and see a terrific art show.

ARTHUR ROSS GALLERY
University of Pennsylvania
220 South 34th Street—19104
898-4401

Hours: Tuesday to Friday, 10 to 5; weekends, 12 to 5. Closed Thanksgiving and Christmas.
Tours: You're on your own.
Cost: Free.
SEPTA: Buses D, 30, 40, 42.
E & H: To avoid 10 steps at main entrance, call ahead to 898-4401 or 898-1479 and arrange to enter at ground level on building's south side and take elevator to gallery level.

It's worth a trip to the Penn campus just to see the magnificently restored 19th-century Furness Building that houses this gallery. In a former time (as recently as my days at Penn in the 1960s) the building housed the University's library. The gallery housed the Trustees' Board Room. This grand Victorian structure became a National Historic Landmark in 1985.

Over 4,000 works of art have been acquired by the University in its almost 200-year history. Five shows a year are drawn from Penn's eclectic collection, the University Museum's collections and from area connoisseurs with outstanding collections.

You could see anything from ancient arts to contemporary treasures. Call ahead if you'd like a preview. And while you're on campus, take time to go next door to see the exciting Institute of Contemporary Art*.

BARNES FOUNDATION
300 Latches Lane
Merion, Pa. 19106
667-0290

Hours: Friday and Saturday, 9:30 to 4:30; Sunday, 1 to 4:30. Closed July, August and holidays.

Reservations: 100 visitors are admitted each Friday and Saturday with advance reservations, and 100 more are admitted without reservations. On Sunday, 50 are admitted with reservations and 50 more without. If there are 6 or fewer in your group, call at least one month ahead. Include the full name and address for each visitor. For those without reservations, more are admitted later in the day as earlier visitors depart. Children under 12 not admitted. Young people 12 to 15 must be with an adult.

Cost: $1.

SEPTA: Bus 44 to Latches Lane and Old Lancaster Road and then a short walk. Barnes is 4 blocks west of City Line Avenue.

Other: No cameras are allowed. You'll be asked to check your loose belongings.

E & H: The first floor is wheelchair accessible if you can negotiate the 3 low steps at the entrance. There is no elevator to the 2nd floor.

In 1961 a court ruling forced the Barnes Foundation to open to the public. Dr. Albert C. Barnes, an eccentric millionaire, died in 1951. But his temperament and influence still control this mansion gallery. His will prohibits the reproduction or loan of any of the collection.

There are hundreds of paintings and sculptures in 23 rooms on two floors. Any one of these rooms would put an art gallery on the map. Each room conveys the spirit of France in the 1920s and 1930s because Parisian artists were among Barnes' favorites.

You'll be startled by the enormity of the collection. There are 180 Renoirs, 60 Matisses, 59 Cezannes and a good representation of works by Picasso, Seurat, Soutine,

174

Modigliani, Rousseau, El Greco, Titian and Tintoretto. Matisse, himself, came to the mansion in 1932 to hang his 42 by 11 foot mural, "The Dancers."

One room is shared with the works of Horace Pippin, the one-armed black primitive artist from West Chester, Pa., and William Glackens, Dr. Barnes' high school classmate. Elsewhere in the mansion is Pennsylvania Dutch bric-a-brac, Mayan Indian ornaments, pewter pieces and 16th century Chinese art.

Don't miss this opportunity to see one of the finest art collections in the world.

BUTEN MUSEUM OF WEDGWOOD
246 N. Bowman Avenue
Merion, Pa. 19066
664-6601

Hours: Tuesday to Friday, 2 to 4:30; Saturday, 10 to 1. Groups of up to 40 can sometimes schedule a lecture-tour at another time. Closed July, August and major holidays. Allow at least one hour.

Tours: There's a 60- to 90-minute lecture-tour on Tuesday to Friday at 2 and on Saturday at 10. Call ahead for reservations. Children must be with an adult.

Cost: Adults, $2.50; senior citizens and students, $2; children with an adult, $1.

SEPTA: Bus 44 to Montgomery and Bowman Avenues and then a short walk.

Other: A gift shop offers books, remainders and Wedgwood special issues for lovely gifts.

E & H: All exhibits and the lecture gallery are on the first floor, but entrance steps and narrow areas limit wheelchair access. Call ahead to arrange for assistance.

If you like Wedgwood, you'll love the Buten Museum on the outskirts of the city. If this is your first experience with Wedgwood, you're bound to be awed.

Over 10,000 pieces in the 10 basic varieties of Wedgwood make up the collection. Only 20 percent are on display at any given time. There's glazed earthenware, the most familiar Wedgwood, porcelain bone china, and the unglazed stonewares that often are overlooked. Some of the most popular pieces are the Portland vases and the Fairyland lustreware.

You'll see Wedgwood you never would have dreamed is Wedgwood. It's in all colors, shapes, sizes and descriptions and it's all imported from England where Josiah Wedgwood began producing it in 1759.

CAMPBELL MUSEUM
Campbell Place
Camden, New Jersey 08101
609-342-6440

Hours: Weekdays, 9 to 4:30. Closed some holidays. Allow one hour.
Tours: Gallery talks are scheduled for groups of up to 50. A 20-minute film, "Artistry in Tureens," can be included with your visit if requested in advance. Children must be supervised. All groups of 10 to 50 must call a few weeks ahead to schedule visit, a gallery talk or film.
Cost: Free.
SEPTA: The museum is about one mile from the Camden City Hall stop of the PATCO High Speed Line which connects with many SEPTA bus and rail routes in Philadelphia. It is a 2-minute drive from the Ben Franklin Bridge and just off the Admiral Wilson Boulevard. It's a good idea to have directions before starting out.
E & H: The museum is all on one level, but there are several steps at the entrance.

"Soup's on!"
The Campbell Soup Company has a rare collection of 300 unusual tureens, bowls and ladles. The exhibits change at least twice a year, so call ahead if you're curious about the current show. When you come here, you'll get an idea of the many ways soup has been served over the past 2,500 years.

Anyone interested in food, the history of food service and the decorative arts will be fascinated by the assortment of porcelain, earthenware, gold, silver and pewter tureens. They're as innocent as a pair of porcelain rabbits, as opulent as a 100-pound ornamental bronze piece, as traditional as a lettuce topped with a playful toad and as bizarre as a life-size boar's head of 18th century porcelain.

The proof is all here that throughout the centuries the soup tureen has dominated the table as the biggest and most decorative service piece.

CITY OF PHILADELPHIA ART PROGRAMS
686-0152 (686-1940 in July and August)

No art-oriented youngster or adult should miss out on art lessons in Philadelphia. If you can't attend a class that's offered by a museum or art school, there are the Department of Recreation art classes.

A variety of arts and crafts programs are offered at recreation centers throughout the city. You can study painting, crafts, drawing, sculpting, enameling or dabbling.

An annual Spring Arts Show presents the best of the year's creations by participants of all ages in programs representing everything from handicrafts to fine arts. Stop by the mall level of the Gallery at Market East, 9th and Market Streets, in late April or May to see some of the terrific work being done at city recreation centers.

Each summer the city sponsors an Arts Camp in Fairmount Park. Four two-week sessions are offered for boys and girls from the ages of nine to 17. A small fee covers costs for materials, lunch, field trips and bus transportation to and from camp.

If you attend the city's Arts Camp, you'll get professional instruction in drawing, painting, graphics and sculpting. And, to stimulate your creativity, you'll visit area museums and exhibitions. The season ends with a show and celebration of the Summer Arts Camp that features the works of campers who attended any one of the encampments.

For additional information, call the Department of Recreation's Cultural and Special Events Section.

THE CLAY STUDIO
49 North 2nd Street—19106
925-3453

Hours: Gallery is open weekdays, 2 to 6; Saturday, 1 to 4; except between shows when it's closed Monday to Thursday.
Tours: Visit the gallery on your own. Tours of the studio and artists' floor can be scheduled during gallery hours or other times by appointment. Call at least 2 weeks ahead for groups of 7 to 20, 4th grade and above. Allow at least 30 mintues.
Cost: Free.
SEPTA: Bus 5 or any Market Street route.
E & H: The gallery entrance is level. A freight elevator can be used by a few; otherwise there are 2 steep stairways to studios and workshops.

Here's where you'll learn first-hand about the art of ceramics.

On the second floor, nine competitively chosen resident artists work with clay in their own spaces. They use the various kilns in the studio, and also teach in the workshop program and exhibit in the gallery.

Downstairs, The Clay Studio School students work at basic pottery, raku, firing and glaze mixing. Classes, workshops and lectures are open to children and adults, both novice and advanced. Youngsters who tour the studio get a chance to play with clay and work a wheel. (Dress accordingly.)

On the street level, the gallery presents monthly shows; five by the resident artists, three invitationals for potters from around the country, a student and a holiday exhibition. An annual schedule is available.

DREXEL MUSEUM COLLECTION
Drexel University Main Building, Room 305
32nd and Chestnut Streets—19104
895-2424

Hours: Weekdays, 10 to 4. Closed holidays.
Cost: Free.
SEPTA: Buses D, 30, 42; Market Street routes; or walking distance to 30th Street Station.
E & H: There are 13 steps at the Chestnut Street entrance, or call ahead to use street level entrance with easy elevator access on 32nd Street.

Drexel's Main Building, which dates back to 1892, is a masterpiece in itself, but neatly tucked away on the third floor is an enormous skylit gallery where you'll discover many artistic masterpieces. The focus is on 19th century paintings, sculpture and decorative arts.

Portraits of Drexel family members cover the walls. Many of them are by the 19th century family artist-turned-banker Francis Martin Drexel.

The floor is filled with fine furnishings of the period. The showcases display valuable silver tea services, pewter, miniatures, antique toys, old wooden utensils, china collections and a service of Sevres china that was made for Napoleon III.

The most historic clock in America is on display here. It's the David Rittenhouse* clock, made in 1773. The clock still ticks away the seconds, minutes and hours, as well as the day and date of the month, the moon's phases, the earth's and moon's orbits, zodiac signs and other technical data.

The Rincliffe Gallery, which adjoins the main gallery, is devoted exclusively to what has to be Philadelphia's largest collection of Edward Marshall Boehm porcelains. These are the true-to-life sculptures of birds and animals that are often chosen for gifts to royalty and heads of state.

A third facet of Drexel's Museum Collection is a changing exhibition gallery in Room 305. These displays are related to the University through its alumni, faculty or permanent treasures.

So don't miss these changing exhibits. And before you leave, don't miss the bronze "Water Boy" by Auguste Bartholdi, the French sculptor of the Statue of Liberty, or the marble bust of Anthony Drexel by Moses Ezekial. They're on the main floor of the Main Building.

Note: Drexel University owns the historic Frank Furness Building on the southeast corner of 32nd and Market Streets. Plans call for its restoration and moving the Museum Collection to its own "new" home.

FLEISHER ART MEMORIAL
719 Catharine Street—19147
922-3456

Hours: October to June, Monday to Thursday, 12 to 5 and 6:30 to 9:30 P.M.; Saturday, 1 to 3. Closed between exhibitions and July through September.
Tours: A gallery talk can sometimes be scheduled along with a brief description of the Sanctuary. Groups of 10 to 30 should call a few days ahead. And if you're coming for art classes, you'll have to sign up.
Cost: Free.
SEPTA: Buses 47, 63.
E & H: Complete wheelchair access.

The Fleisher Art Memorial has three noteworthy divisions: the school, the galleries and the Sanctuary.

Art classes are free from October to July.

Adults can attend evening classes, and children from ages five to 17 can come any Saturday morning or afternoon. There's also an outdoor summer session (Saturdays in May and June) for landscape painting. This is a fabulous opportunity. You only pay for materials and you get first-rate instruction. (A $5 contribution is requested.)

The changing art exhibits are always open to the public. They may include works from a growing collection of contemporary art, sculpture and graphics. Or they may feature work by a faculty member, a student or the "challenge" exhibitions presenting new local talent. Three artists are chosen by competition for each of these shows that are mounted four times a year. Call ahead if you want to know what will be exhibited on a certain date.

There's nothing in Philadelphia that's like Fleisher's Sanctuary. It's an 18th century Portuguese Chapel (the only one of its kind outside Portugal and Brazil) that shares space with an icons collection, medieval sculpture and primitive paintings.

GALLERY OF THE
ART INSTITUTE OF PHILADELPHIA
1622 Chestnut Street—19103
567–7080

Hours: Weekdays, 9 to 5; Saturday, 9 to 12. Closed some holidays. Allow 20 to 30 minutes.
Cost: Free.
SEPTA: Any route on Chestnut Street.
E & H: On street level with complete wheelchair access.

The Art Institute's home is a grand example of 1930s architecture. Much of its art deco splendor has been restored.

The school offers a continuous 24-month program to students aspiring to careers in commercial art, photography, interior design and fashion illustration.

A contemporary storefront gallery features changing exhibits by students, faculty and leading designers and illustrators. Design professionals as well as the public will enjoy this opportunity to keep current with the state-of-the-visual arts.

GOLDIE PALEY DESIGN CENTER
4200 Henry Avenue—19144
951–2860

Hours: Monday to Saturday, 10 to 4. Closed major holidays.
Tours: Groups of no more than 40 should call 2 weeks ahead to schedule a one-hour tour. You'll be divided into smaller groups. You might want to combine this with a tour of the College (see Chapter 13).
Cost: Free admission; guided tour $2 per person.
SEPTA: Bus 32.
E & H: There's one low step at the entrance and exhibits are on one floor.

The Goldie Paley Design Center is part of the Philadelphia College of Textiles and Science*, the oldest and largest college of its type in the country.

The Center has four exhibition rooms, and the shows change every two months. The exhibits could be on fabrics from the fourth century, fabrics from around the world, or possibly work by students, faculty or visiting artists. This is a comprehensive textile museum and resource design center.

More than 200,000 fabric samples from American and foreign textile mills make up a study section that's actually a vast fabric library. You'll get a glimpse at some of these stored materials, and you'll get a chance to look in on workshops where student projects, repairs and restorations are taking place.

Goldie Paley was an artist and she painted at her ranch-style home adjacent to the campus grounds. When she died in 1977, her family donated the house and grounds to the college as a living memorial. Goldie's son, William, was the founder of CBS.

**GOLDIE PALEY GALLERY at
MOORE COLLEGE OF ART**
20th and Race Streets—19103
568-4515

Hours: Weekdays, 10 to 5; Saturday, 12 to 4. June through August, Monday to Thursday, 10 to 5; other times, by appointment. Closed some holidays.
Cost: Free.
Lunch: The nearby student cafeteria is open to gallery visitors.
SEPTA: Buses 32, 38.
E & H: Complete wheelchair access.

The emphasis at Moore is on 20th century art, including contemporary crafts, architecture and the avant-garde. Both American and foreign artists are exhibited. The shows generally run five weeks, and a yearly schedule is available in the fall.

Moore's students have their annual show in the spring. This is when you get to see the textile designs, fashions, graphics, sculpture and photography of tomorrow's talents. A faculty show is held every few years.

Watch for the opening of Moore's Showcase Gallery in the spring of 1987. It will be Philadelphia's newest showcase for Philadelphia artists.

Luckily for Moore students and for the public, the campus and gallery are directly across from the southwest corner of Logan Square...within a flower's scent of the Ben Franklin Parkway.

181

ILE-IFE MUSEUM
OF AFRO-AMERICAN CULTURE
2544 Germantown Avenue—19133
225-7565

Hours: By appointment only, Monday to Saturday at 10, 11, 1 and 2. Allow at least one hour.
Tours: Scheduled at least 2 weeks in advance for groups of 25 to 75, but individuals can call and arrange to join a group already scheduled.
Cost: Adults, $1.50; children under 12, 75¢.
Lunch: A room is available for groups to sit on the floor if they bring their own lunch. Make arrangements when scheduling tour.
SEPTA: Buses 39, 47; trolley 23.
E & H: There are 2 steps at the entrance and exhibits are on 2 floors. Special arrangements can be made for group to remain in one room and artifacts will be brought to you, along with dance and drum demonstrations.

Ile-Ife, Nigerian for "House of Love," is filled with memorabilia from African and Caribbean civilizations. It beautifully depicts the heritage of Afro-American people. This black-operated museum is the first of its kind in Pennsylvania.

The museum and the Ile-Ife Center for Arts and Humanities were founded by Arthur Hall. It's also the home of his world-renowned Afro-American Dance Ensemble*. (In fact, two dances and a drum demonstration are part of your tour.)

You'll also see sculptures and wood carvings, ceremonial swords, masks, fabrics, weavings, paintings and photographs.

Don't be surprised if you leave singing a native tune.

INSTITUTE OF CONTEMPORARY ART
Meyerson Hall, 34th and Walnut Streets—19104
898-5118 or 898-7108

Hours: Daily, 10 to 5; Wednesday and Friday to 8.
Tours: Gallery talks can sometimes be arranged for art students and school groups of no more than 30. Reservations are necessary for groups requesting a gallery talk.
Cost: Free.
SEPTA: Buses D, 30, 40, 42; Market-Frankford Subway-Elevated to 34th Street.
E & H: Call ahead and arrange to enter at ground level

entrance that has no steps. An elevator goes to the gallery.

Four exhibits are presented at ICA during the course of the school year. ICA is a vital part of the University of Pennsylvania. Recent exhibitions have featured Laurie Anderson, Cindy Sherman, The East Village Scene, Siah Armajani, and Arquitectonica. This is where tomorrow's art is exhibited today.

During each exhibit, one hour of a Saturday and Sunday morning is devoted to young people five to 12. These **Children's Workshops** include geared-to-the-young gallery talks (which fascinate parents) and a supervised informal art happening where children have an opportunity to display their own creative talents.

Call the ICA in the fall for dates and information.

LA SALLE UNIVERSITY MUSEUM
Olney Hall, 20th Street and Olney Avenue—19141
951-1221

Hours: Late September through April: Tuesday to Friday, 11 to 4; Sunday, 2 to 4. May through July: Monday to Thursday, 11 to 3. Closed August and holidays. Allow one hour.

Tours: Student "gallery associates" schedule up to 40, at least 9th grade, who are divided into groups of 15 to 20. Call at least a week ahead to schedule tours.

Cost: Free. Donations accepted.

SEPTA: Buses S, 26. There's parking on campus; inquire at the guard house where you enter.

E & H: You can avoid steps by entering at the street level and taking a self-service elevator to the gallery floor.

Each of the five period rooms at LaSalle's gallery exhibits works from a different century. The 16th to 20th centuries are represented with a collection of more than 200 paintings and over 2,000 prints and drawings. These exhibits are supplemented with special shows that change every few months.

The artists include Boudin, Bourdon, Corot, Degas, Eakins, Pissaro, Prevost, Raeburn, Roualt, West and Tintoretto. Almost every style and subject matter is shown.

One of the gallery highlights is the Susan Dunleavy Collection of some 200 finely illustrated and printed Bibles from the 15th century to today. Catholic, Jewish and Protestant versions have the common quality of artistic beauty.

LLOYD P. JONES GALLERY
Gimbel Gymnasium, 37th and Walnut Streets—19104
898-6101

Hours: Weekdays, 12 to 3; Saturday, 2 to 5. Closed some
holidays.
Tours: You're on your own, but call ahead if you're coming
with a group of more than 10.
Cost: Free.
SEPTA: Buses D, 40.
E & H: There are 4 low steps if you approach from the adjacent parking lot. Gallery is on entrance level.

This fine exhibition is bound to please anyone interested in sports.

Lloyd Jones, a member of the University of Pennsylvania's class of 1907, was also a member of the 1908 U.S. Olympic Track Team. R. Tait McKenzie was a surgeon, Professor of Medicine and Director of Physical Education at the University from 1904 till his death in 1938. He also achieved world fame as a sculptor.

The gallery displays 68 of Dr. McKenzie's sculptures. Most of them are bronzes, and almost all of them capture the stance, the equipment or the expression of an athlete or an athletic event.

Also look at McKenzie's lifelike sculpture of "The Scout" standing proudly on the front lawn at the Boy Scouts of America Building*, 22nd and Winter Streets near the Benjamin Franklin Parkway.

MORANI ART GALLERY of the
MEDICAL COLLEGE OF PENNSYLVANIA
Conference Center at EPPI—Room 305
3200 Henry Avenue—19129
842-7124 or 849-2691

Hours: Tuesday and Thursday, 4 to 6; 1st Sunday of each
month, 2 to 4; other hours by appointment.
Tours: You're on your own, or call the curator at 849-2691
to schedule a guided tour.
Cost: Free.
SEPTA: Buses E, R, 32.
E & H: Complete wheelchair access. Gallery is on ground
level.

Dr. Alma Dea Morani graduated in 1931 from what was then called Women's Medical College. She was one of the country's first female surgeons and in 1947 became the first woman member of the American Society of Plastic and Reconstructive Surgery. Dr. Morani is also a world traveler, an art collector and sculptor. She recently gave much of her collection to her alma mater, which, in turn, opened a gallery in her honor.

Among the items on exhibit are bas reliefs, sculptures, antique statuary, paintings, woodcarvings and artifacts from other times from throughout the world.

Some of the sculptures and bas reliefs are by Dr. Morani, some of the artwork is by members of her family; and some are by local artists whose work she collected. There are also sculptures from the Philippines, a Shiva from India, jade from China and Macau and landscapes from Japan, just to name a few.

NORMAN ROCKWELL MUSEUM
Curtis Building, 6th and Walnut Streets—19106
922-4345

Hours: Daily, 10 to 4. Closed Thanksgiving, Christmas, New Year's. Allow 30 to 45 minutes.
Tours: Scheduled for groups of 10 or more by calling in advance.
Cost: Adults, $1.50; senior citizens, $1.25; children 12 and under, free. Group rates for 10 or more, $1. A fee for class tours is set when reservations are made.
SEPTA: Any route to Independence Hall.
Other: The gift shop has the country's largest selection of Norman Rockwell prints, figurines, plates and limited editions ranging from 50¢ to $350.
E & H: There are 9 steps at the entrance and then exhibits are on one level. Or call ahead to check if level entrance at Sansom Street is available.

What's as American as apple pie?

A Norman Rockwell illustration.

Where can you see a complete set of his 324 covers for *The Saturday Evening Post?*

In the Norman Rockwell Museum. And that happens to be in the very same building where *The Saturday Evening Post* was published.

What else will you see here?

Reproductions of Rockwell's "The American Family" series, which was done for the Massachusetts Mutual Insurance Company," his Boy Scout drawings, the "Four Freedoms" posters and at least 50 more canvas reproductions of his work. The exhibit spans 60 years of Norman Rockwell's prolific career. The museum's only original is an unfinished drawing that sits on the easel in a simulation of Rockwell's studio in Stockbridge, Massachusetts.

PEALE HOUSE
1820 Chestnut Street—19103
972-7600

Hours: Tuesday to Saturday, 10 to 4; Sunday, 12 to 4. Closed Thanksgiving, Christmas, New Year's and between exhibits.
Tours: You're on your own.
Cost: Free.
SEPTA: Buses 2, 42, 76, D.
E & H: There are 2 steps at the entrance. Exhibits are on one level except the mezzanine which is visible from below.

The Peale House is a "branch" school and gallery of the Pennsylvania Academy of the Fine Arts*. If you like contemporary and experimental art, visit the Peale Gallery.

Ten shows are presented throughout the year featuring students at the Academy and its graduates. An Annual Student Show is hung each summer.

PENNSYLVANIA ACADEMY
OF THE FINE ARTS
Broad and Cherry Streets—19102
972-7600 or 972-7633 (recorded information)

Hours: Tuesday to Saturday, 10 to 5; Wednesday to 7; Sunday, 11 to 5. Closed Thanksgiving, Christmas, New Year's. Allow one hour or more.
Tours: Regularly scheduled tours are Tuesday to Friday at 11 and 2, Wednesday at 5:30, and weekends at 2. Groups of 10 to 60 must call at least 3 weeks ahead to schedule tours at other times. Museum lessons for school-age groups from kindergarten through high school must also be scheduled 3 weeks in advance. Choose from a variety of study topics and receive pre-tour classroom material and follow-up suggestions. Call 972-7608 for all group and bilingual tour arrangements.
Cost: Adults, $3; senior citizens and students, $2. Free on Tuesday. Memberships (Individual, $30; Family, $40) are available.
SEPTA: Any route to City Hall and walk 2 short blocks north on Broad Street to Cherry.
Other: The contemporary, bi-level triangular gift shop

features art books, posters, stationery, slides, T-shirts, totes, ties and some nifty gift items.

E & H: Complete wheelchair access. There are 7 steps at the main Broad Street entrance, or ring bell at rear Burns Street entrance for level access. Wheelchairs are available. Special tours can be arranged in advance for the visually and hearing impaired; call 972-7608.

If architect Frank Furness were around today to see his creation, he would beam with delight.

This National Historic Landmark built in the Victorian Gothic style was completely restored for the Bicentennial. Every part of the building is as much a work of art as the masterpieces it displays. You have to see it to believe it.

The Pennsylvania Academy of the Fine Arts houses one of the world's finest collections of American paintings and sculpture. The Academy, founded in 1805, is the nation's oldest art museum and school. Its art ranges from the 1700s to today. It's known for its art by local painters like Charles Willson Peale (founder of the Academy) and his sons, Thomas Eakins (who taught at the Academy), Winslow Homer, Horace Pippin, William Rush, Andrew Wyeth and Gilbert Stuart.

The galleries on the second floor are reached by the great stairhall or by elevator. They have natural lighting and individual decors which are appropriate to their exhibits. The major shows change five or six times a year, and they range from historical to contemporary art. A Red Grooms Show drew record crowds to the Academy in 1985. Among the hundreds of paintings on permanent display is Benjamin West's "Penn's Treaty with the Indians."

The special exhibitions in the first floor Morris Gallery feature one-person shows by contemporary artists from the Philadelphia area. The shows here change every eight weeks.

Other popular facets of the Academy are the concerts, lectures and special events which are throughout the year. Call the Academy to find out what's coming up next.

PHILADELPHIA ART ALLIANCE
251 South 18th Street—19103
545-4302

Hours: Monday, Friday, Saturday, 10:30 to 5; Tuesday, Wednesday, Thursday, 10:30 to 9. Closed holidays and August through Labor Day. Allow 30 minutes.
Cost: Free.
Lunch: No facilities unless you're a member.
SEPTA: Buses 2, 9, 17, 42, 90, D.
E & H: There are 8 low steps at the entrance and exhibits are on 3 floors connected by stairs or elevator. Call ahead for ramp to be placed at entrance.

This stately former center city dwelling overlooking scenic Rittenhouse Square is filled with seven galleries of exhibitions that change every six weeks. Even the hall cases and beautiful wooden stairway are utilized for displaying works of contemporary art.

At any given time you might be delighted to see sculpture, paintings, prints, weavings, architectural design, jewelry, glass, metal or wood crafts. Several now-famous artists have been introduced to the public with shows at the Art Alliance. Andrew Wyeth was one.

Lecture, poetry, music and dance programs are also on the agenda. Call the Art Alliance for details.

PHILADELPHIA MUSEUM OF ART
26th and Benjamin Franklin Parkway—19101
763-8100 or 787-5488 (recording of daily schedule)

Hours: Tuesday to Sunday, 10 to 5. Limited access to galleries on Tuesday. Closed holidays. Allow as much time as you can, and then plan to return.
Tours: You have a choice of ways to visit the museum.
    1) Visit on your own and get to know the museum.
    2) Any individual can join the daily one-hour Museum Treasure Tours Wednesday to Sunday at 10:15, 11, 12, 1, 2 and 3.
    3) Family Programs are Sunday at 1 P.M. (arrive when admission is free).
    4) Museum Treasure Tours or Family Tours, for groups of 10 or more, on a special subject or in a foreign language must be scheduled a week in advance. Call the Museum Guides Office, 787-5450. Groups of 10 or more can also be scheduled on Tuesdays.
    5) Members of the museum's professional staff present one-hour gallery lectures from October to June on

Tuesdays, Thursdays and Saturdays at 11 A.M. The gallery and topic changes each week. Folding stools are provided. Reservations are not necessary. Call the Education Department (787-5455) for the current topics.

6) Philadelphia Public Schools: One-hour tours are scheduled for a class 2 weeks in advance on weekdays from 9 to 3. Call the Museum Education Department at the Board of Education, 299-7778, to arrange.

7) Parochial, private and suburban schools: similar tours are arranged by calling Museum Division of Education, 787-5455.

8) Scouts, church, neighborhood and other groups: 45-to 60-minute tours are scheduled 2 weeks in advance for groups of 5 to 100, at least 2nd grade level. Tuesday to Sunday from 10 to 3. Call the Museum Guides Office, 787-5450.

Cost: Adults, $4; senior citizens, students and children, $2; 5 and under, free. $1 more for special shows. Free for everyone on Sunday till 1. On Tuesday, pay what you wish. Group rates for 20 or more: adults, $3.50; senior citizens, students and children, $2. Membership (Student, $15; Individual, $30; Household, $45) entitles you to free admission, special programs and events, the art rental gallery service, newsletters and shop discounts.

Lunch: The cafeteria is open Tuesday to Friday, 10 to 3:30, and weekends from 11 to 3:45. The restaurant is open Wednesday to Sunday, 11:30 to 2:30. A Student Center Cafeteria is available weekdays by reservation to school groups with a scheduled tour and bringing their lunch. Beverage machines are available.

SEPTA: Buses 7, 32, 38, 43, 48. The Fairmount Park Trolley-Bus stops at the west entrance.

Others: There's an expansive Museum Shop, film* programs and an extensive gallery talk schedule. Inquire at the east or west entrance information desks. No flash photography is allowed, and children under 12 must be with an adult. Wheelchairs and strollers are available.

E & H: There are 7 low steps at the west entrance. There is complete wheelchair access to the museum. A ramp entrance is on the museum's south side. Special parking spaces for the handicapped are marked off nearby. Group Tours for senior citizens are scheduled through the Museum Guides Office (787-5450). Tours for visually impaired are scheduled through the Education Department (787-5455). Tours for hearing impaired are scheduled through the Education Department (787-5455) or by calling on TTY phone 787-5458.

It doesn't matter how old you are, or what you like in art, because there are things for everyone to marvel at in the Philadelphia Museum of Art.

When the nation celebrated its Bicentennial, the museum celebrated its Centennial with a major renovation of its classical Greco-Roman home that was built between 1919 and 1928. Over 300,000 art objects are displayed in 200 galleries covering 10 acres. The museum's map will be a big help if you're visiting on your own.

Among the museum's most prized possessions are Van Gogh's "Sunflowers," Picasso's "Three Musicians," Rubens' "Prometheus Bound," DuChamp's "Nude Descending a Staircase," Renoir's "The Bathers," Cezanne's "The Large Bathers," Charles Willson Peale's sons in the artist's "Staircase Group," Benjamin West's "Benjamin Franklin Drawing Electricity from the Sky" and Brancusi's limestone sculpture "The Kiss."

The museum's 20th century wing and the Arensberg Collection make New Yorkers realize they don't have a monopoly at their Museum of Modern Art.

If Renaissance art is more to your liking, don't miss the Johnson Collection represented by most of the great Italian and French masters.

The Philadelphia Museum of Art is more than paintings and sculpture. It's the home of the Kienbusch Armor Collection of weaponry and entire suits of metal, and a tapestry collection big enough to floor anyone.

The museum is also the "new home" of entire buildings, fountains and interiors that have been reconstructed as they were in their own time and place. Where else could you stay under one roof and walk through a 17th century Chinese Palace Hall, a 12th century French Cloister, a 16th century Indian Temple Hall, a Japanese Buddhist Temple and an authentic Tea House?

You can also visit Period Rooms from England, France and America or stand face to face with the 7th century statue of a Buddhist Lord of Mercy. Then visit Rural and Shaker Pennsylvania, see three centuries of magnificent handmade furnishings, glass and silver collections and the works of Thomas Eakins, Winslow Homer, Thomas Sully and Andrew Wyeth, to name a few.

Two pages here hardly does justice to the museum. You'll have to see it for yourself.

THE PRINT CLUB
1614 Latimer Street—19103
735-6090

Hours: Tuesday to Saturday, 11 to 5:30. Call for summer hours. Closed some holidays.
Tours: No tours, but groups of 10 or more should call in advance for reservations.
Cost: Free. Ask about General Membership ($25) that enables participation in lectures, special events, educational programs and discount purchases. If you're an artist, ask about the additional benefits of an Artist Membership ($20).
SEPTA: Buses 2, 42, 76, 90, D.
E & H: There's one step at the entrance, and only the first floor is accessible to wheelchairs.

The Print Club is a non-profit educational and cultural organization that has been operating since 1915. It's in a charming, converted center city townhouse. The gallery features a new exhibition each month presenting new and established artists from the Philadelphia area.

Members are also invited to partake in The Print Club's program of lectures, demonstrations and talks by exhibiting artists and visiting professionals. Schedules are available in the late summer, or you can check the newspapers for announcements.

RODIN MUSEUM
22nd Street and Benjamin Franklin Parkway—19101
763-8100

Hours: Tuesday to Sunday, 10 to 5. Closed holidays. Allow 30 minutes.
Tours: A public tour is the first Saturday of each month at 1 P.M. Adult groups of 10 to 50 can be scheduled any day from 10 to 3. Reservations must be made at least 2 weeks in advance through the Museum Guides Office at the Philadelphia Museum of Art (787-5440).
Cost: Pay as you wish.
SEPTA: Same as for the Philadelphia Museum of Art.
E & H: A combination of 33 low steps and landings lead through the gardens and to the museum entrance. Galleries are on one level.

The City of Philadelphia just saved you a trip to Paris to see the work of French sculptor Auguste Rodin (1840-1917). Philadelphia's Rodin Museum houses the largest single collection of Rodin's work outside of France.

You'll know you're there when you come upon "The Thinker" on the Parkway. Continue through the peaceful gardens to a chateau-inspired building, and revel first at "The Gates of Hell" dominating the museum's entrance.

Inside are nearly 200 magnificent bronze, plaster and marble sculptures so lifelike they seem to breathe. Rodin's favorite themes were interpretations of various strong emotions and the hands and busts of his many famous friends. One small room is devoted to the French poet Balzac. The six bigger-than-life figures of "The Burghers of Calais" dominate the main gallery.

A collection of Edward Steichen's photographs capture Rodin at work and several of his sculptures.

ROSENBACH MUSEUM AND LIBRARY
2010 Delancey Place—19103
732-1600

Hours: Tuesday to Sunday, 11 to 4. Closed August and some holidays.

Tours: Everyone gets a tour at Rosenbach. Groups of 8 to 30, at least junior high school level, must be scheduled in advance.

Cost: Adults, $2.50 for a tour of the house and exhibits, or $1.50 to see only the exhibits; senior citizens, military personnel, students and children under 12, $1.50. Group rates for 8 or more scheduled in advance. Memberships are available from $30.

SEPTA: Buses 17, 40, 42, 90, D.

E & H: There are 4 steps at the entrance and 3 floors of exhibits. No wheelchair access.

It's almost inconceivable that two bachelor brothers could have amassed such an outstanding collection of treasures. Abe Rosenbach collected fine literature and books. Philip concentrated on antiques and decorative arts.

A foundation has maintained the Rosenbach treasures and has continued to acquire them since the brothers' deaths in the 1950s.

Their stately 1863 townhouse has valuable furniture, silver, antiques, porcelain, paintings, rare books and manuscripts. More about the library in Chapter 11.

One room reproduces the living room of poet Marianne Moore. Her furniture, books, bric-a-brac, souvenirs and baseball mementos are just as they were when she died.

Another room features the original drawings of Maurice Sendak, well-known author and illustrator of children's books. Trace the complete production of a Sendak favorite by viewing the artist's preliminary sketches, finished artwork, color separations and finished composition.

The museum is well known for its "Bay Psalm Book" (the first Bible printed in the Western hemisphere), the original manuscripts of Chaucer's "Canterbury Tales" and James Joyce's 877-page handwritten copy of "Ulysses." The works of art include Matisse bronzes, Daumier drawings and William Blake watercolors. And since you're interested in Philadelphia, don't miss seeing the first issue of Benjamin Franklin's "Poor Richard's Almanack."

ROSENWALD–WOLF GALLERY
Philadelphia Colleges of the Arts
333 S. Broad Street—19102
875-1116

Hours: Weekdays, 10 to 5; Friday till 9; Saturday, 12 to 5. Mid-May through July: weekdays, 10 to 5. Closed-August and holidays.

Tours: Groups of up to 30 can be scheduled by calling at least a week in advance.

Cost: Free.

Lunch: The PCA Cafe directly across the street in PCA's Haviland–Strickland Building is open to gallery visitors.

SEPTA: Buses C, 27, 32, 40, 90; Broad Street Subway.

E & H: Complete wheelchair access.

The Rosenwald–Wolf Gallery at PCA offers another fine opportunity to see what's new in contemporary art. The gallery occupies a glass-front street level space in a building that was stunningly restored by PCA in 1985.

And what better way to celebrate an opening than with the East Coast's first major show of "Memphis/Milano: Furniture, Furnishings, Experiments and Ideas in the New Design." Art and design aficionados will appreciate the type of work exhibited here.

Each show runs a month. (The gallery is closed for two weeks between each show.) They might also overflow into the exhibit space in PCA's Haviland–Strickland Building directly across Broad Street. You can't miss the Doric-style portico. It's well worth walking over just to see the "Great Hall" restoration in this historic building that was PCA's home since the 1890s.

ROTUNDA GALLERY at
COMMUNITY COLLEGE OF PHILADELPHIA
1700 Spring Garden Street—19103
751-8040

Hours: September to May, weekdays, 10 to 8; weekends,
  10 to 5. Closed school holidays and between shows.
Tours: You're on your own.
Cost: Free.
SEPTA: Buses 2, 43.
E & H: Complete wheelchair access. Enter at ramp on 17th
  Street side of old U.S. Mint building and take elevator
  to gallery level.

Of the six shows presented here during the school year,
one features work by the College's art faculty; another, by
its students.
  Other shows are brought to the gallery from the outside, but they're always tied in with some aspect of the
curriculum at Community College.
  The gallery is named because of its unique architecture.
The glass-domed show area is at the core of the grand old
United States Mint building.
  Call ahead to ask what's being shown now. You might
want to combine your visit to the gallery with a tour of the
campus (see Chapter 13) or a concert or dramatic presentation (call the Student Activities Office, 751-8210).

STEPHEN GIRARD COLLECTION
Founder's Hall at Girard College
Girard and Corinthian Avenues—19130
787-2600

Hours: Every Thursday from 2 to 4; other times by special
  arrangement.
Tours: Groups of 10 or more must call ahead; groups of 10
  to 50 can be scheduled for guided tours. Allow one hour.
Cost: Free.
SEPTA: Trolley 15 to the College entrance. There's plenty
  of free parking on the campus.
E & H: There are 11 marble steps to the porticoed entrance. Exhibits are on 2nd floor and reached by stairs.

Stephen Girard's name is almost as familiar to Philadelphians as Benjamin Franklin's. A bank used to be named
after him, dozens of businesses and a street were named
after him, and, of course, Girard College where his collection is housed.

Girard came from France to Philadelphia in 1776 and rapidly became one of the wealthiest men in America. As a result, he was able to hire the finest craftsmen and buy the best of everything. His furnishings attest to that.

Antique lovers shouldn't miss this display.

The collection includes 500 pieces of furniture, china, silver, crystal and personal items dating from 1780 to 1830. Everything is carefully documented and preserved by the excellent records that Girard kept.

The furnishings are displayed in six exhibit areas, simulating the rooms at Girard's Water Street home in Philadelphia at the time of his death in 1831.

Founder's Hall, designed by Thomas U. Walter and completed in 1847, is considered to be one of the world's finest examples of Greek Revival architecture. Among Walter's other designs were the four cantilevered stairwells in the corners of City Hall*, the Society Hill Synagogue* at 418 Spruce Street, Andalusia* in Bucks County and the dome of the Capitol building in Washington, D.C.

TEMPLE GALLERY
Temple University Center City
1619 Walnut Street—19103
787-5041

Hours: Tuesday to Saturday, 10 to 6; Wednesday, 10 to 8. June through August: weekdays, 10 to 6. Closed holidays.
Tours: You're on your own.
Cost: Free.
SEPTA: Buses D, 2, 9 or any Chestnut Street route.
E & H: Complete wheelchair access.

The Temple Gallery of Temple's Tyler School of Art came to Walnut Street's upbeat retailing district in 1985. The gallery was designed by Robert Venturi, a leader in today's post-modern architecture movement and a partner in Philadelphia's world-renowned architectural firm Venturi, Rauch & Scott–Brown. The gallery is a welcome respite from the hectic center city pace.

An expansive glass street-front facade invites you inside to view contemporary works by artists, sculptors and craftspeople of international reputation.

Shows change every five or six weeks and, to date, have proven that art can be fun, educational and a rewarding interlude.

UNIVERSITY MUSEUM
33rd and Spruce Streets—19104
898–4000 or 222–7777 (recording of current programs)

Hours: Tuesday to Saturday, 10 to 4:30; Sunday, 1 to 5. Closed Sundays from late June till early September, July 4, Christmas. Allow one hour, at the very least.

Tours: You can visit on your own at any time. 45-minute gallery tours are September through May, Saturday and Sunday at 1:15 P.M. Groups of 10 to 30, at least 3rd grade, can be scheduled for a one-hour tour with a museum teacher by calling the Education Section (898–4015) at least 4 weeks in advance. These tours can be Tuesday to Friday at 10, 10:30, 1, 1:30 or occasionally at other times by special arrangement. One gallery must be chosen from those described below, and preparation is suggested. Teachers conducting their own tours may reserve the desired gallery between 11:30 and 1 or after 2 from Tuesday to Friday. Appointments for class reservations are made by phone in mid-September for the fall, and in mid-December for January through the end of the school year. Call Tuesday to Saturday between 9 and 4.

Cost: $2 donation is requested from individuals. Membership (Individual, $25; Family, $35) offers lectures, newsletters, gallery talks, special events, shop discounts and library privileges. There's a charge for all tours led by museum teachers: $10 for groups from Philadelphia; $25 for groups from out-of-state.

Lunch: The Potlatch Cafeteria offers a wide variety of hot and cold foods at reasonable prices.

SEPTA: Buses 30, 40, 42.

Other: The Pyramid Shop is especially for children and school groups. The Museum Shop carries distinctive museum replicas, jewelry, crafts, books and unusual gift items.

E & H: You can avoid steps by entering from a driveway on the east side of the museum's new wing. Elevators connect all floors, and there is complete wheelchair access. The **Nevil Gallery for the Blind and Sighted** features permanent and changing exhibits. Visitors are invited to read in braille about the museum pieces they can touch. Group tours for senior citizens and the handicapped are free and scheduled as noted above. The 33rd Street driveway entrance permits direct access to the museum's auditorium for special programs. Call ahead to make sure it will be open.

You can wander through thousands of years of history simply by exploring the primitive art and artifacts at the University Museum of the University of Pennsylvania. Many of the museum's relics have come from the almost 300 archaeological expeditions the museum has participated in since 1889. Among its most recent acquisitions is Jordan's Bicentennial gift, an ancient Roman column excavated from the ruins of the Jordanian city of Jerash.

Choose your scheduled group gallery tour from any of the following areas: the ancient civilizations of Egypt, Mesopotamia, Greece, Rome, a combination of Greece and Rome, Palestine, Biblical Archaeology or General Archaeology; Africa, Oceania, Plains Indians or Woodland Indians; Buddhism, Diversity of a Great Tradition; or the culture of the Aztec, Maya, and Inca tribes.

Whether you're with a group tour or on your own, these exhibits give you a fairly good idea about man's daily existence in civilizations that go back thousands of years. Tools and weapons used by North American Indians as long as 3,000 years ago are on display, as well as African fetishes, masks and ceremonial objects.

There's a sphynx and Egyptian mummies from 2490 B.C., give or take a few years. You can "dig" through nine layers of Biblical civilizations from a "tell" that has been excavated at Gibeon near Jerusalem. And don't miss seeing the 2,000 objects in the museum's new Polynesia exhibition.

The museum's film programs are described later in this chapter, and its concerts are described in Chapter 10. Or ask at the Information Desk when you enter for a schedule of the day's events at the University Museum. It's nice to combine a special program with your visit to the museum.

WOODMERE ART GALLERY
9201 Germantown Avenue—19118
247-0476

Hours: Tuesday to Saturday, 10 to 5; Sunday, 2 to 5. Closed weekends in July and August and closed holidays. Allow 45 minutes for group tours.

Tours: Scheduled for groups of up to 30. At least 2 adults must accompany children's groups, and children under 14 must be with an adult. Groups should call ahead, and tours must be scheduled at least 2 weeks in advance.

Cost: Free.

SEPTA: Bus L. There's plenty of parking within the grounds.

E & H: Visitors in wheelchairs should call ahead. There's access to the main gallery and the upper level exhibits. Gallery talks and tours can sometimes be planned-especially for small groups of blind visitors allowing them to handle the works of art.

For almost 50 years, the Woodmere Gallery has been showing fine paintings, sculpture, tapestries, Japanese ivories, vases, porcelain and other objects of art from the valuable collections of the late Charles Knox Smith.

The original house was Smith's grand residence. With its new wing, Woodmere is a veritable museum. You'll be a guest in Smith's own magnificent salon and dining room, with their priceless furnishings. Be sure to notice the fine Miessen pieces, including two delicate all-shell flower arrangements.

You'll hardly be able to miss the huge "Persepolis rug," the largest of the many Orientals. The history of the Persian Empire is portrayed in its woven patterns.

Several special exhibitions are featured each year. Plan your visit when you can see a special exhibit as well as the permanent collections. Call for a schedule.

Art classes are offered for children and adults in the spring and fall, and there are summer classes for children. Call for details.

Movie Theaters

Movie Theaters—Center City, Society Hill and University City—for first-run feature presentations, foreign films and occasional early afternoon specials.

Budco Midtown Twin 1412 Chestnut Street, 567-7021.
Budco Olde City 1 and 2 Sansom Street Walkway between Front and 2nd Streets, 627-5966.
Budco Palace 1812 Chestnut Street, 496-0222.
Budco Regency Twin 16th and Chestnut Sts., 567-2310.
Budco Walnut Mall 3 3925 Walnut Street, 222-2344.
Duke & Duchess 1605 Chestnut Street, 563-9881.
Eric's Mark 1 18th and Market Streets, 564-6222.
Eric's Place 1519-1521 Chestnut Street, 563-3086.
Eric 3 on the Campus 40th and Walnut Streets, 382-0296.
Eric Rittenhouse 3 1907-1911 Walnut Street, 567-0320.
Ritz Five 214 Walnut Street, 925-7900. Frequent foreign films along with prize-winning short subjects. Bargain matinees. "Movies to talk about."
Sameric 4 1908 Chestnut Street, 567-0604.
Sam's Place I and II 19th and Chestnut Sts., 972-0538.

Alternative Movie Theaters

Commercial movie theaters aren't the only places to go to see films in Philadelphia. Many of Philadelphia's cultural and civic centers show full-length feature films and shorts on a variety of subjects throughout the year.

In many instances, they're free. And you'll be able to see excellent films that the regular movie houses don't show.

So forget about the popcorn (or bring your own if you can't see a film without it) and take advantage of a continuous festival of fine films.

If you're a film buff, keep an eye out for announcements from Y's, area colleges, community centers, churches, synagogues, shopping centers and local gathering places that present occasional programs for young people and adults.

EXPLORATORY CINEMA AT ANNENBERG*
3680 Walnut Street—19104
898-6791 or 898-7041

An outstanding film series is presented on Wednesdays at 8 P.M. from late September through April, except during the University of Pennsylvania holidays. The films are in Annenberg's School of Communication. An annual schedule is available in the fall.

This is a rare chance to see classic and contemporary documentaries, features and short subjects from around the world. Most of the films that are shown are produced independently. They're films you probably won't get to see on television. They're sometimes controversial, often unusual and always significant.

FREE LIBRARY OF PHILADELPHIA*
Central Library on Logan Square, and at Branches
686-5322 for general information

The Free Library has free films. Seating is on a first come, first served basis. The programs and times vary with the branches. A schedule with all of the library's programs is available monthly.

Pictures for a Sunday Afternoon (check the dates) are at 2 in Montgomery Auditorium at the Central Library. There are also specially scheduled matinee and evening programs at many of the branch libraries. These might include a series of musicals, films by women, black filmmakers, foreign flicks or travel adventures.

The Free Libraries' films for children are described in Chapter 15. The Free Library also offers films "to go." See Chapter 13.

GEOGRAPHIC SOCIETY OF PHILADELPHIA
563-0127

You probably yearn to see some far-off and exotic places, but you won't be able to swing it this year. So go by way of some beautiful and exciting travel films with live narration by professional film producers. Where would you like to go? London? Paris? The Orient? Australia? Or Africa?

The Geographic Society of Philadelphia conducts travel lecture films at the Academy of Music*, 10 Wednesday evenings at 7:45 from October to April.

These armchair excursions are open to members only, who pay $30 annually Membership entitles you to purchase additional tickets for guests, use the Society's extensive travel library, and take advantage of trips planned by the Society to places of historic, geographic and scenic interest around the world.

For information, call or write the Geographic Society of Philadelphia, Suite 909, 21 S. 12th Street, Phila., Pa. 19107.

NEIGHBORHOOD FILM/VIDEO PROJECT OF INTERNATIONAL HOUSE*
Hopkinson Hall
3701 Chestnut Street—19104
387-5125

An annual series called "International Cinema" brings American and foreign films, along with visiting film-makers, to the International House. They could be premieres, classics, documentaries or experimental.

The season is from September to April. The program breaks when the semester breaks at the University of Pennsylvania. It resumes again in June and July.

Showtimes are Wednesday to Saturday evenings at 7:30 and an occasional Sunday, too. Tickets are $3 for adults, $2.50 for senior citizens and students, $1.50 for children under 12. There are group rates for 10 or more who call a few days ahead for reservations.

Programs for these outstanding Neighborhood Film/Video Project series are available in advance. Or watch for listings in the neighborhood movie directory of the daily newspaper.

PHILADELPHIA MUSEUM OF ART*
Van Pelt Auditorium
26th and Benjamin Franklin Parkway
763-8100 or 787-5488

The museum's Division of Education features an occasional film series on Saturday afternoons. Call or write (P.O. Box 7647, Phila., Pa. 19101) for information about upcoming events.

The museum's film programs for children are described in Chapter 15.

ROXY SCREENING ROOMS I & II
2021–2023 Sansom Street—19103
561-0115 or 561-0114 (recorded schedule)

Philadelphia's smallest commercial movie houses both have 137 comfortable seats. The Roxy I screens foreign and American repertory films. Next door the fare is first-run films that generally don't reach Philadelphia audiences. There are occasional retrospectives as well as revivals.

Admission to either Roxy is $4, or $2.50 for senior citizens or for the first matinee performance daily. Programs are available each season, or consult the daily newspaper's movie directory.

E & H: Complete wheelchair access for Roxy I.

THEATRE OF THE LIVING ARTS
334 South Street—19147
922-1011 or 922-1010 (recorded schedule)

Philadelphia's most unusual theater environment with 400 seats brings you some of the world's most unusual motion pictures. There are rarely seen films by independent filmmakers, comedy favorites, premieres, special interest films and and international classics. What else would you expect from a theater that's in the heart of South Street?

The schedule changes with the season and a new program is available every three months. There's something to see every evening, weekend matinees, sometimes in the late afternoon, and sometimes at midnight. Call or write for the program, or to be placed on the mailing list.

Admission is $4, $2 for children and senior citizens, $2.50 at discount matinees (daily before 5), or $3.50 at midnight shows. Discount cards are also available and are a good idea if you plan to attend often.

E & H: Complete wheelchair access.

TUCC CINEMATHEQUE
1619 Walnut Street—19103
787-1529

TUCC Cinematheque provides film buffs with a rare opportunity to view formerly lost, sometimes forgotten and rarely seen movies. (TUCC is the center city campus of Temple University.)

During the school year, showtime is 7:30 P.M. on Monday to Thursday; 7 and 9:15 P.M. on Friday to Sunday. The "Upstairs" screening room on the fifth floor seats 125. Be there in plenty of time to get a seat for a film you might otherwise never get to see. During June, July and August there are performances every night at 7 and 9:15, in either the "Upstairs" theater or the "Downstairs" lower level theater that seats 200.

The Film Society at TUCC is a club whose members perpetuate the preservation of one-of-a-kind remaining and hard-to-find films. The Society meets on Tuesdays at 7:30 to view and discuss film classics. Join the club ($18 for the calendar year; $8 for the season, there are three a year) and you'll contribute to that worthwhile cause. You'll also get invitations to private functions, free admissions to the Cinematheque (four during the school year, two in a season) and reduced prices for all other admissions.

Tickets to the Cinematheque are $3. Film society members and students with ID pay $2.50.

Pick up a film schedule at TUCC's Information Desk, or call to find out what's "in the can."

E & H: Complete wheelchair access.

UNIVERSITY MUSEUM*
33rd and Spruce Streets—19104
898-4015 or 222-7777 (recorded schedule)

The film programs at the University Museum are free and they're fun. An annual program is available in September by sending a long, self-addressed stamped envelope to the Museum's Education Section. Specify whether it's for children or adults. (The museum's film programs for children are described in Chapter 15.)

An Adult Entertainment Program features full-length motion pictures on Sunday afternoons from October through March at 2:30. These films are about anthropology, archaeology and classic dramas. Children attending these shows must be with an adult.

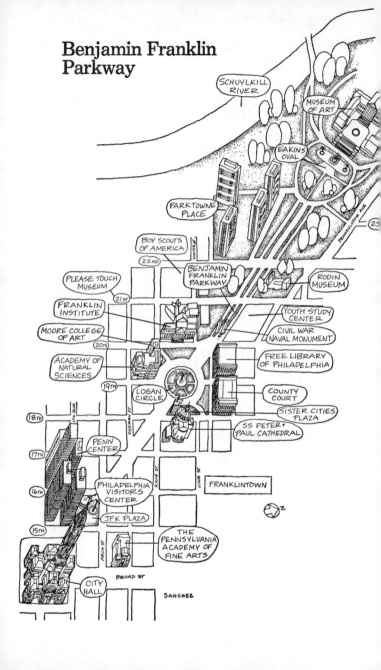

Benjamin Franklin Parkway

SCHUYLKILL RIVER

MUSEUM OF ART

EAKINS OVAL

PARKTOWNE PLACE

PENNSYLVANIA AVE

23

BOY SCOUTS OF AMERICA

22ND

WINTER ST

BENJAMIN FRANKLIN PARKWAY

RODIN MUSEUM

PLEASE TOUCH MUSEUM

21ST

FRANKLIN INSTITUTE

YOUTH STUDY CENTER

CIVIL WAR NAVAL MONUMENT

MOORE COLLEGE OF ART

20TH

ACADEMY OF NATURAL SCIENCES

FREE LIBRARY OF PHILADELPHIA

19TH

LOGAN CIRCLE

COUNTY COURT

18TH

JFK BLVD

CHERRY ST

SISTER CITIES PLAZA

PENN CENTER

17TH

SS PETER + PAUL CATHEDRAL

RACE ST

VINE ST

FRANKLINTOWN

16TH

PHILADELPHIA VISITORS CENTER

N

JFK PLAZA

15TH

ARCH ST

THE PENNSYLVANIA ACADEMY OF FINE ARTS

BROAD ST

CITY HALL

SANCHEZ

Street Art

There's so much sculpture outdoors in Philadelphia that the city's Fairmount Park Art Association has published a thick photo book entitled "Sculpture of a City," as well as an abbreviated paperbound edition called "Philadelphia's Treasures in Bronze and Stone."

The proliferation is partly due to a trend in major cities towards placing monumental contemporary works in public, outdoor places.

In Philadelphia, it's also due to an ordinance that requires one percent of costs for any municipal construction project be spent on artistic embellishment. These works must be approved by the Philadelphia Art Commission prior to purchase and installation.

The city's Redevelopment Authority has a similar requirement. The Authority has the right of eminent domain to acquire blighted land, then clear, package and sell it for public or private redevelopment. The purchasers of this land must agree to spend no less than one percent of their total construction cost for fine arts. In this case, the artwork must be approved by the Redevelopment Authority's Fine Arts Committee.

We're also lucky in Philadelphia because we're a regional district headquarters for the Federal government, and the General Services Administration has a policy requiring that three-eighths of one percent of total construction costs must be devoted to fine arts on new Federal buildings. That gives us even more street art.

These art requirements can be met with murals, mosaics, frescoes, stained glass, bas reliefs, tapestries or ornamental fountains. The most popular is statuary. I call it "Street Art" because most of it is outdoors.

The following list is restricted to works created since 1950. It's limited to sculpture and some works in other mediums that you'll come upon while walking in center city Philadelphia or visiting attractions that are described in this book. It also includes a few major pieces that are inside public buildings, but at least partially visible from the street.

The works are listed by their locations—from Old City to Society Hill and heading west to the Independence Mall area, Washington Square, around City Hall and Penn Center, the Benjamin Franklin Parkway and University City. Sports fans will want to see the bigger-than-life sculptures outside Veterans Stadium* and the Spectrum*.

The site is followed by the artist's name, the year of installation (often a year or two after its completion) and the title of the work.

444 N. 3rd Street
Fred Fisher, 1980
Abstract metal sculpture

2nd and Locust Streets
Society Hill Towers Plaza
Leonard Baskin, 1965
"Young Man, Old Man,
    and the Future"

3rd and Locust Streets
Society Hill Townhouses
    Courtyard
Gaston Lachaise, 1963
    (sculpted 1927)
"Floating Figure"

210-212 Delancey Street
Harold Kimmelman, 1970
"Butterfly"

2nd and Pine Streets
Stamper–Blackwell Court
Margaret Wasserman Levy,
1969, "Mustang at Play"

**Delancey Street
between 3rd and 4th**
Delancey Park*
Sherl Joseph Winter, 1966
"Three Bears"

**North of Pine Street
between 4th and 5th**
Lawrence Court
Harold Kimmelman, 1970
"Kangaroos"

4th and Willings Alley
Bingham Court
Richard Lieberman, 1970
"Unity"

4th and Market Streets
Royal Globe Building (lobby)
George Persak, 1974
"Symbol of '76"

5th and Chestnut Streets
Independence National
    Historical Park
EvAngelos Fradakis, 1982
"The Signer"

5th and Christ Church Walkway
Museum of
    American Jewish History*
Christopher Ray, 1976
"The Seed" (iron relief panel)

5th and Market Streets
Philadelphia National Bank
    Building
Robinson Fredenthal, 1977
"White Water"
Joseph Bailey, 1977
"Gift of the Winds"

6th and Market Streets
Rohm and Haas Building
Clarrk Fitzgerald, 1965
"Milkweed Pod"

**Monument Plaza, 6th Street at
Benjamin Franklin Bridge**
Isamu Noguchi, 1984
"Bolt of Lightning... A Memorial to Benjamin Franklin"

5th and Race Streets
Barbara Hepworth, 1980
"Rock Form"

6th and Race Streets, WHYY
Harold Lehr, 1976
"Clouds"
Eric Parks, 1976
"American Song"

6th and Arch Streets
Beverly Pepper, 1977
"Phaedrus"
Federal Reserve Bank*
    East Courtyard
Alexander Calder, 1976
"White Cascade" (mobile)

6th and Market Streets
U.S. Courthouse*
David von Schlegell, 1977
"Voyage of Ulysses" fountain
Louise Nevelson, 1976
"Bicentennial Dawn" (lobby)

7th and Race Streets
Police Administration Bldg.
Charles Parks, 1977
"Policeman Holding
  Small Child"

7th and Arch Streets
Afro–American Historical
  and Cultural Museum*
John Rhoden, 1976
"Nesaika"

615 Chestnut Street
Philadelphia Life Building
George Segal, 1981
"Woman Looking Through
  A Window"

7th and Washington Square
Hopkinson House
Oskar Stonorov and
  Jorio Vivarelli, 1963
"Adam and Eve"

7th and Delancey Streets
McCall School Playgound
Joseph J. Greenberg, Jr., 1966
"The Bear"

9th and Market Streets
Market East—The Gallery
Harold Kimmelman, 1977
"Burst of Joy"
  (interior and exterior)

900 block Locust Street
9th and Walnut Streets
Wills Eye Hospital (entrance)
George Sugarman, 1981
90–foot grouping of free-
  standing wall sculptures

10th and Walnut Streets
Thomas Jefferson University
Henry Mitchell, 1975
"The Ox"

10th and Market Streets
Market East—Stern's
David Lee Brown, 1977
"Amity"
Charles Madden, 1977
200-color abstract tapestry
(between 3rd and 4th floors)

11th and Market Streets
Market East—Gallery II
J.C. Penney's concourse level
Larry Rivers, 1983
"Philadelphia Then and Now"
Market East Commuter Tunnel
David Beck, 1984
880-foot-long ceramic mural

11th and Market Streets
ARA Building (lobby)
Ronald Bateman, 1985
Three murals
Walter Erlebacher, 1985
Two bronze odalesques
"The Dream Garden"

1234 Market Street
Robinson Fredenthal, 1973
Three metal sculptures
"Falling Water"
  (two interior, one exterior)

Broad and Delancey Streets
Herbert Bayer, 1977
"Horizons"

Broad Street and Kennedy Blvd.
Joe Brown, 1981
"Benjamin Franklin, Craftsman"

15th and Kennedy Boulevard
Municipal Services Building
  Plaza
Jacques Lipchitz, 1976
"Government of the People"

15th and Kennedy Boulevard
John F. Kennedy Plaza
Robert Indiana, 1976
"LOVE"
Henry Moore, 1964
"Three-Way Piece Number 1:
  Points"

207

15th and Cherry Streets
Friends Center*
Sylvia Shaw Judson, 1975
"Mary Dyer" (Quaker martyr)

City Hall West/Dilworth Plaza
Emlen Etting, 1982
"Phoenix Rising"

1500 Market Street
Centre Square*
Claes Oldenburg, 1976
"Clothespin"
Centre Square Galleria
Alexander Calder, 1976
Eight banners
Jean DuBuffet, 1976
"Milord La Chamarre"
  ("Man With a Fancy Vest")

15th and South Penn Square
3 Mellon Plaza
Robert M. Engman, 1974
"Triune"

17th and Kennedy Boulevard
Penn Center Plaza Concourse
Alexander Calder, 1964
"Three Disks: One Lacking"
Seymour Lipton, 1963
"Leviathan"

17th and Chestnut Streets
Chestnut Street Park
Christopher Ray, 1980
"Wissahickon Valley Gates"

17th and Locust Streets
J. Seward Johnson, Jr., 1985
"Allow Me"
  ("Man with an Umbrella")

2300 Chestnut Street
Richard Haas, 1984
Trompe l'oeil wall painting
"William Penn, Ben Franklin,
  the B & O Railroad..."

18th and Market Streets
Timothy Duffield, 1981
"The Family"

16th and Benjamin Franklin Parkway
Jacob Lipkin, 1966
"The Prophet"

16th and Benjamin Franklin Parkway
Isaac D. Levy Memorial Park
Nathan Rapoport, 1964
"Monument to the
  Six Million Jewish Martyrs"

17th and Benjamin Franklin Parkway
Oskar Stonorov and
  Jorio Vivarelli, 1963
"The Tuscan Girl" fountain

18th and Benjamin Franklin Parkway
Cathedral of SS. Peter and Paul*
Walter Erlebacher, 1977
"Jesus Breaking Bread"

20th and Benjamin Franklin Parkway
Youth Study Center Lawn
Walter Raemisch, 1955
"The Great Mother"
"The Great Doctor"

25th Street, foot of North Drive to Art Museum
Khoren Der Harootian, 1976
"Meher"

208

The contemporary sculptors, representing a sampling of works outdoors around the Philadelphia Museum of Art*, include Jacob Epstein, Jacques Lipchitz and Louise Nevelson.

Continuing along **Kelly Drive**, you'll find dozens of statues. William Zorach's "Puma" reposes in the Azalea Garden*. The **Ellen Phillips Samuel Memorial Sculpture Garden***, with works by 16 artists, is just a short distance west of Boat House Row and before you get to the Girard Avenue Bridge.

If you get to **University City**, look for the following:

34th and Civic Center Blvd.
Civic Center Plaza
Harry Bertoia, 1967
"Fountain Sculpture"

3500 Market Street
Monell Chemical Senses Center
Arlene Love, 1975
"Face Fragment"

35th and Market Streets
(lobby mural)
Jennifer Bartlett, 1981
"In the Garden"

3624 Market Street
University City Science Center
James Lloyd, 1974
Untitled 14-foot fiberglas work
on granite base that rotates
periodically to show
revolution and change
Edith Neff, 1976
Untitled mural depicting life in
West Philadelphia (lobby)

34th and Walnut Streets
University of Pennsylvania
Claes Oldenburg, 1981
"Split Button"

34th and Spruce Streets
University of Pennsylvania
Chemistry Building (lobby)
Robert M. Engman, 1977
"After Invengar"

34th Street and Locust Walk
University of Pennsylvania
Alexander Calder, 1979
"Jerusalem Stabile"

36th Street and Locust Walk
University of Pennsylvania
Tony Smith, 1975
"We Lost"

33rd and Market Streets
Drexel University
Henry Mitchell, 1975
"Running Free"
George Rickey, 1985
"Two Open Triangles
Leaning Gyratory"
(3rd floor parapet of library)

3700 Market Street
Founders Plaza
Timothy Duffield, 1976
"Dream of Sky"

3680 Walnut Street
Annenberg Center (lobbies)
Contemporary works by
Harry Bertoia,
Jose de Rivera,
Michael Langenstein,
Seymour Lipton
and Sam Maitin

209

39th Street and Locust Walk
University of Pennsylvania
Alexander Liberman, 1975
"Covenant"

51 North 39th Street
Scheie Eye Institute*
Christopher Ray, 1975
"Phoenix Tree"

At the **Sports Complex** in South Philadelphia, look for sculptor Joe Brown's two "Football Players" and two "Baseball Players" outside gates B, C, E and H of **Veterans Stadium.** On the south side of the **Spectrum** is Gilman B. Whitman's "Hockey Player." These works were installed in 1975 and 1976. And, look for film hero "Rocky Balboa" cast in bronze by A. Thomas Schomberg and installed late in 1982.

Chapter 10.
The Performing Arts.

As we continue in the arts, this chapter tells you about arts where there's action. It's about performances alive with sound and movement in dance, music and theater. Additional programs for children are described in Chapter 15.

Setting the Stage

Some of the names and facilities have already appeared in the preceding chapter, and you'll come across them repeatedly in this chapter. That's because many galleries and theaters cater to more than one of the arts. And many of the performing arts companies can be enjoyed at a variety of locations. The following are some of the most popular. Spend some time in Philadelphia and you'll be familiar with them.

The **ACADEMY OF MUSIC** at Broad and Locust Streets (893-1930), home of the Philadelphia Orchestra*, is also a stage for other musical programs, opera, dance and film events. You can also tour the Academy (see Chapter 13). The Academy seats almost 3,000 in the orchestra pit, parquet, parquet circle, balcony, family circle and amphitheater.

The **ALL STAR-FORUM**, under the direction of Philadelphia impressario Moe Septee, brings concerts, dance and theater in individual performances and series to the Academy of Music. The Forum's offices are at 1530 Locust Street, Phila., Pa. 19102 (735-7506).

Every summer, the **CITY OF PHILADELPHIA Department of Recreation** sponsors cultural events that are scheduled during the day and evenings at several locations throughout the city.
Among the hundreds of happenings are the Monday evenings at Rittenhouse Square and at Gorgas Park and the Wednesday evenings at Pastorius Park and Pennypack Park. The programs include opera, Gospelrama, barbershop singers, dixieland bands, folk and rock concerts, theater and dance. There are series at parks and recreation centers throughout Philadelphia.
On Tuesday evenings you can choose Mummers String Band concerts at the Mummers Museum or the Big Band Sounds at Tarken Recreation Center.

There isn't any charge to attend these performances, and one of the series will be convenient for you.

Most events with a constant schedule are included in Chapters 9 and 10. They're also announced in the Philadelphia newspapers. You can get additional information by calling the Mayor's Office for Information (686-2250) or the Department of Recreation (686-0151).

The **CITY OF PHILADELPHIA Department of Recreation** also has programs where young people and adults can join in workshops, classes and performances of their own. The activities during the fall and winter include ballet, ceramics, dramatics, folk dancing, music, painting, paper-mache, sketching and sculpting.

Many of these programs continue during the spring and summer along with arts and crafts, bands, contemporary music, dramatics, harmonica and guitar lessons. The city also has outstanding cultural summer camps*.

For more information about these programs, call the Philadelphia Department of Recreation, 686-0151. And don't forget about all the special events that happen annually in Philadelphia. They're included in Chapter 19.

The **FREE LIBRARY OF PHILADELPHIA** at Logan Square is more than a place for books (see Chapter 11). It's a showplace for literary exhibits, films, the performing arts, story hours and whatever else those clever people can schedule for their auditorium. Several of these events are described elsewhere in this book. Refer to the Index.

The **PAINTED BRIDE ART CENTER,** founded on a shoestring in 1969, is prospering at 230 Vine Street in Old City*.

By day, the Painted Bride is an art gallery for month-long shows by area painters and sculptors. Gallery hours are Tuesday to Friday, 12 to 6, and Saturday, 2 to 5.

At night it transforms into a 200-seat theater for budding and seasoned talent to recite poetry, dance, sing, act, mime, do puppetry or give musical performances.

The theater is casual and comfortable. Admission to

these performances is always under $10. Discounts are available to groups making reservations at least a week in advance. Watch the local newspapers, or call 925-9914 for a schedule.

SEPTA: Buses D, 5, 17, 33, 42, 48; Market-Frankford Subway-Elevated train to 2nd and Market.

E & H: Complete wheelchair access, but please call in advance.

The **SHUBERT THEATER** at 250 S. Broad Street belongs to the Philadelphia Colleges of the Arts*. It accommodates an audience of almost 2,000 in the orchestra, balcony and family circle. To find out what's appearing, watch the theater announcements in the local newspapers, or call the college at 875-2200.

You can count on the **Y ARTS COUNCIL** to bring to Philadelphians whatever is new and outstanding in films, chamber music, poetry readings and literature programs. Their stage for the performing arts is primarily the auditorium of the Gershman YM & YWHA at 401 S. Broad Street, Phila., Pa. 19147. The Gallery Y Space for innovative artwork occupies a part of the first floor here.

Arts Council events are usually scheduled from October to May. You can subscribe for the year, or purchase tickets for individual programs. Call 545-4400 for details.

ANNENBERG CENTER, the **FORREST THEATER** and the **WALNUT STREET THEATER** are described later in this chapter.

Getting Tickets

You can get tickets for the performing arts by subscription or for individual shows, directly from each company or its box office.

Or, you can get tickets at the **TicketBooth** that's scheduled to be built and operational in 1986 at the northwest corner of 15th and Market Streets.

The TicketBooth is a function of the Greater Philadelphia Cultural Alliance (735-0570), a non-profit service organization representing more than 180 Delaware Valley arts and cultural organizations.

This is where you can get half-price tickets on the same day as a scheduled performance, and full-price tickets for future performances. A computerized listing will show you the area's happenings in both the performing and visual arts.

Dance

Philadelphians are rising to their feet.

The local dance world is no longer dominated by a single ballet company. Several dance troupes have arisen in recent years and are being welcomed by growing audiences. The troupes represent diverse styles and goals, and they provide an opportunity for Philadelphians to attend traditional ballet, modern, improvisational, ethnic and young people's performances. Many of them will bring their performances directly to you (see Chapter 13).

In 1972 the **PHILADELPHIA DANCE ALLIANCE** formed an association of "smaller" companies dedicated to promoting dance in the Philadelphia area. Today its ranks have grown to more than 80 professional dance troupes and schools, from the most prominent to the small and up-and-coming. Dance students and devotees of dance are welcome to join.

Members of the Dance Alliance receive a monthly newsletter announcing public workshops, ticket specials, a professional "dance calendar" and general information.

National Dance Week is celebrated locally at the end of April. Watch for announcements of the special events. The Alliance also schedules occasional dance festivals at popular and convenient Philadelphia stage locales.

If you would like to know more about the Philadelphia Dance Alliance, contact them at 1315 Walnut Street, Suite 1505, Phila., Pa. 19107 (545-6344).

ARTHUR HALL AFRO-AMERICAN DANCE ENSEMBLE
225-7565

This notable ensemble of at least 20 dancers and drummers makes its home at the Ile-Ife Center for the Arts & Humanities. (You get a mini-performance when you tour the center and its museum. See Chapter 9.)

Arthur Hall's inspiration is the black cultures of Africa, the Caribbean, North America and Latin America. Many of their performances are authentic ritual dances, enacted in native costumes.

When they're not on tour, the Arthur Hall Dancers perform a few times a month in Philadelphia. Their schedule can be had by calling on a month-to-month basis.

BALLET DES JEUNES
473-2253

Ballet des Jeunes, founded in 1958, is a professional company of 50 dancers ages 10 to 18. Along with ballet and jazz, their repertoire includes traditional Polish, Russian, Spanish and American ethnic dances.

You can see Ballet des Jeunes during the year at places like The Port of History Museum, the Walnut Street Theater and Zellerbach Theater at Annenberg. They frequently perform outdoors in warm weather.

Ballet des Jeunes also represents Philadelphia as cultural diplomats when they travel around the country and abroad. In recent years they've performed at such faraway places as Monte Carlo, Russia, Bulgaria, Austria and Hungary. They are internationally recognized as the leading performing ballet company of the young in the United States.

Call for a schedule and details to enjoy this delightful young people's dance company.

CITY OF PHILADELPHIA
DANCE PROGRAMS

The Philadelphia Department of Recreation has fall and winter classes in acrobatics, aerobics, ballet, modern and tap dancing for young people and adults. The best dancers are chosen to perform in a Spring Recital at a major performing arts center. A year-round children's program in conjunction with the Philadelphia Dance Alliance also takes place at sites throughout the city. Call 686-0151 to find out which dance classes would be the most convenient for you.

For those who would rather watch, semi-professional and professional dance companies perform in city-sponsored programs throughout the summer. Many of them are described elsewhere in this chapter.

DANCE CELEBRATION
898-6791 (Annenberg box office)
898-1550 (subscription office)
563-5445 (group sales for 20 or more)

Dance Celebration has been bringing Philadelphians the tops in contemporary dance since 1984. Performances are at Zellerbach Theater in the Annenberg Center*.

When we say tops, we mean the likes of Alvin Ailey, Merce Cunningham, Eliot Feld, Martha Graham, Bella

Lewitsky, Jose Limon, Pilobolus and Twyla Tharp. Five companies visit for each year's Celebration, usually with three 8 P.M. performances by each.

Tickets can be purchased for the series or, if you're lucky, for individual performances.

A mini-series of Dance Celebration introduces Philadelphians to three lesser known dance troupes each year in one-night performances.

FOLK DANCING

This is where the star dancing attraction is YOU. There are several places to go when you get the urge to dance. Try one of the following, or consult the dance listing of the weekend newspapers.

The **Philadelphia Folk Dancers** do everthing from the Virginia Reel to polkas, American ragtime and international tunes.

Would-be and seasoned dancers meet on Tuesdays at 7:30 P.M. from May through September on the Art Museum Terrace at 26th and Benjamin Franklin Parkway. The action moves indoors to No. 1 Boat House Row (Plaisted Hall, 686–3119) on Kelly Drive on rainy summer nights. On Monday evenings from October through April, they also meet at 7:30 P.M. at No. 1 Boat House Row.

No one judges your ability, but everyone is enthusiastic and has a good time. Some folks attend just to have an excuse to jump up and down. Bring a partner or come alone.

The word on the Philadelphia Folk Dancers is out, and people from all over the country mosey over to dosey-do when they're in this-here parts. There's circle dancing, line dancing, partner dances, no-partner dances and traditional square dances. Donations of $2.50 are requested to help defray the cost of records and sound equipment. Call 884–4884 or 646–9264 if you have any questions.

The **Folk Dance Center of Philadelphia** meets from September to June on Friday nights at the St. Michael's Lutheran Church, 6671 Germantown Avenue. Be there at 8 P.M. to do your dos-a-dos, or the second Tuesday of each month for a Country Dance. Admission is $1.50 for members and $2.50 for non-members.

Traditional dances are called, along with native folk dances of foreign countries. There's something for everyone, so stop by any evening and "swing your partner." If you want to know more, call 844–3163 and ask for folk dance information.

The **Germantown Country Dancers** have been gathering since 1972. They dance at Calvary Episcopal Church, Pulaski and Manheim Streets, on Wednesday evenings from 8 to 10:30 from mid-September to the end of May. You're welcome to join them on your own or with a partner, no matter what your skill is.

The Germantown Country Dancers are always learning new figures to English and American country dances done to live or recorded music. The fee is $2.50 per session, or you might decide to become a member.

Workshops, with guest callers, or country dance parties are held the first Saturday of each month. These are always fun, too. You can learn more about the Germantown Country Dancers by calling 844–6819, or you can be one of the 25 to 50 enthusiasts who stop by at any of their gatherings.

If you would like to schedule a fully-costumed demonstration by the Germantown Country Dancers at your occasion, see Chapter 13.

PENNSYLVANIA BALLET COMPANY
978–1429

Philadelphia's resident ballet company since 1964 of 32 dancers presents a season of new ballets, repertoire favorites and modern dance at the Academy of Music from September to June. Robert Weiss has been artistic director since 1982.

You can attend single performances, or you can subscribe at discount rates to one of their series plans. There are evening shows and weekend matinees. Tickets for a single performance range from $5 in the amphitheater to $40 for a box seat.

A once-a-year favorite for thousands of Philadelphians is the Christmas week performance of the "Nutcracker." There are matinee and evening shows. Tickets range from $9 to $40, and group discounts are available.

Don't miss a chance to see a ballet company that is a major force in the local and national dance world.

PHILADELPHIA CIVIC BALLET COMPANY
923–4477

The Philadelphia Civic Ballet Company appears on prominent center city stages as well as going out to the community to entertain and introduce Philadelphians of all ages to the world of dance. Many of their performances are at area schools (see Chapter 13), and several through-out the year are available to the general public.

Twenty adults make up the Civic Ballet. Founded in 1955, this is a "veteran" among the local companies. They've appeared on television, in major theaters, at the Academy of Music, historic sites, playgrounds, parks and even in the streets.

The Philadelphia Civic Ballet performs annually at Robin Hood Dell East, at the Free Library and in an Easter program at John Wanamaker Department Store*.

PHILADELPHIA DANCE COMPANY
387–8200

The Philadelphia Dance Company, founded in 1970, has a well-established reputation for exhilarating contemporary and modern dance.

Twenty-three young men and women train and perform with Philadanco. They made a Lincoln Center debut in 1979, and recently appeared at the Walnut Street Theater, Zellerbach Theater at Annenberg and in the 1986 Bermuda Arts Festival.

Members of the company have appeared at the Philadelphia Orchestra's student concerts, the University Museum, Young Audiences and a variety of programs hosted by the city. This is another dance company that goes into the neighborhoods for a full schedule of lectures and demonstrations at schools and recreation centers (see Chapter 13).

Philadanco's 150-seat theater at 9 N. Preston Street in University City* is a comfortable setting for recitals and neighborhood performances.

Call or check the newspapers for the Philadelphia Dance Company's next performance.

WAVES
563–1545

WAVES is a phenomenon in the dance world since its birth in 1982. Founder Shimon Braun describes its three elements as "art, entertainment and 'soul'—the esprit of the dance corps." The "wave" technique involves the entire body in movement that has no beginning or end.

Over 20 men and women mix the grace of ballet with elastic, popular skills like belly-dancing, break-dancing, gymnastics and roller skating. The accompanying music is non-stop, mostly rock. It's very jazzy.

WAVES appears locally several times during the year

219

at the Academy of Music. They've already achieved instant stardom with performances in cities throughout the United States and Europe.

Don't miss this colorful celebration of dancers and dancing. Call to find out when they're appearing. If you'd like to make WAVES just for you and your group, refer to "Tours to Go" in Chapter 13.

Reminder: Other internationally-known dance companies appear in Philadelphia each year thanks to the **ALL STAR-FORUM***. Call them (735-7506) to find out who will be here soon. These performances are usually on a weekend at the Academy of Music.

SMALLER BUT EQUALLY SIGNIFICANT DANCE COMPANIES

You can call these dance companies individually for their performance and ticket schedules, or keep in touch with them by way of the Philadelphia Dance Alliance's monthly calendars.

GROUP MOTION MULTI MEDIA DANCE THEATER (928-1495) is a modern dance company that was founded in 1968. As their name implies, Group Motion's dance is highly improvisational, using innovative lighting and electronic music and requiring boundless energy. They present workshops and perform at their studio (624 S. Fourth Street) and at several other locations throughout the year.

RITA JONES DANCE COMPANY is another professional company performing ballet, jazz and modern dance. Ten members, along with a junior troupe of five, are the resident company of the Mid-City YWCA, 2027 Chestnut Street. They perform throughout the year at area theaters and at outdoor locations in the summer. Call the Y (564-3430) and ask for the Rita Jones Dance Company manager to find out when you can see them on stage.

Along with all the other things happening along South Street, it has also given life to a dance company. The **SOUTH STREET DANCE COMPANY** (925-3619) was founded in 1974. Since then, they've performed at the Painted Bride Art Center, Annenberg Center, Walnut Street Theater, with city festivals and Young Audiences in works choreographed by the company's founder and artistic director, Ellen Forman, and guest artists. If you'd like to see them, call for a schedule of upcoming performances.

ZEROMOVING DANCE COMPANY was founded by its artistic director, Hellmut Gottschild, in 1972 as a highly improvisational dance company. Where Group Motion Dance Theater uses unusual music and sets, ZeroMoving depends only on the eight-member dance ensemble. Their body movements and sounds, along with the audience reactions in movement and sound, complete the dance. Thus much of their work is constantly changing, while other pieces are more definitely choreographed.

If this sounds like an audience you'd like to be part of, call 843-9974 for ZeroMoving Dance Company's upcoming performance schedule.

MORE DANCE COMPANIES? OF COURSE!

These, too, are companies that dance periodically in and around Philadelphia. Watch the local newspapers for announcements of their programs, try to contact them directly, or ask the Philadelphia Dance Alliance if they have any news on their performance schedules.

These include the Dance Company Sybil, Dance Conduit, Germantown Dance Theater, Susan Hess Modern Dance, the Terry Beck Troupe and Voloshky Ukrainian Dance Ensemble.

Music

ALL STAR-FORUM
1530 Locust Street (office)—19102
735-7506

Every year between October and May, the All Star-Forum brings eight exciting concerts to the Academy of Music*. Most are at 8 P.M.; a few are Sunday matinees at 3 P.M.

Orchestras from Boston to Moscow have appeared. And stars like Isaac Stern, Rudolf Serkin, Marcel Marceau, Zubin Mehta, Robert Merrill, Roberta Peters, and Renata Tebaldi have also appeared.

Select-A-Series enables you to choose six concerts in advance for preferred seats and savings. Subscriptions should be ordered by mail, or they can be charged by telephone (735-5266). There may be tickets at the Academy of Music box office prior to a performance.

Special events are also scheduled by the All Star-Forum at the Academy. They might include such greats as Leontyne Price, Van Cliburn, P.D.Q. Bach, the

Preservation Hall Jazz Band and the Vienna Choir Boys. Select-A-Series subscribers get first choice at these tickets also.

Reminder: The All Star–Forum's interest extends far beyond music. Look into their dance and theatrical events, too.

CHORAL GROUPS

If you like vocal music, we've got it. You can either listen to it or participate in it.

The **ACADEMY BOYS CHOIR** of the Performing Arts School of Philadelphia (875–2285) features 50 boys from ages of eight to 15 who attend public, private and parochial schools in the Delaware Valley. They're directed by Dr. Carlton Jones Lake, and they perform with the Philadelphia Orchestra and at concerts throughout the city. Each year, the group represents Philadelphia on a singing tour which in recent years has taken them to England, Wales, France, the Caribbean and Scandinavia.

The **CHORAL ARTS SOCIETY** was founded in 1982 under the direction of Sean Deibler. Members are carefully selected from the tri-state area; a third are professional musicians. They've grown to a 200-voice symphonic chorus that is recognized around the world. The Society's 1986 two-week European tour marked the first time a group of this kind performed in Warsaw, behind the Iron Curtain.

Back home, the Choral Arts Society performs at the Academy of Music and at center city church locales. You can purchase tickets as a series or for individual concerts. Call 545–8634 for a schedule of performances and additional information.

Philadelphia's oldest coed choral group, the **MENDELSSOHN CLUB,** was founded in 1874. Tamara Brooks is their musical director. Among the Club's 150 semi-professional singers are doctors, lawyers, teachers and housewives. They range in age from 17 to 75.

The Mendelssohn Club performs on various occasions throughout the year at the Academy of Music, churches and concert halls. Most of their selections are classical, and many are major choral works that aren't often heard. The 35-voice **MENDELSSOHN SINGERS** are chosen from the Club to perform in chamber concerts. Call 527–1808 for audition or performance information.

PENNSYLVANIA PRO MUSICA, directed by Dr. Franklin Zimmerman, presents rarely heard music, especially from the Baroque and Renaissance Periods.

The company varies with the programs. The concerts usually feature a chorale or solo singers, and they are often accompanied by a chamber orchestra.

You can see Pennsylvania Pro Musica usually one Sunday afternoon a month from October to May at historic churches in Old Philadelphia. Tickets are generally from $4 to $17.50. Discounts are available to students, groups of 10 or more, senior citizens or if you subscribe to a series. For ticket and schedule information, call 222-4517 or write Pennsylvania Pro Musica, 225-A South 42nd Street, Phila., Pa 19104.

The **PHILADELPHIA BOYS CHOIR & CHORALE** sing at concerts and special events both in Philadelphia and around the world. Since their founding in 1968, they've travelled over a million miles and performed in 14 different languages on every major continent.

Dr. Robert G. Hamilton directs this highly acclaimed choir of 75 schoolboys from the ages of eight to 13. They're complemented with a young men's chorale of 25 voices.

Auditions are held throughout the year. If you know someone who would like to try out for this great opportunity, call 546-5544, or write to Suite 305, 311 S. Juniper Street, Philadelphia, Pa. 19107.

If you'd like to see a choir that has performed for the President and heads-of-state, call or watch the newspapers for concert announcements.

The **PHILADELPHIA COLLEGES OF THE ARTS* CHORUS**, directed by Sean Deibler, is composed of 75 students from the college. They perform at the Shubert Theater and on occasion with the Philadelphia Orchestra at the Academy of Music. For an annual performance schedule that's available in September, call 875-2206.

PHILADELPHIA ORATORIO CHOIR performs in December and late February through Easter under the direction of Earl Ness at the First Baptist Church, 17th and Sansom Streets. This is an all-professional choir numbering around 40. There's no charge to attend any of their concerts. Call 563-0397 if you think you might qualify for the one or two openings they have each year. If you enjoy listening to oratorio concerts, call for a schedule during the performance months.

PHILADELPHIA SINGERS is a 30-voice all-professional chorus directed by Michael Korn. They perform from a repertoire of classical choral literature in a series from October to May at the Academy of Music or the Church of the Holy Trinity on Rittenhouse Square.

Philadelphia Singers is also the resident professional chorus (accompanied by the Concerto Soloists Chamber Orchestra*) for the annual Basically Bach Festival of Philadelphia held in November. They've recently made a world premiere recording of Handel's "Roman Vespers" on the RCA Red Seal label, and in 1985 were featured in a P.B.S. telecast, "A Celebration for Handel and Bach."

Tickets for the Philadelphia Singers can be ordered by phone, mail or picked up prior to each concert. Group, student and senior citizen discounts are available. Call 732-3370 for auditions, schedule and ticket details. Or write or stop by Philadelphia Singers, 1830 Spruce Street, Phila., Pa. 19103.

SINGING CITY, founded in 1948, is a 100-voice group of talented amateurs conducted by Dr. Elaine Brown. They sing at community centers throughout the city and with the Philadelphia Orchestra at the Academy of Music. They'll capture your ear with a wide range of music from Hindu chants to Handel's "Messiah." Their music is as diverse as their membership. Call 561-3930 for information.

CITY OF PHILADELPHIA
SUMMER MUSICAL PROGRAMS

Thanks to the city's Department of Recreation, you have a choice of free musical events to attend almost every night of the summer. A few of the series are described later in this chapter. Here are some more.

They're all announced in the daily newspapers. If you prefer to plan ahead, the Department of Recreation (686-0151) can tell you the schedule for citywide locations so you can choose the programs according to your interest and the location.

Music comes to the **Pennypack Park Festival,** at Rhawn Street near Winchester Avenue, on 10 consecutive Thursdays at 8 P.M. from the last week in June. You'll enjoy symphony concerts, opera, a touch of dixieland, the big band sound, jazz or vocalists on any given warm summer night. Many of the same groups also appear at the **Summer Evenings at Rittenhouse Square,** 18th and Walnut Streets, Mondays at 8 P.M.

Big Band Dance Concerts are Tuesday evenings in July and August at Tarken Recreation Center, Frontenac and Levick Streets.

Other summer festivals are Mondays at Martin Luther King Recreation Center, 22nd and Columbia Avenue; Tuesdays at Clark Park, 46th and Kingsessing Avenue; Wednesdays at Pastorius Park, Abington and Roanoke Streets; Thursdays at Schuylkill River Park, Taney and Pine Streets; Fridays at Marconi Plaza, Broad Street below Oregon Avenue; and a half-dozen more parks and recreation centers.

There's lots of music filling the air of lazy, hazy nights of summer.

CONCERTO SOLOISTS
CHAMBER ORCHESTRA OF PHILADELPHIA
735-0202

Founded in 1964 under the direction of Marc Mostovoy, the Concerto Soloists offers an unusual opportunity to listen to distinguished chamber music. It's comprised of 15 strings and a harpsichord. Woodwinds, brass and percussion are added when necessary. Their name comes from the unusual practice of giving the performers a chance to play both solo and supporting roles. They stand while performing.

Baroque and classical music are the Concerto Soloists' specialty, but it isn't the limit of their repertoire. They also play rarely heard music of the 19th and 20th centuries, and each year they premiere the work of a contemporary American composer.

Concerto Soloists presents two concert series. One is six concerts at the Academy of Music on Mondays at 8 P.M. Marc Mostovoy or Max Rudolph conduct. They also perform in a series of six Basically Baroque Coffee Concerts on Sundays at 2:30 P.M. at the Church of the Holy Trinity on Rittenhouse Square. And, they perform with the Philadelphia Singers* in the annual fall Basically Bach Festival and in a series of Concerts for Children that are described in Chapter 15.

Tickets can be purchased in a choice of series plans (or individually before a concert when available) with reduced rates for students and senior citizens. Call or write (338 S. 15th Street, Phila., Pa. 19102) for a schedule and the programs.

Remember: An asterisk(*) indicates that the same place or event appears elsewhere in the book with more details. Look in the Index for additional pages.

THE CURTIS INSTITUTE OF MUSIC*
1726 Locust Street—19103
893-5261

This is a wonderful opportunity to hear the future great musical artists of the world because students from throughout the world come to Curtis to study virtually every musical instrument.

Their recitals in Curtis Hall include opera, chamber concerts, wind, percussion, piano and harp performances. They're at 8 P.M. on Monday, Wednesday and Friday evenings from October to the first week of May, and there's no admission charge.

The Curtis schedule is available a month in advance. Call or stop in for information.

You're probably wondering who Curtis' famous graduates are. Well, among others they include Leonard Bernstein, Jorge Bolet, Gary Graffman, Eugene Istomin, Jaime Laredo and Anna Moffo.

The exterior of The Curtis Institute was prominently featured in the movie "Trading Places."

JAZZ

There's an annual Jazz Festival in Philadelphia that's described under "June" in Chapter 19.

We don't miss a beat in Philadelphia!

MANN MUSIC CENTER
West Fairmount Park
George's Hill near 52nd Street and Parkside Avenue
567-0707

SEPTA: Buses 38, 40, 43, 85 and special Mann Music Center buses that go round-trip from center city. Call for schedule and route. There's plenty of free parking and special parking for Friends of the Dell.

E & H: Complete wheelchair access with restrooms at ground level. An 8- by 130-foot ramp eliminates steep walking and steps. It goes from the top of the theater shell and parking areas directly into the balcony.

The **Philadelphia Orchestra** moves outdoors in summer. They've been making a joyful sound in Fairmount Park since 1929. In 1976 they moved to the dramatic new Mann Music Center.

The world's most popular guest conductors and soloists visit with the orchestra each season for 18 concerts in seven weeks. They begin the third week in June and continue on Tuesday, Thursday and Friday evenings at 8 P.M., except the week of July 4th.

Aficionados can take their choice between tiers of bench seating or grassy slopes (bring a blanket). There's free seating for 10,000 but tickets are necessary. Coupons appear in The Inquirer three weeks prior to each concert. Mail the coupon with a stamped, self-addressed envelope and your tickets will be sent on a first come, first served basis. If you don't have a coupon which indicates a concert, give your concert preference. The address is Mann Music Center Concerts, Department of Recreation, P.O. Box 1000, Phila., Pa. 19105. There's a two-ticket limit for each concert requested.

You can have a reserved seat, under cover, by becoming a Friend of the Mann Music Center. An annual contribution entitles you to a seat at each concert.

Box suppers can be purchased at the two food stands before each concert, and you can picnic on the lawn. Refreshments are also available at intermission.

For concert programs and additional information, call or write The Mann Music Center, 1617 John F. Kennedy Blvd., Phila., Pa. 19103.

Note: The entertainment continues at the Mann Music Center in August and in the absence of the Philadelphia Orchestra. There's ballet, opera, theater, pop and rock concerts. Watch for newspaper announcements, or call to find out who will be there.

MUMMERS STRING BAND CONCERTS
336-3050

Since 1952, the Philadelphia Mummers String Bands have been "showing their stuff" each summer in a weekly concert series. Top bands perform their well-known music along with instrumental solos and duets, vocalists, community singing and impromptu strutting.

Be at the Mummers Museum*, Two Street and Washington Avenue on Tuesdays at 8 P.M. from May through September. But don't come if it rains. (The concerts are held outdoors.) Call the museum at 6 P.M., or listen to KYW Newsradio, for last minute announcements.

And be prepared to go away singing "I'm Looking Over a Four Leaf Clover."

MUSIC FROM MARLBORO
569-4690

The Marlboro Music Festival has brought outstanding

chamber music to Marlboro, Vermont, every summer since 1950. Music From Marlboro has gone on tour to Philadelphia annually since 1965.

Seven chamber concerts are presented in conjunction with the Philadelphia Chamber Music Society at the Port of History Museum* on Mondays from November to May at 8 P.M. Programs include music by Bartok, Beethoven, Debussy, Dvorak, Haydn, Mozart and Schumann, to name a few. Distinguished soloists also perform, all under the artistic direction of Philadelphia's own Rudolf Serkin.

Tickets are available by subscription. Call for details, or write Music From Marlboro, 135 South 18th Street, Phila., Pa. 19103.

OPERA

The history of opera in Philadelphia is as old as the Academy of Music. Its opening performance in February, 1857, was Verdi's "Trovatore" and for the past century opera has flourished here.

Today you have a choice of opera companies. The grand scale, popular productions are presented by the **OPERA COMPANY OF PHILADELPHIA**, formed in 1975 when the local Grand and Lyric companies merged. This is the company that premiered Gian-Carlo Menotti's 17th opera, "The Hero," in June, 1976. It's the company where Luciano Pavarotti makes frequent guest appearances and judged an international voice competition.

The Opera Company of Philadelphia stages five operas a year at the Academy of Music from October to May. The curtain is 8 P.M. and each opera is performed on two evenings in one week. Tickets go on sale in September at the Academy box office or from the company's office at Suite 1300, 1500 Walnut Street, Phila., Pa. 19102. They range from $11 to $35 and can be purchased for individual operas or by subscription. Call 732-5811 for details.

Another opera series is presented each year by the **ACADEMY OF VOCAL ARTS**. They present in the native language four operas a year from November to May at the Walnut Street Theater (two nights for each performance) or their own charming 150-seat theater at 1920 Spruce Street (four nights for each performance).

Tickets are $10 or $15 at the AVA, and $10 to $20 at the Walnut. Call 735-1685 for tickets and schedule information. (A note for the **E & H**: Call ahead to use the ramped entrance on Delancey Street.)

A new concept in opera was introduced to Philadelphia in 1974 by the **PENNSYLVANIA OPERA THEATER** and its artistic director, Barbara Silverstein. Their operas are in English and they stress drama as well as music. Their productions appeal to contemporary audiences of all ages. Recent choices have been Mozart's "The Marriage of Figaro," David Amram's "Twelfth Night," Jacques Offenbach's "The Tales of Hoffmann" and Rossini's "Cinderella."

The Pennsylvania Opera Theater stages two operas each spring, with three 8 P.M. performances of each, at the Walnut Street Theater.

For schedule and ticket information, call 972-0904 or write the Pennsylvania Opera Theater, PNB Building, Suite 1800, 1345 Chestnut Street, Phila., Pa. 19107.

The nation's oldest amateur Gilbert and Sullivan troupe, **THE SAVOY COMPANY** was founded in Philadelphia in 1901. They, too, perform at the Academy of Music. Their performances are one Friday and Saturday each year in May. It's a rare treat to see a fully-staged and authentic production of Gilbert and Sullivan. You'll see why Gilbert and Sullivan are two of America's favorite playwrights. Call the Academy or The Savoy Company (735-7161) for the schedule and ticket information. If you miss them at the Academy in May, there's a repeat performance later in the month or in June at Longwood Gardens* in Kennett Square, Pa.

ORCHESTRA SOCIETY OF PHILADELPHIA
Drexel University
32nd and Chestnut Streets—19104
924-2196

A group of professional musicians who wanted to practice and perform regularly, but didn't want a strenuous concert schedule, founded the Orchestra Society of Philadelphia in 1964. Today they're highly respected innovators in the local musical arena, and they're the resident orchestra of Drexel University. Luis O. Biava, a principal violinist with the Philadelphia Orchestra, is music director and conductor.

The Orchestra Society encourages new compositions and performances by young soloists. They present unusual concerts like Mahler's Symphony 8 (the Symphony of One Thousand), heard in Philadelphia in 1976 for the second time in 60 years.

You can see the Orchestra Society of Philadelphia at

Drexel when they perform in the Main Hall Auditorium. Admission is free. Call or watch for newspaper announcements of the exact dates and programs. Auditions are also held regularly for talented musicians interested in joining the orchestra.

ORGAN CONCERTS
John Wanamaker Department Store*
13th and Market Streets—19101
422-2450

If you like organ music, and if you've never seen a pipe organ, this is where you have a chance to see one. The Wanamaker pipe organ is the largest in the world and one of the finest ever built.

This huge instrument has 451 stops and 964 controls, all within the organist's reach. They're tied in with 30,000 pipes. The 100 gold pipes you see in the loft area overlooking Wanamaker's Grand Court are purely decorative. The real ones stretch out for seven floors behind them!

Mr. Keith Chapman, or one of his associates, gives 45-minute concerts every shopping day at 11:15 A.M. and 5:15 P.M. (The organ has been played at John Wanamaker every business day since its installation in 1911.)

You can be at any point in the Grand Court on the store's main floor to enjoy the music or on any of the upper floors where they overlook the Grand Court. Or you can be one of the lucky few to sit by Mr. Chapman at the great console while he performs. A dozen guests, at the most, can be accommodated at one time. Go directly to the second floor on the 13th Street side of the Grand Court and ask a salesperson to direct you.

If you can't be at Wanamaker's for a concert but you'd like to see and learn more about the organ, the console can be seen at other times by appointment only.

PHILADELPHIA CLASSICAL
GUITAR SOCIETY
259-3767

Classical guitar music is unusual for many of us, so it's an interesting interlude. The Philadelphia Classical Guitar Society presents recitals at 7:30 P.M., usually on the fourth Sunday of each month from September to June (unless it's a holiday). They're held at convenient center city locations so plan to attend something unusual and interesting.

Selections for these recitals include a wide variety of

classical music. Sometimes there's a lecture and discussion of the program. If classical guitar music is new to you, this will be a good learning experience.

Tickets are available in advance or at the door for $4 to $15. Members of the Society get ticket discounts and the opportunity to attend social and educational events as well. A schedule is available from the Society at the end of the summer.

PHILADELPHIA FOLKSONG SOCIETY
247-1300

Come and sing along when the spirit moves you!

Whether you sing along or just enjoy listening, this is another unique musical experience in Philadelphia. The music ranges from blue grass to a good sampling of international favorites. You'll probably find yourself humming a few tunes.

The concerts are held in Hopkinson Hall at the International House*, 3701 Chestnut Street, the second Sunday of each month from October to June at 8 P.M. You can call ahead to find out who's appearing. Concerts are followed by refreshments and an open sing-along. You should be able to make new friends, too.

Admission is $4, or free if you're a member of the Society or under 12 years of age.

The Folksong Society also sponsors the annual **Philadelphia Folk Festival** the last weekend before Labor Day. This is a three-day, rain or shine event with afternoon workshops, evening concerts and overnight camping at the Old Poole Farm campgrounds near Schwenksville, Pa. Tickets are available from Ticketron or the Folk Society for the entire weekend or individual afternoon or evening events. Thousands of folk-lovers participate, so if you're interested be sure to get the details early so you won't be left out.

Just in case you can't make it in August, inquire about the Folk Society's annual **Spring Thing** that takes place during a weekend in May or the **Fall Folk Festival** that happens on a September weekend.

PHILADELPHIA ORCHESTRA
Academy of Music* (performances)
1420 Locust Street—19102 (offices)
893-1900 or 893-1930 (box office)

Hours: About a dozen series of subscription concerts are
at 8:00 or 8:30 on Monday, Tuesday, Thursday, Friday
and Saturday evenings. Matinees are Fridays at 2. The
season is September to May. For summer schedule,
read about the Mann Music Center.

Cost: Individual concert ticket prices are $8 to $38.
They're available at the box office 4 weeks prior to a
performance. Mail orders are also accepted a month
ahead (include a stamped, self-addressed envelope with
your request and check or money order). $2 General
Admission tickets for the Amphitheater go on sale one
hour prior to Friday matinees, Friday and Saturday
evening concerts.

Box Office Hours: Weekdays, 10 to 9, or till 5:30 if there is
no evening performance. Open Sunday only if a performance is scheduled.

E & H: See Chapter 16.

The Philadelphia Orchestra is said to be one of the finest orchestras in the world. (In Philadelphia, we say it's
the finest.) When the first cultural exchange in decades
between the United States and the People's Republic of
China was planned, our orchestra was chosen to make the
historic tour in September, 1973.

The Philadelphia Orchestra is as old as this century.
Following the Leopold Stokowski era from 1912 to 1935,
Eugene Ormandy took over direction of the orchestra in
1936. Riccardo Muti assumed the role of Music Director
and Conductor of the Philadelphia Orchestra in 1980. A
distinguished list of additional guest conductors, in-
strumentalists and vocal soloists appear.

In celebration of the 200th anniversary of the U.S. Constitution, six American composers have been chosen to
create new works that will be premiered by the orchestra
in 1987.

If you want to learn more about the Philadelphia
Orchestra you can tour the Academy of Music (see Chapter 13). The orchestra's **Concerts for Children and Students** are described in Chapter 15.

The Philadelphia Orchestra also presents a series of pre-
concert lectures that are open to the public free of charge.
These **Orchestra Insights** take place in the Academy of
Music Ballroom preceding six Thursday evening concerts.

Another series called **Meet the Composer** enables you to chat with today's top composers in conjunction with concerts that include their works. This program also takes place in the Academy Ballroom and general admission tickets are $3 at the door.

Call for details on both of these exciting opportunities to get really close to the music.

PHILADELPHIA YOUTH ORCHESTRA
c/o Penn Center Academy, 1423 Arch Street—19102
293-9445

Talented young people between the ages of 14 and 21 can audition in May or September for this 100-piece orchestra which is conducted by former Philadelphia Orchestra member Joseph Primavera.

Since 1940, this talented orchestra has had a 35-week annual season of Saturday morning rehearsals at 1423 Arch Street, and concerts for children, a benefit performance and an annual closing concert in late April or May at the Academy of Music.

The orchestra made its first major tour in 1981. They travelled to Australia to perform in the Australia Youth Music Festival. In 1983 they played at the Edinboro Festival in England. In 1985 they played for over 50,000 people in China and Hong Kong.

The Youth Orchestra is the only full-sized symphony of its kind in the area. It's a treat to attend their concerts. It's a bigger treat to be a member. Call or write for information.

PHILLY POPS
735-5266

The Philly Pops was founded in 1980. Under the baton of Peter Nero, and with guest performers like Robert Merrill, Tommy Tune and Tug McGraw (reciting "Casey at the Bat"), they're an overnight sensation.

The Philly Pops performs at the Academy of Music from October to May in a choice of three series of four concerts each. One series is Sunday afternoons at 3 P.M.; one is Mondays at 8 P.M.; the other is a combination of Tuesday and Wednesday evenings at 8.

Tickets can be purchased individually from the Academy box office prior to each concert, if you're lucky, or in a series from the All Star–Forum, 1530 Locust Street, Phila., Pa. 19102. Call for programs and dates and try to see this fun-filled musical entertainment.

233

ROBIN HOOD DELL EAST
East Fairmount Park
Near Kelly and Strawberry Mansion Drives
477–8810 (summer months only)

SEPTA: Buses 7, 39, 54, 61, 85. There's plenty of free
parking.

E & H: Anyone in a wheelchair can be seated comfortably
at the Dell. Try to arrange in advance to park at the lot
that's adjacent to the main entrance. Refreshments are
accessible, but the restrooms are reached by steps.

For spectacular musical events, come to "Summer Festival of Stars" under the stars at Robin Hood Dell East,
compliments of the city's Department of Recreation.

Any Monday, Wednesday or Friday at 8 P.M. in July or
August might feature singers, dancers or musicians from
Philadelphia or around the world. (Rain dates are on the
following evenings.)

Recent audiences were treated to jazz, folk and pop
music programs with Natalie Cole, The Commodores, The
Spinners and The Four Tops. Gospelrama, ethnic festivals
with international flavor, ballet and opera are also on the
schedule.

General Admission is $2; reserved seats are $3, $5 and
$8. Watch for June and July newspaper announcements
with the summer's schedule. Call for ticket information,
or write to the city's Cultural and Special Events Office,
Belmont and Parkside Avenues, Phila., Pa. 19131.

ROCK AND POP CONCERTS
Call 976–HITS or The Spectrum, 389–5000

The latest jazz, folk and rock shows head first to Philadelphia—all compliments of the **Electric Factory Concerts.** Lines have been known to form for blocks around
the Spectrum as fans anticipate the crush for tickets.

Billboard Magazine has named Electric Factory Concerts as the nation's top promoter of rock concerts. At the
same time, they named the Spectrum* as the nation's top
facility for rock concerts.

Electric Factory Concerts also stages programs at the
Tower Theater with approximately 3,000 seats at 69th
and Ludlow Streets in Upper Darby (352–0313), the
Academy of Music, John F. Kennedy Stadium, Mann
Music Center, the Walnut Street Theater and area college
campuses.

For more night club entertainment, see Chapter 18.

UNIVERSITY MUSEUM* CONCERTS
33rd and Spruce Streets—19104
898-4015

The Museum String Orchestra, under the direction of Philadelphia Orchestra member Donald Montanaro and other great artists, performs at this concert series that's usually held in winter and spring on four Sunday afternoons at 3.

The programs generally include music that is rarely heard in this area. There's also an annual tribute to Johann Sebastian Bach.

Admission is free and no tickets are necessary. Children who attend must be accompanied by an adult; these concerts are billed as "Adult Music Programs."

Call the museum for information, or send a long, self-addressed stamped envelope with your request for an "Adult Entertainment Program" and schedule for "Music at the Museum." They're available in September.

VALLEY FORGE MUSIC FAIR
Route 202 at Devon Exit
Devon, Pa. 19333
296-9994

The Valley Forge Music Fair is a 45-minute drive from center city Philadelphia (west on the Schuylkill Expressway Route 76 and south on Route 202 at King of Prussia). It's theater-in-the-round—open year-round.

There are one-night stands, weekend attractions and week-long runs of concerts and shows. The Music Fair bills only the best entertainment for its audience of 2,800. Tickets are sold for each show and they can be ordered by mail or phone with Visa or Master Charge (644-5000) once you know the date and ticket price of your choice. There's plenty of free parking for everyone and special group rates are available in advance. Call 647-2307 for group reservations.

To find out what's coming up, either call or look in the daily papers. **Children's Musical Theater** at Valley Forge Music Fair is described in Chapter 15.

There are a number of other orchestras and musical groups that periodically perform throughout Philadelphia. There are also musical celebrations that take place annually.

The **AMERICAN SOCIETY OF ANCIENT INSTRUMENTS**, the first of its kind in the United States, was founded in Philadelphia in 1929. This chamber orchestra is devoted to playing baroque and Renaissance music on authentic 18th century instruments. Performances take place at museums, cultural centers, college campuses and an annual festival held three Sunday afternoons in May at the Pennsylvania Academy of the Fine Arts*.

After each concert you have a chance to talk with the musicians and see their antique instruments. This is a rare opportunity to touch a pardessus de viole, viola da amour or viola da gamba and see if you can tell the difference from their contemporary counterparts. If you can't get to a concert and would like to see an exhibit of the instruments, they're on permanent display at the Fleisher Collection of the Free Library of Philadelphia*.

There's no charge to attend performances by the American Society of Ancient Instruments, but contributions are accepted. For additional information, call 247-7823.

You've already read briefly about **THE BASICALLY BACH FESTIVAL**, under direction of Michael Korn, with the Philadelphia Singers and Concerto Soloists Chamber Orchestra. The celebration is in November at locations in Chestnut Hill*. World-famous artists perform, many on authentic period instruments as they would have for Bach's 18th century audience. Don't miss this rare opportunity. Call 247-4070 after Labor Day for a schedule and ticket information.

CONCERTS BY CANDLELIGHT are six summer Sunday evenings at 7:30 at Laurel Hill* in East Fairmount Park. They usually feature soloists or chamber groups. A reception follows each concert. Tickets are $7. For tickets and schedule information, call Women for Greater Philadelphia at 627-1770.

MOZART ON THE SQUARE takes place for two weeks in May on and around Rittenhouse Square*. It's been an annual musical celebration since 1979 with chamber music, opera, orchestral concerts and recitals. All of the noon events are free. Tickets for evening chamber concerts are $4 and $6; for orchestral concerts, $10 and $12. There are senior citizen and student discounts. Call

988-9830 for festival information. Mozart would have loved this series.

The **PENNSYLVANIA ORCHESTRA,** under the baton of Maurice Kaplow, is the resident orchestra of the Pennsylvania Ballet*. On occasion, they expand their ranks to a full-size orchestra and do concerts on their own. Their program selections range from 13th century to contemporary pieces. Call 978-1400 if you'd like more information.

The **RELACHE Ensemble for Contemporary Music** was formed in 1977. A core of 15 inspired musicians and vocalists develop and present contemporary music, mainly by American composers, and mostly that you might not otherwise hear. Much of what they perform is experimental music.

Relache is "in residence" at Mandel Theater of Drexel University where they perform several concerts annually. They also present three concerts each year at The Painted Bride and produce the "Praxis" series of four concerts each year at Drexel featuring composers and performers of international renown.

Tickets for Relache concerts are $6, or $4 for students and senior citizens. You can buy them in advance or just prior to a concert. Call 844-2018 or 387-4115 for additional information.

A final note: If you're a fan of the late Mario Lanza, you'll want to stop by the **MARIO LANZA MINI-MUSEUM** at 1414 Snyder Avenue (468-3623). Hours are Monday to Saturday, 10 to 6.

The Mario Lanza Institute was organized to pay tribute to the singer and to provide inspiration and scholarship awards to aspiring young vocalists. The Institute also established this mini-museum in one room of a South Philadelphia record shop that's not far from where Lanza was born and raised. It's chock-full of photographs and memorabilia.

Theater

Where are the major shows and Broadway productions in Philadelphia? Many of Philadelphia's stages for the performing arts are described at the very beginning of this chapter. You've read about the **SHUBERT** and the **PAINTED BRIDE**.

The **FORREST***, 1114 Walnut Street (923-1515), was completely refurbished in 1977. It has 1,800 balcony, mezzanine, box and staggered orchestra seats.

Several theater companies present live **theater for children**. These are described in Chapter 15.

Where else can you see provocative and entertaining drama in Philadelphia? Read on.

ANNENBERG CENTER*
3680 Walnut Street—19104
898-6701 (program information)
898-6791 (ticket information and phone reservations)

SEPTA: Buses D, 40, 42; subway–surface cars (all except #10) to 36th and Sansom Streets.
E & H: See Chapter 16.

You can indulge yourself in a showcase of innovation and classic drama at any of the Annenberg Theaters: Studio (smallest, with 120 seats), Harold Prince (200 seats), Annenberg School Theater (382 seats) or Zellerbach (most frequently used, with 970 seats).

Six plays are presented as part of Annenberg's annual subscription series. Three are co-produced with other Philadelphia area theaters and festivals, namely the American Music Theater Festival, the Philadelphia Festival Theater for New Plays and the People's Light & Theater Company. (All are described later in this chapter.)

Some of the stars who've appeared here in recent seasons are Zoe Caldwell, Jose Ferrer, Estelle Parsons, Rachel Roberts, Robert Shaw, Liv Ullman and Mary Ure.

The admission prices vary. Tickets are available individually or on a discount subscription plan. Group, senior citizen and student discounts are available.

Annenberg also offers a series of **Very Special Events** in addition to its series. "The Flying Karamazov Brothers" and Steve Reich in Concert are indeed very special events.

Annenberg Center Theater for Children is described in Chapter 15.

Zellerbach is also home for the Philadelphia Drama

Guild. Harold Prince is home for the Philadelphia Festival Theater for New Plays. You'll be reading about these later in the chapter.

Be sure to get your seasonal program.

And don't say that Philadelphia doesn't provide unusual and exciting theatrical experiences.

CAFE THEATER OF ALLENS LANE
Allens Lane and McCallum Street—19119
848-9384 or 438-4222

SEPTA: Bus H to McCallum Street and Mt. Pleasant Avenue, and then a short walk.
E & H: There's one step at the entrance. Theater is on 2nd floor and reached by stairs only.

A 50-member ensemble company works and studies together every year to present four classic or avant-garde shows. Curtain time is 8 P.M. on Fridays and Saturdays. Each of the productions runs for six consecutive weekends, starting in late September, mid-November, January and April. Tickets are $9 on Friday, $10 on Saturday, or $4.50 on Friday night for students and senior citizens. Group rates can be arranged in advance.

Acting classes are held here, too. You may decide to audition for the permanent company in January or June.

This is appropriately called a cafe theater because of its unique setting in Fairmount Park. The theater opens 45 minutes before curtain so you can picnic before the show. The intermission is time for coffee and cake at your candle-lit table. If you prefer, bring wine and cheese. Discussion with the cast sometimes follows the performance.

Allens Lane Children's Theater is described later in Chapter 15.

CITY OF PHILADELPHIA'S
DRAMA GROUPS TO JOIN

The Department of Recreation conducts an extensive four-part drama program each fall and winter at its indoor facilities throughout the city.

Creative dramatics involves pre-schoolers to 12-year-olds in spontaneous acting out of stories, poetry and their daily lives.

Formal dramatics offers basic training in acting, movement, dialogue and stage craft. Skits and plays are the end result of practical exercises and classes in theory.

Environmental theater offers workshops in scenery, lighting, music, costumes, make-up and the like—all with the goal of being able to create a complete production.

Talent shows are conducted at local recreation centers, followed by district shows and two play festivals showcasing the city's top amateur talents. Who knows where the stars will go from here? After all, Philadelphia is a City of Stars. Just ask Bill Cosby, Joey Bishop, David Brenner, Fabian, Eddie Fisher, Jack Klugman, Lola Falana, Wilt Chamberlain or Bobby Rydell.

The talent shows and dramatics workshops continue in summer months at local recreation centers on an individual basis. Call your neighborhood recreation center for their schedule, or the Department of Recreation's Cultural and Special Events Division (686-0151) to see if there's a program beginning soon near you.

Youngsters from ages six to 16 get together at neighborhood recreation centers each summer to write and produce original **Fire Prevention Plays.** They're based on an annual theme which is chosen by the Philadelphia Fire Department. Local fire battalions give helping hands.

Competitions are held in the districts and the winners compete at a citywide finals production. The top four finalist groups present their plays at Kennedy Plaza.

You'll be surprised how amateur talents can dream up and act out imaginative stories about hazards like faulty heaters, oily rags and open flames.

On second thought, you won't be amazed. When you look at television commercials, you know that a 10-year-old can probably come up with better ideas.

Don't forget about the other **summer camp*** opportunities provided by the city. Of course, there are those that focus on sports and recreation. There's also a Summer Arts Camp and there's a Carousel House Camp that combines a variety of recreational and cultural activities for handicapped youngsters.

DINNER THEATER
(See Chapter 18.)

FORREST THEATER*
1114 Walnut Street—19107
923-1515

SEPTA: Buses D, 9, 42; trolley 23.
E & H: Theater entrance and orchestra seating are street
    level. There are 6 orchestra locations for people in
    wheelchairs. You must notify the theater in advance.

Restrooms are either up or down a long flight of stairs.

Four or five Broadway productions make up the Forrest Theater Subscription Series each year. Subscribers are guaranteed seats to see top stars in smash hits. Recent shows have been "Cats," "Dreamgirls," "La Cage aux Folles" and "My One and Only."

Subscriptions to the Forrest Series are ordered c/o The Shubert Organization, P.O. Box 1006, Times Square Station, New York, NY 10108. For details, call 1–800–233–3123.

Showtimes are Monday to Saturday evenings, a weekday and Saturday matinees. Tickets are also available at the Forrest box office prior to and during each show's run.

The Forrest remains lit most of the year, even when it isn't alive with the Broadway series. Musical and dramatic hits are booked for short stays. Watch the newspapers for announcements, or call for a schedule.

FREEDOM THEATER
1346 N. Broad Street—19121
765–2793

SEPTA: Buses C, 57; Broad Street subway to Girard Avenue.

E & H: No wheelchair access. The theaters are on the lower level and reached by stairs.

Freedom Theater is a unique showplace in the Heritage House, where the great American actor Edwin Forrest once lived. Forrest was born in Philadelphia in 1806 and we have a theater named in his memory. Freedom Theater is Philadelphia's oldest and most active black theater. There are actually two theaters: one seats 120, the other, 130.

A dozen or so talented actors and actresses stage six productions a year in addition to a special summer happening, "Moments of Sharing." There could be musicals, dance, drama, poetry, or who knows what.

Recent productions have been "A Scattering of Seeds," "12 Going on 20" and "Under Pressure." Many of Freedom Theater's performers have gone on to successful careers in television and theater.

Shows are usually on Friday, Saturday and Sunday and there are 12 performances of each. Tickets are $10 or $15, or $8 for children under 16, with discounts for senior citizens and groups of 25 or more.

Freedom Theater also brings its dramatic talents to

schools and centers in the community (see Chapter 13). A school for performing arts is conducted at Heritage House for adults and young people. Auditions are held for all study programs, and there's an open casting for all of Freedom Theater's productions. If you're interested, call for specifics.

LA SALLE MUSIC THEATER
20th Street and Olney Avenue—19141
951-1410

Hours: July and early August, Wednesday to Friday evenings at 8, Saturday at 6 and 9:30, Sunday at 7.
Cost: $12 and $13.50. Discounts are available for students, senior citizens, groups and early subscribers. Tickets can be ordered by mail or at the box office.
SEPTA: Bus 26.
E & H: Wheelchairs can be accommodated, but you should notify the theater ahead on the day that you'll be attending.

Since 1962, the LaSalle Music Theater has been presenting outstanding musical shows every summer.

Recent productions have included "Gypsy," "No, No, Nanette" and "Sweet Charity." Call for information and a schedule for this summer's show.

The 380-seat theater doesn't go dark the rest of the year. The **Masque Theater of LaSalle** raises the curtain for a fall and spring production and for student drama workshops.

Tickets for these shows are $4, or $3 for students and senior citizens. The selections are drawn from musicals, comedy or drama.

THE PHILADELPHIA COMPANY
592-8333

The Philadelphia Company was founded in 1974 to present Philadelphians with new plays by American writers. Their stage is the Plays and Players* Playhouse at 1714 Delancey Street.

Four or five shows are presented each year from November to June. Each has a two to three week run. Tickets are $9.50 to $16, but if you subscribe to the series, you get one play free. There are also student discounts.

Among the company's recent Philadelphia premieres are "Extremities," by William Mastrosimone, "Painting Churches," by Tina Howe and "Nuts" by Tom Topor.

They've also performed "True West" and "Fool for Love" by Sam Shepard.

If gutsy, provocative, innovative drama appeals to you, call for a schedule, or write to The Philadelphia Company, The Bourse, Suite 735, 21 S. 5th Street, Philadelphia, Pa. 19106.

PHILADELPHIA DRAMA GUILD
563-7530 or 898-6791 (Annenberg box office)

The Philadelphia Drama Guild began in 1971 as the city's only professional production company. Five well-known plays and frequent premieres starring well-known talents are brought to Zellerbach Theater at Annenberg* every year from October to May. Each show has a three-week run. There are 7:30 or 8 P.M. curtains Tuesday to Sunday, and Wednesday and Sunday matinees at 2.

Tickets can be purchased prior to each show (if you're lucky) or by a season subscription that offers two shows free. The subscription hot-line is 563-PLAY. Discounts for students, senior citizens and groups are available in advance.

Call the Drama Guild for their schedule and brochure, or write to them at 112 S. 16th Street, Philadelphia, Pa. 19102, and watch for announcements in the local newspapers.

PLAYS AND PLAYERS
1714 Delancey Street—19103
735-0630

SEPTA: Buses 2, 90, or a short walk south from Chestnut or Walnut Streets.
E & H: The entrance and lobby are level and a ramp leads to the theater. Wheelchair access.

This is one of the oldest little theater groups in the Philadelphia area, and it certainly enjoys a fine reputation. This charming 324-seat structure on quaint Delancey Street is historically certified.

Four shows are presented from October to May. They run three weeks each with Thursday to Saturday evening performances at 8 and one Sunday matinee at 2:30 for each show. The fare is comedy, light drama and suspense.

Tickets are $7 for general admission, $6 for students and senior citizens. Inquire in advance about group rates for 14 or more.

Classes for teens and adults involve workshops and

productions. Admission to these shows is $1. Call for specifics.

Memberships to the Plays and Players Club are available at various levels: single, couple, student, out-of-towners and so forth. This is a great opportunity if you're interested in theater. The club has a cocktail hour in the evening; the atmosphere is social and the talk is stimulating.

The **Children's Theater** of Plays and Players is described in Chapter 15.

SOCIETY HILL PLAYHOUSE
507 South 8th Street—19147
923–0210

Hours: October to mid-June with each show having a designated run. Wednesday to Saturday evenings at 8:30, and sometimes Sunday evenings and weekend matinees.
Cost: Tickets are $12 to $17.50, with discounts for subscribers and groups who arrange in advance, and sometimes for students.
SEPTA: Buses 47, 90.
E & H: Theater is on 2nd floor and there's no elevator.

An open acting company has been providing the drama at Society Hill Playhouse since 1960. It's thought of as Philadelphia's oldest professional off-Broadway theater. Four or five shows are presented each year. Recent productions have been "Nunsense," "Quilters" and Bertolt Brecht's "The Good Woman of Setzuan."

In addition, the S.H.P. Second Stage series presents premieres of new plays to area theater-goers.

There are acting classes for adults and an opportunity to audition for the Playhouse's productions.

Call or watch for newspaper announcements to find out which shows might interest you.

PHILADELPHIA YOUTH THEATER performs at Society Hill Playhouse as well. This is an Alternative Program for students between the ages of 15 and 18 who live in Philadelphia or surrounding communities.

The productions are a group effort. It's a training ground in real theater for budding actors, actresses and technicians. In addition to acting, students get to work on sets, props and costumes.

Their approach to drama is young and fresh. A contemporary version of "The Taming of the Shrew" was recently adapted by youth and for youth in this "almost adult" theater.

One play is produced early in December, Shakespeare is in February and another show is in the last two weeks of May. There isn't any charge to see any of these performances. And who knows what future stars you might get to see?

TEMPLE UNIVERSITY
Tomlinson Theater
13th and Norris Streets—19122
787-1122

SEPTA: Bus C on Broad Street; trolley 23 on 11th or 12th Streets. There's free attended parking in Lot #6 adjacent to the theater (enter on Diamond Street).

E & H: Special arrangements must be made in advance for people in wheelchairs to enter by side door. Otherwise, there are steps.

The productions at Temple theaters are under the auspices of Temple's drama department. This is where you might see tomorrow's stars today.

Main Stage productions take place on Temple's main campus at the 480-seat Tomlinson Theater. Each show usually has a two-week run during the college year with evening curtain times and Sunday matinees. Musicals, comedies, classics and contemporary drama make up the season. Smaller productions take place at the more intimate Randall Lab Theater or at Stage Three (see below). Inquire about these, too.

Tickets can be purchased for Tomlinson and Stage Three productions individually or in a series. Naturally, student discounts are available as well as special rates for senior citizens and groups.

Schedules for Tomlinson Theater and Stage Three are available in the late summer. They can be mailed, or you can call or stop by the information desk at Temple University Center City, 1619 Walnut Street, to get yours.

Stage Three
1619 Walnut Street—19103
787-1122 or 787-1619

SEPTA: Buses 2, 9, 42, D; Market or Chestnut Street routes.

E & H: Entrance is level with street and there's an elevator to basement theater.

Temple University's Center City campus opened in

1973 and the 180-seat Stage Three was inaugurated in the spring of 1974. The theatre was once the home of the Mike Douglas Television Show.

Many of Stage Three's productions are Philadelphia premieres. They're presented two weeks at a time, and they have evening and Sunday matinee performances. **Children's Theater** at T.U.C.C. is on frequent Saturdays. See Chapter 15 for more about this.

THEATER CENTER PHILADELPHIA
622 South 4th Street—19147
925-2682

Hours: The season begins in mid-October and at least 5 major productions are presented. Each show runs for 4 weeks with 20 performances on Wednesday to Saturday nights at 8:30 and Sundays at 3 P.M.

Cost: $8 to $12. Student, senior citizen, series subscription and group rates available.

SEPTA: Bus 50.

E & H: Theater is on ground floor and there are no steps.

The concept of Theater Center Philadelphia (T.C.P.) is unique in Philadelphia. Local playwrights arrange in advance to present their new works at the weekly **Playwright's Workshop.** The public is invited to listen to and critique them on Tuesdays at 8 P.M. Admission is $3. Many of the pieces read in these open forums go on to become T.C.P. productions.

T.C.P. also stages modern and experimental plays that are rarely or never seen in Philadelphia. The works of Brecht, Pirandello, Sternheim and Wedekind are among those that have been "rediscovered" at this double storefront theater in the heart of the South Street district. Seating is arranged for each production to accommodate an audience of about 125.

Acting workshops are held for children and adults who are beginners or advanced performers. There's an open casting when it's necessary for additional roles. There's also an occasional **children's theater** on weekend afternoons.

Another facet of T.C.P. is its annual summer **Black Theater Festival.** Philadelphia or world premieres of works by Afro-Americans are staged from late June to early October. The plays might be contemporary or revivals of classics. Showtime is Wednesday to Saturday nights at 8 and Sundays at 7, and ticket prices are the same as above.

If you've considered yourself a would-be actor or

playwright, Theater Center Philadelphia is an ideal place to try out your talent.

WALNUT STREET THEATER
9th and Walnut Streets—19107
574–3550 or WALNUT–5

SEPTA: Buses D, 9, 38, 42, 47, 61 or any Chestnut Street route.
E & H: See Chapter 16.

The Walnut Street Theater is the oldest continuously operating theater in the English-speaking world. It opened in 1808 with a gala circus performance. It was designated a National Historic Landmark in 1964, and a two-year total renovation of the Walnut was completed in 1971. The Walnut was the site of the historic first debate between then-President Gerald R. Ford and Jimmy Carter in September, 1976.

The Walnut Street Theater Company produces five mainstage plays a year from November to March, including musicals and Shakespeare. Subscriptions are available, and there are discounts for early purchases, students, groups and senior citizens. Tickets for individual performances are also available at the box office.

There are evening performances during the week and Saturdays, as well as a weekday and weekend matinees. This is a popular series, so call in advance to find out what's scheduled.

In addition to its two-level, 1,052 seat theater, the Walnut has two more intimate theaters in its adjoining building at 825 Walnut Street where you can enjoy four plays a year. Most of the plays are new, as part of the Studio Theater series.

When the Walnut Street Theater Company isn't presenting plays, its stages are home to theatrical road shows, dance, opera and musical programs. The Walnut is a center for all of the arts.

THE WILMA THEATER
2030 Sansom Street—19103
963-0249

SEPTA: Buses D, 9, 17, 42 or a short walk from Market Street routes.
E & H: There's one step outside. Call ahead for ramp to be placed. Complete wheelchair access in the theater.

The Wilma Theater also gives Philadelphians a pot-pourri of innovative drama. There are original works, multi-media presentations and staging that provokes the imagination. Four shows are presented each year from October to June. Each runs about three weeks.

Curtain is Tuesday to Friday at 8 P.M., Saturday at 5 and 9, and Sunday at 2. Tickets are $12 to $17, and there are discounts for subscribers, students, senior citizens and groups of 12 or more.

There's something for everyone on stage in Philadelphia.

Philadelphians can revel in two local annual theater festivals born in the 1980s.

The **AMERICAN MUSIC THEATER FESTIVAL** takes place six weeks in September and October on stages at Annenberg, Mandell Theater at Drexel University and the Walnut Street Theater. Look for world premieres during the celebration, and don't be surprised to find that many of the works go on to be hits in New York. Watch for newspaper announcements, call 988-9050 for festival information, or write to the American Music Theater Festival, Suite 905, 1617 John F. Kennedy Boulevard, Philadelphia, Pa. 19103.

The **PHILADELPHIA FESTIVAL THEATER FOR NEW PLAYS** is professional, non-profit theater devoted exclusively to the production of new plays by American playwrights. Thousands are submitted from around the country, and four or five are selected each year. Almost seventy-five percent of the plays presented since the festival began in 1981 have since been published or presented elsewhere.

Harold Prince Theater at Annenberg is the festival's stage every spring. Each production has a two-week run. Subscriptions and group discounts are available (call 222-5000) and series holders also can plan to attend performances followed by discussion with the playwright. For single ticket information, call 898-6791. This is rightfully billed as "the only theater event of its kind in Philadelphia."

Many theaters and little groups in and around Philadelphia offer a variety of outstanding and unusual productions. They often look for members to participate, as well as for audiences to enjoy their shows. Here's a few.

BIG SMALL THEATER was founded in 1981 to present original musical shows of a political and social nature. They frequently interact with the audience; their music combines jazz and contemporary styles; their stage is simple and realistic at the Painted Bride, community centers, churches and schools. big SMALL Theater makes you think about human issues. If you think you'd like to participate in this theater experience, call 662-0441 or write to them at 3601 Locust Walk, Philadelphia, Pa. 19104 for a schedule and ticket information.

Four plays and popular children's theater are presented from October to June at the 140-seat CHELTENHAM PLAYHOUSE at 439 Ashbourne Road in Cheltenham, Pa. (379-4027). The schedule is available in late June. This is part of an extensive cultural program from the Cheltenham Arts Center (379-4660).

ETAGE produces mostly experimental theater and original drama. Most of it involves mixed media with a mixed bag of theatrics. ETAGE stands for "environmental theater and gallery experiment." If you're looking for avant-garde performances in Philadelphia, call 978-0494 to find out the details.

A charming old mill was converted in 1923 into the 135-seat HEDGEROW THEATER on Rose Valley Road in Moylan, Pa. It had operated almost continuously since then as a year-round community theater. Fire gutted the historic Hedgerow in 1985. Until it's rebuilt, the dedicated resident company of 12 is presenting their dramas, mystery and comedy at the Theater of Widener University at Route 320 and 16th Avenue in Chester, Pa. Performances are every Thursday, Friday and Saturday at 8 P.M. Call 565-4211 for details. They also go on tour to area schools with delightful children's productions. The Hedgerow Playhouse also enjoys an outstanding reputation for their acting classes. They're really quite famous in Philadelphia.

OLD ACADEMY PLAYERS presents six performances each, of six popular shows from September to June at their theater (which used to be a church) at 3544 Indian Queen Lane. Cake and coffee are served to 130 theater-goers at intermission.

Curtain for each show is at 8:30 P.M. on Friday and Saturday for three consecutive weekends. Tickets are $5, with discounts available for groups of 15 or more.

This is a delightful way to see a favorite comedy, mystery or drama. For a schedule, call 849-7406.

Contemporary and classic drama is electrifying when it's performed by the **PEOPLE'S LIGHT AND THEATER COMPANY** located at 39 Conestoga Road in Malvern, Pa. 19355 (644-3500). It's worth the 40-minute drive from center city Philadelphia to see this dynamic troupe in their dramatic country home: a magnificently converted 200-year-old stone barn that's now a top caliber 400-seat theater.

Four mainstage productions are presented annually, each with a month-long run. Performances are nightly except Monday, with a matinee on Sunday (a nice time to picnic before the show).

People's Light also produces an annual New Play Festival in August and September. This is another outstanding opportunity to see untried new one-act and full-length American plays. Call for additional information.

If you've never experienced *mime,* make it a point to see **THE QUIET RIOT COMEDY THEATER.** Their show includes some verbal story-telling, but most of it is silent. It incorporates clever costumes, dance, gymnastics, creative lighting and sound backdrops to tell the tale.

The Quiet Riot Comedy Theater has appeared at the Walnut Street Theater, the Philadelphia Museum of Art, the Philadelphia Folk Festival and almost every area college theater. They frequently appear on stage at the Free Library of Philadelphia...a logical place for a silent performance. Shh!

The Quiet Riot Comedy Theater also brings its show to you (see Chapter 13). For information, call 885-8825.

Chapter 11.
Libraries.

A library is more than a place to do research and home-work assignments. A library can be a source of fun. A place for enjoyment and self-improvement.

In Philadelphia, we're fortunate in having libraries of all types and sizes. Many are part of museums, cultural and historical attractions. Those listed in this chapter with an asterisk (*) appear elsewhere in this book with more details. Refer to the Index.

Some libraries require you do your reading there, while others allow you to borrow their books. In some cases you have to be a member to use the facilities. Some libraries even offer tours.

If you have questions on a particular subject, it's wise to call the library in advance to see if they can help you.

"The Fabulous Freebie"

FREE LIBRARY OF PHILADELPHIA
Central Library—Logan Square
19th and Vine Streets—19103
686-5322, for instant information

Hours: Monday to Wednesday, 9 to 9; Thursday and Fri-day, 9 to 6; Saturday, 9 to 5; Sunday, 1 to 5. Closed Sun-day in summer and 15 holidays during the year. Hours vary with the branches and the season, so call ahead to be sure. All branch libraries are listed under "Free Library" in the White Pages of the Philadelphia Tele-phone Directory.

Tours: Scheduled a month in advance for groups of no more than 15 (larger groups will be divided) for week-days from 9 to 4. Allow one hour. An adult must accom-pany students. For children through 8th grade, call the Office for Work with Children, 686-5372; for 9th grad-ers through adults, call the Office for Work with Adults-Young Adults, 686-5344. Tours of the Rare Book Department are weekdays at 11; groups are sched-uled at other times by appointment. Call 686-5416.

Cost: There is no charge for tours or any of the special events at the Free Library. Membership is available, free, to any resident of or student in Philadelphia, to workers who pay the City wage tax and non-residents over 65 years old. For anyone else, the annual cost is $15.

Lunch: A cafeteria on the Central Library's 4th floor is open to the public weekdays, 9 to 4, and Saturdays, except in summer, 10 to 2. Groups are not permitted between 11 and 1:30.

SEPTA: Buses 32, 33, 38.

Other: The Library Store offers unusual stationery, jewelry, posters, books and items you'd like for your personal library.

E & H: See Chapter 16.

The Free Library of Philadelphia houses over four million bound volumes in the Central Library and 49 neighborhood branches. About one-third of those books are in the Central Library. The three regional branches are Northeast at Cottman Avenue and Oakland Street (725-3377), Northwest at Chelten Avenue and Green Street (843-9800) and West Philadelphia at 52nd and Sansom Streets (823-7424).

The Free Library has grown from its original three-room home in 1894 in City Hall to one of the country's largest library systems with a main building that's among the biggest of its kind in the country.

The Free Library is for you. Members of the Free Library may borrow as many as 12 books at one time for as long as 21 days, and sometimes for the entire summer. Besides having books, the Free Library has changing exhibits, displays and special programs.

A good place to start your visit to the Free Library is the General Information Department on the second floor. The knowledgeable staff answers thousands of questions each month by phone and to visitors. These people can make your research easier. General Information also houses all telephone directories for Pennsylvania, Delaware and New Jersey as well as for all U.S. cities with populations over 100,000.

The Computer Based Information Center (686-2860) is also housed on the second floor. You have five minutes to search at no charge for news items from The Inquirer or Daily News on one of the Center's five different information systems. Over a million abstracts are stored in nearly 400 data bases. The "V.I.C.S." system here and in the three regional branch libraries provides career information for high school students, people making career changes and those re-entering the job market. There's no charge for use of the V.I.C.S. The Computer Center is open weekdays from 9 to 5.

Are you looking for a particular newspaper? The Free Library subscribes to over 130 newspapers, including several foreign ones. This is a great way to practice a foreign language, to find out what's going on back home or to look up the news from an important day in your past.

The Social Science and History Department's collection includes almost 100,000 maps, charts and guidebooks to most major cities. It's also where you'll find the Regional Foundation Center to research fund-raising and proposal writing. An appointment is necessary (686–5423) if you're a first-time user of these resources.

There are more than 12,000 completely scored musical compositions in the Fleisher Collection of Orchestral Music, making this the largest collection of its kind in the world. Most of the classical, jazz or show music can be listened to on earphones.

The Free Library has one of the world's finest collections of literature on cars, motorcycles, bicycles and carriages in the Automobile Reference Collection. You'll be interested to know that almost all of the 10,000 or so annual U.S. government's publications are in the Government Publications Department.

We think every conceivable hobby and profession is covered in the Business, Science and Industry Department. (Business books, financial books, magazines and popular literature are the specialty of the **Mercantile Library** at 1021 Chestnut Street, 592–5584.)

The Rare Book Department is like a rich Uncle Henry's private paneled library. It's lavishly furnished to display hundreds of old manuscripts like Edgar Allan Poe's "Murders in the Rue Morgue" and "The Raven." And for those who have grown up to love her tales, Beatrix Potter's first editions and many of her original drawings are here. Special tours of the Rare Book Department are available as described above.

The Film Department allows borrowers to take home 16mm films and video cassettes. And there are 2,000 films and over 650 videos to choose from. There's more about this service in the section of Chapter 13 on tours "to go."

Most branches feature a **Children's Department** which you'll be reading about in 30 seconds.

Of course, the Free Library has fiction. With over 40,000 volumes, it's the largest collection in Pennsylvania. Over 125,000 books on all subjects are available for borrowing from the Central Lending Department. We could obviously fill a book on all of the departments, books, events and services at the Free Library. Is it any wonder it's called "The Fabulous Freebie"?

The Children's Department
Central Library
686-5372

Hours: Weekdays, 9 to 6; Saturday, 9 to 5; Sunday, 1 to 5, except when the Central Library is closed.

Tours: Call at least a month in advance to schedule groups of no more than 15 and up to 8th grade level. Allow one hour for story time, a short film and discussion of the library. Groups can visit the Rare Book Department and outside the Children's Department by special request.

Cost: There's no charge for tours. Membership is open, free, to any Philadelphia youngster who is able to write his or her full name. Up to 5 books may be borrowed at a time for a 3-week period.

E & H: See Chapter 16.

The shelves of the Children's Room are crammed with fairy tales, magazines, fiction, picture stories and other informative books for youngsters from pre-school to eighth grade. (There's a Parents Room and there are special collections for adults to use with children.)

This is the largest collection of books for children and for those studying children's literature in Philadelphia.

In Philadelphia, children are encouraged to become acquainted with books at an early age. The library holds Story Hours* for pre-schoolers, Picture Book Story Hours for kindergarten to second graders and Story Hours for school age children.

An Annual Spring Book Review with displays, reviews and reading lists of the year's outstanding children's books is given to parents, teachers and librarians. A "Welcome Gifts" book list is available in mid-November for suggested holiday giving.

Every summer the library encourages youngsters from fourth through eighth grades to join the eight-week Vacation Reading Club. The club has a meeting each week (at the Central Library and every branch library) where its members discuss books they've read from among specified categories of fiction and non-fiction. The members must read at least eight books to finish the program and receive a certificate.

Book Concerts*, Story Hours*, Film Festivals* and an occasional Lecture Series are regularly scheduled at the Free Library. They're usually on Sunday afternoons at 2 at the Central Library. You can stop by any branch library to pick up a monthly calendar of events that includes activities at all of the libraries.

Or for more information about special events, the Vacation Reading Club for youngsters or other programs sponsored by the Free Library, call the Office for Work with Children (686-5372) or the Office for Work with Adults-Young Adults (686-5344).

General Interest

RYERSS MUSEUM-LIBRARY*
Cottman and Central Avenues—19111
745-3061

Hours: Friday to Sunday, 10 to 5.

In 1895, Robert W. Ryerss willed that his stately mansion's library be open free to the public. His trust gives area residents an opportunity to use its resources.

Membership at Ryerss is open to residents of the Burholme Park neighborhood and surrounding communities.

Ryerss is divided into departments for adults and children. Over 15,000 volumes of fiction, non-fiction and reference works make up the circulating collection. There's also a very special collection of Victoriana and books about that era which are available for use at the library.

In case you didn't know, Philadelphia is a college town.

It's the home of more than 30 colleges and universities. Among them are the University of Pennsylvania, Temple University, Drexel University, LaSalle University, St. Joseph's University, Thomas Jefferson University, Philadelphia Colleges of the Arts, Bryn Mawr College, Haverford College and the Philadelphia Community College. All of these schools have outstanding libraries.

While you can't borrow their books if you aren't enrolled there, you're welcome to browse and do research.

Incidentally, many of these libraries are worth visiting just to see.

AMERICAN-SWEDISH HISTORICAL MUSEUM* (389-1776) has catalogued more than 12,500 volumes, manuscripts, rare books and genealogy charts to research American and Swedish history and immigration to the middle-Atlantic colonies. An appointment is necessary at the Nord Library and it's helpful if you can read Swedish or German since three-fourths of the collection is in those tongues.

BALCH INSTITUTE* (925-8090) has a non-circulating research library of more than 50,000 books, in addition to thousands of manuscripts, microfilms and a collection of newspapers representing ethnic and minority groups who have immigrated to North America. These resources are available to the public and there is no charge. The hours are 9 to 5, Monday to Saturday.

CATHOLIC HISTORICAL SOCIETY* (925-5752) is bound to have information for your research on Catholicism. See Chapter 5 for details.

JEWISH ARCHIVES CENTER* (925-8090) is what the name implies. See Chapter 5 for details.

JOSEPH HORNER MEMORIAL LIBRARY of the German Society of Pennsylvania* (627-4365) has more than 80,000 volumes, 85 percent in the German language. Annual membership (Student, $5; Adult, $20; Family, $30) entitles you to library privileges and regularly scheduled activities of the German Society.

The **MENNONITE CHURCH LIBRARY*** (843-0943) will be of interest to researchers of Mennonite and Germantown history. Call for an appointment.

PRESBYTERIAN HISTORICAL SOCIETY* (627-1852) is another religious archives center, specializing in Presbyterianism in the U.S. and abroad. Call ahead to see if they have the material you need, and make an appointment to do your research.

YEARLY MEETING LIBRARY at the Friends Center Complex, 1515 Cherry Street (241-7220), is of general interest to Quakers. Books can be borrowed by Friends School teachers, members and attenders of the Yearly Meeting and other Quaker affiliates. The public is welcome to use the books at the library. Ask about a library subscription if you'd like borrowing privileges. Hours are weekdays, 9 to 5, except a few weeks in August and holidays when the library is closed.

Probing into History

ATHENAEUM OF PHILADELPHIA
219 South 6th Street—19106
925-2688

Hours: Weekdays, 9 to 5. Closed holidays.
Tours: Groups of 10 to 30, 4th grade and above, are scheduled by calling at least a week ahead. Allow about one hour and specify if you want a general tour or emphasis on architecture or literature.
Cost: Free.
SEPTA: Bus 90 or Walnut Street routes.
E & H: There are 6 steps at the entrance. An elevator connects the 3 floors.

The Athenaeum welcomes you back to Victorian Philadelphia. This private library, named for the Greek goddess of wisdom, was founded in 1814 as a literary society. Charles Dickens and Edgar Allan Poe were among the famous writers who used its facilities.

Today the Athenaeum is one of the country's most complete 19th century libraries. Its strongpoints cover Victorian architecture, interior design, periodicals, literature, the French in America, travel, exploration and transportation.

Borrowing privileges are limited to members only, but students, writers and researchers are welcome to use the Athenaeum's books and reference works. Call ahead to see if the material you need is available, and to make an appointment.

Tours of the Athenaeum go beyond the literary collections. They focus on the distinctive period furnishings, artwork and architecture. The building was completed in 1847 and was one of Philadelphia's first "brownstones." It was also America's first major building in the Italian Renaissance Revival style. Now it's a National Historic Landmark and completely restored.

CIVIL WAR LIBRARY AND MUSEUM* (735–8196) specializes in books about Abraham Lincoln and the Civil War period. Many of the 12,000 volumes are old and one-of-a-kind so you won't be able to borrow them. The reading rooms are comfortable, though, and the surrounding exhibits get you into the appropriate mood.

GERMANTOWN HISTORICAL SOCIETY'S LIBRARY at Baynton House* (844-0514) goes into the past of Germantown and its residents. If you're tracing local history or genealogy, this is a good place to start.

HISTORICAL SOCIETY OF PENNSYLVANIA* (732-6200) was the first of its kind in the state. It serves as a center for research on Pennsylvania and American history. The Society has been gathering and preserving old documents since it was founded in 1824.

Scholars and book lovers from around the world come to see the treasures that start with the archives of the Penn family and continue through three centuries.

Over 14 million pieces are included in the manuscripts collection. Another 8,000 bound volumes of newspapers relate to Pennsylvania history. There is also a superb collection of Pennsylvania maps.

If your ancestors were Pennsylvanians, you might be able to use the material here to trace your family tree. The collections of the Genealogical Society of Pennsylvania are also maintained by the Historical Society and include over 10,000 printed family ancestries, manuscripts, family, church and civil records.

The Society insists that reference work be done in its reading rooms. The material cannot be taken out. The hours are Tuesday, Thursday, Friday, 9 to 5; Wednesday, 1 to 9; and closed holidays.

There's a $5 daily fee for use of the reading rooms. Annual membership of $30 allows free use of the reading rooms and also gets you subscriptions to "The Pennsylvania Magazine of History and Biography" and "The Pennsylvania Correspondent."

LIBRARY COMPANY OF PHILADELPHIA
1314 Locust Street—19107
546-3181

Hours: Weekdays, 9 to 4:45. Closed holidays.
Tours: Groups of no more than 25 high school students or adults can be scheduled for hour-long tour that includes the current exhibit. Call at least a month ahead.
Cost: Free. Or you might consider purchasing a share in the library for a nominal amount. That is an old and honorable tradition shared by signers of the Declaration and distinguished citizens through the centuries.

SEPTA: Buses D, 42, 90 or Broad Street routes.
E & H: The entrance is at ground level so there's wheelchair access.

In addition to everything else Benjamin Franklin founded, he also founded this library in 1731. It was the first of a long list of Franklin's "finds" to follow.

This is the oldest circulating library in the country. The first books were brought from England in 1732. The library currently houses over 300,000 books that tell you about America from Colonial times to the Civil War era.

Among the Library Company's treasures are Lewis and Clark's guidebook to their 1804 expedition, Thomas Jefferson's personal copy of his first published book and the James Logan collection, which was the most important library in the colonies.

The Library Company's building is an award-winning design of contemporary architecture. It's next door and connected to the Historical Society of Pennsylvania.

Note: This library is open to students, scholars and the curious for research purposes only, and their work must be done here.

LIBRARY HALL* (627-0706) is the venerable library of the American Philosophical Society. It's also part of Independence National Historical Park and described previously in Chapter 2.

NATIONAL ARCHIVES
Philadelphia Branch
9th and Market Streets—19107
597-3000

Hours: Weekdays, 8 to 5; 1st and 3rd Saturdays of each month, 9 to 1. Closed holidays.
Tours: You're on your own to view exhibits and use resources. Hour-long educational programs are offered from October to June at 10 A.M.: Tuesday and Thursday in October, December and February; Monday and Wednesday in November, January and April. Groups of no more than 35, grades 5 to 10; or special programs for grades 11 and 12 and college classes. Reservations are necessary a week in advance. See below for topics.
Cost: Free.
SEPTA: Any Market or Chestnut Street route.
Other: Items for sale include books, postcards, posters

and games related to U.S. history as well as family-tree charts and books related to family history.

E & H: Wheelchair entrance from Market Street side.

The National Archives of the United States in Washington, D.C. houses the records that document our nation's history from 1775 to today.

All of the documents that are considered to be of permanent value from all three branches of the Federal government are stored here. Among the millions of documents at the main branch of the National Archives are the Declaration of Independence, the Constitution of the United States and the Bill of Rights.

Several Federal depositories are located around the United States, and Philadelphia is one of 11 field archives. The local holdings include federal records from agencies in Pennsylvania, Delaware, Maryland, Virginia and West Virginia; the U.S. District Courts; the U.S. Court of Appeals for the Third and Fourth Circuits; the U.S. Army Corps of Engineers and the U.S. Navy.

Microfilm holdings include census records from 1790 to 1910, Civil War records, Revolutionary War records, passenger list indexes from ships that arrived in Philadelphia from 1800 to 1948 and Baltimore from 1820 to 1952, and indexes for Naturalization Petitions in the Federal Courts of Baltimore, Pittsburgh, Philadelphia and Wilmington from 1795 to 1968.

These resources are all available for your use.

The museum exhibits are drawn from the Archives' vast resources. The exhibits change twice a year.

Groups can schedule visits and choose from one of four topics. They'll learn what an archives is and how to use it. Original documents, microfilm, a slide show, tour and demonstration are part of the program.

You can focus on "Searching for Your Roots," "Introduction to Historical Documents," "Archives and the Three Federal Branches of Government" or a special program based on the current museum exhibit.

It's practically impossible to visualize the scope of the National Archives. A visit to the Philadelphia Branch will heighten your understanding and certainly aid any research in these areas.

Researching a Special Interest

Many of these libraries are in museums where there is an admission charge. The fee, however, is usually waived if you are visiting specifically to use the library.

ACADEMY OF NATURAL SCIENCES* (299-1040) has a research library specializing in biology, geology and the natural sciences. The public may use the reading room but books are loaned only to members. The hours are weekdays, 9 to 5.

The **COLLEGE OF PHYSICIANS OF PHILADELPHIA LIBRARY,** 19 South 22nd Street (561-6050), ranks among the top 10 collections of its kind in the United States. Dr. John Morgan, who formed the library in 1789, was a founder of the College of Physicians and the nation's first medical school at the University of Pennsylvania. Dr. Morgan donated 25 volumes to the library.

Today there are almost 600,000 volumes and one of the most complete collections of medical periodicals in the world. Almost 2,500 medical journals arrive here each year.

You're welcome to use the library's reference materials in the library. If you would like borrowing privileges, ask about membership. Hours are weekdays, 9 to 5, except holidays when the College is closed.

The Mutter Museum* is also here at the College of Physicians and worthy of your visit.

The **FEDERAL RESERVE BANK*** has a research library (574-6543) for people interested in banking, finance and the economy. There are current books and periodicals, as well as periodicals dating back to the early 1800s and all Federal Reserve publications. All research must be done at the library. Hours are weekdays, 9 to 4. A guard will direct you when you enter the building and sign in.

HENRY GEORGE BIRTHPLACE* (922-4278) contains a library devoted to economics and the particular economic philosophy of its namesake. There's also a small collection on Chinese language and philosophy. You're welcome to visit the house and browse through its books, but only students of the Henry George School of Social Science are permitted to borrow them.

JENKINS MEMORIAL LAW LIBRARY (592-5690) is the place to go if you're interested in law. It's at 841

Chestnut Street and open weekdays, except holidays, from 9 to 5. The stacks and comfortable reading areas are available to the public, and books may be borrowed by members of the library and the Philadelphia Bar Association.

The library at the **NEW YEAR'S SHOOTERS & MUMMERS MUSEUM*** (336-3050) contains historic Mummerabilia, a collection of English Mummers' plays and the latest in video-tape and copying equipment to aid in your research since you won't be able to borrow any of the materials. It's open by appointment only.

PENNSYLVANIA HORTICULTURAL SOCIETY* (625-8268) maintains a growing library of books and periodicals about horticulture, plants and gardens. Members of the Society are welcome to borrow from its bulging shelves; others can dig into the books while there. If you thought about starting a garden, it is a good place to find out how to do it.

At the **PENNSYLVANIA HOSPITAL*** (829-3971) in the Old Pine Building, you'll find the country's most complete collection of medical books from 1750 to 1850, and some that go back as early as the 16th century. This was the first and finest medical library in the colonies, located here in 1847 and elegantly restored in 1977. There are over 13,000 volumes. Obviously, these books aren't available for loan. A compact new medical library is upstairs.

PHILADELPHIA MARITIME MUSEUM* (925-5439) has a non-circulating library for those of you doing research on maritime life. If you're a museum member or serious researcher, call ahead for an appointment during museum hours.

The **PHILADELPHIA MUSEUM OF ART*** (763-8100 Ext. 259) has an extensive library of books on art, art history, decorative arts and art sales that museum members are welcome to use at the museum on Wednesdays, Thursdays and Fridays from 10 to 4. Members are admitted free. There's a $5 annual fee for teachers and graduate students, and it's $10 a year for anyone else having reciprocal arrangements to use the resources.

ROSENBACH MUSEUM* (732-1600) is a veritable goldmine of rare books, priceless manuscripts and the thousands of books collected by A.S.W. Rosenbach during his lifetime and by the foundation established after his death. Read about some of them in Chapter 9, or, better yet, go there. You have to see it to believe it. Rosenbach's library is open by appointment and for research only.

The library at **SCHUYLKILL VALLEY NATURE CENTER*** (482-7300) is restricted to borrowing by members only, but anyone is welcome to use the resources here. The 4,000 books are all about nature, ecology and the environment. If you're interested in borrowing privileges and activities at the Center, inquire about membership.

The reference library at the **WAGNER FREE INSTITUTE*** (763-6529) is valuable if you're doing research on natural history or scientific subjects. There are more than 25,000 bound volumes and 150,000 pamphlets, magazines and periodicals, including many foreign titles. Hours are Tuesday to Friday, 10 to 4; Sunday, 12 to 3.

Chapter 12.
International Philadelphia.

This chapter is for visiting foreigners or anyone who seeks a taste of foreign lands.

If you're a visiting foreigner or have an interest in foreign lands and peoples, you have several sources of special assistance with tours and interesting programs. The most obvious source, of course, is the city's official **VISITORS CENTER*** on John F. Kennedy Boulevard at 16th Street (568-1976). Here are some others.

INTERNATIONAL HOUSE
OF PHILADELPHIA
3701 Chestnut Street—19104
387-5125

This well-designed, modern high-rise is a home-away-from-home for 450 foreign students. A small number of short-term accommodations are also available for visitors interested in unique housing (see Chapter 20).

International House provides social and service programs for its residents, including at-home hospitality extended by Philadelphia hosts. In return, International House invites you to its outstanding facilities with a smorgasbord of happenings.

There's the Neighborhood Film/Video Project* and frequently scheduled cultural events with guest musicians, ethnic performers and speakers on international issues. Many of these events are described in Chapters 9 and 10 of this book.

There's a gourmet cafeteria restaurant, Eden, at International House. The International Bazaar sells arts and crafts from around the world.

All of this proves that you don't have to go far in Philadelphia to get a foreign taste. Most of the activity at International House is planned around the academic year. If you're interested, call for details.

INTERNATIONAL VISITORS CENTER
OF PHILADELPHIA
3rd floor, Civic Center Museum
34th Street and Civic Center Boulevard—19104
823-7261

Foreign visitors who need emergency translation for medical or other reasons, should call the **IVC language bank** at 879-5248 anytime, day or night. Over 300 volunteers are available to translate over 60 languages over the phone, usually within five minutes.

The International Visitors Center of Philadelphia arranges professional appointments, home hospitality, and tours led by multi-lingual Philadelphians for over 3,000 sponsored foreign visitors each year. IVC also refers foreign visitors to service committees and organizations that could be of interest.

If you're a Philadelphian who would like to have the opportunity to meet and help welcome foreign guests to your city, then call IVC and ask about being a volunteer.

NATIONALITIES SERVICE CENTER
1300 Spruce Street—19107
893-8400

If you're coming to live in Philadelphia from another country, you'll find that this agency can be very helpful.

The Nationalities Service Center is a United Way agency that serves the social, educational and personal needs of immigrants and their descendants. It helps refugees and non-English-speaking people with problems resulting from language or cultural differences.

The NSC teaches English as a second language to newcomers, provides social activities and prepares immigrants and refugees for the naturalization process. They also have changing exhibits of foreign arts and crafts.

The NSC sponsors the popular Philadelphia Folk Fair at the Civic Center on even years in November (see Chapter 19).

WORLD AFFAIRS COUNCIL
563-5363

Another opportunity for Philadelphians to get involved in foreign affairs is the World Affairs Council. It invites you to participate in its program of luncheons, dinners, discussions, seminars, films, trips and tours.

Special activities are planned and coordinated for area students and teachers. A Young Adults group involves local professional people in their 20s and 30s. They meet three or four times a month for lectures, luncheons, cocktails and special events.

The World Affairs Council guarantees to stimulate your interest in international subjects. They keep you informed of what's going on in the world today. Call if you'd like to find out more about this dynamic organization.

Foreign Intrigue

Philadelphians and foreign visitors alike will be interested in touring "foreign" Philadelphia.

Architecture of the British colonial period dominates the historic area. The Benjamin Franklin Parkway, Logan Circle and City Hall have obvious French influences. There are also many classic examples of Greek Revival and Italian Renaissance styles, and they're mentioned throughout this book. Germantown* was predominately settled by Germans. The Swedes founded Old Swedes' Church, and they're highlighted in the American-Swedish Historical Museum*. Mikveh Israel* was the first synagogue in the colonies. The prominence of Ukrainians in Philadelphia is explored when touring the Cathedral of the Immaculate Conception of the Blessed Virgin Mary*. Afro-Americans can trace their roots at the Afro-American Historical and Cultural Museum*.

The tastiest way to pay a local visit to faraway lands is to sample their foods. And in Philadelphia you can almost dine your way around the world. You can have Chinese food (with chopsticks, of course), crepes from France, German schnitzel, moussaka from Greece, Italian pasta, Japanese food with a tea ceremony, shish kebab from the Middle East or tacos and beans from Mexico.

Restaurants representing many different countries are plentiful in Philadelphia. You'll find them listed by nationality in the Yellow Pages, and you'll also find many of them in Chapter 18. You'll find many of them casual-style under one roof at the Reading Terminal Market*.

And now, more about International Philadelphia.

BALCH INSTITUTE
18 South 7th Street—19106
925-8090

Hours: Monday to Saturday, 10 to 4. Closed holidays. Allow one hour.
Tours: If you're on your own, everything is self-explanatory. Groups of 10 or more should be scheduled at least 2 weeks in advance. Programs are geared to any school level or to adults and can include a choice of films.
Cost: Adults, $1; children under 18, 50¢; senior citizens, free. Groups of 10 or more adults, 50¢.

SEPTA: Any Market Street route to 7th Street, or a 2-block walk from Independence Hall.
E & H: Complete wheelchair access.

This is where you'll relive the experience of your parents, grandparents or great-grandparents when they immigrated to America. You'll sit on a bench immigrants once sat on when they came to Ellis Island. You'll see exhibits on new immigrants telling what it's like to be in America.

Since one-third of the 50 million immigrants to the United States between 1820 and 1980 entered through ports other than New York, you'll be interested in a major exhibition, "Freedom's Doors: The Other Ports of Entry to the United States." Important documents, clothing, household objects and cherished personal belongings brought by foreigners to America help tell the story.

This is all very timely as centennials are celebrated by the Statue of Liberty and Ellis Island.

This is where you can learn about your ethnic heritage. An hour here gives you the total immigration experience.

You can dig further for your roots at the Balch Library described in the previous chapter.

CHINATOWN

There are no regularly scheduled tours of Chinatown in Philadelphia, but you can explore this pocket of center city on your own and discover a wealth of Oriental lore and excitement.

The neighborhood is centered around Race Street from 8th to 11th, and from Vine to Market Street.

The **Chinese Cultural and Community Center** at 125 N. 10th Street is worthy of your inspection. Its original structure dates back to the 1830s. It's designed after a Peking Mandarin Palace. The colorful tilework that decorates its facade is actually from China. Authentic New Year's Banquets are held here every winter in conjunction with the Chinese New Year. Every year, chefs are invited from different regions of China to present Philadelphians with a traditional 10-course dinner. Call 923-6767 for the schedule, price information and reservations.

South of the Community Center, spanning 10th Street north of Arch, is the spectacular 40-foot-high **Chinese Friendship Gate.** In 1983, a team of artisans from Philadelphia's sister city Tianjin, China, came here with 142 cases of colorful tiles to build and paint the gate in dazzling colors and symbols. It's a magnificent tribute to the friendship between two distant cities.

Chinatown is famous for its outstanding restaurants. The first restaurant opened in Chinatown in 1880. Today, there must be at least 40 restaurants serving Canton, Szechuan and Hunan cuisines as well as Japanese and Vietnamese fare.

You can shop for Oriental groceries and household items at a number of markets and gift shops. Be sure to stop for fortune cookies at Yep's Bakery at 127 N. 11th Street. Pick up chow mein or lo mein noodles from Ding Ho at 933 Cuthbert Street or New Tung Hop at 133 N. 11th Street. If your timing is right, you might see fortune cookies or noodles being made.

All of the streets of Chinatown are identified with signs in both English and Chinese. The phone company has thoughtfully placed pagoda-style booths on the sidewalks. The sidewalks themselves have a stylized Chinese symbol for long life called a "shou."

You'll get the flavor of the Orient just by strolling through Chinatown.

Good appetite!

GERMAN SOCIETY OF PENNSYLVANIA
611 Spring Garden Street—19123
627-4365

Hours: Wednesday and Thursday, 11 to 5; Saturday, 10 to 4. Closed Saturdays in July; closed all of August.
Cost: Free.
SEPTA: Buses 43, 47.
E & H: No wheelchair access.

In Chapter 3 you read about Germantown and the early German settlement in Philadelphia. You might recall that Holy Trinity Roman Catholic Church* was founded for German-speaking Philadelphians in the late 18th century.

The German Society of Pennsylvania, founded in 1764, is the oldest of its kind in America. The Society provides its members with a cultural program of language classes, concerts, exhibits, films and lectures.

The German Society's Joseph Horner Memorial Library was founded in 1817. Call for additional information and see Chapter 11.

ITALIAN MARKET
9th Street, from Wharton to Christian Streets

Hours: Tuesday to Saturday, early mornings till about 6 at night. Some activity on Sunday mornings.
Tours: See "Reading Terminal Market" in Chapter 13.
Lunch: There are several restaurants along 9th Street, or munch on fresh fruit, Italian bread and cheese.
SEPTA: Buses 47, 63, 64.
E & H: No stairs to climb, but the walking can be treacherous.

The Italian Market in the heart of South Philadelphia* is different from any market you've ever seen. The neighborhood merchants jam-pack their stores and display their overflowing merchandise on sidewalk tables and pushcarts.

The market is stretched along five city blocks with the hub at 9th Street and Washington Avenue.

You'll find anything that's in season. The stalls are decked with fresh fruits, vegetables, poultry, baked delicacies, pasta and cheeses. An assortment of skinned animals adorns butcher shop windows while chickens and rabbits wait in coops to be selected for someone's dinner.

Hucksters call out the merits of their cod, mackerel, octopus and crabs that are ready to be scooped up from barrels. Even clothing hanging from canopies is for sale.

The prices are reasonable, and the markets are a beehive of activity, especially towards the end of the week when the shoppers stock up. Most of the shops are closed on Sunday and Monday.

As a note of interest, every candidate for office campaigning in Philadelphia, from the President of United States on down, makes it a point to visit the Italian Market. You've also seen 9th Street in a number of movies... like "Rocky," "Rocky II" and "Rocky III."

JAPANESE EXHIBITION HOUSE
Fairmount Park Horticultural Center*
Lansdowne Drive east of Belmont Avenue
West Fairmount Park
686-0096

Hours: April to October, Wednesday to Sunday, 10 to 5.
Call ahead to be sure. Allow 30 minutes or more.
Tours: Japanese guides in kimonos will greet you and
explain the function and reason for each of the home's
features. Call ahead if you're bringing a group.
Cost: Adults, $1; children under 12, 50¢.
Lunch: No food permitted within the house gates, but you
can picnic nearby in Fairmount Park.
SEPTA: Walk from Bus 38 stop on Belmont Avenue, or
take the Fairmount Park Trolley-Bus. There's plenty of
free parking.
E & H: Wheelchair access difficult within the gates; the
walkway is narrow and there are a few steps.

Nestled among the trees in scenic Fairmount Park is an
authentic replica of a 16th century Japanese home. It's
known as a "shoin" and represents the typical living quarters of a scholar, priest or government official of the time.

It's surrounded by Japanese gardens, walkways, waterways and a pond. By today's standards, the house is modern and spacious. And the furnishings are authentic.

Sliding and removable screens separate the rooms to
give an open, airy feeling. The "fusama" (sliding screen
doors) and "shoji" (sliding paper doors) were restored and
painted by Japanese artisans. Tables, chests and bedding
are stored away when not in use. Floor cushions provide
the seating, and they're covered with "tatami" (rice-straw
mats).

The Japanese always remove their shoes before entering the house. It's considered unsanitary to wear shoes
indoors, and it also prevents damage to the "tatami."

You might be lucky enough to see "Ikebana," the Japanese art of flower arranging; "Origami," the Japanese
art of paper folding; or "Cha-No-Yu," the ancient tradition of the symbolic tea ceremony. If you're especially
interested in one of these arts, call ahead for a schedule.

While you're at the Japanese House, don't miss the
Horticultural Center that's just a stone's throw away.

Chapter 13.
Philadelphia at Work.

This chapter takes you into the workings of Philadelphia's government, businesses and industries. It tells how you can tour various city and federal offices, private companies, public utilities and institutions.

Philadelphia is one of the country's leading cities in business and industry, and it's a regional headquarters for several agencies of the federal government. If your group is interested in a particular field that's not shown here, don't hesitate to call a company, institution or department in that area. Many of Philadelphia's prominent banks, brokerage houses, manufacturers, medical facilities and public agencies will accommodate you with special tours.

The last section of this chapter features people who will bring programs to your location.

It's called "Tours to Go."

Tours of City Installations

CITY HALL
Broad and Market Streets—19107
686-1776 (general information)

Hours: Weekdays, 9 to 5. The City Hall Tower* closes a half-hour earlier. Closed holidays. See below for specific activities.

Tours: Call 567-4476 for tour information, in addition to what's noted below, or stop by Room 121 for a "Do-It-Yourself Tour." One-hour guided tours are weekdays at 12:30, departing from Conversation Hall, Room 201, along the north corridor of the 2nd floor (enter through North Broad Street portal). Group tours are by appointment only, weekdays at 10:30 A.M. Philadelphia Public School classes grades 3 to 12 can be scheduled in advance by calling 686-2840.

Cost: Free.

SEPTA: Buses 12, 17, 27, 32, 33, 76, C; trolleys 10, 11, 13, 34, 36; or either subway route.

Lunch: No facilities, but there are refreshment stands at the northwest and southeast corners.

E & H: To avoid steps, enter under archways to courtyard on south, east or west sides and go to corners of building to use elevators to all 7 floors.

This is where you'll learn how Philadelphia works.

Our City Hall is the largest City Hall in the country, and till 1987, the tallest building in Philadelphia. Its vast size and beauty always amaze visitors. Philadelphians, unfortunately, take it for granted. They're hardly aware of what goes on inside, unless they get in trouble.

City Hall took 30 years to complete, and it cost over $23 million. Just take one look and you'll understand why.

If you're on your own, the best place to start is at the northeast corner, the direction William Penn faces from his perch on top of City Hall.

The cantilevered stairwells at each of the building's four corners are six stories tall. They were designed by Thomas U. Walter, who designed the dome of the U.S. Capitol.

Take the stairs or an elevator to the second floor. The Mayor's Reception Room (202) is where dignitaries are greeted, proclamations are presented and official ceremonies are held. Walk in, look at the gold-leaf ceiling, the magnificent chandelier, the Honduras mahogany paneling, the portraits of many former Philadelphia mayors and the carpet with the City Seal woven into its center.

Another example of our ornate City Hall is Room 400, the City Council Chamber. City Council usually meets on Thursday mornings at 10. Its 17 members are elected every four years to serve a simultaneous term with the Mayor. It's fascinating to see what goes on when they meet. Groups of 10 or more should make reservations by calling the Assistant to the President of City Council at 686-3432.

While you're here, don't miss viewing Art in City Hall.* That's described in Chapter 9.

Court Sessions are open to the public. There are over 40 courtrooms in City Hall for criminal and civil cases. This is an excellent learning experience for school children. For one thing, it shows them why they should stay out of trouble. For another, it might prompt your son or daughter to become an attorney, a court stenographer or court officer. Visiting arrangements must be made in advance for groups of no more than 20 (larger groups will be divided) by calling the Public Information Office of the Philadelphia Court of Common Pleas and Municipal Court at 686-7932. Discretion should be used in choosing the types of cases that youngsters observe.

Arrangements can be made for small groups of high school students or adults to observe Traffic Court hearings on weekdays. Requests must be put in writing at least two weeks in advance to the President Judge of Traffic Court, 800 N. Broad Street, Phila., Pa. 19130. Use school or organization stationery to make your request and give two or three dates when your group could attend.

Back to City Hall. A trip here isn't complete until you see William Penn atop the **City Hall Tower***. Take an elevator on the north side to the seventh floor, and then follow the red lines directing you to the tower elevator.

When you've returned to the ground, walk through City Hall's **courtyard**. There are maps of Philadelphia, plaques commemorating historic events in Philadelphia and the history and development of Centre Square and City Hall.

If you have specific questions while you're at City Hall, visit the **Mayor's Office for Information** in Room 121.

FIRE ADMINISTRATION BUILDING
3rd and Spring Garden Streets—19123
592-5952

Hours: By reservation only, weekdays, except holidays, 2 to 4 P.M. Allow 45 minutes.

Tours: Scheduled for groups of no more than 50, at least elementary school age. One adult must accompany every 10 children. All tour requests must be made at least a few weeks in advance by writing to the Deputy Commissioner of Operations at the above address.

Cost: Free.

SEPTA: Buses 5, 43; Market-Frankford Subway-Elevated.

E & H: Complete wheelchair access.

The Philadelphia Fire Department has a contemporary administration building where special care went into the design and construction. These details will be explained as you tour the facility. You'll see the rooftop helipad and learn about the special facilities that are always ready here in case of a disaster.

Every call for rescue wagons and fire engines in Philadelphia is received and dispatched from the Fire Department Communications Center which is located in the basement of the building. The center always elicits amazement and respect from visitors.

FIRE TRAINING ACADEMY
Delaware River and Pennypack Street—19136
592-5952

Hours: Weekdays, 10 to 4. Closed holidays. Allow at least one hour.
Tours: Scheduled for groups of no more than 50, at least elementary school age. One adult must accompany every 10 children. For reservations, see Fire Administration Building.
Cost: Free.
SEPTA: Bus 20.
E & H: Wheelchair access.

This is where you learn how to be a firefighter.

In Philadelphia, if a child's father is a fireman and if his grandfather was or is a fireman, chances are he or she will be a firefighter. It runs in the family.

Try to arrange a tour of the Academy while there's a class in training. It's exciting to watch future firefighters practicing how to climb ropes, use ladders and squirt the hoses. You might also see a class of veteran firefighters getting advanced training in the latest firefighting methods.

FIREBOAT STATION
Pier 11 North, Delaware Avenue and Race Street
592-5952

Hours: Daily, anytime. Allow 20 minutes.
Tours: Stop by this city-owned pier on your own, or schedule in advance for a group to visit. For group tour arrangements, see Fire Administration Building.
Cost: Free.
SEPTA: Buses 17, 33, 48; Market-Frankford Subway-Elevated.
E & H: Wheelchair access.

The firehouse at the end of Pier 11 is where firemen are stationed aboard the "Bernard Samuel," one of Philadelphia's two fireboats.

Although you're required to stay on the pier, you can still see the 89-foot red boat, the special uniforms worn by the firemen and an interesting photographic exhibit of the firemen at work.

A fireman will tell you about his job on the waterfront. In addition to fighting blazes on the Camden or Philadelphia side of the Delaware River, the firemen fight oil spills, help distressed boats and aid in rescue operations.

Fireman's Hall* is just two blocks away from the Delaware at 2nd and Quarry Streets. The 4th and Arch Streets firehouse is one of the most modern in the city. From these three locations, you can trace the Philadelphia Fire Department's earliest efforts to its present day record of efficiency and excellence.

FIRE HOUSE—Local Installation
592-5952

Hours: Daily, anytime. Allow at least 20 minutes.

Tours: Visit on your own, or schedule in advance for a group visit. For group tour arrangements, see Fire Administration Building.

Cost: Free.

Other: Fire Service Recognition Day is usually the second Saturday in May. All Philadelphia firehouses celebrate by holding Open House. Fire Prevention Week is always the full week that includes October 9. It commemorates the great Chicago fire of October 9, 1871. Again, all firehouses hold Open House. There are also float displays, home fire drills and a series of educational programs to promote fire safety. Watch the newspapers for a schedule.

E & H: Wheelchair access.

Fire prevention is the best way to fight a fire. Nothing impresses that on a child more than a visit to a firehouse. There are 70 firehouses in Philadelphia.

Every local firehouse has a hook and ladder truck, rescue wagon, mobile intensive care unit, the battalion chief's car and, of course, the red fire engines. The equipment varies according to the size of the station.

A fireman will talk to your group and tell you about his job. When you go on a class tour, ask the fireman about the Junior Fire Department Program.

The Fire Department's Fire Prevention Division also conducts **Fireama** programs three times a day in July and August at city recreation centers. Activities include two fire safety games, "Beat the Hazards," a home and school fire safety quiz, and "Play it Safe in 50 States," an historical quiz. Boys and girls from throughout the city are urged to attend. Prizes are awarded to the winners. Call 592-5967 to find out when Fireama will be at your local recreation center.

MUNICIPAL INCINERATOR (Northwest)
Domino Lane and Umbria Street, Roxborough—19128
686-5552 (Department of Streets, Sanitation Division)

Hours: Weekdays, except holidays, 10 to 4. Allow 30 minutes.

Tours: Scheduled for groups of no more than 30, at least 6th grade. One adult must accompany every 10 children. Call a week in advance for reservations.

Cost: Free.

SEPTA: Bus 61

E & H: No wheelchair access.

The study of ecology and the environment is even more relevant when you visit one of our city's waste disposal facilities.

Groups can see the trash pits and the cranes in action, and they can learn how waste material is processed as sanitation trucks deposit it into the incinerator.

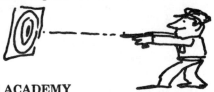

POLICE ACADEMY
State Road and Ashburner Street—19136
686-3380 (Police Community Relations)

Hours: Weekdays, 10 to 4. Closed holidays. Allow one hour.

Tours: Scheduled for groups of no more than 30, at least 3rd grade. Write at least 2 weeks in advance to the Philadelphia Police Commissioner, Police Administration Building, 7th and Race Streets, Phila., Pa. 19106.

Cost: Free.

SEPTA: Buses 28, 84, Y.

E & H: Wheelchair access.

This tour gives visitors a bird's-eye view of the modern facility in which "Philadelphia's finest" receive their 13-week training. You'll see the gymnasium and training areas, and you'll learn about the rigorous curriculum.

The canine unit also trains here. If you're lucky, one of the dogs will give you a demonstration.

You might also see a display of firearms, recruits at physical training, lectures on crowd control or patrol procedure.

POLICE ADMINISTRATION BUILDING
7th and Race Streets—19106
686-3380 (Police Community Relations)

Hours: Weekdays, 10 to 4. Closed holidays. Allow one hour.
Tours: Same procedure for scheduling and reservations as the Police Academy.
Cost: Free.
SEPTA: Buses 47, 48, 61 or Market Street routes.
Other: National Police Week is celebrated one Saturday in May with Open House from 10 to 3. Everyone is invited to see drill teams, the bugle corps and firearms displays. You can tour the building and perhaps ride in a police vehicle.
E & H: Wheelchair access.

Legend has it that the "Roundhouse" was designed with a pair of handcuffs in mind because of its shape.

Tours are geared according to the group's age level. You'll learn about chemical analysis and ballistics. You might see the communications center, a lie detector machine, fingerprinting or any number of other methods of crime prevention being put to work.

POLICE HARBOR PATROL
Pier 11 North, Delaware Avenue and Race Street
686-3380 (Police Community Relations)

Hours: Daily, anytime. Allow 30 minutes.
Tours: Same procedure for scheduling and reservations as the Police Academy.
Cost: Free.
SEPTA: Buses 17, 33, 48; Market-Frankford Subway-Elevated.
E & H: Wheelchair access.

Everybody gets a thrill out of seeing the Police Marine Unit and the city's fleet of four blue and yellow police boats that are moored here. The 52-man river patrol's diving gear and headquarters are also here. The marine unit patrols both the Schuylkill and Delaware Rivers.

If the weather's right, and if you're lucky, one of the unit's five scuba diver police officers will demonstrate diving techniques.

While you're here, stop by Fireboat Station No. 2*. The pier is also just a short distance from Penn's Landing* and all of its attractions.

POLICE STABLES
Chamounix. North end of Chamounix Drive in West Fairmount Park, 686-0181.
F.D.R. 17th Street and Pattison Avenue, 686-1797.
Krewstown. Krewstown Road and Rising Sun Avenue, 673-7040.

Hours: Weekdays, 8 to 4. Allow at least one hour.
Tours: Scheduled for groups of no more than 60 at a time, and an adult must accompany every 10 children. Call at least one week ahead. Your tour will be confirmed by a return call.
Cost: Free.
E & H: Wheelchair access to observe outdoor activity only. If you want to enter the stables, one adult must be able to accompany each person in a wheelchair.

Since the city's mounted police force was reinstated in 1972, the handsome horses and their riders-in-blue have become a friendly and familiar sight.

A Mounted Training and Services Tour familiarizes you with patrol and stable headquarters near you.

An officer will give you a tour of the stable. He'll show you how the horses are saddled, how the riders are trained, and how the horses are prepared for duty. If the blacksmith is in, he'll show you how he puts shoes on horses. This tour is a must for everyone who loves horses.

WATER POLLUTION CONTROL PLANT
8200 Enterprise Avenue—19153
492-4000

Hours: Weekdays, except holidays, 10 to 4. Allow one hour.
Tours: Scheduled for groups of no more than 25 adults, college or senior high school students. Call a few weeks in advance for reservations.
Cost: Free.
SEPTA: Bus M.
E & H: Much of the tour is outdoors and there's a lot of walking. You'll also go into several buildings. There's limited wheelchair access to everything but the laboratories.

If you're an environmentalist, engineer or technician, this tour will be given to you in technical terms. If not, you'll learn about ecology and water pollutants in simple, easy words. Either way it's a sophisticated look at the environment and what we can do to hurt it or improve it.

Philadelphia's Southwest Water Pollution Control Plant is a contemporary facility and ranks among the finest of its type in the country. It's also one of the largest—1½ miles long and a ½ mile wide.

You can see the sedimentation basins, the digester tanks, a separate airblower building and the laboratories that are used for analysis and experimentation. And don't forget the sludge heaters and grit building that are also involved in wastewater treatment.

WATER TREATMENT PLANTS
1) Belmont—Ford Road and Belmont Avenue
2) Queen Lane—3545 Fox Street
3) Samuel S. Baxter—9001 State Road
592-6144

Hours: Weekdays, 10 to 4; weekends, 2 to 4. Closed holidays. Allow one hour.
Tours: Groups of 10 to 35 are scheduled daily. Families and smaller groups can visit on weekends. All individuals and groups must call in advance.
Cost: Free.
SEPTA: 1) Buses 38, 85. 2) Buses E, R, 32. 3) Bus 84.
E & H: No wheelchair access.

If you're interested in ecology, you should visit a water treatment plant, because this is a splendid way to learn how Philadelphia deals with pollutants in the water.

Our drinking water is the most purified in the country. You can follow the process in any one of our plants' modern pushbutton facilities. (The Baxter Plant is one of the largest in the country.) Water filtration starts directly at the river and the process continues until it's ready for you to drink. The pollution becomes apparent when the filter is washed clean of all non-purified elements.

A visit to the Baxter Plant includes a tour of a pilot project that is the first of its kind in the country. An experimental unit within the filter plant building is studying how to remove trace organics from water. These are the barely discernible particles that have caused concern throughout the country. In Philadelphia, we're setting the pace to do something about this.

Tours of Federal Installations

Over 3,000 Federal government workers serve you from their offices at the 10-story **WILLIAM J. GREEN FEDERAL BUILDING** at 600 Arch Street.

You can contact your United States Senators and Congressman through their offices here.

Information is available from the regional offices of the Internal Revenue Service, Passport Agency, Census Bureau, U.S. Civil Service Commission, U.S. Department of Labor, Federal Trade Commission, Atomic Energy Commission and the Social Security Administration. You can even tour the National Weather Service.

For general information about these and other government offices and services, call the **Federal Information Center** at 597-7042 from 8 A.M. to 5:30 P.M. (There are other Federal offices at different locations in the city.)

A **Government Printing Office Bookstore** is on the ground floor of the Federal Building (and scheduled to move in 1986 to the ground floor at 100 North 17th Street). You can browse here, or purchase practically every publication that is printed by the United States Government. The current list of hardbacks, paperbacks and pamphlets available from Washington numbers 25,000. Twenty-five hundred of them are on display here. A "New Books Catalogue" is published four times a year and describes the 1,000 currently most popular titles. It's available free from the bookstore. The subjects are as varied as the public library's.

The bookstore's hours are weekdays, except holidays, from 8 to 4. If you're interested in a specific title, call 597-0677 to see if it's in stock.

The Federal Building can be reached by **SEPTA** bus 48. It's just one block from any Market Street route.

The **elderly and handicapped** can avoid steps by entering the building from 6th or 7th Streets. Once inside, there's complete wheelchair access.

A 22-story Federal Courthouse adjoins the Federal Office Building.

UNITED STATES COURTHOUSE
601 Market Street—19106
597-9368 (Clerk's Office)

Hours: Court is in session weekdays, except holidays, 9:30 to 4:30. Allow at least 30 minutes.

Tours: Individuals can report to the Clerk's Office, Room 2609, for trial information. You'll be directed to a court session. School groups, at least 5th grade, are scheduled in advance. All groups must call 2 weeks ahead for a date. You will then be directed to confirm your request in writing.

Cost: Free.

Lunch: There's a large cafeteria in the adjoining Federal Office Building.

SEPTA: Any Market Street route.

E & H: Complete wheelchair access.

Twenty-three Federal judges, five U.S. magistrates and three Federal referees in bankruptcy preside here over criminal and civil cases for the U.S. District Court for Eastern Pennsylvania.

They hold trials in the 26 courtrooms at the handsome high-rise U.S. Courthouse. The building also houses the U.S. Court of Appeals for the Third Circuit.

The court facilities are thoroughly modern, comfortable and secure. Each courtroom has its own jury room and individual offices for the judge, the official court reporter and the clerk. Holding cells for defendants are on most floors, and they're directly accessible to courtrooms and elevators. So unless a defendant is free on bail, you'll never meet one in the corridors.

A courtroom visit is a worthwhile educational experience for anyone interested in the legal profession and criminal justice system.

AGRICULTURAL RESEARCH SERVICE
U.S. Department of Agriculture
600 E. Mermaid Lane
Wyndmoor, Pa. 19118
233–6634

Tour Day is once a year on a weekday in April. Two-hour tours are by reservation only at 10 A.M. and 1:30 P.M., for groups of no more than 40, at least junior high school level. Call after January 1 for the date and additional information.

Cost: Free.

SEPTA: Bus X. There's ample space for parking.

E & H: Wheelchair access possible for one or two members of group.

The U.S.D.A. Research Center is a unique city "farm" where scientists work to help consumers. This isn't a traditional farm. The "farmers" here are researchers looking for ways to develop new and improved products, upgrade nutritional value, open new domestic and foreign markets, expand existing ones, reduce marketing costs, eliminate health-related problems, use waste products that are potential pollutants and provide improved quality and economy to the consumer—you and me.

The commodities include animal fats, dairy products, fruits, hides and leather, maple sap and syrups, honey, meats, potatoes and other vegetables.

Your tour will include stops at four of the 14 laboratory stations, if it's pertinent to your reason for being there. You could see a 15-minute film on the Agricultural Research Service, and there will be time for questions and answers.

DEFENSE PERSONNEL SUPPORT CENTER
2800 South 20th Street—19145
952-2311

Hours: Weekdays, 9 to 4. Closed holidays. Allow one hour.
Tours: Scheduled for groups of 20 to 30, at least 12 years old. Call at least 2 weeks in advance.
Cost: Free.
Lunch: Arrangements can be made when scheduling tour to bring-your-own or purchase lunch at the cafeteria.
SEPTA: Buses 2, 17.
E & H: No wheelchair access.

Uniforms for all branches of the United States Armed Forces are manufactured here. You'll see these garments being produced, and you'll visit the testing labs for government clothing textiles and medical supplies.

The local Defense Personnel Support Center can boast about something they do that no one else in the world does. They have a hand-embroidery flag shop where each seamstress works an average of three months to complete one flag. This is where all hand-embroidered flags for the President, his Cabinet and officers of general rank are made.

FEDERAL RESERVE BANK OF PHILADELPHIA
100 North 6th Street—19106
574-6114 (Public Services)

Hours: The ground floor Eastburn Court is open to the public, weekdays, 9 to 3. Closed holidays.

Tours: Groups of no more than 30 high school or college students, or adults interested in banking or related work, can usually be scheduled by calling at least a month ahead.

Cost: Free.

SEPTA: Buses 47, 48, 50, 61 or two blocks from Independence Hall.

Other: The ground floor 180-seat auditorium is the site for a concert series from October to April, as well as other occasional public events. Call for a schedule.

E & H: You can avoid steps by entering from 7th Street.

The Federal Reserve Bank isn't like any other bank. It's not a commercial bank. It's a bank for financial institutions, and it's governed by the Federal Reserve System.

The Federal Reserve Bank of Philadelphia serves a district that includes Eastern Pennsylvania, Southern New Jersey and all of Delaware. You can come here to purchase U.S. Savings Bonds and Treasury securities. You'll see the tellers' booths on the ground level of the Eastburn Court.

The Federal Reserve Bank is a monumental eight-story building which covers a whole city block. It's built around two sun-lit courts.

Alexander Calder's 100-foot "White Cascade" mobile is suspended from the Eastburn (East) Court facing Independence Mall. You can't miss it; it's the largest mobile in the world.

Rare U.S. coins and currency are also on permanent display in this court. And, you can push a button and see a three-minute video show on the Federal Reserve Bank.

Combining this visit with a tour of the U.S. Mint* across Independence Mall provides on-site education about money flow in the United States.

NATIONAL WEATHER SERVICE
William J. Green Federal Building
600 Arch Street—19106
627-5575

Hours: Weekdays, 1 to 3. Allow 30 minutes.
Tours: Scheduled for groups of no more than 20, at least
5th grade level. Call at least one week ahead. Hold the
line till the recorded weather forecast is finished.
Cost: Free.
E & H: Wheelchair access.

Sometimes we love them, sometimes we hate them. But
we always rely on them. Who? The weather forecaster.

Here at the weather bureau, a staff of meteorologists
issues general, marine and aviation forecasts every six
hours, 24 hours a day, and you can see how they do it.

A tour of the office highlights forecast and communications procedures, weather maps and charts. (Since this is a
forecast office only, you won't see any weather instruments.)

You'll also see the operation of radio station KIH 28
that's broadcast 24 hours a day from and by the National
Weather Service. If your radio is equipped with a Public
Service band, tune in to 162.475 megahertz. You'll hear
weather reports, updated hourly, along with the marine
forecast, travelers' advisories and storm warnings. And,
you'll hear educational tapes about the weather and
forecasting.

The weather people spend time providing members of
the legal profession with certification of weather on
specific dates. Building contractors try to use long range
forecasts as an aid to estimating contract and construction deadlines.

And unless you were born before 1871, the weatherman
can check the records for the temperature and precipitation on the date of your birth.

PHILADELPHIA NAVAL BASE
End of South Broad Street—19112
952-7626

Hours: 4 tours will be scheduled every Friday and Saturday at 9 and 11 A.M. Group tours for 25 or more can sometimes be arranged for other times. Allow one hour.
Tours: Call or write a few months in advance to the Public Affairs Office at the Base. A bus that seats a maximum of 35 is provided on arrival, or you can stay on your own bus. All tour-goers must be at least 8 years old.
Cost: Free.
SEPTA: Buses C, G, 17.
Other: United States citizens only, and no cameras are allowed.
E & H: Everyone remains on the bus for the tour. Wheelchairs cannot be accommodated on the Naval Base bus.

The Philadelphia Naval Base is a city within the city on 713 acres where the Schuylkill River meets the Delaware. The nation's largest aircraft carrier, the U.S.S. Saratoga was completely overhauled here.
The Navy Base is a fascinating place to visit for anyone interested in ships, the waterfront, life at sea, or the life on a military base.
A public affairs representative and a bus will meet your group at the base entrance. Your guide will point out the various ships, the shipbuilding center, the drydocks and the land facilities. He'll identify the mothball fleet's assorted craft including battleships, an aircraft carrier, submarines, cruisers, destroyers, tugs and cargo ships.
Note: If you would like to board a Navy or Coast Guard vessel, or if you want to find out more about the Armed Forces, turn to "May" in Chapter 19.

UNITED STATES MINT
5th and Arch Streets—19106
597-7350

Hours: Monday to Saturday, 9 to 4:30. Closed holidays. Allow 45 minutes.
Tours: They're self-guided at your own pace. Call ahead if you're bringing a large group.
Cost: Free. No samples.
SEPTA: Buses 48, 50, or Market Street routes.
Other: There is a sales counter where you can buy commemorative medals and uncirculated coins.

E & H: Complete wheelchair access.

It's hard to imagine that most of the coins in the United States are made right here in Philadelphia. Of the country's three mints, ours is the largest.

The Mint has a self-guided audio visual tour that explains the stages involved in making nickels, dimes, quarters and pennies...all of which we take for granted. You'll see the processes of melting, casting, pressing and cleaning, inspecting, counting and bagging.

Six coin denominations are manufactured at the country's biggest money factory. This is the mint that made the Bicentennial coins now in circulation which are double-dated 1776-1976. It's also where the John Wayne commemorative medals and Statue of Liberty coins were made.

A museum in the mint exhibits historical objects related to coin-making. And don't miss the seven Tiffany stained glass mosaics that depict the coinage processes of ancient Rome. The circular murals were preserved from the former Philadelphia mint when it closed in 1969.

While you're in the neighborhood, stroll around the corner to see the bust of Benjamin Franklin* on Arch Street, just below 4th. He was made out of 80,000 Philadelphia copper pennies.

UNITED STATES POSTAL SERVICE
30th and Market Streets—19104
596-5333 (Public Information Office)

Hours: Weekdays, 10 to 3. Closed holidays. Allow one hour. No tours are scheduled from November 15 to February 1.
Tours: Scheduled for groups of 10 to 30, at least 13 years old. One adult must accompany every 10 children. Call or write at least a few weeks ahead. You'll set the tour date and then be told to send a letter to confirm.
Cost: Free.
SEPTA: Buses D, 9, 30, 31, 42, 45 or Market Street routes.

E & H: There are steps at entrance and considerable walk-ing in hectic areas. Visitors in wheelchairs should enter at Chestnut Street. Arrangements can be made in advance for a few people to use elevator.

Do you know how 8 million pieces of mail are handled in Philadelphia every day? And how they're sorted for delivery to your door? You'll find out when you visit the Main Branch of the Philadelphia Post Office.

A tour of the building lets you chart the various stages of mail processing from the time it's deposited in a mailbox until it's bundled for delivery to its destination.

The mailman who makes box collections drops his pick-up bags at the post office. They go by conveyor belt to the collection center for sorting and separating. The letters are then automatically canceled at the rate of 20,000 per hour. Next they're sorted according to ZIP codes at the rate of 60 per minute. Then they're bundled and labeled and sent down the chutes to a platform for final pick-up and area delivery.

If all this sounds exhausting, we haven't even mentioned what happens to Special Delivery and the 35,000 pieces of first class mail scanned each hour by the Optical Character Reader.

Stamp collectors will be interested in the **Philadelphia Philatelic Center** of the United States Postal Service. It's located at the 9th and Market Streets Post Office. Hours are 8 to 4:45 on weekdays and 9 to 3:45 on Saturdays.

The Center sells American commemoratives, mini-albums, opening day cachets and a variety of items of interest to philatelists. Call 592–9652 to see if they have what you're looking for.

Many of the same items are also available at the **B. Free Franklin Post Office** in Franklin Court* at 314 Market Street. This is also where all outgoing mail gets specially hand-canceled, and there's an interesting Postal Museum.

Institutional Tours

ACADEMY OF MUSIC
Broad and Locust Streets—19102
893-1935

Tours: On specific Tuesdays at 2 P.M. during the orchestra season from October to May. Allow one hour. Reservations are necessary at least a few days in advance. Groups can be accommodated, but no one under 12 is permitted.
Cost: $3. Proceeds go to the Academy.
SEPTA: Buses C, 27, 32; Broad Street Subway.
E & H: There is no wheelchair access for the tour, and there's a good bit of walking.

The Academy of Music is the home of the world-famous Philadelphia Orchestra*, and as part of the tour, you can stand on the stage where the orchestra performs. Then you can walk backstage, through the ballroom, the reception room, and the dressing rooms of the orchestra and their guest performers. If you would like, you can try out some of the Academy's 2,929 seats.

The Academy, which opened in 1857, is acoustically among the world's finest concert halls because of a 20-foot-deep well that's in the basement. The well is also on the tour.

You'll find out about the features that contribute to the excellent sound of the great musicians who perform here.

And, hopefully, you'll come back again when the Academy is filled with beautiful music and beautiful people.

AMERICAN RED CROSS
23rd and Chestnut Streets—19103
299-4198

Hours: Weekdays, 10 to 3. Allow 45 minutes to one hour.
Tours: Groups of no more than 40 can be scheduled, at least junior high school age. Write or call 4 weeks in advance to the Public Education Office.
Cost: Free.
SEPTA: Buses D, 7, 9, 12, 42 or Market Street routes.
E & H: The tour goes to two buildings, with wheelchair access to only one of them.

The Penn-Jersey Region of American Red Cross moved

to these handsome new headquarters in 1972. Their increased services, the community's interest and special programs necessitated their expansion in 1977 to additional space in an adjacent building on 23rd Street. Further expansion was completed in 1981 with a new building across 23rd Street.

The tour includes visits to the blood donor center, blood processing laboratories and the dispatching area where blood is refrigerated, packed and prepared for shipment to hospitals. You'll see the pheresis unit where donors contribute a specific component of their blood to be used to treat cancer patients. You'll see the emergency services department and services to military families, and you'll visit the operations department where computers store information on donors and the inventory of available blood and components.

If you're between 17 and 65 years old, weigh at least 110 pounds and are in good health, ask about the benefits of being a blood donor.

BOY SCOUTS OF AMERICA
Philadelphia Council
22nd and Winter Streets—19103
988-9811

Hours: Weekdays, 8:30 to 4:30. Allow 30 minutes.
Tours: Groups of up to 50 can be scheduled. Call or write in advance to the Public Relations Office for a group tour. Individuals can stop by to browse.
Cost: Free.
SEPTA: Buses 7, 32, 48.
E & H: 8 steps at entrance prevent wheelchair access, but the building's exterior can be admired from the sidewalk. Ask about scout troops with special programs to accommodate boys with just about any type of handicap. A ramp will be available in 1987.

The Philadelphia Boy Scout Council was founded in 1910 and completed construction of its own headquarters building in 1930. The Italian Renaissance-style structure houses administrative offices for the camping, activities, training, advancement and specialized programs that include more than 28,000 youth members in 895 Philadelphia cub, scout and explorer units. It's the oldest continuously used Boy Scouts office in America.

Scouts and friends of scouting from around the world take great pride in this building. Its entrance facade is

inscribed, "Youth Prepared Safeguards the Nation...
This house dedicated to the training of boys for useful
leadership."

The building is covered inside and out with the many
symbols of scouting. Look for the 12 points of the Scout
Law, the universal Scout Badge, all of the merit and Veteran Scout badges along with several more noteworthy
inscriptions.

You'll also see the seals of Philadelphia, Pennsylvania
and the United States. The Golden Book of Scout Heroes
is exhibited under glass, and a cabinet display includes
assorted emblems, flags, medallions, statuettes and cita-
tions of local scouting.

A life-size bronze statue of "The Scout" looks out to the
Benjamin Franklin Parkway as it greets you in front of
the building. It was sculpted in 1937 by Dr. R. Tait
McKenzie, whose works are also exhibited at the Lloyd P.
Jones Gallery*.

Note: This is the only place for members of the Boy
Scouts' "Order of the Arrow" to explore the complete
history of that elite group.

COMMUNITY COLLEGE OF PHILADELPHIA
1700 Spring Garden Street—19130
751-8040

Hours: Weekdays, 10 to 5. Closed school holidays. Allow
one hour.
Tours: Groups of up to 15 should call a week ahead.
Cost: Free.
SEPTA: Buses 2, 43.
E & H: Complete wheelchair access. Enter at ramp on
17th Street side of old U.S. Mint building.

High school students and prospective college students
of any age will benefit from this tour. You'll hear about
the diverse course offerings available in day and evening
programs, and you'll see some of the up-to-date facilities
used by those attending classes.

High tech areas like the TV studio and the computer-
aided drafting labs used by architecture students are
always interesting to see. If you're a would-be or accomplished artist, you'll want to see the art department and
ceramics studios.

You'll be impressed by the preserved grandeur of the
old United States Mint building and marvel how it has
been adapted to classroom, library and academic use.

You can combine your tour with a visit to the Rotunda

Gallery*. If you would like to know what concerts and plays are being presented at the Community College, call the Student Activities Office at 751-8210.

CURTIS INSTITUTE OF MUSIC
1726 Locust Street—19103
893-5275

Hours: October to May, weekdays, 10 to 3. Allow 45 minutes.
Tours: By reservation only, and some interest in music is a prerequisite. Call the Public Relations Office at least 2 weeks in advance to schedule groups of no more than 15.
Cost: Free.
SEPTA: Buses D, 40, 42, 90.
E & H: There are 9 steps at the entrance and 3 flights of stairs inside.

Since its founding in 1924, the Curtis Institute of Music has trained nearly 3,000 musicians for concert performance. Students from around the world are given a strenuous audition and, once they're accepted, they receive the Institute's coveted free education.

Leonard Bernstein, Judith Blegen, Eugene Istomin, Gian-Carlo Menotti, Anna Moffo and 47 current members of the Philadelphia Orchestra are graduates of Curtis.

Josef Hofmann, Gregor Piatigorsky, Rudolf Serkin, Leopold Stokowski and Efrem Zimbalist have served on the distinguished Curtis faculty.

A visit to the school is a treat to the eye as well as to the ear. While you won't attend any classes, the chances are good that you'll hear lessons and practice sessions. When you tour the magnificent buildings and unusual classrooms, you'll see wonderful art, antiques and furnishings from the collections of Curtis founder Mary Louise Curtis Bok Zimbalist and her family.

If you're interested in attending Curtis concerts, pick up a monthly schedule from the receptionist, or refer back to Chapter 10.

MASONIC TEMPLE
1 N. Broad Street—19107
988-1917

Tours: Weekdays, promptly at 10, 11, 1, 2, and 3. Saturdays (except July and August) at 10 and 11. Closed July 4, Thanksgiving, Christmas, New Year's. Allow one hour. Call ahead if you're coming with 20 or more.

Cost: Free.

SEPTA: Any route to City Hall.

E & H: There are 10 steps at the entrance. The tour includes a lot of walking and steps. An elevator is available.

If you haven't been on a fancy movie set, you can pretend you're on one when you visit the Masonic Temple, because this place is unbelievable.

The Masons keep deep, dark secrets about their organization. Their secrecy is symbolized by two handsome Egyptian sphinx figures that flank the members' entrance on Broad Street. Each month, members from 92 lodges in the Philadelphia area hold their meetings here.

The building is the headquarters for the Pennsylvania Masonic Order. It was designed by a 27-year-old member, James A. Windrim, and it was dedicated in 1873. Windrim planned each of the seven huge Lodge Halls to represent a period in history. These halls are among this country's finest examples of Corinthian, Ionic, Italian Renaissance, Norman, Gothic, Oriental and Egyptian architecture.

Renaissance Hall, the most modern of the Temple's styles, will remind you of a three-story 15th century Italian cathedral with its marble columns and stained glass windows bearing the symbols of Masonry. The perfect hieroglyphics of Egyptian Hall were copied from eight Temples in Egypt.

The museum collections associate early Philadelphia and America to the Masonic Order. There are assorted emblems, gavels, symbolic jewels, decorative chinaware and an apron embroidered by Madame Lafayette. President Washington wore the apron when he laid the cornerstone of the new United States Capitol building in ceremonies that were in part Masonic ritual.

The Masonic Temple's cornerstone opened a few years ago. Construction tools and objects of the day from 1873 are beautifully preserved and on display in the museum.

**PENNSYLVANIA COLLEGE
OF PODIATRIC MEDICINE**
8th and Race Streets—19107
629-0300 Ext. 219 (Public Relations)

Hours: Weekdays, 9 to 4. Allow one hour.

Tours: Scheduled for groups, at least 4th grade level, with at least one adult for every 15 students. Call at least 2 weeks ahead.

Cost: Free.
SEPTA: Buses 47, 61.
E & H: The tour includes a lot of walking, but there's wheelchair access.

Podiatry applies to foot health and the proper medical and surgical care of human feet. There are only seven colleges of podiatric medicine in the United States, and you can visit one right here in Philadelphia. The college grants the degree of Doctor of Podiatric Medicine to students who successfully complete its four-year curriculum.

Your tour of the six-story education building covers several facets of contemporary teaching. You'll visit classrooms, laboratories and the Foot Health Center where 100 patients are treated every day by upperclassmen and professional staff. You'll see the instructional communications center that enables students to witness surgery by closed-circuit TV.

While you're here, stop by to see the Shoe Museum*. Happy walking!

PENNSYLVANIA S.P.C.A.
350 E. Erie Avenue—19134
426-6300

Hours: Tuesday and Thursday at 10. Allow one hour.
Tours: Groups of 10 to 35, at least junior high school age, are scheduled several weeks in advance.
Cost: Free.
SEPTA: Buses 47, 50; trolleys 53, 56.
E & H: Complete wheelchair access.

When you visit the Society for the Prevention of Cruelty to Animals you'll see the garage where rescue equipment and animal transport vehicles are kept and the receiving area where animals are checked in and given physicals. There are kennels for puppies, kittens, guinea pigs, hamsters and other creatures that turn up at the S.P.C.A. There's even a stable for horses.

Weather permitting, you'll visit the bird sanctuary and feed the resident chickens, ducks and geese.

Everyone leaves with a souvenir and information on proper pet care.

PHILADELPHIA COLLEGE
OF TEXTILES AND SCIENCE*
School House Lane and Henry Avenue—19144
951-2851 (Public Relations)

Hours: October to mid-May, weekdays, 9 to 4. Closed holidays. Allow one hour, and an additional hour if you include a visit to the Goldie Paley Design Center*.

Tours: Groups of high school students or adults should call at least 2 weeks ahead to schedule.

Cost: Free.

Lunch: Reservations can be made at the same time for the student cafeteria.

SEPTA: Buses J, 32.

E & H: No wheelchair access. The tour goes into a few buildings and there's considerable walking and steps.

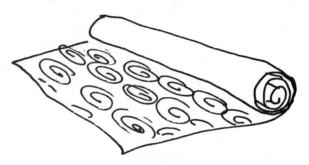

Let a knowledgeable student be your guide at the country's oldest and largest college of textiles. This is where students major in textiles, science and business while they earn a four-year Bachelor of Science degree.

You won't visit any of the classrooms, but you'll get an insider's view of the laboratories and learn about other facets of the 86-acre campus.

The emphasis of the tour is on textiles, but it can be designed to coincide with the interests of your group. You'll see a fragment of thread on its way to becoming a fabric. That includes the process of spinning, dyeing, design-making, silk screening, card weaving, hand or commercial weaving on a variety of looms.

In the Apparel Research Center you'll be introduced to a variety of mannequins and machinery.

You'll leave this tour with a greater appreciation of your wardrobe.

THE PHILADELPHIA INQUIRER
400 N. Broad Street—19101
854-5502 (Public Affairs Office)

Hours: By appointment only, weekdays, 10 A.M. to Noon.
Allow one hour.
Tours: School groups of 10 to 30, 7th to 12th grades, will
be scheduled by written request from the teacher to:
Public Affairs Dept., *The Philadelphia Inquirer,* Box
8263, Phila., Pa. 19101. Give your preferred date and an
alternate.
Cost: Free.
SEPTA: Bus C; Broad Street Subway.
E & H: No wheelchair access.

Journalism students will be interested in tours of *The
Philadelphia Inquirer.* Philadelphia's major morning
newspaper has a daily circulation of 490,000; on Sundays
it's 900,000.

When you visit The Inquirer's headquarters you'll see
the work that goes into putting out a major daily newspaper. You'll tour the newsroom. You'll see reporters at
work covering the metropolitan desk, national and foreign
news. Practically everything in today's newsroom is processed on video display terminals.

From there you'll see the production facilities, and
you'll learn what it means when they say: "Roll the
presses."

If you can't get to tour The Inquirer, read further in this
chapter about bringing The Inquirer to you. And we don't
mean home delivery.

PHILADELPHIA STOCK EXCHANGE
1900 Market Street—19103
496-5000

Hours: Action on the trading floor is weekdays, 9:30 to 4.
Tours: You're on your own to observe. See below.
Cost: Free.
SEPTA: Any Market or Chestnut Street route to 19th.
E & H: No wheelchair access.

This is the nation's oldest stock exchange, and one of
the busiest. Transactions are made on more than a thousand securities and options. Foreign currency options
traded here have put the Philadelphia Stock Exchange in
the international marketplace.

Even though you can't go directly on the trading floor,
there's much to learn and observe. The Philadelphia Stock

Exchange is the most modern exchange in the country. It moved to its new headquarters in 1981.

The building alone deserves a visit. It's built around a block-long, eight-story, enclosed skylit atrium. Stock and options trading can be viewed through window walls dividing the hectic marketplace from the lush, green, lower-level garden.

The atrium has 6,000 plants, 23 varieties of trees, nine pools, seven fountains and wonderful seating areas.

Watch the people on the trading floor and try to figure out the various roles they play. Look at the ticker tapes and try to read their codes.

The exchange's reception area is on the street level. Brochures are available here that explain how to better understand the stock exchange.

SCHEIE EYE INSTITUTE
51 North 39th Street—19104
662-8100

Tours: Weekdays, 10 to 4. Closed holidays. Allow at least 30 minutes. School-age groups to visiting professionals can be scheduled and tours are geared accordingly. Call ahead to make reservations.

Cost: Free.

Lunch: There is a large cafeteria in the adjoining Presbyterian Hospital.

SEPTA: Buses 30, 40; Market-Frankford Subway-Elevated to 40th Street.

E & H: Entrance ramp and elevators enable wheelchair access.

The Scheie Eye Institute is a round building that serves as an in- and out-patient hospital facility and research center for the University of Pennsylvania's Ophthalmology Department.

On the lower level you'll see the education department's modern classrooms and auditorium with complete audiovisual facilities. You'll see the examining equipment and, if conditions allow, a demonstration of a laser beam.

The second floor is for out-patient surgery. Moving upstairs, a central nursing core is surrounded by patients' rooms. In the top floor research center, a staff member might be available to describe current projects underway at Scheie.

After you've toured Scheie you'll know why the building has received several architectural awards.

C. A. ASHER CONFECTIONERS
5537 Germantown Avenue—19144
438-3774

Hours: Weekdays, 9 to 3. Closed major holidays. Allow 30 minutes.
Tours: Call at least 3 days ahead to schedule for no more than 40. One adult must accompany every 10 youngsters, and all children must be supervised.
Cost: Free, but you might be tempted to buy a treat.
SEPTA: Buses E, K, XH, 26; trolley 23. Or, ask about parking arrangements when scheduling tour.
E & H: Everything is on street level making wheelchair access possible. You'll be standing for entire visit.

Who wouldn't love to visit a candy factory? C.A. Asher has been making assorted chocolates since 1892, and this year they'll be making around one-and-a-half million pounds worth.

Asher's products include sandwich mints, caramels, chocolate-covered marshmallows, chocolate-covered pretzels, raisin clusters, butter creams, cashew pralines, cherry cordials and almond bark, to name a few. For the calorie conscious candy eater, they thoughtfully make dietetic varieties as well.

On any given day you could see mint souffle being handmade, truffles being poured, molasses paddles getting their chocolate coating or hostess mints being layered. You'll follow the assembly line from production to weighing and packaging.

Since C.A. Asher is in the heart of Germantown, you should combine your visit with stops at one or two of Germantown's historic attractions (see Chapter 3). That would make Mr. Asher very happy. You might also go to the next block (and the next paragraph) and tour the Cunningham Piano Co.

CUNNINGHAM PIANO CO.
5427 Germantown Avenue—19144
438-3200

Tours: By appointment only, Monday to Saturday, 9 to 3. Allow one hour. Call a week ahead to schedule groups of up to 10.
Cost: Free.

SEPTA: Buses E, K, XH, 26; trolley 23.
E & H: Wheelchair access to showroom only. Factory is on the 2nd floor.

Cunningham Piano Co. started manufacturing pianos in 1891 and continued until the 1940s.

Today, pianos are restored in their factory around the corner on Coulter Street to the tune of 300 a year. (No pun intended.) This is the only factory of its kind in Philadelphia.

Your tour starts in the showroom where you'll see several kinds of new and used pianos. Do you know the difference between a spinet, grand, console, upright and player piano? If you don't, you'll find out quickly from the 60 or so models on display.

Twelve pianos at a time are usually in various stages of restoration or repair at the factory. Old-world craftsmen may be replacing a sounding board, rebuilding a keyboard or adjusting strings. Many of the employees have been here 25 or 30 years and they're proud to show you their work.

Next, you might want to visit some of the historic sites along Germantown Avenue (see Chapter 3) or C.A. Asher Confectioners* on the next block.

FOOD DISTRIBUTION CENTER
East of Broad Street, from Packer to Pattison Avenues
3301 Galloway Street—19148

Cost: Free.
SEPTA: Buses G, 17.
E & H: No wheelchair access. There are steps and a good bit of walking on either tour.

The city's Food Distribution Center moved from its cramped and outmoded Dock Street headquarters in 1959 (now the site of the Society Hill Towers at 2nd and Locust Streets).

Today this $100 million, 380-acre complex is a perfect example of how a large city's food distribution should operate. The Center has food processing, warehousing, wholesaling and distribution. The occupants range from a banana importer and a dairy producer to a variety of meat, poultry and fish packers. Over 10,000 people work here day and night.

You can visit the wholesaling centers as follows:

301

Fruit and Produce
336–3003

Hours: Some weekdays at 10 A.M. Allow 45 minutes.
Tours: Scheduled for groups of 10 to 20, college students or people involved in the food industry. Call one month in advance.

The hustle and bustle of activity starts here at 4 A.M. Bushels and baskets of farm-fresh foods are brought in by the 40 wholesalers who occupy the row. Retail merchants, hucksters, restaurant buyers and thrifty housewives arrive before the sun rises to buy the day's or week's provisions. Tours are led by the terminal manager. He might focus on shipping, food handling, display or whatever the particular interest of the group.

Seafood
336–1051

Hours: Weekdays, 8:30 to 9:30 A.M. Allow 30 minutes.
Tours: Scheduled for groups of 20 to 25, at least 4th grade. Call at least two weeks in advance.
Other: The floors are slick and wet. Wear sneakers or rubber-sole shoes.

Seafood is the only thing that's sold in this market, and most of it is gone by 9:30 in the morning. The procedures of receiving and delivery will be explained. And all of the different varieties of seafood and fish will be pointed out.

NATIONAL BISCUIT COMPANY
Roosevelt Boulevard and Byberry Road—19116
673–4800 Ext. 62

Hours: January to April, Tuesday and Thursday mornings at 10 sharp. Allow one hour.
Tours: Scheduled for groups of no more than 20 (including adult chaperones), at least 5th grade or 10 years old. Call at least a month in advance, and have some alternate dates in mind.
Cost: Free.
SEPTA: Bus B.
Other: Cameras are forbidden.
E & H: There are a lot of steps and strenuous walking, so wear comfortable rubber-sole shoes. No high-heels are allowed, no canes or walkers, and there's no wheelchair access.

This is Nabisco's main plant in this area for baking

biscuits, cookies and crackers. You'll watch the entire baking and packaging process for some of your favorite snacks.

You'll know by the aroma that you're near Nabisco, even if you don't see the sign.

PHILADELPHIA ELECTRIC COMPANY
2301 Market Street—19101
841-4121 (Consumer Affairs Division)

Tours: A variety of programs, films and demonstrations is available for student groups, youth and adult organizations at several P.E. locations or "to go" (as described later in this chapter). They last anywhere from 20 minutes to a few hours. Call or write for information on programs and films available from Philadelphia Electric's speakers bureau.

Cost: Free.

SEPTA: Routes will vary according to the specific location. Buses 7, 12, 31, 45 to 23rd and Market.

E & H: Informative and entertaining programs planned specifically for senior citizens are held monthly, September to April, at 2301 Market St. Small or large groups are welcome. Call 841-4121 for details on Senior Citizen Days. No wheelchair access.

Philadelphia Electric Company wants you to be informed about energy use and supply. They want you to know more about the energy situation we're all concerned about, and they want you to know the practical ways of conserving electricity.

Over 200 employees from all levels of P.E. make up a speakers bureau that can talk to your group on any topic that deals with electricity, energy saving, conservation tips, nuclear power, natural gas or electrical safety.

Many of the programs involve films, slide shows or demonstrations. They can be presented at your location, or sometimes at a nearby P.E. facility.

Since you consume electricity, you should find out about these programs Philadelphia Electric offers, in Spanish as well as English, and take advantage of them.

READING TERMINAL MARKET
12th and Filbert to Arch Streets—19107
922-2317 (market information)
925-0948 or 546-2690 (tour information)

Tours: October through March, daily, except Sunday; April through September, weekdays, at 10 A.M. Other

303

times can sometimes be scheduled. Allow 2 to 3 hours for groups of 8 to 20.

Cost: Call for details.

Lunch: There's an abundance of places and menus to choose from.

SEPTA: Bus 48; trolley 23 or any Market Street route.

E & H: Enter from Arch Street and everything is on one level.

The Reading Terminal, completed in 1893, is an architectural wonder. This is the country's only surviving single-span train shed and one of the largest that was ever built. That's why the U.S. Department of the Interior includes the Reading Terminal on its list of National Landmarks.

The trains have been relocated to the new Market East Station (see Chapter 1). But you shouldn't miss the world-famous Reading Terminal Market beneath the old station. It's another Philadelphia phenomenon.

Over 40 merchants are on hand with a vast assortment of fruit and produce stalls, butcher shops, seafood stands, bakeries, restaurants, cheese shops, dairy and ice cream bars and markets for every delicacy imaginable. The Pennsylvania Dutch bring their specialties to the market on Thursdays, Fridays and Saturdays.

You can wander around the market on your own and sample some cookies and ice cream, or you can get a group together and take a guided tour to meet the vendors and learn about their goods.

Tours are led by two local ladies who have written a book, "To Market, To Market, Philadelphia's Reading Terminal Market." Special emphasis can be placed on meat cutting demonstrations, spices, cheeses, international foods, poultry or seafood. You'll be interested in the history, the restoration and future plans for Reading Terminal.

The same two ladies can also take your group on a tour of the Italian Market (see Chapter 12). Don't say we don't have unique places to shop in Philadelphia!

SAMUEL YELLIN METALWORKERS AND YELLIN MUSEUM
5520 Arch Street—19139
472-3122

Hours: By appointment only, weekdays, 9 to 3. Allow one hour.

Tours: Up to 25 can be scheduled by calling or writing in advance. All visitors must be at least high school seniors and interested in the fine arts, ornamental metalworks or blacksmithing.

Cost: Free.

SEPTA: Bus 31 or Market Street elevated train to 56th and Market; bus G to 56th and Arch. There's plenty of street parking space.

Other: Dress comfortably and appropriately for visiting an ironworks studio.

E & H: No wheelchair access.

A visit to Samuel Yellin Metalworkers is a multi-faceted experience. The two-story Spanish-style building dates from 1920 when Samuel Yellin opened his shop. Mr. Yellin died in 1940, but his studio continues to create masterpieces in metal in the same tradition.

A first-floor museum houses hundreds of samples of Yellin craftsmanship and fine examples of metalwork from around the world. Locks, keys, altarpieces, gates, railings, andirons, lighting fixtures and purely decorative objects are embellished with sculpted asps, birds, animals, flowers, leaves and ornamental patterns.

Yellin ironwork can be seen across the country. In center city Philadelphia you can see the exquisite designs at the First Pennsylvania Bank entrance on the southeast corner of 15th and Chestnut Streets, the Curtis Institute of Music* at 1724 Locust Street, the iron-clad red doors of St. Mark's Church at 1625 Locust Street, and the Rosenbach Museum* at 2010 Delancey Street.

Samuel Yellin Metalworkers also has a library on wrought iron art and architecture and a medieval-style room with many of Mr. Yellin's favorite furnishings and artwork. The blacksmiths and metalworkers in the ironworks use many of the tools that Samuel Yellin used more than 60 years ago. While much of their current work is in iron, other metals such as bronze, stainless steel and aluminum are used. Depending on what's in production, you might be lucky enough to see iron being shaped by one of the many tools or methods that make the art possible.

C. SCHMIDT & SONS
127 Edward Street—19123
928-4121

Hours: Weekday mornings, by reservation only, or call ahead to ask if you can join a tour already scheduled. Allow 1½ to 2 hours.

Tours: Scheduled for groups of no more than 35. Youngsters must have parental consent and adult supervision. Call or write to "Tours" at least 2 weeks ahead.

Cost: Free.

SEPTA: Bus 5; trolley 15; Girard stop of Market–Frankford Subway–Elevated.

Other: Wear comfortable shoes. A sweater or jacket is suggested since the processing requires temperature changes from 34 to 85 degrees.

E & H: No wheelchair access. Everyone must be ambulatory. There's considerable walking on several floors.

Schmidt's has been brewing beer in Philadelphia since 1860. It's the nation's ninth largest brewer. Schmidt's produces over four million barrels of beer a year.

You'll find out how pure water, malt, cereal grains, hops and cultured yeast are processed into beer and then bottled or canned or kegged under Schmidt's or any of their 20 other labels.

You'll discover what distinguishes different beer flavors and what makes a beer "light" in calories or "light" in color. If you aren't already, you'll become a connoisseur of Schmidt's fine beer.

SMITH KLINE AND FRENCH
LABORATORIES
1500 Spring Garden Street—19130
751-4412

Hours: Weekdays, except holidays, in morning or afternoon. Allow one hour.

Tours: See below.

Cost: Free.

SEPTA: Buses C, 43; Broad Street Subway.

E & H: Wheelchair access.

Some of the world's best known pharmaceuticals come from the laboratories of Smith Kline and French, a division of SmithKline Beckman Corporation.

Tours of the production areas are limited to professional groups in related fields, and juniors or seniors in area high school classes who are at least 16 years old and interested in science.

Reservations for group tours must be made at least a week in advance, and larger groups will be divided into smaller groups of ten each.

TERMINI PASTRIES
1523 South 8th Street—19147
334-1816

Hours: Daily for business, 8 A.M. to 8 P.M.

Tours: By reservation only, weekdays, 9 to noon. Call a week ahead for groups of no more than 25, with 4 adults accompanying any group of children. Allow about 30 minutes. No tours are scheduled around holidays.

Cost: Free, but we think you'll be tempted to purchase a reminder of the visit.

SEPTA: Bus 47; trolley 29.

Other: Wear appropriate clothes to be in a bakery and standing for entire tour.

E & H: Everything is on street level, but no wheelchair access.

Tantalizing pastries have been rising from the ovens of this South Philadelphia family bakery since 1921. The second generation has joined in the all natural and handmade preparation of popular items like chocolate whipped cream cake, strawberry shortcake, brown derby cake with a whipped cream center, donuts, streudel, napoleons, muffins, sticky buns and gingerbread men.

More exotic temptations are a fresh fruit ambrosia, clove-flavored "bones" and zuccardi cookies from Sicilian recipes, sfogladelli from Naples and a "stork's nest" from Northern Italy.

Their most famous product, though, is the cannoli. You can see cannoli-making on Wednesday, Thursday and Friday mornings. A cannoli is sinfully delicious. (I saw President Reagan's face light up when he sampled a Termini cannoli.)

What you'll see at Termini's depends on the day and the season, but whatever you see will be tempting.

Audience Television Shows

If you would like to be part of a live television audience, there are opportunities in Philadelphia.

AM/PHILADELPHIA, hosted by localites Lizabeth Starr and Wally Kennedy, has guest stars each day as well as regular features. It's televised live from WPVI-TV, Channel 6, City Line and Monument Road, every weekday morning from 10 to 11.

The program schedule is available three weeks ahead and reservations must be made at least a few days ahead. The audience numbers 125 and, sorry, no one under 16 years old is permitted. Call 477-4040, weekdays 11 to 3, for reservations, and plan to be at the studio by 9:30 A.M.

PEOPLE ARE TALKING with Richard Bey is live from KYW-TV, Channel 3, weekday mornings from 10 to 11. Richard chats with guest stars and gets into controversial and timely issues with visiting celebrities and newsmakers. He also goes into the audience for questions and answers.

If you would like to be in the audience, call 238-4940, or write to the producer of "People Are Talking" at KYW-TV, Independence Mall East, Phila., Pa. 19106. The program schedule is available a month in advance. Groups of up to 40 can be accommodated and the minimum age is 16. You're due at the station by 9 A.M.

Tours to Go

Many Philadelphia businesses and industries will bring their programs to you.

Their shows might be educational, they might be entertainment, or they might be both. There are several programs on tour from the city's performing arts groups, museums and sports teams. The selection is plentiful and often there's no charge.

Reminder: An asterisk (*) indicates that the same place or event appears elsewhere in this book with more details. You'll find that place in the Index.

Films, slide programs and lectures are available to please any audience. Reservations for most of them must be made at least a month in advance.

The **ARCHDIOCESE OF PHILADELPHIA** offers hundreds of films and videotapes to schools, churches and religious organizations. One of the selections is a 30-minute production, "Neumann." It portrays the events that led to the Blessed John Nepomucene Neumann's appointment as Bishop of Philadelphia in 1852. Call the Archdiocese Media Center at 332-2958 for additional information.

BELL OF PENNSYLVANIA offers without charge a choice of six films and lectures about communications. They're given to civic, social and religious groups of 20 and more. Call the Bell Speakers Bureau at 466-4111 for details or to schedule your event.

FIRST PENNSYLVANIA BANK lends more than money. They loan 16mm films on banking, business and short subjects of general interest. They also schedule bank employees to discuss topics related to money and personal finances. These interest-free loans are available to schools, community organizations and social clubs. There are subjects appropriate for elementary school age youngsters to adults. Call the bank's Public Relations Department at 786-8420 if you would like to take advantage of their film library or speakers bureau.

The **FREE LIBRARY OF PHILADELPHIA*** loans films to anyone over 18 years old with a library membership card. They have over 2,000 16mm features, documentaries, short subjects and cartoons. The only condition to borrowing a film is that you can't charge admission or ask for donations when you show.

Film catalogues are sold at the Central Library and available for reference at every Free Library branch. The films, which must be ordered through the Films Department of the Central Library (686-5367), can be picked up and deposited there or at the Northeast, Northwest or West Philadelphia Regional Branches.

The Free Library also loans VHS videocassettes from a growing collection. They can be borrowed overnight or over the weekend once you've signed the library's videocassette service agreement card and meet their requirements.

Same day service is available at the Central Library from the Films Department. Pick-ups can also be made at the three regional branches with reservations made a week in advance.

"American and International Films on Videocassettes" and "Videocassettes for Children" catalogues are available free at the Central Library and three regional branches.

Hours at the Central Library Films Department are weekdays, 9 to 5.

INDEPENDENCE NATIONAL HISTORICAL PARK offers two ways to preview the park experience and both are free.

School and civic groups can borrow a 12-minute, previsit slide program called **"The Independence Experience."** It has 60 slides in a carousel, a cassette tape and a copy of a script that can also be ordered in Spanish. The program is geared to 5th and 6th graders but it's appropriate for anyone planning to visit the National Park. The package is available on a first come, first served basis, so it's a good idea to request the kit at least a month before your group intends to see it. Write to: Pre-Visit Kit, Independence National Historical Park, 313 Walnut Street, Phila., Pa. 19106.

Independence National Historical Park also loans to schools and civic groups the 16mm, 28-minute film **"Independence"** that's shown at the Visitor Center*. Again, requests are filled in the order they receive them, so plan your private show a few months ahead. Write to: Visitor Center "Independence" loan, Independence National Historical Park, 313 Walnut Street, Phila., Pa. 19106

Both the film and the slide program must be returned

within 10 days of receipt so be sure to plan your schedule accordingly.

The **PHILADELPHIA ELECTRIC COMPANY*** will bring to your group, organization or school a film, slide presentation, demonstration, or a well-known speaker to bring you up-to-date on electricity, energy use, safety and conservation. P.E. has free programs and films for third-graders to adults, from 15 minutes to an hour or more.

Call the Electric Company's Consumer Affairs Division at 841–4121. Ask for details, or request the booklet on programs and films available from Philadelphia Electric's speakers bureau.

The **PHILADELPHIA FIRE DEPARTMENT** has a fire prevention program that's worthwhile for any school, community, civic or residential group. A Philadelphia fire-fighter will address your audience at your locale on the warning signs of a fire, prevention measures and safety tips. Call the Fire Prevention Division at 592–5967 to schedule this very important discussion.

THE PHILADELPHIA INQUIRER* sends its staff members and journalists to address interested groups. Write at least a month in advance to the Public Affairs Department, The Philadelphia Inquirer, Box 8263, Phila., Pa. 19101. Tell them your group, the topic and the type of speaker you would like, business or editorial, and they'll give you an informative program.

The **PHILLIES*** will include you on their road trip schedule. You have a choice from the Phillies Film Library of an annual 30-minute "Phillies Highlights" production, baseball instructionals for would-be professionals or films about All-Star games and World Series spectaculars. Call 463–6000 Ext. 291 for details. There's a small charge to cover mailing and your deposit is returned when the borrowed film is returned.

Many of Philadelphia's performing arts groups, museums and organizations have shows "to go." Here are some of them.

The **ACADEMY OF NATURAL SCIENCES*** takes its "Eco Show on the Road" to schools, homes or any institutions where the audience won't exceed 350. You have a choice of different auditorium or animals-only shows.

They're each 45 to 60 minutes long and they include a speaker-naturalist, slide presentation and five or six live animals. There's a fee for "Eco Show on the Road." Call the Academy's Education Department at 299–1060 for details. The critters are happiest when they go on tour.

The **CHILDREN'S MUSEUM** is the ultimate entry for the category of tours "to go." It's a museum without walls. All of its displays and workshops are designed for visits to schools, libraries and scout groups. Workshops on animals, plants, theater, toys and games are for as many as 50 youngsters from four to 12-years-old. Traveling displays feature the elements of time, shapes, bones, weights and sizes. For rates and details, call 247-7235 or write to the Children's Museum, c/o 137 W. Mt. Pleasant Avenue, Phila., Pa. 19119.

CONCERTO SOLOISTS OF PHILADELPHIA* provides recitalists and ensembles for special corporate and social gatherings. You can help choose the program. Call 735-0202 for additional information.

FREEDOM THEATER* travels to schools, churches, prisons, community groups and career conferences. You can choose from their repertoire a play that can be anywhere from 15 minutes to a full-length, full-scale production. The fee is charged accordingly. Call 765-2793 at least three months in advance to make arrangements.

GERMANTOWN THEATER GUILD and **PHILA-
DELPHIA THEATER CARAVAN*** takes its professional shows, puppet plays and mime theater for children and young adults to audiences of at least 50 in
schools, libraries, churches, recreation centers, camps,
club or organization gatherings. The fee depends on the
size of the cast, the traveling props and the group's ability
to pay. The productions are 35 to 60 minutes. For available dates and rates, call 849-0460 or 898-6068.

PHILADELPHIA MARIONETTE THEATER* will
pack up its puppets and bring them to your gathering.
Choose a show of fantasy or humor. This isn't just kids
stuff—you'll be fascinated by the variety. For details on
arranging a visit from the Marionette Theater, call
879-1213.

HEDGEROW THEATER* (565-4211) and the **PEO-
PLE'S LIGHT AND THEATRE COMPANY***
(647-1900) also have children's theater that goes on tour.

PENNSYLVANIA OPERA THEATER* sends a mini-
company on tour to senior citizen groups and community
organizations in the Delaware Valley. From September to
April they'll give either a one hour survey of musical theater or a look at the season's offerings with the company's
artistic director. For information about "Opera Around
Town" call 972-0904.

The **PHILADELPHIA MUSEUM OF ART*** brings you a 45-minute mini-slide tour on one of 11 topics that you're free to choose from. If you can supply the screen, an art museum guide will supply everything else to give you a memorable tour. These slide programs are $25 to groups within a 45-minute drive of the museum. For topics and reservations, call at least a month ahead to the Museum's Park House Guides office, 787-5449.

PLEASE TOUCH MUSEUM* has **Traveling Trunks** for rent. Each trunk is chock-full of objects that provide hands-on learning experiences on the following subjects: The Circus, Dinosaurs, Native Americans, India, Space, Water, Puerto Rican Panorama, and Head to Toe (Clothing from Around the World). A teacher's guide is also included with explanations and activity suggestions.

The trunks are available for two-week rentals, and a one-hour introductory show can be scheduled for an additional fee. Call the museum's director of programming and marketing (963-0667) for fee information and reservations for a traveling trunk.

THE QUIET RIOT COMEDY THEATER* can't keep this quiet. The three-person company will appear at your school, club or community gathering with a 45- or 90-minute mime show. For details, call 885-8825, or write to them at 131 Woodland Road, Wyncote, Pa. 19095.

The **UNIVERSITY MUSEUM*** has "mobile guides" who take artifacts and treasures to third to sixth grade audiences in the Philadelphia Public Schools. A mini-museum on "Woodland Indians" or "Ancient Egypt" becomes a part of the host classroom. For details, call the Volunteer Services Office at the Board of Education at 299-7774. There is a fee for the program, and they'll explain it. If you would like to volunteer as a "mobile guide," call the museum at 898-4277.

Remember: An **asterisk(*)** indicates that the same place or event appears elsewhere in the book with more details. Look in the Index for additional pages.

YOUNG AUDIENCES introduces local students from kindergarten through high school to the performing arts. Professional musicians, singers and dancers from Philadelphia's finest companies visit school assemblies to demonstrate string instruments, brass, percussion or woodwinds and to perform opera, dance, jazz or orchestral numbers. Poetry workshops, mime, puppetry and theater are performed by a professional cast as well. Smaller workshops with 10 to 40 students allow greater audience participation.

The Philadelphia Chapter of Young Audiences, Inc. arranges for school programs anywhere in Southeastern Pennsylvania, the Lehigh Valley and South Jersey. For further information, call 732–8369. Reservations should be made early in the school term, or at least a month in advance.

At least four of Philadelphia's dance groups will perform at the place and time of your choice. Their programs are as flexible as their well-trained bodies. In each instance, there is a fee depending on the size of the company, distance traveled, accompanists and so forth.

GERMANTOWN COUNTRY DANCERS* go on tour evenings and weekends with a full-length program of English and American country dances in traditional costume. The audience usually joins in after the show. Allow as much notice as possible. For more information, you can call 477–0546.

PHILADELPHIA CIVIC BALLET COMPANY* goes on tour with "Dance, the Language of Movement." Four or five professionals dance in the 45-minute show at public and parochial schools in and around Philadelphia, for private groups and organizations. Over 600,000 youngsters and adults have seen the program since it started in 1971. Call 923–4477 for details and make reservations as early as possible in the school term.

315

PHILADELPHIA DANCE COMPANY* goes on tour to schools, community groups and senior citizen centers with a 45- to 60-minute concert-lecture-demonstration program. Arrangements must be made at least two weeks in advance. Call Philadanco (387–8200) for details.

There are portable **WAVES***, too. Call them (563–1545) at least two months in advance to arrange for as few as four or as many as the entire company to appear for your audience. It's non-stop entertainment for 15 minutes to an hour.

Chapter 14.
Philadelphia at Play.

Spectator Sports

Philadelphia is fortunate to have a professional team and first-rate facility for every major sport.

And because Philadelphia's a college town, there's a full schedule of college games for every sport you can think of. And some you wouldn't think of. Like cricket.

Our sports complex, the nation's largest, is 10 minutes from City Hall at the southern end of Broad Street.

The **Spectrum**, opened in 1967, has a seating capacity of over 17,000. **Veterans Stadium**, opened in 1971, can seat over 65,000 for baseball and 73,000 for football. **John F. Kennedy Stadium**, opened in 1926, can seat as many as 102,000. (The elderly and handicapped should refer to Chapter 16 for helpful information regarding these stadiums.)

The best SEPTA routes to the complex are bus C south on Broad Street or the Broad Street Subway south to Pattison Avenue. Check with SEPTA for special express trains and other routes to the stadiums.

Sports events are also held at the Civic Center's Convention Hall, 34th Street and Civic Center Boulevard, and at the Palestra, 33rd near Walnut Street.

Tickets for sporting events are available at the stadiums, at the respective team's office, at all Ticketron outlets (call 885-2215 for the Ticketron location nearest to you) and at commercial ticket agencies.

Don't forget to check the Calendar of Annual Events in Chapter 19 to keep up with sporting spectaculars like the Penn Relays, the Army-Navy Football Game, the BIG FIVE Tournament and the U.S. Pro Indoor Tennis Championships that take place every year.

BASEBALL—PHILLIES
Veterans Stadium (ticket office)
463-1000 (ticket, inclement weather and daily game information)

The Phillies play 80 home games at **Veterans Stadium** during the baseball season which runs from April through early October. Over two million fans turn out each year to cheer the 1980 World Champions and the 1983 National League Champions.

There are day games, night games, occasional twi-night doubleheaders and mid-week afternoon businessperson specials.

You can get tickets at one of 75 ticket agencies in and around Philadelphia, at the Phillies ticket office at the stadium or in the lobby of Mellon Bank at Broad and Chestnut Streets. Call the Phillies to find out which is most convenient.

Since the Phillies ticket sales are completely computerized, you get the best available tickets from whichever location you buy them. You can even purchase by phone using any of three major credit cards. Your tickets will be mailed if time permits, or held at the "will call" window at the stadium.

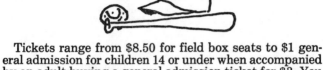

Tickets range from $8.50 for field box seats to $1 general admission for children 14 or under when accompanied by an adult buying a general admission ticket for $3. You can take advantage of Family Day with special $1 reductions. There are always special reductions available for senior citizens. There are often group rates for 25 or more on specific dates. For group information (25 or more) and season tickets call 463-5000 or write Phillies Group Service, Box 7575, Phila., Pa. 19101.

Groups of 40 to 80 can also reserve the new 400-level superboxes, "Philadelphia Suite" or "Legends," for a sit-down or buffet-style dinner during the game. Call Group Service as early in the season as possible to make these arrangements.

If you would really like to go first class, call the Stadium Restaurant (271-2300) for reservations to dine and watch the game from the glass-enclosed restaurant above the first base line. If you would like to see the Phillies at a time and place of your choice, see Chapter 13 on tours "to go."

The Phillies' two Phanavision scoreboards constantly dance with names, numbers, pictures, songs, cheers, games and cartoons. You can have a birthday party at the Vet, and YOUR NAME can be on the scoreboard. The entertainment continues at your seat. (Call Group Service for these plans, too.) The Phillie Phanatic is also a constant source of amusement.

The Phillies are as big on promotions as they are on winning. There are events like T-shirt Day, Hat Day, Jacket Day, Beach Towel Day and Glove Day. There are many special occasions to celebrate during baseball season.

BASKETBALL—76ERS
The Spectrum
339-7676 (ticket office at Veterans Stadium)

The 76ers play 41 home games at the **Spectrum** from late October to April. When you see them, you'll be watching some of the best and the brightest basketball stars of the National Basketball Association and the 1983 World Champions.

If the game doesn't provide enough excitement for you, the promotions and special programs will. The half-time shows are colorful, and special nights are designated for children 14 and under. The purchase of any full-price ticket guarantees youngsters a 76ers ski cap, equipment bag, basketball or jacket on certain promotional days.

Tickets are $8 to $20, and group rates are available in advance for groups of 25 or more. Call or write the 76ers Group Sales Office at Veterans Stadium, Broad Street and Pattison Avenue, Phila., Pa. 19148. (339-7600).

There are more opportunities to watch top-notch basketball in Philadelphia each winter. The **BIG FIVE** (LaSalle, University of Pennsylvania, St. Joseph's, Villanova and Temple) play at their respective campuses and at the Palestra. Call 898-4747 for a schedule and ticket information.

BOXING AND WRESTLING

Boxing is a sometimes occurrence at the **Spectrum.** When important bouts aren't on the local schedule, the Spectrum provides closed circuit television viewing of them. World Wrestling Federation matches are once a month at the Spectrum, too, usually on Friday or Saturday nights. For a recorded announcement of what's coming up in the ring at the Spectrum, call 389-5000. Ticket prices vary with the event. Group rates for 25 or more are available by calling 463-4300.

Wrestling is also monthly on the agenda at **Convention Hall** at the Civic Center, 34th Street and Civic Center Boulevard (686-1776 or 823-7280). Call or watch the newspapers for announcements.

CRICKET

Did you ever wonder where Americans got the game of baseball? It's derived from cricket, a game played with a ball and stick that originated and still draws huge crowds in countries of the British Commonwealth.

In cricket, the batter scores as many runs as possible after a hit by going back and forth between two wickets, or bases, that are 22 yards apart. Eleven men play on each team and their uniforms are long white pants and white shirts. You can generally distinguish a team by the color of its players' hats or belts, and you can pick out the wicket keeper because he wears gloves. That's cricket.

The **PRIOR CRICKET CLUB** (878-2552) plays its matches on Saturdays and Sundays from late April through September at Cedar Grove Cricket Field, Edgely Road east of Belmont Avenue in West Fairmount Park. Starting times vary from noon till 2 and games often last five or six hours.

INTERNATIONAL CRICKET CLUB (747-9068) has a similar season and they compete on the cricket field next to Memorial Hall.

Other local teams include Bramley, United and the University of Pennsylvania. They all meet teams from all along the East Coast, Canada, Jamaica, Australia and Great Britain. Call any weekend during the season for a specific schedule. These events are free to the public.

FOOTBALL—EAGLES
Veterans Stadium (ticket office)
463-5500 (ticket information)

The Eagles are Philadelphia's long-time popular delegation to the National Football League. Since Philadelphia is, was and will always be a football town, fans will brave the rain, cold and the snow to cheer the "Birds" on to victory. The Eagles wound up the 1980 season against Oakland in Super Bowl XV.

Sixteen games are on the schedule from September to December. Eight are at home on Sunday afternoons with 1 or 4 P.M. kick-off at **Veterans Stadium**. Tickets are $20, and there are group discounts for 25 or more.

One or two pre-season games are played in August at the Vet. These seats are available at the same prices.

HORSE RACING

Philadelphia Park, on Street Road (Route 132) between I-95 and Roosevelt Boulevard, in Bensalem, Pa. (639-9000), features afternoon flat racing from mid-June through mid-February. The first race is at 1 P.M. You can bet on the thoroughbreds six days a week, but never on Monday. You can also make reservations to have lunch in the clubhouse. Admission is $2.50 and it includes parking.

There's no admission charge if you arrive after the seventh race.

Garden State Park, just across the Benjamin Franklin Bridge on Route 70 in Cherry Hill, New Jersey (609-488-8400), has thoroughbred racing from February through June and harness racing from September through December. Post time is 8 P.M. daily, except Sunday.

Admission is $2 for the grandstand, $3 for the clubhouse, and $4 for the Phoenix. Garden State is a state-of-the-art race track and entertainment center that opened in 1985. The physical beauty of the track and the exclusive restaurants are worth a trip in itself.

These tracks are also close to Philadelphia: Brandywine and Delaware Park in the nation's first state, Delaware; Penn National in Harrisburg, Pa.; and Atlantic City, near the New Jersey seashore.

Philadelphia also hosts two of the country's most prestigious **HORSE SHOWS.** You can attend the **Devon Horse Show** each spring and the **American Gold Cup** in September. Both are described in Chapter 19.

ICE HOCKEY—FLYERS
The Spectrum (ticket office)
465-4500 or 755-9700 (ticket information)

The Flyers play 40 games at the **Spectrum** from October to early April. Tickets are from $9.75 to $20.50. Many of the Spectrum's 17,211 seats are sold out to season ticket holders, but a number of seats go on sale for each game.

Tickets are sold at all Ticketron locations and at the 14 Showcase Stores in malls throughout the area.

Most of the Flyers are fearless Canadians. The 20-minute periods move as quickly as the puck that speeds across the ice. Tempers flare, so be prepared to witness some fights. The Flyers have been Patrick Division Champions at the end of the 1983, 1985 and 1986 seasons.

If you're lucky enough to go to a game, be sure to dress warmly. The playing floor chills even the hardiest of fans.

REGATTAS
The Schuylkill Navy
No. 4 Boat House Row, Kelly Drive
686-2176 (Fairmount Park Information Office)

Rowing races along the **Schuylkill River** are on 10 weekends from spring to late fall. Among the annual events are
the May Day Vail Regatta (the world's largest inter-
collegiate regatta), the Independence Day Regatta and
the Frostbite Series in November.

The Schuylkill sculling course is close to center city in
scenic Fairmount Park*. Its calm, sheltered flow makes it
one of the world's most popular rivers for regattas. Artist
Thomas Eakins has immortalized sculling on the
Schuylkill; the United States Postal Service issued a commemorative stamp honoring it.

Most races begin north of the Strawberry Mansion
Bridge and end 2,000 meters downstream towards center
city. You can watch the races from the Schuylkill Grand-
stand on Kelly Drive (about a mile-and-a-half west of Boat
House Row) or from anywhere you choose along the
river's eastern shore. You might decide to follow the races
while biking along the Kelly Drive bike path. Of course,
there's no admission charge to watch any of these events.

There are few things more graceful than these sleek
shells skimming rapidly across the water. If you walk by
the 19th century boat houses on Boat House Row (just
west of the Museum of Art and the Azalea Gardens),
you'll be able to examine the shells. A single shell can cost
rowers up to $10,000.

Ten boat clubs comprise Boat House Row, and they all
have open memberships. If you've ever considered joining
the Schuylkill Navy, call to find out which club might be
appropriate for your schedule, skills, competitive or recreational rowing interests.

For a schedule of the season's regattas, look in the newspapers or call the Fairmount Park Information Office.

RUGBY

Rugby bears some resemblance to football, but no forward passing or blocking is allowed. This is another sport
most Americans have never seen. You can watch first-
class rugby any Saturday afternoon from March through
May and early September through November at the
Memorial Hall field, Belmont and Parkside Avenues in
West Fairmount Park. It's free and wholesome sports
entertainment, and in Philadelphia rugby has gone coed.

323

The **Whitemarsh-Philadelphia Rugby Football Club** (642-9899) and any of the 30 rugby clubs within 50 miles of Philadelphia compete in two, three or four games beginning at 1:30 P.M. Each game runs 30 to 40 minutes nonstop, and neither team of 15 is allowed more than two substitutes. And then it's only for an injury. Call the club for a schedule, and come out and see the action.

SOCCER

The **PHILADELPHIA SOCCER 7** provides an opportunity to see outdoor college soccer each fall. Drexel (895-2551), LaSalle (951-1605), Philadelphia Textile (951-2852), St. Joseph's (879-7447), Temple (787-7445), University of Pennsylvania (898-6128) and Villanova (645-4121) are pitted against each other and visiting teams from along the East Coast. Call the school closest to you to find out when you can see them play.

TENNIS

Professional tennis comes to Philadelphia on several occasions each year.

The **U.S. PRO INDOOR TENNIS CHAMPIONSHIPS** pit 48 of the world's top male players against each other in eight sessions of singles and doubles at the **Spectrum** for a week in the end of January or early February. Tickets are $15, $17.50 and $20 for individual sessions. Call 947-2530 for details, or watch for newspaper announcements.

If you've never seen tennis played on grass, watch for newspaper announcements each summer for **NATIONAL GRASS COURT TOURNAMENTS** at the Germantown, Merion and Philadelphia Cricket Clubs. Not only is this a terrific opportunity to see top players, but it's also fun to see any of the country's few and finest grass court clubs that are usually open to members only.

Participation Sports

CITY OF PHILADELPHIA
Department of Recreation, 686-0150 or 686-3612
Fairmount Park Commission—Division of Recreation
686-0052

The Department of Recreation, along with the Fairmount Park Commission, coordinates and supervises hundreds of activities for young people and their parents.

Philadelphia has 200 recreation centers and playgrounds. There are over 80 swimming pools, an abundance of tennis courts, golf courses, ball fields and ice skating rinks, all of which are strategically located throughout the city. There are facilities for just about every sport you could want to try, and the activities are continuous throughout the year.

BASEBALL

Baseball is the most popular non-professional sport in Philadelphia. Each year, almost 50,000 people play in the city's programs in three major divisions on a thousand teams in almost 200 leagues competing in 8,000 games. So you see, when we say "baseball" in Philadelphia, we really mean baseball.

"A" and "B" divisions (uniformed and non-uniformed) are coached by Recreation Department staff and volunteers. The "Independent" division consists of teams that are privately sponsored by churches, clubs and businesses.

There are four age divisions for players under 19 and another for adults. The teams compete at neighborhood ball fields throughout the summer in order to earn a place in the citywide playoffs for the annual championship.

With this kind of organization, there's no excuse for anyone interested in baseball not to be out there playing.

BASKETBALL

Some of the country's top basketball players are graduates of Philadelphia's Department of Recreation programs.

Players and teams should register at local playgrounds for indoor league competitions in the winter and outdoor leagues that compete in the summer. Boys and girls from under 12 to under 20 are divided into age groups with league games leading to citywide playoffs and a championship.

N.C.A.A. rules are used, but the length of time periods is determined by age. Boys and girls, divided into age categories, can also compete in a national Pepsi/N.B.A. Hot Shot Program from summer through fall.

BICYCLING

The city's bicycling program has grown in accordance with the popularity of the sport. There are 23 miles of scenic bike paths in Fairmount Park, alone. You can ride the paved routes along the Kelly and West River Drives, in the Wissahickon Valley from Ridge Avenue to Rittenhouse Street, for five-and-a-half miles of gravel bridle path along Forbidden Drive adjacent to the Wissahickon*, the eight miles paved along Pennypack Creek and on trails in other parts of the park.

Special biking events are planned by the city from March to October. They include a Bike Safety Rodeo, rides with local celebrities and professional groups, and the Youth Sprint Bicycling Championships held in late spring in conjunction with the Core-States U.S. Pro Cycling Championship.

Call the Department of Recreation (686-0150) for your annual cycling schedule. Call the Fairmount Park Commission (686-0052) for a listing of Bicycle Clubs in Philadelphia and its suburbs.

If you don't own a bike, you can rent one by the hour or by the day at Plaisted Hall, No. 1 Boat House Row on the Kelly Drive just west of the Art Museum. The shop is open year-round: weekdays, 10 to 8; weekends, 8 to 8; weekends only in winter, 10 to 7. Call 236-4359 for specific rates and deposit requirements. The bike rental shop will give you a map of bike trails in Fairmount Park.

If you would like to join an easy bike ride, the Fairmount Park Commission and the Center City Touring Club sponsor easy rides every Sunday starting at noon from Plaisted Hall. Riders learn the rules of the road while taking a leisurely three-hour excursion.

Other, more vigorous bike trips are sponsored by American Youth Hostels (925-6004).

If you're an avid bike rider and would like to ride with fellow bicyclists or work on improving conditions for bike riders in Philadelphia, write to the Bicycle Coalition of the Delaware Valley, P.O. Box 8194, Phila., Pa. 19101, or call them at 222-1253. Members in the Coalition (Friends, $10;

Family, $15) receive newsletters, an annual biking wall calendar, commuter and touring service and discounts at area bike shops. Thanks to their efforts, bicyclists can now pedal across the Benjamin Franklin Bridge. They have the city building and improving more and more bike routes, and they also publish a helpful Regional Commuters' Bike Map.

BLOCK PARTIES and PLAY STREETS

The City of Philadelphia wants you to have fun. They'll close off a street temporarily so you can have a **Block Party.** All you have to do is submit an application along with a petition representing more than 75 percent of the block's residents who want the party. The city must receive the request at least three weeks before the planned event. There's a $5 fee for the permit. For additional information and an application form, write to the Contract and Permit Office of the Highway Division, Philadelphia Streets Department, 820 Municipal Services Bldg., Phila., Pa. 19107. Or call 686-5501.

If you live on a residential block with a lot of children, you might want to have it closed to traffic on summer days. This is a good idea if you're getting a fire hydrant spray cap (described under "Swimming").

The city must receive all applications from April to early June and streets can be closed off from May through August. Call 978-2728 for additional information about **Play Streets.**

BOATING

Few American cities offer boating on a placid river in a beautiful park near the center of town. Philadelphia does, at the East Park Canoe House, Kelly Drive south of the Strawberry Mansion Bridge (225-3560). You can rent rowboats ($7), canoes ($7) and sailboats ($10) by the hour from April to October. Refreshments and souvenirs are also available. The hours are 11 to 9 on weekdays and 10 to 9 on weekends, but it's a good idea to call ahead and be sure. (There are no boat rentals when regattas are taking place on the Schuylkill.) One member of your crew must be at least 16.

It doesn't matter if you're going out for serious rowing or for relaxation. Boating along the Schuylkill River is fun on a beautiful day.

Happy sails to you!

BOXING

If you're anxious to test your strength and physical fitness, the Department of Recreation gives you a chance in their non-competitive amateur boxing program. Boxing rings are located at centers throughout the city where one exhibition is usually held each month.

The bouts consist of three two-minute rounds. The pairings are determined by age (four groupings from ages 10 to 18), weight (12 classes from 90 to over 181 pounds) and experience.

CHECKERS and CHESS

Checkers and chess players are attracted in droves to neighborhood tournaments at recreation centers, followed by district and citywide playoffs.

The city encourages chess playing, so there's an annual citywide tournament. Contestants are divided into seven age groups from Pee Wee (12 and under) to Senior (over 18). International rules govern the play.

FISHING

Bring your own equipment (it doesn't have to be fancy) and try your luck.

A license is required if you're over 16. It costs $12.50 for a calendar year if you live in Pennsylvania, or $2.50 if you're a senior citizen. (If you're over 65 you can purchase a lifetime license for $10.50.) Non-residents pay $20.50, or $15.50 for a seven-day tourist license. You can get one in the Municipal Services Building concourse, 15th Street and Kennedy Boulevard (686–2489), or at a local sporting goods store.

The Schuylkill River (from Manayunk through Fairmount Park, center city and southwest Philadelphia) and F.D. Roosevelt Lake (20th Street and Pattison Avenue) have carp, catfish, muskellunge, panfish, sunfish, striped bass and yellow perch.

Five miles of the Wissahickon (from Germantown Pike to the Walnut Lane Bridge) and Pennypack Creek (from State to Pine Roads) are stocked with trout in mid-April and several more times before Labor Day. Sometimes the catch is good at Concourse Lake (44th Street and Parkside Avenue). Check in advance with the Fairmount Park Commission; they might be able to tell you where the fish are biting.

They also sponsor the two-day annual Fall Festival

Fishing Contest when thousands of dollars of fishing equipment is awarded as prizes. Call 686-0052 for the dates and details.

GOLF

Philadelphia has six public golf courses which are in operation year-round. They are J.F. Byrne, Frankford Avenue and Eden Street (632-8666); Cobbs Creek and Karakung, 72nd Street and Lansdowne Avenue (877-8707); Juniata, M and Cayuga Streets (743-4060); Walnut Lane, Walnut Lane and Henry Avenue (482-3370) and F.D. Roosevelt, 20th Street and Pattison Avenue (462-8997). All of them can be reached by SEPTA.

Golfing fees are $8 on a weekday and $9.50 on weekends and holidays, except at Cobbs Creek where it's $9 and $11. There are special prices for season pass holders and senior citizens. Each course has a new snack bar and pro shop.

The Philadelphia Publinks Golf Association sponsors an Annual Open Junior Championship Tournament on a weekday in August. The tourney is open to young golfers from 14 to 17 in the Pennsylvania-New Jersey-Delaware region who regularly play on public golf courses.

HIKING

Here's a sport that requires no special equipment other than sturdy shoes and uncomplaining feet. Hiking is something you don't have to practice. You compete only with yourself.

The Department of Recreation's Wanderlust Hiking Club offers supervised four- to eight-mile hikes along scenic trails in and around Philadelphia every Saturday afternoon at 1 or 1:30. For a schedule of weekly routes, call 686-0150.

Other hikes are organized locally by American Youth Hostels (925-6004) and the Batona Hiking Club (836-4185). Call them for details.

HOCKEY

Philadelphia has hockey fever. Remember when millions of fans turned out to celebrate each time the Flyers won the Stanley Cup? Thousands of those fans also participate in hockey programs which are sponsored by the city's Department of Recreation, including clinics led by members of the Flyers.

There are street, floor and ice hockey leagues for boys.

They're divided into teams according to age. The street and floor games are played at neighborhood centers, while the ice hockey battles are fought at the Cobbs Creek, Rizzo, Scanlon, Simons and Tarken rinks (see "Ice Skating" in this chapter). All of the leagues follow traditional rules. Parents don't have to worry about dental bills because the rules prohibit malicious play.

HORSEBACK RIDING

Over 80 bridle paths wind through Fairmount Park, the Wissahickon and Pennypack Park. And every mile of them is great for horseback riding.

If you don't have your own horse, there are stables listed in the Yellow Pages under "Riding Academies."

Call them for hours, rates, directions and additional information.

And by all means, "get a horse."

ICE SKATING

The Department of Recreation holds sessions at five outdoor ice skating rinks two or three times a day from mid-December to March.

The rinks are Cobbs Creek at Cobbs Creek Parkway and Walnut Street (748-3480), Scanlon at J and Tioga Streets (739-5515), Simons at Woolston Avenue and Walnut Lane (424-9857), Tarken at Frontenac and Levick Streets (743-3266) and the Ralph Rizzo, Sr. Rink under I-95 at Front Street and Washington Avenue (686-2925).

There's a nominal charge to skate: adults, $1; children three to 15 and senior citizens, 50¢. (Spectators are charged 25¢.) Ice hockey clinics and instructions are sometimes provided and there are occasional speed and figure skating competitions. An annual ice extravaganza at the Scanlon rink casts over a hundred skaters from the neighborhood.

Also, frozen creeks and ponds are sometimes declared safe for skating by the Fairmount Park Commission. They include (only when the park police say it's okay) the Wissahickon at Valley Green, sites along Pennypack Creek, and Concourse Lake at 44th Street and Parkside Avenue.

You have a choice of places to skate indoors throughout the year. Call ahead for their rates and hours. You can rent skates at most of these rinks, which is a good idea for children with rapidly growing feet and for children who want to find out how much they like the sport before investing in a pair of skates.

You can skate at the University of Pennsylvania Class of '23 Rink at 3130 Walnut Street (898–1823), providing the Penn ice hockey team isn't playing there.

The Wissahickon Ice Skating Club at Willow Grove and Cherokee Avenues (247–1907) is open to the public on Friday, Saturday and Sunday evenings.

There are suburban rinks in Ardmore, Elkins Park, Havertown, Villanova and Willow Grove. Check with Bell Telephone Information if one of these locations is more convenient for you.

JOGGING and RUNNING

If you would rather jog than walk, you can go out on your own when it's convenient. Jogging is non-competitive and you go at your own pace. All jogging trails in Fairmount Park are posted with half-mile markers. One of the most popular is the eight-and-a-half mile loop starting at No. 1 Boat House Row on Kelly Drive.

Running, on the other hand, pits you against other runners in competition. Special events in Fairmount Park bring runners together in organized races throughout the spring and fall seasons. Most runs are five or 10 kilometers, also originating at No. 1 Boat House Row.

If you're a competitive runner, you might also want to inquire about the annual 10–mile Broad Street Run on the first Sunday in May, or the Greater Independence Marathon, on the last Sunday in November.

For additional information, call 686–0150 or 686–0052, or jog by No. 1 Boat House Row (Plaisted Hall) west of the Art Museum.

PLAYGROUNDS

The Department of Recreation operates over a hundred playgrounds reaching into all parts of the city. In the summer some of them are supervised for group games, organized sports and arts and crafts projects. Call to find out which is most convenient for you.

Smith Memorial Playground was established in 1899 as a lasting memorial to Richard and Sarah Smith's son, Stanfield. Their trust fund enables youngsters to frolic indoors and outside among a potpourri of amusements. The house contains a mini-village where small-frys under five learn to drive mini-cars through mini-streets with pint-sized traffic meters, street lights and buildings.

Another playroom, a reading room and a nature den provide additional entertainment resources.

The playground itself is for children under 12, with a smaller playground within it that's reserved for preschoolers. It's landscaped with a variety of equipment from small swings and climb-ons to a sliding board for 10. There's an outdoor wading pool and a swimming pool for youngsters to enjoy from June 1 to mid-August. There are picnic groves and a refreshment stand that's open from mid-May to Labor Day from 10 to 2:30.

Smith Memorial Playground is in East Fairmount Park. It's about a two-block walk from the SEPTA bus 32 stop at 33rd and Oxford Streets. You can drive to it by turning onto Fountain Green Drive (at the Grant Statue) from Kelly Drive and make the next three right turns. Hours for the house are Monday to Saturday, 10:30 to 3:30, and the playground is open 9 to 4:30 in winter and till 5 in summer. It's closed Sundays, Good Friday, Thanksgiving, Christmas and New Year's. If you have any questions, call 765-4325.

ROLLER SKATING

Philadelphians have joined the trend to skate. It's another fun way to get your aerobic exercise.

Several indoor, year-round "Skating Rinks" are listed in the Yellow Pages, along with "Skating Equipment and Supplies" you can rent to take outdoors. Call for hours, rental information and rates.

Get rolling!

SLEDDING and SKIING

There are advanced hills and beginner's slopes in Fairmount Park for folks who want to participate in either of the above activities. Bring your own vehicle, even if it's only a homemade slab of cardboard or a trash can lid.

Among the most popular hills are those in Burholme Park at Cottman and Central Avenues, Clifford Park at Wissahickon Avenue and Walnut Lane, Tacony Creek Park at Roosevelt Boulevard and F Street, Cobbs Creek Park at Haverford and Lansdowne Avenues and Bennett Hill at 7300 Emlen Street near Allens Lane.

And don't forget the Belmont Plateau near the Playhouse in the Park, behind the west entrance of the Art Museum, and the hills at the public golf courses.

Fairmount Park is also ideal for cross-country skiing. If you're a beginner on the slopes, try renting equipment from any of the shops listed in the Yellow Pages under "Skiing Equipment."

Novice down-hillers would be wise to ski the small hills of Fairmount Park before heading for the big slopes. There are several ski areas within a short distance of Philadelphia, and there are 42 of them in Pennsylvania. Write to the Pennsylvania Bureau of Travel Development, Department of Commerce, South Office Building, Harrisburg, Pa. 17120, for maps and information on ski trails, ski schools and accommodations. Also, refer to the Philadelphia Yellow Pages for ski tours.

SOCCER

The country's fastest growing sport is enjoying increased popularity in Philadelphia. Young people of both sexes are playing soccer, so soccer clinics are now part of the fall and winter recreation programs at neighborhood centers.

In addition, a major indoor soccer program for boys and girls 19 and under begins in January at city recreation facilities and school gymnasiums.

There are frequent competitions in three age categories. An Annual Soccer Tournament brings the winning teams together.

SOFTBALL

There's a citywide softball tournament for boys in all age divisions. Slo-Pitch and Fast-Pitch Tournaments are held at neighborhood recreation centers. The tournaments eventually go on to semi-finals and city finals.

Girl's softball leagues play throughout the summer in three age groups for Slo-Pitch and Fast-Pitch. They use shorter pitching distances. The league playoffs for boys and girls are followed by competitions in the Gold Medal Softball Tournament.

SUMMER CAMPS

Summer camps are a specialty in Philadelphia. The Department of Recreation sponsors several day camps at various locations for thousands of children. Registration is required for all camp programs. A nominal fee is charged, lunch is usually provided, and transportation is often arranged.

There are one-week periods for seven- to 11-year-olds at Camp Overbrook on the grounds of St. Charles Seminary at City Line and Wynnewood Road. The camp program includes organized nature study, hikes, arts and crafts, singing, stunts, storytelling, campfires and games.

The P.D.R. Swimming Day Camp is at Memorial Hall's Kelly Pool in West Fairmount Park. It's for youngsters who already know how to swim but want to improve their skills and train in aquatics. Youngsters six to 12 years old can attend.

Additional summer camps include the Summer Arts Camp (see Chapter 9) and Carousel Camp for the handicapped (see Chapter 16). William Penn overnight camp takes 350 boys and girls from nine to 11 years old on each of four two-week encampments in the Poconos.

Call the Department of Recreation (686-0150) or get the details on any of these camping opportunities at your neighborhood recreation center or playground.

As if this wasn't enough, the Fairmount Park Commission runs six outdoor day camps for boys and girls from eight to 12 years old. Each camp schedules three two-week sessions during the summer. Again, registration is necessary and there's a small enrollment fee to pay for refreshments, supplies and camp trips. The activities include swimming, crafts, drama, games, camp songs and some camp trips. Check with the Fairmount Park Commission (686-0052) for the camp location nearest you.

SWIMMING

The Department of Recreation operates 80 outdoor pools at neighborhood centers throughout the city. The Fairmount Park Commission has four. You can swim alone or together with friends or family in special events that are scheduled according to the pool and its location. The pools are open daily all summer. For specific hours, call 686-3612.

Most pools hold a variety of programs that include Swim-to-Live classes, family night, splash parties, meets, modified water polo, water carnivals and junior and senior life-saving for certification. Swim meets place swimmers of all ages in competition for individual and team championships.

If you aren't close to a swimming pool this summer, take advantage of the city's refreshing **street shower** program. Starting June 1 and depending on the city's water supply, 2,500 **spray caps** are distributed free of charge through neighborhood police stations. A cool spray of water shoots out when the cap is attached to an all-orange fire hydrant.

Applications for spray caps are available at any police station. A cap and permit is given to any responsible adult who fills out the simple form.

The low flow spray caps protect children and property while they save water and preserve water pressure. It's against the law to open a fire hydrant any other way.

TABLE TENNIS

Ping-pong tables are at most of the city's recreation centers. So practice your table tennis and enter the annual tournament. There are both singles and doubles competition.

Competitors are divided into five classifications of boys and girls from under 12 years old to 17 and over. They compete in a citywide tournament in April each year. United States Table Tennis Association rules govern all play.

TENNIS

If you want to play tennis, there's no excuse for not playing it in Philadelphia.

Over 100 all-weather courts are in Fairmount Park (686-0052), and free instruction is offered to children on weekdays throughout the summer. Call for a schedule and locations that are convenient to you.

Another 150 all-weather courts are at various Department of Recreation sites throughout the city (686-0150). Some of the courts are equipped for nighttime playing.

More than 4,000 youngsters participate in the Department of Recreation/National Junior Tennis League of Philadelphia each summer. There's a minimal fee to enroll. Boys and girls from ages eight to 18 play at beginner, intermediate and advanced levels. Rackets and balls are provided by the instructors at the courts. Of course, you can bring your own. Each participant also gets a team T-shirt.

Morning and afternoon clinics are held at 70 locations from late June through August. A round-robin tournament in August determines who the city champions will be. Some have gone on to Middle States junior rankings...which is pretty good, if you're up on tennis. If you would like to sign up, or know someone who would, call 686–3612 or 424–5300 (July and August only).

The Fairmount Park Commission sponsors an annual Fairmount Fall Festival Tennis Championship, the largest amateur tennis tournament held in the Philadelphia area. It's held at the Chamounix courts in late September. There are junior singles events and adult events including singles and doubles for men and women. Call (686–0052) in August for rules and information and to request an entry blank.

A once-a-year Saturday clinic attracts thousands of young tennis enthusiasts. It's held in conjunction with the U.S. Pro Indoor Tennis Championships* at the Spectrum. Some of the best players in the world conduct the clinic.

TRACK AND FIELD

Kids from all over the city are keeping fit by doing dashes, jumps, sprints and relays. At the latest count, over 15,000 boys and girls have participated in local, district and citywide contests. There's an indoor and outdoor season with many meets.

The Little Quaker Track Meet brings together boys and girls five to nine years old to do sprints, relays and field competitions. Other events include development meets, an all-girls meet, summer relays, and the Jesse Owens Meet.

The Recreation Department's annual coordinated Track Carnival is a week of track and field in January. Some of the events are 60-yard dashes and hurdles, mile relays, mile runs, mile walks, pole vaults, weight throws and shot puts.

All of these activities require practice and fitness.

TUMBLING AND GYMNASTICS

Over 45 recreation centers sponsor fall and winter programs for boys. They're divided into four age groups: small frys (nine and under) to advanced (14 to 18). Dual, district and citywide meets are held.

Girls can compete in an equally lively tumbling program. Their meets also precede a city championship.

VOLLEYBALL

Almost 100 teams play volleyball throughout the year at city facilities. Intermediate players are up to age 15, juniors to 17, and 18 and over for seniors. Local competitions lead up to a citywide playoff. An outdoor championship is held each summer.

An annual springtime Volleyball Jamboree for adult men and women separates teams into power and recreational divisions. It's fun for an April evening no matter where you play.

If none of the preceding sports turns you on, maybe one of these will interest you:

AEROBICS classes are at several neighborhood recreation centers. Call the one nearest you to see if an exercise program is on the schedule.

BRIDGE is played indoors at clubs in center city Philadelphia that welcome your membership. The clubs are listed in the White and Yellow Pages.

DOG FRISBEE contests are sponsored each summer by the Department of Recreation. If your dog is good at catching frisbees, you can participate together as a team. Call ahead (686-0151) for the dates so you don't miss this June event. Start practicing now and sign up at your neighborhood center early in June.

RACQUETBALL and **SQUASH** are popular sports in Philadelphia, but they're limited to playing at private clubs where you can buy time by the hour. Racquetball and squash clubs are listed in the Yellow Pages.

If you're still not motivated, take another look at the chapters on "The Arts" and "History" and think about becoming an artist or a scholar.

Chapter 15.
Philadelphia for Children.

Many of the attractions described throughout this book are suitable for children. But this chapter is about the places and events that are designed *especially* for children. Grown-ups are welcome, of course, but they're requested to adequately supervise their little folk.

Reminder: An **asterisk(*)** indicates that the same place or event appears elsewhere in the book with more details. You'll find that place in the Index.

Just Watching

CONCERTS

Children can enjoy the **Philadelphia Orchestra's Children's Concerts** just as their parents and grandparents did when they were young. Conductor William Smith makes music fun at the Academy of Music*. Each concert features narration, illustration, ballet, choral groups or an unusual solo.

The Philadelphia Orchestra* gives one-hour **Concerts for Children**, ages five to 11 years old, on five Saturday mornings at 11 during the concert season.

Tickets are $10 to $30 per seat for the series, and all seats are reserved. These concerts are usually sold out well in advance by subscription, but frequently tickets are returned to the Academy's box office prior to concerts. You might get lucky.

The Orchestra's **Concerts for Middle School Students** are on two weeknights during the school year from 8 to 9:30 P.M. Tickets are $4 to $10 for the series, and you can attend as part of a school group or on your own.

One adult should accompany every group of 10 youngsters for both concert series. Call 893–1900 for additional information.

Concerts for High School and College Students are also two weeknights during the school year from 8 to 9:45 P.M. Tickets are $4 to $10 for this series, which really doesn't belong in a chapter for children!

One or two children's concerts are also presented outdoors by the Philadelphia Orchestra in the summer at the Mann Music Center*. These performances always feature talented young soloists and there's no charge to attend. Watch the newspapers for announcements of these concerts, or call 567–0707 early in the summer for details.

A combination of music and books is the main attraction at the Free Library of Philadelphia's* popular **Book Concerts for Children,** ages six to 12. Each concert has a theme and includes some facet of the performing arts. It could be a fairy tale, a dance or an adventure story told with music. Nine of these programs are presented at the Logan Square Main Library during the school year. They last from 60 to 90 minutes, with time to visit the library before and after the concert.

Reading lists and lending books, which are available after the concerts, encourage youngsters to follow up on the musical programs they've just heard. It's a creative as well as painless way to combine reading, music and the arts for children who aren't inclined towards these subjects. Call 686-5372 for a schedule and details.

Concerto Soloists Chamber Orchestra of Philadelphia * presents a series of four **Concerts for Children** at the Walnut Street Theater* on Saturdays at 11 A.M. Marc Mostovoy conducts and a young soloist performs at each one-hour program.

Children are introduced to classical music along with narration and audience participation. Tickets for individual concerts are $4, or you can subscribe to the series and save. Group rates are available. Call 735-0202 for additional information.

ARTS AND SCIENCES

The **Philadelphia Museum of Art*** (763-8100) has workshops that enable pre-schoolers and school-age children to discover the museum and explore various art techniques. The museum also has Family Programs on Sunday afternoons each month.

The **Institute of Contemporary Art*** (898-5118) has an occasional Saturday afternoon Children's Day to coincide with their exhibitions. These gallery talks and art happenings are planned especially for youngsters 13 and under.

The **Academy of Natural Sciences*** (299-1000) is the ultimate indoor stop for little people who love animals and want to know more about them. The exhibits, live animal shows and children's classes are described in Chapter 7. Outside In is described later in this chapter.

A special program just for children under seven years old is on Saturday mornings at 10:30 in the **Fels Planetarium*** (448-1200). It's a nifty way to learn about the phases of the moon, the stars and what's happening in the skies. Admission is 75¢ in addition to the regular admission to the Franklin Institute. All adults must be accompanied by children.

FILMS

The **Free Library of Philadelphia*** (686-5322) has free films at the Main Library and many of the branch libraries. There are film programs for pre-schoolers on weekday mornings, and after school for their older brothers and sisters. Friday Flicks (and other days, too) are shown in late afternoons and early evenings at some branch libraries. There are afternoon showings during the summer.

The **Philadelphia Museum of Art*** (763-8100) has a film festival for young people on occasional weekends during the school year. They're part of the Family Programs described earlier in this chapter. The price is generally included with the admission to the museum.

The **University Museum*** (898-4015 or 222-7777) shows all kinds and lengths of films for children on Saturday mornings at 10:30 from October through March. They're chosen especially for children from eight to 14 years old.

LIVE AND ON STAGE

Allens Lane* Children's Theater (248-0546) raises the curtain in February and March for Friday, Saturday and Sunday performances. The **Teen's Theater** performs later in March. Tickets for all shows are usually $2. Since the shows are always sellouts, reservations are a must. Call the Center in the fall for a schedule or watch for announcements in the papers.

The Allens Lane Kaleidoscope afterschool program offers children's classes in art, dance, music and drama. Each spring, an original play is presented on two weekends by the class members who write the show, make the sets, gather the props and perform in it. This is always great fun for a cast of children to perform for an audience of children.

Note: Allens Lane also presents occasional weekend matinees of magic, puppet shows and crafts workshops for children of all ages. Children under 6 must be with an adult. Call 247-7727 for a schedule or ticket information.

American Theater Arts for Youth (563-3501) is a non-profit theatrical company of professional adult performers produced by localite Laurie Wagman, and Laurie really knows what young people like to watch.

Theater Arts for Youth presents musical shows that are especially related to school curriculums for children of all ages. Prepared study guides are included for teachers.

Most of the audiences are filled with groups, but the public is invited, too. Most of the school-year productions are weekdays (at 10 A.M. and 12:30 P.M.) and Saturdays (at 11 A.M.) at the theater in the Port of History Museum*. A seven week summer series has morning shows twice a week. Tickets are $5.75 and group rates are available. Reservations are necessary.

The repertoire changes each year, but "Babes in Toyland" is an annual fall classic. Be sure to call for the schedule. Look into this and give the young folks a real treat.

Annenberg Center* (898-6791) presents three productions a year in a top-notch Theater for Children series. Dynamic companies from around the world bring four performances of each show to the Zellerbach stage on Fridays and Saturdays. Recent shows have included children's opera, giant puppets and "potato" people. Study guides are available for each production. This is a popular series, so get your schedule early in the fall so you won't miss anything.

The **Germantown Theater Guild and Philadelphia Theater Caravan*** (849-0460 or 898-6068) is the only local group, and one of few in the country, to be honored by the American Theater Association. An award-winning professional adult cast gives four children's shows during the school year.

The plays are aimed for children at least five years old, but chaperoning adults have been known to enjoy them as well. Sometimes, the audience is involved. The setting is a carriage house at 4821 Germantown Avenue called "The Little Theater." It seats 140 and dates back to the Revolutionary period.

Each show usually plays for two or three consecutive weekends with 2 P.M. curtains on Saturday and Sunday. Tickets are $4. One adult must accompany each group of five to 15 youngsters.

Note: There are no steps at the theater and four wheelchairs can be accommodated at each performance. Advance notice is necessary.

The first **Philadelphia International Children's Festival** in 1985 was a huge success. So now it's bigger and better. For five full days in early June there are over a hundred performances of theater, mime, puppetry and dance along with juggling, face painting, balloon art and street performances. Professional children's theater companies from around the world are here to perform at the fete, and everything is geared to children.

Many of the events take place at Annenberg Center* which is the core of the six-square block festival site in University City*. Call the Annenberg box office (898-6791) early in May for information. (Groups should call 898-6683.)

Plays and Players* (735-0630) has plays for children. Five original and/or classic plays are presented from September to May, each on two consecutive Saturdays at 11 A.M. and 1 P.M. They're planned for an audience of pre-schoolers to 5th graders. Tickets are $2 for children and $3 for the adults who accompany them. Find out what's coming up and give a child a treat.

Children's Theater at Temple University Center City* (787-1122) is on Stage Three at 1619 Walnut Street. Two delightful productions are held during the school year. The showtimes are at 11 A.M. and 1 P.M. on three consecutive Saturdays for each play. Tickets are $2 and group rates are available.

Children's Musical Theater at Valley Forge Music Fair* (644-5000) is on Wednesdays in July and August at 11 A.M. and 2 P.M., and occasionally on Saturdays during the rest of the year and during school holidays.

A rollicking musical with charming costumes and scenery is presented in-the-round. Tickets are $4. Group rates and series rates are also available (call 296-9820).

Youngsters never seem to get enough of "Cinderella," "Pinnochio," "Alice in Wonderland" or "The Wizard of Oz." If your children will be home this summer, give them this joyful entertainment. If you can't wait till summer, check the newspapers or call to find out what's scheduled during the rest of the year.

The **Free Library of Philadelphia*** has free **Story Hours for Children** at the Main Library's Children's Department and at neighborhood branch libraries. These Story Hours spark the imaginations of Philadelphia children from preschool through elementary school ages. The Library's animated reading program takes youngsters into a world of fantasy. It encourages children to become interested in books.

Pre-registration is required for pre-school Story Hours. They're usually one morning or afternoon during the week at specified branch libraries throughout the city. Story Hours for school children are scheduled for 4 P.M. Bedtime Story Hours are after dinner at some neighborhood libraries. Youngsters are invited to attend in pajamas, listen to stories and go home ready for bed. The schedule is available each month at the Free Library. Or call your local branch (listed in the Philadelphia White Pages) or the Office for Work with Children at 686-5372.

This project, alone, shows that Philadelphia is a great city for children. (The Free Library's extensive Children's Department is described in Chapter 11.)

ALMOST LIVE AND ON STAGE

Children love puppets, so Philadelphia has plenty of puppet shows.

You'll have to watch for newspaper announcements or keep up with schedules of places like Allens Lane Art Center, the Free Library and Painted Bride Art Center to know when they'll be performing.

The **Philadelphia Marionette Theater*** performs in its fantasyland at Playhouse in the Park*. A one-hour performance includes magic, puppets, live organ music and a marionette show from a happy repertoire that's guaranteed to make you smile.

Tickets are $3.50, with group rates available. Reservations are necessary. Curtain is weekdays at 10:30 A.M. (except September and October), and there are occasional Saturday shows. Call 879-1213 or watch the newspapers for a schedule. Don't miss this fabulous opportunity to have someone pull the strings for you.

If you're interested in making your own puppets, the City's **Department of Recreation** (686-0151) sponsors occasional classes in puppetry. Participants create their own characters from cloth, cardboard, paper or plastic scraps. Then they create the dramas in which their puppets perform. Check with your neighborhood recreation center to find out when these programs will be held near you, and then be ready to pull the strings.

If you're interested in making your own dolls, the Department of Recreation, in conjunction with the Pennsylvania Ballet Company*, has an annual fall "Nutcracker Doll Contest." The participants listen to a synopsis of the ballet, choose a character from the story and create a doll in the image of their chosen character. Members of the ballet company judge the entries, and the creators of the winning dolls receive tickets to "The Nutcracker." If you know someone who would like to try their hand at this, call the Department of Recreation to find out the closest participating recreation center.

If you're still looking for something to do "just watching," go back to Chapter 13 and consider a tour of a cookie factory, a candy factory or a bakery.

Joining the Fun

When the weather is nice, it's nice to be outdoors, exploring nature and visiting some animals.

Within the Philadelphia Zoo* is a two-acre **Children's Zoo** where youngsters can touch and feed the animals and be right there when the zookeeper takes care of the creatures. The inhabitants are also known to perform for their little visitors.

Daily events (except in winter from January to March) include sea lion demonstrations, cow milking, sheep dog demonstrations, pony rides and an animal show.

The ZooStop (open daily 11 A.M. to 3 P.M.) is a discovery room with animal exhibits that invite children to learn while having fun as they touch, sniff and listen to the likes of ants, bugs, a beehive and tarantulas.

There's a 50¢ admission to the Children's Zoo in addition to regular zoo admission. Group rates are available for 15 or more.

Another zoo with a petting zoo for children is in Norristown. The **Elmwood Park Zoo*** is described under Montgomery County in Chapter 17.

And, if you can do it, plan a day at **Great Adventure*** in New Jersey (also described in Chapter 17) where thousands of wild animals roam the safari park.

Guided and/or informal **nature walks** are healthy and fun for people of all ages. They can be enjoyed at Morris Arboretum, Pennypack Environmental Center, Schuylkill Valley Nature Center and Tinicum National Environmental Center, all described in Chapter 7. Workshops and special events for youngsters are planned at Pennypack and Schuylkill Valley.

Within the Academy of Natural Sciences* (299-1060) is a Children's Nature Museum called **Outside In.** It's a mini-museum created for youngsters 12 and under who, along with their adult chaperones, can explore nature by using all five of their senses. It's billed as the "touchable world of woodlands, streams, beaches and quarries. It's where you meet some of the creatures who live in these outdoor spaces."

There are live animals to touch, environments to sample, sounds to make and natural objects to examine. Everything is cleverly designed to involve visitors while they enjoy learning about nature and their surroundings. Demonstrations and live shows occur frequently on the "back porch."

Hours at Outside In are weekdays, 1 to 4 P.M., weekends and holidays, 10 to 5. Children must be with an adult. Groups are admitted with advance reservations only. Admission to Outside In is included with admission to the Academy.

Wagner Free Institute of Science* (763-6529) also has a mini-museum created just for children called the **Discovery Room.** It's another unique place for small-fry to touch, smell, rub and piece objects together while having fun learning about natural science.

Please Touch Museum at 210 North 21st Street (963-0666) is the only museum in the country designed especially for children seven and younger. (Please Touch is directly across from the Franklin Institute's parking lot.)

Everything at Please Touch is meant to be explored, touched, climbed on, tried on or played on. The Cultural Corridor provides hands-on exhibits from a variety of cultures. Calliope teaches about sound. The Nature Center houses small animals to watch and pet. The Tot Spot is for toddlers to crawl around and explore. You can be anything you want to be when you use your imagination and try on masks, wigs, hats, costumes and uniforms on hand.

Programs in the informal 120-seat Virginia Evans

Theater might include music, mime, puppets, films or storytelling that's guaranteed to intrigue any small-fry crowd. Special exhibits are always fun and educational, too. There's a new topic every six months or so. A Resource Center is also available at Please Touch for children, parents, educators and students. It's a place to find books, games, work kits and objects that help explain mysteries like magnetism, electricity, fossils and webs.

It's only natural that children are comfortable and curious at Please Touch and their learning is uninhibited. Their social skills benefit, too, as they meet and play with others their size. And parents will learn about their children too!

Hours at Please Touch are Tuesday to Saturday, 10 to 4:30; Sunday, 12:30 to 4:30. Children must be accompanied by an adult (one adult for every three children), and groups are requested to make reservations. No strollers are allowed on the gallery floor. For the **handicapped**: Physically and mentally handicapped youngsters also benefit from Please Touch. It's recommended for handicapped children 12 and under. There is complete wheelchair access.

Cost is $3, and group rates are available on weekdays only. Again, group reservations are necessary. Membership (Supporting, $20; Family, $35) allows free admission, a quarterly newsletter, invitations to preview events, and shop discounts.

Please Touch also rents "Traveling Trunks" (see Chapter 13). A museum shop has high quality, low price books, games and toys reflecting the Please Touch environment.

Summer camps and recreation programs offered by the City of Philadelphia are described in Chapter 14, along with professional sporting events you can watch from the sidelines.

The ultimate educational and recreational park for children three to 13 is **Sesame Place**. Since it's in Bucks County, you'll have to read more about it in Chapter 17.

This is as close as anyone can come to guaranteeing your child will be happy.

Chapter 16.
Philadelphia for the Elderly and Handicapped.

This chapter is especially for people who have limited walking ability or are confined to wheelchairs. A disability shouldn't necessarily preclude visiting historic, educational and recreational attractions in Philadelphia. In many instances there are attractions just for the handicapped.

A concerted effort has been made throughout this book to specify for the elderly and handicapped the accessibility to each attraction. They are described as having "wheelchair access" or "no wheelchair access" based on a building's entrance, door widths and connections between floors.

"Complete wheelchair access" means that not only is the entrance level and manageable, but also there are special restroom facilities, elevators and other considerations. Details are given where it's pertinent. If further information is desired, call ahead before you visit.

You'll recognize the International Symbol for Accessibility at all public places where there are no architectural barriers and where all conveniences are at an accessible height.

You'll also appreciate the curb cuts and sidewalk ramps at all center city intersections in Independence National Historical Park, along the Benjamin Franklin Parkway, on the Chestnut Street Transitway (which also has depressed curbs midway on each block), on Walnut, Market, Juniper and Filbert Streets and John F. Kennedy Boulevard, and at least 100 prominent city intersections where there are public buildings nearby.

Wherever special provisions are made for the **visually and hearing handicapped**, they, too, are mentioned.

You can also write or call the **Mayor's Commission on People with Disabilities,** Room 143 City Hall, Phila., Pa. 19107 (686–2798). They can provide additional details on hotels, places of worship, branch libraries, banks, post offices, government office buildings and other places frequently visited.

Hearing handicapped people with telephone-teletype equipment can call the City Hall TTY phone at 564–1782.

The office is anxious to help Philadelphians and visitors to the city. They'll also refer you to agencies serving people with specific disabilities.

The **Mayor's Commission on Services to the Aging** is on the 9th floor at 1401 Arch Street, Phila., Pa. 19102 (686–3504).

Special Services

SEPTA

Call SEPTA at 574-7365 to get fare information for senior citizens and the handicapped, or write to SEPTA, 130 South 9th Street, Phila., Pa. 19107.

Those with TTY equipment can call SEPTA's TTY phone at 574-7853, weekdays from 8:30 to 4:30, for schedule, route and fare information.

Special ID cards from SEPTA enable handicapped persons to ride SEPTA vehicles at half-fare during off-peak hours. Application forms are available from the 130 South 9th Street office.

Special fares for senior citizens are described under "SEPTA" in Chapter 1.

There are three steps to get on or off the SEPTA buses and trolleys. The first step is approximately 12 inches from the ground. The next two are less.

SEPTA Paratransit is a special van service for people unable to use regular SEPTA vehicles. It operates daily and by reservation only. All riders must be registered with SEPTA. Write to the 9th Street office for Paratransit information, or call 574-2780.

ASSOCIATED SERVICES FOR THE BLIND
919 Walnut Street—19107
627-0600

The transcription of correspondence to braille, large-type copies or tape recordings of your material are provided for a nominal fee for supplies by Associated Services for the Blind.

A two-week training program is available to blind people interested in the Opticon Program which enables them to read through vibrating rods. Call for the cost and details.

Sense-Sations, the A.S.B.'s shop, has clever as well as practical tools for the blind and vision-impaired customer. The merchandise includes canes, braille wristwatches, talking calculators, speech synthesizers for computers, large-type playing cards and books, games and kitchen utensils. Braille playing cards are free for blind people from this agency. A mail/phone order catalogue is available for those who can't get in to the shop.

Ask about other services, like job placement, instruction in mobility, daily living skills and cooking classes that are provided by Associated Services for the Blind.

CAROUSEL HOUSE
686–0160 (Department of Recreation)

The city's Department of Recreation, under auspices of
Carousel House, sponsors year-round indoor and outdoor
programs for handicapped Philadelphians. Sadly, the original Carousel House in West Fairmount Park was
destroyed by fire in 1981. Other locations have been
expanded to keep the programs alive until a sparkling
new Carousel House is complete and ready for use in the
fall of 1986.

A summer camp run by Carousel House in Fairmount
Park is a rewarding experience for emotionally, mentally
and physically limited youngsters who participate in recreational, educational and therapeutic activities. There
are two four-week encampments in July and August.

Tours planned by Carousel House provide unique opportunities for the handicapped. Participants get to visit historic and cultural attractions around the city.

Reservations are necessary for all Carousel House
events and activities. If you know someone who should be
taking advantage of these activities, call the Department
of Recreation for programs and the dates to enroll.

ELWYN–NEVIL CENTER
FOR DEAF AND HEARING IMPAIRED
4031 Ludlow Street—19104
895–5509 (TTY: 895–5695)

This agency provides several vital services to deaf,
hearing impaired or communication-disordered people, as
well as their families, friends, employers and co-workers.
The staff is concerned with deaf people as well as people
who can hear and are interested in the hearing impaired.

Among the services offered are vocational and personal
counseling, social work, information and referral. Also,
there's referral within Elwyn Institutes for speech and
language therapy, audiology, and vocational evaluation
and training. They can help you contact government, public and private agencies providing special services. They
can provide a list of religious services, social organizations and recreational clubs for the deaf. They occasionally sponsor workshops and seminars, and they can refer
you to classes for sign language whether you hear or not.

The Center is open weekdays from 8:30 to 4:30.

A Deaf and Hearing-Impaired Senior Citizen Group (for those 55 and over) is also at the Center. There's a popular "drop-in" room, bi-weekly meetings, frequent social events, educational events and trips. The members are from throughout the Delaware Valley. Call 895-5567 (voice or TTY) for more information.

FREE LIBRARY OF PHILADELPHIA
Library for the Blind and Physically Handicapped
919 Walnut Street—19107
925-3213

Talking books, records, tapes, large print books and braille books are available along with traditional library materials from this special branch of the Free Library.

The resources are available to anyone who can't read ordinary print or hold a book because of a temporary or permanent visual or physical disability.

This library was built especially for the handicapped. It has level entrances, restrooms, phones and an adjoining parking lot to accommodate the blind and physically handicapped. Hours are weekdays, except holidays, 9 to 5.

Books and brochures on blindness are at the Library for the Blind and Physically Handicapped.

Materials and services for the hearing impaired are at the Central Library on Logan Square and at six branch libraries. A teletype machine at the Central Library's General Information Department enables deaf people to converse with the library staff. You can call the Library's TTY phone at 561-0942.

For access to the Free Library, refer to the next section of this chapter.

HUTCHINSON GYM POOL
University of Pennsylvania
33rd and Locust Streets—19104
898-8387

The University of Pennsylvania offers a special opportunity to people who enjoy swimming, but have a physical disability. Hutchinson Gym's pool has depths of three-and-a-half to 10 feet and is equipped with two lifts to lower swimmers into the water. Anyone in a wheelchair or on crutches can take advantage of this if they can swim and are accompanied by an adult swimmer. There's no admission charge for this year-round activity.

The pool hours are weekdays, except holidays, from noon to 6; weekends during the school year, from noon to 5. Call a day in advance to confirm this and to be sure a lifeguard will be on duty. The east entrance of the Hutchinson Gym has a ramp, and the two parking spaces closest to this entrance are designated for the handicapped.

RADIO INFORMATION CENTER
FOR THE BLIND (RICB)
919 Walnut Street—19107
627-0060 Ext. 205

More than 4,000 blind or print-handicapped people within a 50-mile radius of Philadelphia tune in daily to RICB's closed-circuit FM radio station. They hear readings from daily newspapers, magazines and books and live talk shows featuring useful information. Some call-in shows offer the audience a chance to air their questions and comments.

Broadcast hours are weekdays, 5 A.M. to midnight, and weekends, 7 A.M. to 11 P.M.

RICB is a charitable non-profit radio station under the auspices of the Associated Services for the Blind. If you know a print-handicapped person who would benefit from this one-of-a-kind opportunity, call the station for an application. Radios, provided for $15 annually, enable listeners to help defray station expenses and to support its outstanding services.

If you have some spare time, call RICB and volunteer to read aloud for their listeners.

TRAVEL INFORMATION SERVICE
Moss Rehabilitation Hospital
12th Street and Tabor Road—19141
329-5715 Ext. 2233 (TTY: 329-4342)

The Travel Information Service at Moss is where you can get facts on hotels, ships, planes, trains and tourist attractions in the United States and abroad to make your travel easier. They can tell you where you'll have wheelchair access, and where you won't. For $5 to cover postage and handling, they'll send you information on three travel destinations or topics.

If you would like the Service to assist you with a trip, call them with the idea of your proposed itinerary. They won't book any of your accommodations, but they can offer invaluable suggestions and information, as well as contacts for other agencies and travel services for the disabled.

A **Resource and Information Center** at Moss offers a variety of materials on all aspects of physical disability and rehabilitation. The library has information on special programs for the disabled, job possibilities, services, facilities, benefits and the legal rights of the handicapped. You can find information on making a home more accessible, clothing more comfortable and adaptability more complete. The resources are in pamphlets, books and magazines.

The Resource Center has complete wheelchair accessibility, but if you can't get to the Center, call and have materials mailed to you.

Another service at Moss is the **Rehab Line**. Taped messages answer queries about a hundred topics of interest pertaining to the disabled. Brochures listing all of the topics are available. Call 969-7878 for this information.

The Resource Center at Moss is open weekdays from 9 to 5. The facility offers invaluable information to people interested in the physically handicapped.

Each of the following theaters, stadiums and gathering places is mentioned more than once elsewhere in this book. They are popular sites for events in sports, visual and performing arts.

Museums and arts groups with specific programs and exhibits for the handicapped are described with that attraction under "E & H."

ACADEMY OF MUSIC
893-1935

Arrangements must be made in advance for people who plan to attend an event in a wheelchair. The best thing to do is buy designated seats in the parquet circle where the seat can be removed to accommodate a wheelchair. Ushers will assist with seating.

There are six steps at the main entrance on Broad Street. If you call ahead, an usher will meet and assist you at the ramped entrance on the Academy's south alley. Restrooms on the main floor have complete wheelchair access.

ANNENBERG CENTER AT THE UNIVERSITY OF PENNSYLVANIA
898-6791 (TTY: 898-6994)

All of Annenberg's theaters and restrooms are accessible to wheelchairs. Call ahead for special arrangements to enter at the most convenient door. There's limited space in each theater for individuals to remain in wheelchairs, and ushers will assist others into regular seats.

Viewers with up to 75 percent hearing loss can enjoy shows at Zellerbach Theater with a "magic eye" that gets sound signals through infrared light from the theater's master sound system. $2 rents the device for individual seats prior to each performance.

For information on all Annenberg Center handicapped services and programs, call 898-6683.

CONVENTION HALL
Philadelphia Civic Center 823-7350

A portable ramp is placed at the front entrance prior to all events. If you don't see it, ask a guard. Once inside, the main floor is level and there's elevator service to other levels. Restrooms are wheelchair accessible.

FREE LIBRARY OF PHILADELPHIA
686-5322

The Central Library at Logan Square is accessible to wheelchairs. There are automatic doors at the front entrance and six low steps in three tiers. A ramped entrance at the 20th Street end of Wood Street on the library's north side is always open. Designated parking is on Wood Street.

Call the Free Library for information on the branch libraries (28 of them are wheelchair accessible), and read the beginning of this chapter for the library's special services for the handicapped.

INTERNATIONAL HOUSE
387-5125

As you enter from Chestnut Street, there are eight steps in two tiers that take you to the main floor shops. You can avoid those steps by following the outdoor plaza to a ramped entrance on the building's east (37th Street) side.

There are four low steps at the entrance to Hopkinson Hall in the International House.

JOHN F. KENNEDY STADIUM

Gate 6 at the main entrance is street level. To get to the spectator seats, you have to go through portals and then up or down rows of steps to bleacher seats without armrests. Restrooms are on the concourse level. Parking is adjacent to the stadium. To arrange in advance for special parking, call 686-1776 Ext. 84-200.

MANDELL THEATER
AT DREXEL UNIVERSITY
895-2528

A ramp at the Chestnut Street entrance allows access to the building without steps. There are several steps into the auditorium, or there is special level access to the audience left side where room is allocated for six wheelchairs. For assistance with wheelchairs, ask for the house manager on arrival. Complete wheelchair access to restrooms.

MANN MUSIC CENTER

Complete wheelchair access with restrooms at ground level. An 8- by 130-foot ramp eliminates steep walking and steps. It goes from top of the Center and parking areas directly into the balcony.

PAINTED BRIDE ART CENTER
925-9914

Complete wheelchair access. Call ahead and space is reserved at front of theater for people who wish to remain in wheelchairs.

PALESTRA
898-6151

The main entrance (west side) is level. An area in the upper stands, Section WA, is set aside for eight wheelchairs. These spaces must be reserved in advance. Ushers will assist others into seats. Restrooms are accessible.

PLAYHOUSE IN THE PARK
879-1213

The entrances and aisles are ramped. Special arrangements should be made when tickets are bought, so visitors can remain comfortably in wheelchairs. Restrooms in an adjacent building are designed for wheelchairs.

SHUBERT THEATER

Entrance and orchestra seats are level, but it's advisable to get aisle seats since no one can remain in a wheelchair for a performance. Restrooms can only be reached by stairs.

The Shubert is equipped throughout with an "audio loop." It will benefit hearing handicapped members of the audience wearing a hearing aid adaptable to the telecord.

SPECTRUM
336-3600

When buying tickets for any event, specify if a spectator will be in a wheelchair. To reach a level entrance of the Spectrum, approach the building's east or west side from 10th Street. Special parking is designated for the handicapped. A ramp enables you to enter to the main floor without climbing steps. Restrooms, telephones and water fountains nearby are designed for the wheelchair-bound. If you are to remain in a wheelchair for the program, go directly to the Information Room (behind Section U on the main level) on arrival. A folding chair is provided for the person accompanying the wheelchair-bound. You'll then go to the special seating area behind Row 21. For additional information, call the Spectrum's security office.

VALLEY FORGE MUSIC FAIR
644-5000

Check with a parking attendant to be directed to a level entrance. Visitors can remain in wheelchairs around the audience perimeter. There are restroom facilities for the handicapped.

VETERANS STADIUM
Phillies, 463-1000; Eagles, 463-5500

There's one curb step from the adjacent parking lots to the entrance gates. Everything else is accessible by ramps and an elevator. The seats most convenient for fans in wheelchairs are in the 300s sections and reached from Gate D. Restrooms nearby have complete wheelchair access. When you buy tickets specify that they're for handicapped persons. To arrange in advance for special parking, call 686-1776 Ext. 84-200.

WALNUT STREET THEATER
574-3550

The orchestra section entrance is level, but you should call ahead to arrange to remain in a wheelchair or to be transferred to your aisle seat. Restrooms are on the balcony or lower level and reached by stairs.

An "audio loop" in the orchestra section enables better hearing for those wearing a hearing aid adaptable to the telecord. The Walnut was the first theater to offer this.

Chapter 17.
Beyond Philadelphia.

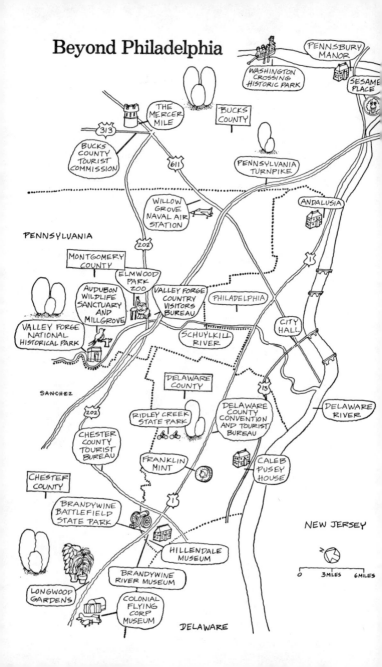

Beyond Philadelphia

PENNSBURY MANOR

WASHINGTON CROSSING HISTORIC PARK

SESAME PLACE

THE MERCER MILE

BUCKS COUNTY

313

BUCKS COUNTY TOURIST COMMISSION

611

PENNSYLVANIA TURNPIKE

WILLOW GROVE NAVAL AIR STATION

ANDALUSIA

PENNSYLVANIA

202

MONTGOMERY COUNTY

ELMWOOD PARK ZOO

AUDUBON WILDLIFE SANCTUARY AND MILLGROVE

VALLEY FORGE COUNTRY VISITORS BUREAU

PHILADELPHIA

VALLEY FORGE NATIONAL HISTORICAL PARK

SCHUYLKILL RIVER

CITY HALL

SANCHEZ

DELAWARE COUNTY

202

RIDLEY CREEK STATE PARK

DELAWARE COUNTY CONVENTION AND TOURIST BUREAU

DELAWARE RIVER

15

CHESTER COUNTY TOURIST BUREAU

FRANKLIN MINT

CALEB PUSEY HOUSE

CHESTER COUNTY

BRANDYWINE BATTLEFIELD STATE PARK

NEW JERSEY

1

HILLENDALE MUSEUM

0   3 MILES   6 MILES

LONGWOOD GARDENS

BRANDYWINE RIVER MUSEUM

COLONIAL FLYING CORP MUSEUM

DELAWARE

A book could be written on Philadelphia's neighboring counties: Bucks, Chester, Delaware and Montgomery.

This chapter attempts only to highlight the most outstanding and popular attractions that are within an hour's drive of center city Philadelphia. You'll see some of America's most beautiful farmland and countryside. In most cases, you'll have to provide your own transportation. Or you can check with the suburban train and bus routes. (The more accessible museums and tours are included with the appropriate chapters.)

Additional information is available from the Philadelphia Convention and Visitors Bureau* or the tourist bureau of each county.

Bucks County

ANDALUSIA
Just north of Philadelphia, on the Delaware River
Andalusia, Pa.
848-1777 (Cliveden)

Hours: By reservation only, Tuesday to Saturday, 10:30, 12:30 and 2. Allow one hour.

Tours: One guide takes up to 8 visitors, and up to 40 can be scheduled for each time. Reservations are absolutely necessary. Call or write one month in advance to Cliveden*, 6401 Germantown Avenue, Phila., Pa. 19144.

Cost: $30 minimum for up to 5 adults. After the first 5, it's an additional $6 per person.

E & H: There are 3 steps at the entrance and the tour is on the main floor.

Andalusia's main house was the first great example in this country of Greek Revival architecture. It sits on a 220-acre estate. The home was redesigned in 1834 by Thomas U. Walter for its owner, Nicholas Biddle. It's still owned by his descendant, James Biddle, who established the Andalusia Foundation and, in conjunction with the National Trust for Historic Preservation, opened the house to the public.

Go no further if you've never been to Athens to see the Theseum. Andalusia's riverside facade is an exact copy of the Greek structure. You'll get a lovely view of the Delaware from its portico.

Your tour of Andalusia includes the yellow parlor, ottoman room, library, music room, study, hallway and dining room with its enormous Duncan Phyfe mahogany table. Other furnishings are original Hepplewhite, Sheraton and Federal pieces. An exquisite fireplace is in every room. The magnificent chandeliers were never electrified. (Inside plumbing and electricity were installed in 1915.)

Art work at Andalusia includes oil paintings by Thomas Sully and Gilbert Stuart. There are rare engravings and busts of Napoleon and Alexander Hamilton.

Other original 19th century buildings on the estate include the cottage, pump house, billiard room and grotto. The grounds are especially beautiful in the summer when boxwood and rose gardens are in bloom.

THE MERCER MILE

Doylestown is the charming early 19th century town that serves as Bucks County's seat. Dr. Henry Chapman Mercer (1856–1930), an eccentric historian, architect, anthropologist, archaeologist and tile maker, lived and left his legacy there in the shape of three fantastic buildings and their contents within a mile of each other. The signs are strategically located to direct you, but you can't miss the towering structures.

Fonthill
East Court Street and Swamp Road (Route 313)
Doylestown, Pa. 18901
1–348–9461

Hours: Daily, 10 to 5 (with last tour at 4). Closed Thanksgiving, Christmas, New Year's. Allow one hour for tour.
Tours: Guided tours only. Groups of up to 8 depart throughout the day. Larger groups are divided. Reservations are suggested for all visitors, and groups of 10 to 50 must make reservations in advance.
Cost: Adults, $3; senior citizens with ID, $2.50; students, $1.50; children under 6, free. Group rates by reservation: 50¢ less for 10 or more.
E & H: Fonthill is multi-level and there are stairs everywhere. No wheelchair access.

Dr. Mercer designed and built his first building, his home, in the summers of 1908 to 1910. He acted as his own architect, employed eight to 10 unskilled day laborers and was among the first builders to use reinforced concrete.

Fonthill resembles a Tudor castle. It's decked with towers and turrets and filled with Moravian tiles from Dr.

Mercer's factory, and others collected from his travels abroad. All of his designs were fascinating. Plans were developed from the doctor's recollections of buildings overseas and his desire for showplaces. He started building from the inside, and the outside followed as a consequence. Fonthill is built around an 18th century farmhouse. You really have to see it to believe it!

Moravian Pottery and Tile Works
East Court Street and Swamp Road (Route 313)
1-345-6722

Hours: Daily, 10 to 5 (with last tour at 4). Closed Easter, Thanksgiving, Christmas, New Year's. Allow 45 minutes for tour.
Tours: All visits begin on the hour or half-hour with a 15-minute slide presentation and talk on the history and production of the Tile Works. Call in advance to schedule groups of no more than 30.
Cost: Adults, $2; senior citizens from outside Bucks County, $1.50; students, $1; children under 6 and local senior citizens, free; family, $4.50.
Other: Approximately 300 varieties of tiles produced here today are available for sale at the tile shop.
E & H: The entrance is level, enabling wheelchair access to the first floor. The 2nd floor is reached by stairs.

This huge factory is another one of Dr. Mercer's fantastic designs. The building was completed in the summers of 1910 to 1912.

Your guide, as well as the slide show, will tell you about the different tiles that have been manufactured during the company's history. You can walk through the plant and see the original kilns and tools and some of the original tiles—including the ones that tell Bible stories. You'll also see tiles as they're being made today by ceramists working for Bucks County.

Tiles from Dr. Mercer's factory have been used for decoration everywhere from the Capitol at Harrisburg, Pennsylvania, to the National Press Club in Washington, D.C.

Mercer Museum
Pine and Ashland Streets
1-345-0210 (Bucks County Historical Society)

Hours: Monday to Saturday, 10 to 5; Sunday, 1 to 5. Closed Thanksgiving, Christmas, January and

February. Allow at least one hour.

Tours: You're on your own. Call in advance if you're coming with 20 or more.

Cost: Adults, $3; senior citizens with ID, $2.50; students, $1.50; children under 6, free. Group rates by reservation: 50¢ less for 10 or more.

E & H: An elevator that holds one wheelchair enables access to all but one level.

This is where you can find over 40,000 colonial artifacts representing at least 50 crafts.

You'll see a conestoga wagon, a stagecoach, a horse-drawn fire engine, a whale boat, a log cabin and a schoolroom, along with the tools and machinery needed for survival, education, recreation, clothing making and the trades.

The world's largest collection of its type is housed in an equally extravagant building. Dr. Mercer's Americana fills the museum he designed and built from 1914 to 1916. It, too, is made entirely of concrete and it, too, must be seen to be believed!

Dr. Mercer's museum was also his castle.

The **Spruance Library** of the Bucks County Historical Society (1-345-0210) adjoins the Mercer Museum. It houses the Bucks County archives dating from 1682 to the present, a huge collection of Bucks County history and genealogy, as well as vast collections on early American crafts, trades, industries and folk art.

The library's holdings include almost 20,000 books as well as an extensive collection of maps, manuscripts, photographs, newspapers, microfilm and other source materials. They preserve the history of Bucks County and interpret the collections of the Mercer Museum and Fonthill. All research must be done at the library. Hours are Tuesday, 1 to 9; Wednesday to Friday, 10 to 5. Admission is $3.

PENNSBURY MANOR
Route 9
Morrisville, Pa. 19067
946-0400

Hours: Tuesday to Saturday, 9 to 5; Sunday 12 to 5. Closed all holidays except Memorial Day, July 4 and Labor Day. Allow at least one hour.

Tours: Start with the 15-minute slide-show orientation in the Visitor Center. Period-costumed guides lead tours at least once an hour through the manor house, outbuildings and gardens. Groups of 18 or more should call ahead to schedule tour and group rate. Tours in any of 8 foreign languages can be scheduled 2 weeks in advance.

Cost: Adults, $2.50; senior citizens and groups with reservations, $1.75; children 6 to 17, $1; under 6, free.

E & H: Complete wheelchair access to all but the 2nd and 3rd floors of the manor house. Gardens are ramped; paths are packed gravel. Wide-tire wheelchairs are available. Signed tours can be scheduled 2 weeks in advance.

You'll feel welcome at William Penn's beautiful country plantation, 24 miles north of Philadelphia on the Delaware River. If you use I-95, it's roughly a 50-minute drive from Independence Hall.

Penn and his second wife, Hannah, entertained here. When you see the plantation, you'll see why. You'll see how Hannah set the table with damask, pewter, silver and glassware. And you'll see the kitchens where vast quantities of food were prepared.

While the family spent only two years here, Penn meticulously planned the house and gardens down to the last detail. The manor house was rebuilt on its original foundations in 1939, and it looks exactly as it did when Penn occupied it in 1700 and 1701. The mansion, with its setting on the river, is so realistic that you'll find it hard to believe it was rebuilt.

The furnishings are in the Jacobean style, and they include what is probably Pennsylvania's largest collection of 17th century antiques. Everything in the mansion reflects Penn's fine taste.

You'll also see the stable, the ice, smoke, bake and brew houses. The kitchen and formal gardens are a lovely part of the visit. The scenery changes according to the season.

SESAME PLACE
100 Sesame Road (just off Route 1)
Box 579
Langhorne, Pa. 19047
757-1100 (recording) or 752-7070

Hours: Early May to mid-June and first week of September, daily, 10 to 5; mid-June through August, daily, 9 to 8; mid-September to mid-October, weekends only, 10 to 5. To avoid summer crowds, try to arrive early or later in the day. When the park is full, it's closed till the crowds diminish and others can be admitted.

Tours: Groups and school classes of 25 or more should

write or call 752-4900 for reservations and to arrange special rates.

Cost: May, June, September, October: adults, $8; children, $10; July, August: $1 more. Children under 2, free. All admission charges plus 10% amusement tax. Computer tokens are 3 for $1. Parking is additional and adjacent to the entrance.

Lunch: The Food Factory serves reasonably priced food that's good for you and tastes good. And, you can watch the preparation.

Other: Most of Sesame Place is outdoors so try to come in good weather. In warm weather, bring a change of clothing for children because some of the play elements involve water. Lockers are available. Mr. Hooper's Store has Sesame Street toys, games, books, puzzles, dolls and clothing. An Adult Oasis is where moms and dads can sit in a shaded, quiet area but still share the fun.

E & H: While the play elements will probably be off limits, there's wheelchair access to the Computer Gallery, Sesame Studios, the Food Factory, Mr. Hooper's Store and restrooms. Call ahead to schedule your visit (752-4900).

The ultimate play-and-learn park designed especially for three- to 13-year-olds and their parents is just 20 miles northeast of center city Philadelphia.

Forty outdoor play elements have youngsters push, climb, pull, slide, crawl and "swim" through the likes of Rubber Duckie Rapids, Rainbow Pyramid, the Sesame Streak, Slippery Slope, the Count's Ballroom, the Monster Maze, Oscar's Obstacle Course, Big Bird's Court and Bert's Balancing Beams. (The author of this guidebook has been seen trying them, too.)

The indoor computer gallery challenges the most nimble of minds with 70 games, puzzles and scientific riddles. Courses for adults and children in BASIC and LOGO are available at The Computer Campus. For information on these courses, cost and times, pick up the brochure or call 752-4900.

Hands-on science exhibits in the Sesame Place Studios make it fun and easy to learn some of the concepts of television production. This is where visitors see themselves on closed circuit television in a replica of the Sesame Street studio. Jim Henson's Sesame Street Muppets also perform on stage, in person. Don't miss Big Bird, Bert & Ernie and the Honkers.

We're fortunate that the Children's Television Workshop and Busch Entertainment Corporation chose our area for the country's first educational play park.

WASHINGTON CROSSING HISTORIC PARK
Routes 32 and 532, on the Delaware River
Washington Crossing, Pa. 18977
1-493-4076

Hours: The park is open daily, 9 A.M. to sunset. The buildings are open 9 to 5 Monday to Saturday, and Sunday noon to 5. The buildings are closed holidays on an alternating basis.
Tours: A 30-minute film, "Washington Crossing the Delaware," is at 9, 10:30, 12, 1:30 and 3. A 45-minute tour follows at 9:30, 11, 12:30, 2 and 3:30. Groups of 10 or more should call at least 2 weeks in advance.
Cost: The film is free. For Thompson-Neely House, Mahlon K. Taylor House and Old Ferry Inn tour: adults, $1.50; senior citizens, $1; children 6 to 17, 50¢. Group rates by reservation only.
Lunch: Picnic pavilions can be rented by groups when making reservations.
E & H: The Visitor Center, some historic buildings and the Wildflower Preserve are accessible. Call for details.

This 500-acre state park (35 miles north of center city Philadelphia) is the site where George Washington crossed the Delaware River on December 25, 1776, to launch the Revolutionary attack on Trenton.

An exact copy of Emanual Leutze's famous painting, "Washington Crossing the Delaware," is on display at the **Memorial Museum.** It's also the place to listen to a short narrative of these momentous events and see the film noted above. (Why was George Washington standing in the boat?)

The **Thompson-Neely House** was the riverside headquarters for the Revolutionary forces. It's where Washington and his officers met to plan the fateful assault.

They say Washington dined at the **Old Ferry Inn** before he took his historic boatride. (Did he stand up all the way?) The **Mahlon K. Taylor House** belonged to a founder of the town of Taylorsville, also known as Washington Crossing. All of these historic buildings are restored and furnished from the colonial period.

The **Boat Barn** houses four replicas of the durham boats. These are one of the types of boats Washington and his troops used to make their famous crossing.

The **Frye Spinning House** is where occasionally you can see a demonstration of that colonial craft.

A 100-acre **Wildflower Preserve** is at the **Bowman's**

Hill section of the park. You'll pass endless varieties of Pennsylvania trees, plants and flowers on its 22 miles of hiking trails. Call at least a month in advance to schedule a one-hour tour for groups of no more than 30. The teacher-naturalist can emphasize plants, animals or both. The talk and walk will be geared to the group's age level.

Bowman's Hill is where you'll get a magnificent view of the Bucks County countryside and a chance to pretend you're a soldier guarding your territory along the river. Bowman's Hill Tower is open April through October, daily, except Tuesdays, 10 A.M. to 4:30 P.M. Cost: adults, $2; senior citizens, $1.50; children, 50¢; group rates by reservation, and reservations are absolutely necessary.

Picnic tables and benches are throughout the park. Large groups can make reservations to rent any of the five pavilions. Canoes can be rented on the outskirts of the park; ice skating is allowed when conditions make it safe.

What else should you see in Bucks County?

Bucks County is known for its 13 covered bridges and its quaint, historic towns. **FALLSINGTON** is a colonial village that's built around a 17th century Friends Meeting House where William Penn worshipped. Many of the town's homes are from Penn's time, and the Stagecoach Tavern is also restored. Fallsington is at Tyburn Road, off Route 1. Guided tours of Fallsington can be scheduled on Wednesday to Sunday afternoons from March 15th to November 15th. Call 1-295-6567 for details.

PEDDLER'S VILLAGE is a recently built community of antique shops, boutiques and restaurants in Lahaska, off Route 202. It's five miles south of the original artists' colony of **NEW HOPE**. This charming little town is only 35 miles north of Philadelphia. New Hope is lined with galleries, workshops, studios, shops and restaurants. (It's the town that Sausalito copied.)

You can ride a mule-drawn barge along the Delaware Canal, daily from April 1st to early in November. (Call 1-862-2842 for hours and cost.)

You can see a show at the Bucks County Playhouse

from May through December (call 1-862-2041 for the schedule and reservations), or you can browse among the shops for a delightful afternoon or evening. New Hope's historic landmarks are clearly identified.

Bucks County Tourist Commission
152 Swamp Road (Route 313)
Doylestown, Pa. 18901
1-345-4552

Chester County

COLONIAL FLYING CORP. MUSEUM
New Garden Airport
Newark Road
Toughkenamon, Pa. 19374
1-268-2048

Hours: Weekends, 12 to 4, except in very cold weather when it's closed. Allow 45 minutes.
Tours: Someone is on duty to answer questions at the museum.
Cost: Adults, $1; children under 12, 50¢. Call ahead for group rates.
E & H: The museum is on 2 levels with ramp entrances and connections.

Did you ever visit a museum on the corner of an airfield? This one is. The Colonial Flying Corp. Museum has an unusual collection: an assortment of interesting bicycles, motorcycles, engines, cars and planes. There are seven automobiles that date from 1909 to as recently as 1950. The small airplanes are vintage World War II.

To get your bearings, the museum and flying field are less than a mile south of Route 1, five miles west of Kennett Square, Pa., and only six miles from Longwood Gardens.

LONGWOOD GARDENS
Route 1
Kennett Square, Pa. 19348
1-388-6741

Hours: Gardens: daily, 9 to 6 (till 5 in winter). Conservatories: daily, 10 to 5. Evening hours for special holiday displays and cultural events. Half-hour fountain displays are Tuesday, Thursday and Saturday nights at 9:15 from mid-June through August, when the conservatories also remain open till 10:30 P.M. Allow at least 2 hours.

Tours: All guided tours are scheduled in advance with the Group Visits Office and payment is due a week ahead. A 90-minute gardens tour or a 2-hour Peirce–duPont House and gardens tour is available for groups of 15 or more any day from 10 to 3. Tours are conducted indoors in inclement weather. At least one adult must accompany every group of 10 youngsters with or without a guided tour.

Cost: Adults, $5; children 6 to 14, $1; under 6, free. Group rates are available for 30 or more when making tour reservations.

Lunch: The Terrace Restaurant offers self-service informality or casual restaurant dining. Call 1-388-6771 for information or reservations.

Other: Wear comfortable shoes. No pets, bicycles or camera tripods are allowed. The Visitor Center provides a multi-image slide orientation. The Gift Shop sells film, books, stationery and plants.

E & H: Wheelchairs and special maps are available at the entrance, and there's access to the grounds and most buildings.

If you were visiting in Europe, you would go hundreds of miles out of your way to see the late Pierre S. duPont's estate. Longwood Gardens is less than an hour's drive from center city Philadelphia.

There are over 350 public acres (including four acres under glass) of magnificent gardens with all of the trees, plants and flowers carefully identified. There's a maze of hedges to navigate through, a conservatory and greenhouse, a bonsai room, experimental and "sample" gardens, fountain displays, a lily pond and water gardens. They're all in various stages of bloom throughout the year.

You're bound to relax at Longwood Gardens, so while you're there inquire about their concerts, lectures and theater productions. Or, call ahead and plan your visit according to seasonal displays or another special event. Picnic facilities are also available, and bring your camera.

WHARTON ESHERICK MUSEUM
Box 595
Paoli, Pa. 19301
644-5822

Hours: By reservation only, March through December, Saturday, 9 to 5; Sunday, 1 to 5. Groups of 8 or more can sometimes be scheduled weekdays.

Tours: All visits are by one-hour guided tour scheduled in advance for up to 8 people. Directions to museum will be provided with tour confirmation.

Cost: Adults, $3; children under 12, $2. $25 minimum for weekday tour.

E & H: Limited wheelchair access.

In 1913, Wharton Esherick, a native Philadelphian, moved to an old stone farmhouse near Paoli in Chester County. He studied painting at the Pennsylvania Academy of the Fine Arts. Esherick spent the rest of his life here, painting scenes of the rural surroundings, sculpting and making furniture.

His studio and collection looks today as it did when he died in 1970. Over 200 paintings, woodcuts, prints, wood, stone and ceramic sculptures, furniture and furnishings are displayed. The five-level studio itself was 40 years in the building. When you see each detail, you'll know why.

Esherick's work has been exhibited around the world and is in permanent museum collections throughout the country. It's a special experience to see his work and the way he worked.

Chester County is rich in flora and fauna.

The **STAR ROSE GARDENS** of Conard-Pyle Rose Company, on Route 1 south of Kennett Square (1-869-2426), is the place to see infinite varieties of star roses. The gardens are open to the public from late May to early fall, daily, from dawn till dusk.

The **SWISS PINE GARDENS**, in Malvern (1-933-6916), is lush with authentic Japanese and Polynesian gardens, herbs, heaths, heathers and a fern trail. A wild bird pond is popular with the youngsters in migratory seasons. This arboretum and wildlife haven is open weekdays from 10 to 4, and Saturday mornings from 9 to 11. It's closed holidays and from December 15 to March 15.

Chester County is also **mushroom growing** territory. In fact, it's the center for the nation's mushroom industry.

You'll see indications of this from the roadside stands, signs and the unusual long, low buildings in Kennett Square, Toughkenamon and along Route 1.

You can tour a museum with a scale model mushroom farm at **PHILLIPS MUSHROOM PLACE** on Route 1 in Kennett Square (a half-mile south of Longwood Gardens). Allow 30 minutes for the visit which includes a short film on mushroom growing, followed by seeing the real thing. Hours are 10 to 6 daily and groups should call ahead for reservations (1-388-6082). Cost: adults, $1.25; senior citizens, 75¢; children 7 to 12, 50¢; 6 and under, free; a busload, $10. And you might be tempted to purchase some of Phillips' luscious fresh mushrooms, pickeled mushrooms and dozens of other mushroom products.

There are also a number of historic sites that are fun to explore in Chester County.

ST. PETER'S VILLAGE, just off Route 23 in Knauertown, is a restored 19th century granite quarry village with stables, shops, a restaurant, French Creek Falls, a quarry and a park. It's a nice visit into the past.

The **CHESTER COUNTY HISTORICAL SOCIETY** at 225 N. High Street in West Chester (1-692-4800) is where archives are preserved and regional antique furnishings, clocks and decorative arts are exhibited. Hours for the museum and library are Tuesday, Thursday, Friday and Saturday, 10 to 4; and Wednesday, 1 to 8. Admission is $2 for adults, $1 for senior citizens and 50¢ for students. Group rates are available for 10 or more when making reservations.

You can also stop at the historic **CHESTER COUNTY COURTHOUSE** in West Chester, and at the Chester County Tourist Promotion Bureau on West Gay Street. While you're there, ask about the **PAOLI MEMORIAL GROUNDS** in Malvern and the **FREEDOMS FOUNDATION** near Valley Forge.

If you would like to go on an all-day tour of historic homes, buildings and landmarks in Chester County, ask about the annual **Chester County Day** that's usually held the first weekend in October.

Chester County Tourist Promotion Bureau
117 W. Gay Street
West Chester, Pa. 19380
1-431-6365

BRANDYWINE BATTLEFIELD STATE PARK
Route 1
Chadds Ford, Pa. 19317
459–3342

Hours: The grounds are open weekdays, 8 to 5; Saturday, 9 to 5; Sunday, 12 to 5. The houses are open June, July and August: daily, except Monday, 10 to 4:30; and weekends only the rest of the year. The Visitor Center is open daily, except Monday, 9 to 5. Closed some holidays.
Tours: Guides are on duty at the houses to answer questions. Special arrangements can sometimes be made in advance for groups to visit out-of-season.
Cost: Adults, $1; senior citizens and groups, 75¢; children 6 to 17, 50¢; under 6, free.
E & H: The houses are level with the ground; steps lead to the 2nd floors. There are many hills and gravel paths.

This is where George Washington and the American Revolutionary troops suffered defeat at the hands of the British on September 11, 1777. Re-enactment Weekend is celebrated at the park annually on the weekend closest to that date in history.
The Lafayette and Washington Headquarters are restored and furnished from the period. Picnic facilities are also available throughout the 52–acre park.

BRANDYWINE RIVER MUSEUM
Route 1
Chadds Ford, Pa. 19317
459–1900

Hours: Daily, except Christmas, 9:30 to 4:30. Allow one hour.
Tours: Call the tour coordinator at least 2 weeks ahead to schedule a one hour tour for school or adult groups.
Cost: Adults, $2.50; senior citizens 65 and over, students with ID and children 6 to 12, $1.25; under 6, free. Group rates available by reservation in February, March, July, August.
Lunch: A self-serve 120–seat restaurant is open 11 to 3. Group reservations are suggested.
Other: The Museum Shop sells art and environmental books, gift items, stationery and reproductions.

E & H: Complete wheelchair access. There's a wheelchair entrance and elevator that enables access to all floors.

This 19th century grist mill on the Brandywine Creek has been restored and converted under the auspices of the **Tri-County Conservancy** of Brandywine, into one of America's most popular art museums. It opened in June, 1971, as a three-story gallery connected by a glassed-in circular silo. 1984 saw the completion of a three-story brick, glass and wood addition. It's a masterpiece in design.

The works of Howard Pyle, three generations of Wyeths (N.C., Andrew and James) and others of the Brandywine School have lured a steady stream of visitors from 80 nations.

The Conservancy and the museum are dedicated to the preservation of the Brandywine and the land that is the artists' inspiration. The permanent and the changing exhibits reflect ecology, land and water conservation.

The museum is an enchanting natural environment for concerts, lectures, antique shows and a fall harvest market in the courtyard.

After you visit the museum, leave through a cobblestone courtyard and follow the mile-long nature trail into the museum's surrounding acreage. You'll be self-guided through woods, meadows and swamps toward **John Chadd's historic home.** The interesting flowers and shrubs are labeled.

CALEB PUSEY HOUSE
Landingford Plantation at 15 Race Street
Upland, Pa. 19015
874-5665 or 876-9206

Hours: June, July and August: Tuesday to Friday, 10 to 4; weekends, 1 to 4. May and September: weekends, 1 to 4. Closed holidays. Arrangements can sometimes be made for groups to visit at other times. Allow 30 to 45 minutes.
Tours: Groups of 5 or more are scheduled if you call or write in advance.
Cost: Adults, $1; children under 12, 75¢.
E & H: The grounds are level and there's one step at the entrance.

Caleb Pusey was Pennsylvania's first historian and the manager of the colony's first English industry, a mill at Landingford Plantation. Grain was ground here, and lumber was sawed for the colonists.

Pusey, who built this two-room stone home in 1683, was often visited by his friend William Penn.

See what the 17th century way of life was like in Pennsylvania. See what is said to be the oldest remaining home of any English settler in the colony.

Other attractions on the 12-acre tract include an 1849 school house (now a museum and gift shop), the barn and the log house.

FRANKLIN MINT MUSEUM
Route 1, at Wawa
Franklin Center, Pa. 19063
459-6168

Hours: Tuesday to Saturday, 9:30 to 4:30; Sunday, 1 to 4:30. Closed holidays.

Tours: You're on your own. No reservations necessary, but groups are requested to call or write ahead.

Cost: Free.

Other: The adjoining Franklin Mint Gallery (459-6884) sells original jewelry, sculpture, clocks, miniatures, home furnishings and collectors items that you can't buy elsewhere.

E & H: Museum is on one level, but there are several steps at the entrance. A chairlift enables complete wheelchair access.

The world's largest private mint is a 45-minute drive from center city Philadelphia. The Franklin Mint produces limited edition heirloom quality collectibles, commemorative coins and medals that have (since the mint's conception in 1965) honored more than 3,500 people, places and events in world history. They also create commemorative objects in pewter, porcelain and crystal.

If the process of coin making fascinates you, so will this coin-shaped museum. It's also a way to recall American history, nature, science, art and the subjects that are imprinted on coins, medals and ingots that are on display. There are also leather-bound books, philatelic issues, traditional and contemporary jewelry, heirloom dolls, crystal, porcelain and sculptures in silver, bronze and pewter.

Continuous showings of the film, "Of Art and Minting," give you a better picture of the creativity and manufacturing that goes into these various art objects.

RIDLEY CREEK STATE PARK
Sycamore Mills Road
Media, Pa. 19063
566–4800

Hours: The park is open daily, 8 A.M. till dusk. The office
is open Memorial Day to Labor Day, daily, 8 to 4; weekends only the rest of the year.
Cost: Free, unless you partake in any of the concessions.

Less than an hour's drive from center city Philadelphia
is a 2,600–acre state park with some unusual features. It
has playgrounds, picnic and barbecue facilities, nature
trails and markers for walking, horseback riding and bicycling. There are stables to rent horses, streams for trout
fishing and a farm that takes you back 200 years.

Colonial Pennsylvania Plantation
Ridley Creek State Park
Media, Pa. 19063
566–1725

Hours: Weekends during Daylight Saving Time, 10 to 5;
Eastern Standard Time, 10 to 4. Closed December
through March. By reservation only, Tuesday to Fri-
day, for group tours. Call ahead to be sure and to ask
about special events.
Tours: Call weekdays (9:30 to 1:30) or write a month in
advance to schedule groups of 15 to 80.
Cost: Adults, $2; senior citizens and children under 12, $1.
Family rate for parents and 2 or more children, $5.
Group rates for 10 or more, $1.
Other: Wear sturdy shoes.
E & H: Call in advance to arrange wheelchair access.
There's one steep gravel hill and everything else is
level.

You can already tell that Ridley Creek State Park is far
from the ordinary. In fact, the **Bishop's Mill Historical
Institute** has recreated and manages within the park an
18th century plantation and working farm that operates
today (just as it did in the 1700s).
The colonial-costumed volunteers and a farmer work on
the 112-acre plantation using the tools and methods of
200 years ago. You'll witness the everyday life of a farm
family as they tend their livestock and fields. Cows,
horses, sheep, pigs and chickens live here. Watch as the
staff milks the cows, cuts curd for cheese, bakes bread,
spins flax and does whatever else is on the day's agenda.

What else is there to see in Delaware County?

The **DELAWARE COUNTY INSTITUTE OF SCIENCE** is at 11 Veterans Square (566–5126) in the center of Media, Delaware County's seat of government. The Institute was founded in 1833. Its formidable red brick home dates back to 1867.

This museum features a wide range of mineral collections, a herbarium of Delaware County plants, mounted birds and animals, fossils, shells, corals and an unusual collection of microscopes. The library has an extensive collection of natural science books and periodicals.

Admission is free. Hours are Monday, 10 A.M. to noon and 7:30 to 9:30 P.M., and other times by appointment. Group tours can be arranged. Call 566–3491 for additional information.

And there's lots more to see in Delaware County, especially if you're a history buff.

The **1724 COURTHOUSE** at 5th Street and Avenue of the States in Chester is the oldest public building in continuous use in the United States.

OLD SWEDES CEMETERY is an 18th century burial ground and the oldest Swedish cemetery in America.

The **JOHN MORTON HOUSE,** built in 1654 and fully restored, is a reminder of the Swedish settlement in the county.

The **THOMAS MASSEY HOUSE,** built in 1696 and restored, is a reminder of Pennsylvania's English Quaker settlement.

GOVERNOR PRINTZ PARK is named for Johann Printz, the man who founded Pennsylvania's first permanent settlement of white men at this site in 1642.

Delaware County Convention & Tourist Bureau
602 E. Baltimore Pike
Media, Pa. 19063
565–3679
Delaware County 24-hour "Funline" 565–3666

AUDUBON WILDLIFE SANCTUARY
and MILL GROVE
Audubon and Pawlings Roads near Route 363
Audubon, Pa. 19407
666-5593

Hours: The grounds are open daily, except Monday, from 7 A.M. to dusk. The house is open Tuesday to Saturday, from 10 to 4; Sunday, 1 to 4. Closed Mondays, Thanksgiving, Christmas, New Year's.
Tours: You're on your own, but groups of 12 or more should call 2 weeks in advance to arrange for an introductory talk.
Cost: Free.
Other: No food allowed. Bicycles are allowed on main road only.
E & H: Wheelchair access to Mill Grove's first floor only. The 2nd and 3rd floors are reached by steps.

John Audubon was an artist and naturalist who lived from 1785 to 1851. He was the first person to paint birds and wildlife with naturalism. The Audubon Society was founded in 1905 for the preservation of wildlife. A bird called Audubon's Warbler is also named after him.

John Audubon made his home in America on this 130-acre estate overlooking Perkiomen Creek, two miles north of Valley Forge National Historical Park.

You can walk along several miles of wooded hiking trails where Audubon walked. And you can visit his home, Mill Grove, which is now a memorabilia museum. All of Audubon's published works are on display.

ELMWOOD PARK ZOO
Harding Boulevard
Norristown, Pa. 19401
272-8080 (Borough Hall)

Hours: Daily, except Monday, 10 to 4:30. Closed Thanksgiving, Christmas, New Year's.
Tours: You're on your own. No reservations necessary. Groups of up to 30, at least school age, can call a few weeks ahead to schedule 45- to 60-minute tour. One adult must accompany every 10 youngsters, and larger groups will be divided into smaller groups of 10.
Cost: Free.

Lunch: Bring your own, or buy something at the refreshment stand that's open in warm weather. Picnic facilities are available.

E & H: Limited wheelchair access.

Norristown, the Montgomery County seat, is a borough of 40,000 people. It also boasts of a municipal zoo with a population in the hundreds.

There are deer, elks, goats, llamas, lambs, lions, monkeys, prairie dogs and a huge aviary with many bird species. A children's zoo within the zoo enables visitors to pet the farm animals. (The children's zoo closes in winter so the animals can go inside to stay warm.) A realistic exhibit recreates North American animal life at the time of the Revolution.

If you're within a 15 mile radius, Elmwood Park also has a "traveling zoo." Call the curator several weeks in advance to schedule this hour-long live animal presentation at your location. The fee depends on the program and the audience.

GLENCAIRN MUSEUM
1001 Papermill Road
Bryn Athyn, Pa. 19009
947-9919

Hours: By appointment only, weekdays, 9 to 5.

Tours: Call in advance to schedule 2-hour tour at 10 A.M. or 2 P.M. for groups of up to 20. Children under 12 must be with an adult.

Cost: Adults, $3; children and students, free.

E & H: There are 2 steps at main entrance. Cloister entrance is level and can be used, except in inclement weather, by special arrangement. An elevator goes to all 9 floors and can accommodate one wheelchair.

In Chapter 5, you read about the Bryn Athyn Cathedral and the work that went into its unique building. Now you can visit the equally unusual home of the man who supervised the Cathedral's construction.

Glencairn, the Romanesque-style former home of Raymond and Mildred Pitcairn, was built from 1928 to 1939. The same principles and craft shops were again used to create a unique family home as well as a depository for the family collection of medieval objects. The multi-level structure itself is embellished in stone, wood, glass and metal with artistic symbols of the teachings of the New Church.

The main floor looks as it did when it was occupied by

the Pitcairns. It serves as a community and cultural center. Rooms on the upper floors are individual galleries housing art and artifacts of Egypt, the Near East, Far East, Greece and Rome, French sculpture and stained glass of the 12th century, American Indian objects, and the medieval collection. If you're in a contemplative mood, don't miss the Chapel and the Cloister.

VALLEY FORGE NATIONAL HISTORICAL PARK
Route 23 and North Gulph Road
Valley Forge, Pa. 19481
783-1076 and 783-1077

Hours: The park is open daily from 8:30 A.M. to dusk. The Visitor Center and Washington's headquarters are open from 8:30 to 5. Allow at least 3 hours.

Tours: Visit on your own, or from April through October call the park concessionaire (783-5788 or 265-6446) for details on a cassette tour to take in your car or a guided tour by bus. SEPTA Rambles* and Gray Line Bus Tours* also go to Valley Forge.

Cost: It's free if you visit on your own. Charges vary for car cassette and bus tours.

Lunch: There are plenty of picnic areas and a refreshment stand.

E & H: There's one step into the Visitor Center and a ramp into the auditorium.

George Washington and his 11,000 weary troops survived the cold winter of 1777-1778 here.

Today Valley Forge Park is a 3,000-acre scenic national park filled with dogwood trees, botanical gardens and reminders of the American Revolution.

Start your tour at the Visitor Center. A 15-minute historic orientation film is presented on the hour and half-hour from 9 to 4:30. A museum is also here.

Also visit Washington's headquarters, the Memorial Chapel, Bell Tower and National Memorial Arch. What once was the soldiers' winter encampment grounds are now hills dotted with cannons, trenches, forts, log cabins, reconstructed soldiers' huts, markers and monuments.

WILLOW GROVE NAVAL AIR STATION
Route 611
Horsham, Pa. 19090
443-1776

Hours: By reservation only, April through October, Thursday and Friday at 10. Allow 1½ hours.

Tours: Call or write to the station's Public Affairs Office at least 6 weeks in advance. Groups of 10 to 30 (including chaperones), at least 6 years old, can be scheduled. One adult must accompany every 4 children. Individuals or smaller groups should call a few days ahead to see if there's a tour group they can join.

Cost: Free.

Lunch: Make reservations when planning tour to buy moderately priced meal at the enlisted dining facility.

E & H: Complete wheelchair access.

Anyone who loves airplanes will love this tour. You'll get to board a military aircraft if one's available. You'll drop by the parachute loft and learn how jump equipment is packed for flight. You'll also visit the base firehouse to see the special engines that are always on the ready at the airport.

No trip to the Willow Grove Naval Air Station is complete without a ground inspection of the World War II aircraft display. If you can't arrange to take the tour at Willow Grove, you can see the old planes from the parking lot on Route 611.

What else should you do in Montgomery County?

See the **MAIN LINE**. It's where some of the nation's grandest estates are located. Why the name? It was, and still is, the "main line" for the Pennsylvania (now Con-Rail) Railroad's commuter route from center city Philadelphia to the western suburbs. We told you about the stops back in Chapter 1.

The train tracks are parallel to Lancaster Pike (Route 30), the original route to the **PENNSYLVANIA DUTCH (or AMISH) COUNTRY** of Lancaster County.

Valley Forge Country
Convention & Visitors Bureau
Box 311
Norristown, Pa. 19404
278-3558 or 275-4636 (24-hour Fun Line)

The Amish Country

It would be an oversight not to mention a few of the famous attractions that are just beyond Philadelphia, and within an hour or two of center city.

AMISH COUNTRY in Lancaster County, Pennsylvania, is about one-and-a-half hours west of Philadelphia on Route 30 beyond Chester County. If you saw the movie "Witness," you had a glimpse of the Amish Country. It's the locale of towns such as Bird-in-Hand, Blue Ball, Intercourse, Lititz, Paradise and Smoketown in some of America's most beautiful farm regions.

Amish Country is a mecca for antique and hand-made quilt shoppers, and for gourmands of German-style cooking followed by fresh fruit or shoofly pies.

You'll be enchanted by the Amish people, their dress, buggies, one-room schoolhouses and colorful hex signs that adorn their barns. Stop by the Mennonite Information Center just off Route 30, or the Pennsylvania Dutch Tourist Bureau on Hampstead Road, for some good and plenty information.

HOPEWELL FURNACE, a National Historic Site, is west of Philadelphia beyond Valley Forge and just a few miles south of Birdsboro on Route 345. It's about an hour-and-a-half from center city Philadelphia.

The village was founded in 1771 as an ironmaking community to supply cannon and shot for the Revolutionary forces. Today Hopewell Furnace looks as it did from 1820 to 1840. It's open daily, from 9 to 5, year-round except Christmas and New Year's (with "living history" programs in July and August) so you can get a true picture of how you might have lived in such a community at the time. Guided tours are scheduled for school groups of 15 or more.

For details write to the Hopewell Furnace National Park Service Superintendent, R.D. 1, Box 345, Elverson, Pa.˙ 19520, or call 1–582–8773.

HERSHEY (Chocolate City), Pennsylvania, is a two-hour drive west from Philadelphia. It boasts three seasons and 23 acres of floral displays in the Hershey **Rose Gardens and Arboretum;** 36 rides (including a Kiss Tower), entertainment and 11 acres of native North American wildlife at ZooAmerica in **Hersheypark** (open mid-May to September); the **Hershey Museum of**

American Life; and a magical ride through **Hershey's Chocolate World** where you'll follow a cacao bean on its way to becoming a Hershey Bar. And Hershey is no doubt the world's only city where streetlights resemble chocolate kisses. For details write to Hershey Guest Information Center, Hershey, Pa. 17033.

State of Delaware

The state of Delaware is less than an hour's drive south of Philadelphia.

Among its attractions are the **HAGLEY MUSEUM** at Routes 141 and 100, three miles north of Wilmington. It's on the 200-acre site of a 19th century industrial community where the DuPont Company began almost two centuries ago. Indoor and outdoor exhibits take you through the original powder and spinning mills to learn the industry's evolution from colonial times to the present.

E.I. duPont built an elaborate country house here for his family in 1803. You can tour "**ELEUTHERIAN MILLS**" and admire generations of the duPont family's furnishings from the 18th and 19th centuries. Plan to spend at least three hours.

Call (1-302-658-2400) or write to the Tour Office, Hagley Museum, Box 3630, Wilmington 19807 for details.

WINTERTHUR MUSEUM is nearby on Route 52 in Winterthur, Delaware 19735. Henry Francis duPont's fabulous 200-room mansion–museum built in 1839 is also open to the public. It's filled with the largest and finest collection of early American (1640 to 1840) furnishings and accessories.

Call (1-302-654-1548) or write for hours, admission charges and details about train rides and tours of various parts of the house–museum and beautiful gardens.

Head east from Philadelphia across the Delaware River and you're in New Jersey.

SIX FLAGS GREAT ADVENTURE, in Jackson, New Jersey, about 45 minutes from center city Philadelphia, has America's largest safari park. It's open from late March through September.

You can actually drive your car through a natural habitat that has been recreated for more than 2,000 wild animals from around the world. Be sure to bring a camera!

The entertainment park has thrill rides for the entire family, an enchanted forest, roaring rapids, a log flume ride, a "dream street," restaurants and arenas for regularly scheduled superstar concerts, musical revues, a Bugs Bunny extravaganza and aquatic shows. A one-price ticket for children and adults includes everything but refreshments and souvenirs and the superstar shows.

Missing Great Adventure is like being in Los Angeles and not seeing Disneyland. Call 201-928-3500 (recording of special events) for directions and details. For group sales information, call 245-8868.

WHEATON VILLAGE is just off of Route 47 in Millville, New Jersey 08332. It's 42 miles south of Philadelphia by way of the Walt Whitman Bridge, or 35 miles west of Atlantic City by way of the Black Horse Pike and Route 552.

Wheaton Village has roots that date to 1739 when Southern New Jersey's first successful glass factory was founded. Years later, Dr. T. C. Wheaton acquired the Shull-Goodwin Glass Company of Millville and gave it his name. His son and grandson have painstakingly recreated a typical late-19th century glassmaking community so that the skill and tradition of South Jersey glassmaking is preserved.

A visit to Wheaton Village is a magnificent look into the past. You'll tour a vast Museum of Glass with Victorian period rooms and glass treasures dating from 300 B.C. to today. You'll visit an exact replica of Dr. Wheaton's 1888 Glass Factory, and you'll actually see artisans making glass by hand. You can browse in the General Store, have something to eat and visit the craft shops.

Wheaton Village is open daily from 10 to 5, except Easter, Thanksgiving, Christmas and New Year's, and January through March when hours are Wednesday to

Sunday, 10 to 5. A one-day admission ticket enables entrance to all exhibits, crafts shops and the museum. Call 609-825-6800 or write for additional information.

Atlantic City, New Jersey

Area code 609. ZIP code 08401

The sun, sand and surf of the New Jersey coast are just about an hour from center city Philadelphia. Take a gambol to Atlantic City! For information, write or call the Atlantic City Convention and Visitor's Bureau, 2314 Pacific Avenue in Convention Hall, Atlantic City (348-7100). The hours are 9 to 5 on weekdays.

You can drive to Atlantic City by way of the four bridges crossing the Delaware River from Philadelphia. Then head for the Atlantic City Expressway (a toll road), the Black Horse Pike (Route 322) or the White Horse Pike (Route 30).

Transport of New Jersey buses to Atlantic City from center city Philadelphia depart frequently from the Greyhound Terminal at 17th and Market Streets and the Trailways Terminal at 13th and Arch Streets (see Chapter 1). Fare for the 75- to 90-minute trip is $6.75 one-way or $12.50 for the round trip. The buses come into Atlantic City at the Municipal Bus Station, Arkansas and Artic Avenues.

If you would like to spend six hours in or around one of the major casino hotels, and if you're at least 18 years old, then take one of the frequent casino package trips from various locations in Philadelphia. The price for any of these is between $10 and $25 round trip, but you'll get most of the price back in quarters when you get there. Ask Greyhound or Trailways, or look in the papers for ads about these trips. It's a terrific deal, but of course the hotels hope you'll spend your time gambling in their casinos.

Transportation in Atlantic City is best accomplished by taxicab, bus, jitney or the boardwalk tram. Jitneys are mini-buses that take only as many passengers as they have vacant seats. They travel along Pacific and Ventor Avenues from one end of Atlantic City to the other (from Gardner's Basin to Jackson Avenue) and the fare is 75¢. There's always a jitney in sight, and if you've never had the experience, it's a fun way to ride. Atlantic City Transportation Company (344-8181) buses travel the length of Atlantic Avenue, and the fare is also 75¢.

The boardwalk tram is an open-air vehicle that runs on

Atlantic City

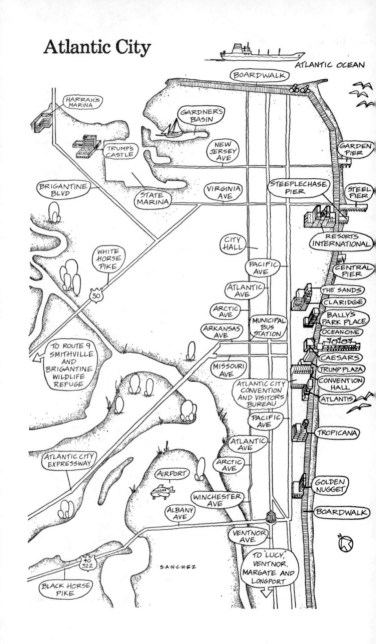

the boardwalk between Resorts International Hotel and the Golden Nugget Hotel. The tram operates every day of the year, till 2 A.M. during the week and throughout the night on weekends. The one-way fare is $1; senior citizens and children under 12 pay 75¢. This is a tireless way to see the boardwalk attractions.

Casino gambling, and the changes it has brought since gambling was approved by New Jersey voters in 1976, is something to see. The change is most evident in the luxurious new hotels. Casinos are a day and night activity. Hours are 10 A.M. to 4 A.M. on weekdays and 10 A.M. to 6 A.M. on weekends. The games are slot machines, blackjack at tables and on electronic machines, baccarat, craps, roulette and the wheel of fortune. Youngsters under 21 aren't allowed in the casinos.

The hotels give you a choice in size, theme and ambience. Entertainment abounds. Superstars appear at some of the casino hotels, while others have glittering variety shows. All of the casinos have lounge acts. There are currently 11 casino hotels, with two more scheduled for 1987.

ATLANTIS CASINO HOTEL Florida Avenue and the Boardwalk (344-4000 or 800-257-8672). Atlantis' sleek black 500-room hotel tower boasts 52,000 square feet of casino on three floors, each with an ocean view. Shangrila and Le Club Lounges have nightly entertainment, and the 1,000-seat Cabaret Theater presents the "Superstars and Stripes" revue. There are three gourmet restaurants, a 24-hour cafe and an indoor pool with saunas and a health club.

BALLY'S PARK PLACE CASINO HOTEL Park Place and the Boardwalk (340-2000 or 800-225-5977). Bally's Park Place offers 512 guest rooms, a 60,000-square-foot casino with more than 1,600 slot machines, 13 restaurants and lounges, complete wheelchair access, a video arcade, an outdoor swimming pool, and a Cabaret Theater (340-2709) with "An Evening at La Cage" variety show. Billy's Pub is the other spot for nightly entertainment at Bally's. The casino is enhanced by waterfalls cascading parallel to lengthy escalators that go up from and back to the gambling floor.

CAESARS ATLANTIC CITY HOTEL CASINO Arkansas Avenue and the Boardwalk (348-4411 or 800-257-8555). Top-rate off-Broadway shows and big-name stars like Burt Bacharach, Anthony Newley, Joan Rivers and Red Skeleton are headliners at Caesars' Circus Maximus. The Arena and Forum Lounges also have entertainment. A smart shopping complex, rooftop tennis, a health spa, five restaurants and a 60,000-square-foot casino are among the amenities at the 645-room hotel.

CLARIDGE CASINO HOTEL Indiana Avenue and the Boardwalk (340–3400 or 800–257–8585). One of Atlantic City's grand old structures was completely refurbished and given a new addition to create the Claridge. There's a gourmet French restaurant, a 24-hour Garden Room, lunch and dinner buffets and a deli. The Palace Theater provides big-name entertainment, as well as the Celebrity Cabaret. The Claridge has 504 guest rooms, a glass-enclosed year-round pool and health club, and a 30,000-square-foot, multi-level casino.

GOLDEN NUGGET HOTEL AND CASINO Boston Avenue and the Boardwalk (347–7111 or 800–257–8677). Return to the gay '90s at the Golden Nugget. Everything is a rollicking blend of Victorian and Western with a background mixture of Scott Joplin music. There's Victoria's gourmet restaurant, Lilly Langtry's for elegant Chinese dining, the Cornucopia for 24-hour fare, an ice cream parlor, three lounges and the Opera House Theater. Cowboys and gals keep an eye on things in the "turn of the century" 40,000-square-foot casino. All of the 504 guest rooms have an ocean view (56 have complete wheelchair access), as well as the glass-enclosed indoor pool. An amusement arcade is designed especially for youngsters.

HARRAH'S MARINA HOTEL CASINO 1725 Brighton Boulevard (441–5000 or 800–242–7724). Harrah's sparkling building was the first casino hotel to rise on Atlantic City's bay. It has a beautiful, sweeping view of the marina, 506 guest rooms and free indoor park-it-yourself space for your car. The entertainment is continuous in the afternoon and evening in the Bay Cabaret and Atrium Lounge. Harrah's Broadway by the Bay features big name stars. Car buffs will enjoy Harrah's world-famous automobile collection decorating the lobby and 44,000-square-foot casino.

RESORTS INTERNATIONAL CASINO HOTEL North Carolina Avenue and the Boardwalk (344–6000 or 800–438–7424). Resorts was the first casino after gambling was approved in Atlantic City. The 727-room hotel with a 60,000-square-foot casino opened in May, 1978. It features two gourmet restaurants, Le Palais and Camelot. The Rendezvous Lounge offers nightly entertainment. As the name implies, Resorts' Superstar Theater (340-6434) gets superstars like Perry Como, Lola Falana, Manhattan Transfer, Lou Rawls and Don Rickles. Resorts is topped off with a roof-top year-round pool, health spa and squash club.

THE SANDS HOTEL AND CASINO Indiana Avenue and Brighton Park (441-4000 or 800-257-8580). If you're overwhelmed by the size of the larger casino hotels, The Sands might be more to your liking. It's set back from the boardwalk in a high-rise with 500 guest rooms and a 45,000-square-foot casino. There's continuous music in the Players Lounge and the Punch Bowl. There's dancing and live entertainment on weekends from midnight to 5 A.M. at the Copa Club. David Brenner often appears here. The Food Court offers dozens of moderately priced fastfooderies with international menus.

TROPICANA HOTEL AND CASINO Iowa Avenue and the Boardwalk (340-4000 or 800-843-8767). The 521-room Tropicana with a 48,000-square-foot formal casino, a six-story sky-lit atrium and glass-enclosed elevators, offers the luxury of Monte Carlo and elegance reminiscent of the South of France. There are three gourmet restaurants, a 24-hour coffee shop, deli and buffet dining. Continuous music is in the Wild Swan Lounge and Top of the Trop. The newest faces in stand-up comedy appear at Comedy Stop at the Trop. Big-name stars are at Tropicana's Showroom. There's a year-round health club, an outdoor pool, tennis and paddleball courts.

TRUMP CASINO HOTEL Mississippi Avenue and the Boardwalk (441-6000 or 800-242-7724) opened in 1984 with 600 rooms and 60,000 square feet of casino. There's nightly entertainment in Viva's and the Casino Lounge, and a theater that presents the likes of Tony Bennett, Joel Grey and Andy Williams. Don's miss Ivana's Restaurant; it's one of the prettiest in town. There's an indoor pool, outdoor tennis, a gym and spa, and a video arcade for the youngsters.

TRUMP'S CASTLE HOTEL & CASINO Huron Avenue and Brigantine Boulevard (441-2000 or 800-441-5551). Trump's Castle on the marina treats everyone "like the king of the Castle." There's a three-acre recreation deck, free indoor parking for 3,000 cars, 60,000-square-foot casino, five gourmet restaurants, continuous entertainment in Jezebel's and Trump's Lounges, and "City Lites" presented in King's Court Theater (441-8300) following several years on stage in Las Vegas.

Under construction and scheduled to open in 1987 are another **RESORTS INTERNATIONAL** and the **SHOWBOAT CASINO.**

There are dozens of other hotels and motels in Atlantic City that are convenient to the beach, boardwalk and casinos. The Atlantic City Visitor's Bureau or a travel agent can provide you with additional information.

Or, you can call Atlantic City Reserve-a-Room, a central clearing number for information and reservations. In New Jersey, call 347-1900; from out-of-state, call 800-227-6667.

There's more to see in Atlantic City, and these are some of the more popular attractions that appeal to the entire family.

ATLANTIC CITY HISTORICAL MUSEUM (347-5844) is at the Atlantic City Art Center on Garden Pier, on the boardwalk at New Jersey Avenue. The exhibits include furnishings from old and bygone hotels, along with related art and sculpture. The postcards and similar memorabilia will appeal to nostalgia buffs. While you're here, visit the Art Center's two galleries. The exhibits, which change monthly, feature paintings, sculpture and photography by regional artists. Hours are 9 to 4 daily. Admission is free.

Atlantic City's **BOARDWALK** has been immortalized by the game of Monopoly and a song or two. Despite the fact that it's five miles of wooden boards and used primarily for walking, the name comes from Alexander Boardman. In the 1860s, Boardman came up with a plan of wooden platforms so people could remove wet sand from their feet before entering shops and hotels from the beach. Can you imagine what would have happened if his name was Alexander Metalman?

Bicycling is permitted on the boardwalk daily from 6 to 9 A.M. Beach badges are not necessary in Atlantic City. Life guards are on duty during the summer from 9:30 to 5:30 daily.

Going to Atlantic City and not seeing the boardwalk is like going to New York City and missing Fifth Avenue. And seeing the boardwalk without sampling a **salt water taffy** is like visiting Philadelphia and not having a soft pretzel or a cheesesteak.

EDWIN B. FORSYTHE NATIONAL WILDLIFE REFUGE—Brigantine Division (652-1665) is on the mainland north on Route 9, about a mile east of Ocean-ville. Its 20,000 acres of protected land attracts almost 300 species of wildlife. Ducks, geese and an occasional bald eagle are spotted migrating to and from the south. Most of the area is coastal salt marsh, but there is brush and woodlands with wildlife trails, observation towers and a visitor center. If you don't have the proper footwear, stay in your car for an eight-mile auto tour around the preserve. Bird lovers should bring binoculars. The admission is free. Hours are daily from dawn to dusk.

NOYES MUSEUM on Lily Lake Road in Oceanville (652-8848) is adjacent to the Brigantine Wildlife Refuge. It's a perfect setting for their collection of decoys. There are decoy carving demonstrations, a permanent contemporary art collection and changing exhibitions. Call for hours and a schedule of special events and admission charges.

HISTORIC GARDNER'S BASIN (348–2880) is at North New Hampshire Avenue and the Bay in Atlantic City. It's a charming reconstructed maritime village with shops, restaurants, outdoor exhibits and seasonal events.

Every youngster who has ever come to Atlantic City remembers Lucy. **LUCY THE ELEPHANT** (823–6473), at 9200 Atlantic Avenue in Margate, is now a National Historic Landmark. Lucy was built in 1881 as a real-estate promoter's dream to lure visitors to the Jersey shore. Lucy has recently been restored, and in warm-weather months you can climb up and around inside her six-story structure. Call for hours and cost.

A 900-foot "oceanliner" **OCEAN ONE** is permanently anchored at the Boardwalk and Arkansas Avenue. Its decks include a self-service food court, sit-down restaurants, exhibits, amusements and a shopping mall extraordinaire.

STORYBOOK LAND (641–7847) is 10 miles west of Atlantic City on the Black Horse Pike (Routes 40 and 322) in Cardiff. Fifty buildings, displays and animals bring fairy tales and nursery rhymes to life. There are also rides, a playground, picnic areas and a snack bar. Call for a schedule of admission, hours and seasonal events.

The **HISTORIC TOWNE OF SMITHVILLE** (652–7777) is also on the mainland on Route 9, about 20 minutes and 12 miles north of Atlantic City. Founded in 1787, Smithville today is a charming conglomeration of some 30 specialty and craft shops, a recreation of the historic Old Village working community that was built around the county's first Quaker Meeting House, and the popular dining attraction of Smithville Inn.

There are several noteworthy and popular **restaurants** in Atlantic City, in addition to those in the casino hotels. Here are a very few representing a choice of cuisines and ambience. Some are closed in the winter. So call them for specific hours, dress code, reservations and credit card information.

Abe's Oyster House 2301 Atlantic Avenue (344-7701) is a local landmark serving fresh seafood and prime beef for more than a half-century.

Dock's Oyster House 2405 Atlantic Avenue (345-0092) serves outstanding oysters, crabs, fish, shrimp, scallops and steaks. The owner is the chef, his wife is the hostess and the atmosphere is nice and relaxing. People drive from New York and Philadelphia to enjoy dinner here.

Irish Pub St. James Place at the Boardwalk (345-9613) is a 19th century-style friendly saloon that serves sandwiches, steaks, chops, Irish specialties and Irish entertainment day and night. Moderately priced.

Knife & Fork Inn Atlantic and Pacific Avenues (344-1133) has been serving gourmet fresh seafood dinners to the Jersey shore's elite since 1927.

Le Grand Fromage 25 Gordon's Alley at Pennsylvania Avenue (347-2743) has open face sandwiches, quiche and daily specials for lunch and superb country French cuisine for dinner. Dine inside or on the porch.

Los Amigos 1926 Atlantic Avenue (344-2293) is akin to Philadelphia's Los Amigos, for authentic Mexican cuisine and decor.

Peking Duck House Iowa and Atlantic Avenues (344-9090) is known for Peking duck carved tableside and fried ice cream for dessert. Elegant decor for Szechuan, Mandarin and Cantonese gourmet cuisine.

The White House 2301 Arctic Avenue (345-1564). You shouldn't visit Atlantic City without trying a steak sandwich or submarine from The White House. If you don't know what that is, it's all the more reason to try one. Be prepared to wait. There are some booths, but most of the service is take-out.

As we said, this is just a small sampling of places to eat in Atlantic City. One thing for sure, you won't go hungry!

Chapter 18.
Restaurants.

Philadelphia is celebrating a true renaissance in restaurants and night life. So many creative restaurants have opened in the past few years that it's difficult to keep track of them all. Stories are constantly being written about Philadelphia restaurants in national publications. And they're really good articles.

I wouldn't attempt to rate restaurants, because I'm not a great believer in reviews. Food and atmosphere are subjective, and service can vary in the best of them. So I tried to give an idea of the menu, the ambience and unique features of each of them. I tell if they're moderately priced or if they're expensive, casual or formal, avant-garde or establishment, romantic or for the family, for fun or for business.

I think I've covered the major restaurants in Philadelphia. But if I didn't, you have my apologies.

Restaurants by Locations

Did you ever wonder which restaurants are within a given area? Well, you don't have to wonder any longer. Here are restaurants by sections of the city.

Center City (east of Broad Street and south of Market Street): Apropos. Celery Stalk. Deux Chiminees. Frankie Bradley's. Hoffman House. Irish Pub. La Buca. La Camargue. Locust Street Oyster House. More Than Just Ice Cream. Natural Foods Eatery. New London. Sechuan Garden. Silveri's. Two Quails.

Center City (west of Broad Street and south of Market Street): Arthur's. Astral Plane. Bogart's. Bookbinders Seafood House. Bread & Company. Carolina's. Cavanaugh's. DeLancey. Chameleon. Commissary. Copa, Too! Corned Beef Academy. Day by Day. Deja Vu. DiLullo Centro. ECCO. Eden. elan. El Metate. Empress. European Dairy Restaurant. The Fish Market. Frankie's Trattoria. Fratelli. Friday, Saturday, Sunday. Frog. Gaetano's. The Garden. The Happy Rooster. Harry's Bar & Grill. Harvest. Houlihan's. Hu–Nan. Il Gallo Nero. Irish Pub. Jimmy's Milan. Kelly's. L'Americaine. La Chaumiere. Le Beau Lieu. Le Bec Fin. Le Wine Bar. Linoleum. Magyar. Mandana. Marabella's. Maxwell's. New Wave Food Co. Not Quite Cricket. Out to Lunch. Pikkles Plus. The Restaurant. Rib-It. Rindelaub's. Saladalley. Sansom Street Oyster House. 16th Street Bar

& Grill. S.P.Q.R. Taylor's Country Store. Thai Royal Barge. Three Three's. Top of Centre Square. Waldorf Cafe.

Center City (The Parkway area, Fairmount, Franklintown): Adrian. Cafe Royal. Corned Beef Academy. Fountain Restaurant. Horizons. Jack Kramer's. London. Mace's Crossing. Mirabelle. Morton's. North Star Bar. Rose Tatoo. Tavern on Green.

Center City (east of Broad Street and north of Market Street): The Abbott Cafe. Chinatown. The Gallery at Market East. Reading Terminal Market.

Old City/Northern Liberties (Chapter 3): The Bourse. Cantina del Dios. Corned Beef Academy. DiNardo's. Fish & Company. Heart Throb Cafe. Khyber Pass Pub. La Famiglia. La Truffe. Liberties. Los Amigos. Middle East. October. Ray Haldeman. Rib-It. Sassafras. Shackamaxon Commissary. Siva's.

Queen Village and South Street (Chapter 3): Alouette. Bread & Company. Bridget Foy. Cafe Nola. Catherine's. Cefalu. Copabananacabana. Downey's. Famous. Hikaru. Jimmy's. Jim's Steaks. Judy's Cafe. Knave of Hearts. La Grolla. Levis. Lickety Split. Marakesh. Monte Carlo Living Room. PhilaDeli. Pizzeria Uno. Primavera. Pyrennes. Russell's. Spaghetti Factory. Tang's. Tuly's. Ulana's. Walt's King of Crabs.

Society Hill (Chapter 3): Any Thyme. Bookbinder's, Old Original. Borgia Cafe. Cafe de Costa. City Bites. City Tavern. Dickens Inn. Head House Inn. Kanpai. Lautrec. Le Champignon. Rusty Scupper. Society Hill Hotel. Tea Garden at I.N.H.P. J.B.Winberie.

South Philadelphia (Chapter 3): Annin Cafe. Cafe Lido. Cent' Anni. Dante & Luigi's. Marra's. Melrose Diner. Norm & Lou's. Osteria Romano. Palumbo's Nostalgia. Pat's King of Steaks. Philip's. Priori's. Ralph's. Saigon. Salloum's. The Saloon. Snockey's. Strolli's. Torano's. Triangle Tavern. Victor Cafe. Villa di Roma. Vinh Hoa Vietnam.

City Line Avenue, Manayunk, Roxborough: Charley's Place. D'Allesandro's. Falls Catfish Cafe. Jamey's. Rosemary's. T.G.I.Friday's. U.S. Hotel Bar & Grill.

Germantown and Chestnut Hill (Chapter 3): Chautauqua. Chestnut Hill Spice Shop. Chiyo. The Depot. Flying Fish. Roller's. 21 West. Under the Blue Moon. Valley Green Inn. J.B.Winberie.

Northeast Philadelphia: DiLullo Fox Chase. Gourmet Restaurant. 94th Aero Squadron. Tacconelli's.

University City (Chapter 3): Cavanaugh's. Eden. The Gold Standard. La Terrasse. Le Bus. New Deck Tavern. Palladium. Saladalley. Smart Alex. White Dog Cafe.

On the Waterfront (Chapter 6): Chart House. Daniel's Riverfront. Moshulu. Spirit of Philadelphia.

A Multitude of Restaurants

Each restaurant description includes a code for the credit cards they accept: American Express (AE), Carte Blanche (CB), Diners Club (DC), MasterCard (MC) and Visa (V).

"BYO" means bring your own wine or liquor if you want a drink with your meal, because the restaurant doesn't have a liquor license. It's a little inconvenient when there's no bar, but your tab will be lower.

Bon appetit!

The Abbott Cafe 201 N. Broad Street, 977-9988. In the newly-restored Abbott Building, convenient to the Pennsylvania Academy of the Fine Arts and City Hall. Chic and contemporary in tones of gray and rose with a handsome bar and dining room that seats 80 overlooking Race Street. Breakfast, lunch and dinner weekdays from 7 A.M. to 11 P.M.; Saturday lunch and dinner, except in summer. Reasonably priced and fun to start the day with simple, clever and amazing eggs; lunch on salads, pasta, burgers, sandwiches, deli and platters; dinner from 4 P.M. on soups, salads, entrees, pizza and burgers. (AE, DC, MC, V)

Adrian 747 N. 25th Street, 978-9190. This charming little two-room restaurant in the Art Museum area has good food that's cooked to order from a menu that changes daily. The prices are reasonable, the service is friendly, the bar is good, and there's live music in the evenings. Lunch weekdays; dinner except Sunday. Reservations. (AE, MC, V)

Alouette 528 S. 5th Street, 629-1126. An old tin ceiling, hardwood floors, exposed brick walls, classical music, three small rooms with a candle and fresh flowers on each table make this a warm and friendly place for dinner. The Thai-French cuisine (prepared by the owner-chef) includes

400

seafood, veal, steak, chicken and duck. Closed Tuesdays. Reservations. (MC, V)

Annin Cafe 1167 S. 12th Street, 467-1099. South-Philadelphia home-style Italian menu and bright white decor. Frank Sinatra watches over while you dine on a large variety of pasta, veal, chicken and seafood dishes followed by homemade desserts. Hearty portions; soup and salad come with every entree. Seats about 35; also a small bar at the rear. Dinner daily. (AE, CB, MC, V)

Any Thyme 414 S. 2nd Street at Head House Square, 922-4325. A popular, casual spot for extravagant treats from the ice cream and soda fountain, as well as fun foods for the entire family. Stop by any day or night of the week for lunch, dinner or a late evening surprise. (AE, MC, V)

Apropos 211 S. Broad Street, 546-4424. An American bistro open daily for breakfast, lunch, dinner, after theater and concert. On Sunday, it's dinner only. Contemporary decor in tones of charcoal and mauve. Elegant but informal. A popular bar and Broad Street sidewalk dining area as well. Interesting menu that changes often with items like quail, rabbit and blackened redfish. Unusual salads and exotic pizzas. Don't miss the marvelous desserts and baked goods. Reservations suggested for lunch and dinner. Live musical entertainment Friday and Saturday nights. (All major cards)

Astral Plane 1706 Lombard Street, 546-6230. A funky, fun Victorian place to dine, with an international menu that changes regularly. Reservations. Lunch weekdays; dinner daily; Sunday brunch. (All major cards)

Bogart's 17th and Walnut Streets (Latham Hotel), 563-9444. This is one of the hotel restaurants where the locals eat because the food is good, the choice is extensive and the mood is elegant. The atmosphere is Casablanca; hence the name. Reservations are suggested for dinner daily; breakfast and lunch, Monday to Saturday; Sunday brunch. (All major cards)

Bookbinder's, Old Original 125 Walnut Street, 925–7027. Philadelphia's most famous restaurant outside of Philadelphia. You'll never know who you'll see here, because Bookbinder's caters to movie stars, athletes, politicians and local celebrities as well as tourists. Seafood is the specialty, but the menu includes beef and chicken. There are model fire engines, unusual wall decor and photographs of people you know. The lobster tank and desserts are also special. Lunch and dinner daily. Reservations. Group arrangements for up to 250. (All major cards)

Bookbinder's Seafood House 215 S. 15th Street, 545–1137. The fourth generation of the Bookbinder family presents gourmet seafood and other excellent dishes. Bookbinder's is popular with business people and celebrities as well as tourists. It's convenient to the Academy of Music and City Hall. Lunch and dinner daily. Group arrangements for up to 150. (All major cards)

The Borgia Cafe 408 S. 2nd Street, 574–0414. Genuine French cabaret posters of the 1920s add to the downstairs bistro atmosphere at **Lautrec**. Daily, except Monday, Continental dinner and late supper. Features piano and vocal entertainment. Lively and chic; not for the kids. (All major cards)

The Bourse at Independence Mall East. A variety of restaurants dominate the 3rd level of this magnificently restored 1890s structure. **Saladalley** features a wine bar, homemade soups and deluxe salad bar. **Bain's** features hefty sandwiches. **Grand Old Cheesesteak** has cheesesteaks and hoagies. **Lots a Licks** dips homemade ice cream. **Cafe Berretta** has Italian pastries and espresso. **Athens Gyro** has Greek fare. **Canton International** has Chinese food. **International Sausage Shop** has what the name says. **Nandi's** has authentic Indian food. **Beeftech** has burgers and toppings. **Hot Chips Cookie Company** is just how it sounds. You can eat while overlooking tiers of elegant shops and activity. **Piccolo Mondo** for Italian cuisine in plush contemporary surroundings is on the lower level reached from the 4th Street side. **The Heart Throb Cafe** (described later) is reached from 5th Street. There's something for everyone to enjoy a casual lunch or dinner at The Bourse.

Bread & Company 216 S. 16th Street, 545–4430 and 425 South Street, 625–2993. Marvelous breads, croissants and pastries are the temptation for Continental breakfast, light lunch, quality dinner and a pleasant Sunday brunch in this bakery that doubles as an informal restaurant. Monday to Saturday, 7:30 A.M. to 9 P.M.; Sunday, 10 to 3. (No cards; no liquor)

Bridget Foy's 200 South Street, 922-1813. A friendly, lively, comfortable bar and restaurant serving popular wholesome food. Salads, soups and starters precede light entrees, individual pizzas, a variety of lean cuisines, and entrees of beef, pork, chicken, pasta and seafood. Lunch Tuesday to Saturday; Sunday brunch; dinner except Monday. Reservations are a good idea. (AE, DC, MC, V)

Cafe de Costa 2nd and Pine Streets in NewMarket, 928-0844. The charm and romance of an old-world brick and cobblestone grotto with a menu that offers American, Italian and Nouvelle French cuisines. Lunch daily; dinner except Sunday. An outdoor cafe in the courtyard when weather permits. (All major cards)

Cafe Lido 738 S. 8th Street, 922-8380. A South Philadelphia neighborhood restaurant for lunch weekdays and dinner daily. Specialties include an Italian salad bar at dinner and desserts for anytime. (All major cards)

Cafe Nola (as in New Orleans, LA) 328 South Street, 627-2590. Head to South Street for Cajun cooking; the likes of fresh seafood, jambalaya, gumbo, Po' Boy Sandwiches and a real oyster bar. Have lunch Tuesday to Saturday (from the raw bar only during midweek), dinner daily, or Sunday brunch to the taped sound of dixieland, pop and light jazz. This handsome art deco bar and dining room seats fewer than 50 people and is also available for private parties. (All major cards)

Cafe Royal 18th and Benjamin Franklin Parkway, 963-2244. A fine French restaurant in the Palace Hotel. Exquisite preparation and presentation of dishes like veal medallions, lamb saddle, loin of venison, duck breast and grilled red snapper or prime sirloin. Expensive but opulent and worthy of mature tastes. Breakfast daily; lunch weekdays; Sunday brunch; dinner from 6 to 9:30 daily, with live music except Sunday. Reservations. (All major cards)

Cantina del Dios 225 Church Street, 625-8686. Enjoy Mexican food and drink in the lower level cantina of a former sugar refinery that's now a unique apartment building in Old City (between 2nd and 3rd Streets, just north of Market). The portions are large, not too hot and spicy. It's traditional south-of-the-border fare. An ethnic dining experience in an interesting old brick interior. Lunch weekdays; dinner daily; Sunday brunch. (All major cards)

Carolina's 261 S. 20th Street, 545-1000. This 1986 addition to the Rittenhouse Square dining scene has attained instant success. A huge bar in one room is popular with the neighborhood crowd; the dining room is equally bustling and fun. Trendy, noisy and friendly for good, basic American food at popular prices. Reservations are necessary. Lunch weekdays; weekend brunch; dinner daily. (All major cards)

Catharine's 782 S. 3rd Street, 592-6580. A cozy Paris-style bistro seating no more than 50 in the heart of Queen Village, and serving dinner from 6 to 10, Tuesday to Saturday. The regular menu features ten entrees of beef, chicken, veal, duck and seafood. A cuisine minceur menu of six items includes the calorie and sodium counts. (AE)

Cavanaugh's 120 S. 23rd Street, 567-9335. An earthy, fun and moderately priced neighborhood bar and three dining rooms. There are steaks, chops, seafood, a salad bar and a decidedly Irish character. Jimmy Carter had lunch here when he campaigned against Ronald Reagan, and the table is identified. Lunch, dinner and late snacks except Sunday. (No cards)

Cavanaugh's 3132 Market Street, 386-4890. A West Philadelphia landmark that's known for large portions at reasonable prices. The favorites are steak, lobster, a special of the day and a Friday night smorgasbord. Lunch and dinner, except Sunday. Evening entertainment Wednesday to Saturday. Convenient to 30th Street Station, University City Science Center, the U. of Pa. and Drexel. (All major cards)

Cefalu 404 South Street, 627-6766. The name comes from a village on the island of Sicily where the owner also has an interest in a restaurant-cafe on the main square. Here it's a chic, sometimes intimate little restaurant with walls and chairs of black, contrasted with white tablecloths. Good Italian cooking and exotic drinks. Dinner till late except Monday. Not for youngsters. Reservations suggested. Salut! (CB, DC, MC, V)

Celery Stalk 716 Chestnut Street, 925-9463 and 1623 Walnut Street, 563-1274. A bright and natural cafeteria salad bar restaurant where for one low price you can have all the various salad greens, garnishes, soup, yogurt, pita bread sandwiches, fresh fruit and dessert you want. Lunch weekdays from 11 A.M. to 3 P.M.; dinner till 7 Wednesday to Friday on Walnut Street. BYO. (No cards)

Cent' Anni 770 S. 7th Street, 925-5558. Old world Italian cooking in the heart of South Philadelphia's Italian neighborhood. Specializing in a variety of veal dishes, large portions and complimentary desserts. Dinner daily. (All major cards)

Chameleon 1519 Walnut Street, 636-4434. A gourmet cafeteria, food shop, bakery for breakfast, lunch and dinner, except Sunday, from 7:30 A.M. to 9 P.M. The menu changes daily for a creative, original and wholesome variety at reasonable prices. Sinful desserts. Upbeat, bright and airy bi-level dining area with oak panelling and tones of gray and rose. (All major cards)

Charley's Place 555 City Line Avenue, 667-9717. Good food in a relaxed atmosphere. A large, colorful room with a big copper collection and an eclectic menu. Popular with the Main Liners; fine for the family. Lunch except Sunday; dinner daily. (All major cards)

Chart House 555 S. Delaware Avenue at South Street, 625-8383. Welcome aboard this dazzling new dining addition to Penn's Landing. A huge cocktail deck and bi-level dining areas with nautical motif and waterfront views. Known throughout the country for fresh seafood and hearty beef, a huge salad bar and even bigger desserts. Dinner daily; Sunday brunch. Reservations taken only for large parties. Be prepared to wait, but it's a pleasant place for cocktails or a riverside stroll. (AE, MC, V)

Chautauqua 8229 Germantown Avenue, 242-9221. Tucked neatly in the second floor rear of the quaint Chestnut Hill Hotel, Chautauqua offers a bright and cheery dining experience. A cocktail and oyster bar occupies one room. The other is a large and airy contemporary room. The food is all fresh and original. Lunch except Monday; dinner daily; Sunday brunch from noon to 3. Reservations suggested. (AE, DC, MC, V)

Chestnut Street Transitway* Choose from a variety of restaurants and fast food establishments while shopping, working or walking along the transitway. We've already mentioned the **Celery Stalk,** and **Eden** and **Hu-Nan** are coming up. There are steak and hoagie shops and fast food stops including Arby's, McDonald's, Roy Rogers and Wendy's.

Chestnut Hill Spice Shop 8123 Germantown Avenue, 242-5449. This charming little restaurant is nestled in two small rooms behind an aromatic spice shop. It's popular with the Germantown, Mt. Airy and Chestnut Hill crowd. Everything's fresh and the menu changes with what's in season. Lunch and dinner, Tuesday to Saturday. Reservations suggested. BYO. (MC, V)

Chinese Food Chinatown* is the home of dozens of Chinese restaurants that feature traditional Chinese cooking, Cantonese, Mandarin and Sechuan-style food. They're all good, and to name a few: **Ho Sai Gai** at 1000 Race Street is open daily from 11 A.M. to 5 A.M. and offers authentic Cantonese, Mandarin, Peking and Sechuan styles. The **Mayflower** at 1010 Cherry Street can cater to large parties and specializes in Mandarin, Sechuan and Pritikin cooking. The **New Imperial Inn** at 142 N. 10th Street has authentic dim sum for lunch daily as well as the **Joy Tsin Lau** Chinese Restaurant at 1026 Race Street. **Riverside** at 234 N. 9th Street has tablecloths, cocktails and delicious chicken, duck, pork and seafood a la Chinese. **Sang Kee** is a fresh seafood restaurant at 1004 Race Street. **Tang Yean** at 220 N. 10th Street is an atypical Chinese restaurant. It's beige and pastel with tablecloths, fresh flowers, handwritten menus and serves Chinese health food. There's no beef, duck, lamb or pork. There's chicken, seafood and a Chinese-style soyburger along with very fresh vegetables. And guess what they serve at **Joe's Peking Duck House** at 925 Race Street. For a complete list of Chinese restaurants, in Chinatown and elsewhere in the city, look in the Yellow Pages. The **Empress, Hu-Nan** and **Sechuan Garden** are also in center city and described later.

Chiyo 8136 Germantown Avenue, 247-8188. You can choose between chopsticks or flatware to dine on an authentic Japanese dinner served in the traditional style by waitresses in kimonos. You'll sit at a low table, but you can keep your shoes on. Closed Monday and Tuesday. Reservations. BYO. (No cards)

City Bites 212 Walnut Street, 238-1300. Eclectic menu with lots of fun and finger foods; reasonably priced. Dinner and cocktails daily from 5:30 P.M. Live rock-and-roll bands for your dancing pleasure Wednesday, Friday and Saturday nights. Casual and convenient to Society Hill, Old City and the Ritz Movies. The decor is unique in Philadelphia. Featured in national design magazines; Memphis inspired and whimsical. (All major cards)

City Tavern 2nd and Walnut Streets, 923-6059. Thanks to the diligence and high standards of the National Park Service, you can return to an exact replica of the 18th century tavern that was frequented by Ben Franklin, Thomas Jefferson and our other famous forefathers. You'll relive the colonial atmosphere and enjoy a delightful "Early American" (or 20th century, if you must) lunch or dinner. There's live harpsicord music in the cocktail lounge and garden dining in the summer. Group arrangements for up to 200. A treat for the whole family. (AE, MC, V)

The Commissary 1710 Sansom Street, 569-2240. This is America's best gourmet cafeteria, but maybe we're a little prejudiced. Everything is in good taste here, including the food. You'll find a wonderful array of salads, omelets, pastas, entrees, pastries, coffees and wines that changes daily for breakfast, lunch, dinner and anytime snacks. Seating is at tables or at the bar counters where you can browse through a library of international cookbooks. The art on the walls is by local artists and it's for sale. Lunch and dinner are served upstairs at The Commissary at the USA Cafe every day (except Sunday) and reservations are a good idea. The adjoining **Piano Bar** is open weekdays for lunch and every evening for cocktails and a delectable choice of salads and sandwiches. Since you'll be tempted, almost everything can be packaged to go from The Commissary or its Market around the corner at 130 S. 17th Street. (All major cards)

Copabananacabana 4th and South Streets, 923-6180. Welcome to Mexico...South Street style. It's neon, glitter, funky and very casual for Tex Mex and Islands fun food. Open daily for lunch and dinner till very late. A great place to dine, drink and South Street people watch. (All major cards, with $20 minimum)

Copa Too! 263 S. 15th Street, 735-0848. An offshoot of the above, Copa Too! is bright and casual with a woodsy and nautical motif on two levels. There are fancy burgers, fancy drinks, Tex Mex and Islands specialties, with some South American and Spanish choices, too. Lunch weekdays; dinner till late except Sunday. (All major cards, with $15 minimum)

Corned Beef Academy 121 S. 16th Street, 665-0460; 400 Market Street, 922-2111; and 18th and Kennedy Boulevard, 568-9696. This is an informal, friendly and fun restaurant that does justice to corned beef, brisket, turkey,

407

ham, salami and tuna salad. Open for breakfast (with eggs and cottage fries) and lunch weekdays. (No cards; no liquor)

D'Alessandro's Henry Avenue and Wendover Street, 482-5407. Go straight to Roxborough for super steak sandwiches, Italian hoagies and ham hoagies. Daily, except Sunday, from 11 A.M. to 1 A.M. A few counter seats and bare tables, but mostly take-out. (No cards)

Daniel's Riverfront Delaware River at Poplar Street, 925-7000. Watch the ships go by as you dine at Daniel's Riverfront. Make your own salad, then choose from a menu that includes large, fresh portions of beef, veal, fowl, seafood and family-style vegetables. Bring the kids. Reservations are suggested. There's parking for boats if you radio ahead, and a dinner theater that's described later. Lunch Tuesday to Saturday; dinner Tuesday to Sunday. Group arrangements for 25 to 500. (All major cards)

Dante and Luigi's 762 S. 10th street, 922-9501. Another of South Philadelphia's more popular, reasonably priced, traditional Italian family-style restaurants. Authentic atmosphere. Lunch and dinner daily (except Sundays in July and August) share the same menu. (No cards)

Day by Day 21st and Sansom Streets, 564-5540. A great little tasteful and contemporary restaurant that's open for lunch weekdays from 11:30 to 3. Dinner is packaged to go. Choose from the day's pates, pastas, cheeses, salads, fresh baked breads and desserts. Popular with people in publishing. (No cards)

Deja Vu 1609 Pine Street, 546-1190. Dining at Sal Montezumas' is like having a party for 30 at a friend's elegant townhouse. There's a private table for six or eight in two of the wine cellars. Deja Vu has over 5,000 bottles, much of it rare. It's formal, intimate, with interpretive French cuisine, rococco decor and a fixed price or a la carte. Dinner Tuesday to Saturday; closed part of August. Reservations a must. (All major cards)

DeLancey 1500 Market Street in Centre Square, 988-9334. Two levels of mahogany, etched glass and polished brass, and a bright balcony overlooking the galleria, make this a combination clubby and/or airy site for a convenient and reasonable lunch or light dinner. Weekdays only. (AE, DC, MC, V)

The Depot 8515 Germantown Avenue, 247-6700. All

aboard for gourmet burgers, all-American favorites and duck specialities. Lunch and dinner daily; Sunday brunch. Memorabilia of the Chestnut Hill local adorns the interior. (All major cards)

Deux Chiminees 251 S. Camac Street, 985-0367. The name comes from the dual fireplaces on one wall that resulted when two 19th century townhouses were joined into one. The food is prepared from French recipes and the menu changes each season. You'll feel like you're dining in a friend's lovely home, and the meal is delicious. Dinner daily; reservations suggested. (AE, MC, V)

Dickens Inn 421 S. 2nd Street in NewMarket, 928-9307. Dining at Dickens Inn is like visiting an English pub. In fact, it's modelled on and managed by its namesake by the Tower of London's Thameside. Roast beef, Yorkshire pudding and steak and mushroom pie are among the "veddy British" dinner entrees. Vegetables are served family-style, and there's a tempting dessert wagon. Lunch and dinner daily. (All major cards)

DiLullo 7955 Oxford Avenue in **Fox Chase**, 725-6000. The restaurant is a brilliant work of contemporary Italian design, and your dinner, which is served every night, is as it would be in Northern Italy. Everything is fresh and simple, and you can see the pasta being made. Order a la carte, or choose a fixed price dinner on Sunday. The gelati is prepared daily on the premises. The zuppa inglese is magnificent. This is one of the restaurants we like to leave center city to visit. After dinner (Wednesday, Friday and Saturday night), visit the glamorous **Ciao!** disco upstairs. (All major cards)

DiLullo Centro 1407 Locust Street, 546-2000. The magnificent marble, brass, glass and mural interior is matched by a menu of finely prepared and beautifully presented Northern Italian and Continental fare. A private wine cellar can accommodate private parties of up to 12. It's hard to imagine this was once the lobby of the Locust Theater. Reservations a must for this elegant and pricey lunch weekdays or dinner except Sunday. (All major cards)

DiNardo's 312 Race Street, 925-5115. DiNardo's saved us a trip to Wilmington when they opened in Old City Philadelphia to serve their famous Baltimore-style hard-shell crabs and other seafood specialties. Informal. Lunch and dinner from 11 A.M. till late, except Sunday when they're open 4 to 9. (All major cards)

Downey's Front and South Streets, 629-0525. A lively drinking house and dining saloon. The bar is from a former Dublin bank, the walls are covered with memorable newspapers, and the ceilings display artwork. There's an old-time radio collection and the favorite finds of proprietor and former broadcaster Jack Downey. Lunch, dinner and late supper daily; Sunday brunch with an omelet bar. There's an oyster bar, outdoor tables, a TV at the bar, and an elegant second floor dining room. Popular with Phillies players and movie stars when they're in town. Also famous for their Irish whiskey cake. (All major cards)

ECCO 1700 Lombard Street, 735-8070. A trendy small neighborhood corner restaurant that seats around 35 and serves fresh food daily. You can watch the preparation. Comfortable and casual in tones of gray and peach. Lunch weekdays; dinner daily; Sunday brunch except in summer. Nice for a date or friendly meal, but not recommended for children. (CB, DC, MC, V)

Eden 1527 Chestnut Street, 972-0400 and 3701 Chestnut Street (in International House*), 387-2471. A bright, cheerful, well-designed cafeteria-style restaurant with an imaginative menu that changes daily. There are soups, salads, quiche, gourmet burgers, stir-fry and a fresh catch of the day. A variety of croissants and muffins are served at breakfast weekdays at the center city location. Wine is available with lunch and dinner. Outdoor dining at the International House. Center city Eden is closed Sunday. (MC, V)

elan 17th and Locust Streets (The Warwick), 546-8800. This swinging bar and disco is also a glamorous place to dine and a fun place to people-watch. Continental menu for dinner except Sunday, by reservation only. Not for youngsters. A bountiful Sunday brunch buffet. (AE, DC, MC, V)

El Metate 1511 Locust Street, 546-0181. The name comes from a stone that's used by Mexicans to grind corn for tortillas. El Metate is a traditional Mexican-style restaurant for those who like their food hot or not so hot. It's relaxed, reasonably priced and a fun place for a south-of-the-border meal. Lunch weekdays; dinner daily except Sunday in summer. Typical Mexican-style drinks, too. (AE, DC, MC, V)

Empress 1711 Walnut Street, 665-0390. Trudie Ball's

famous Washington establishment has a northern relative. The specialties include Peking duck, Sechuan and Mandarin dishes. The atmosphere is more elegant than most Chinese restaurants. There's a bar, and the prices are moderate. Lunch weekdays; dinner daily except Sunday. (AE, DC, MC, V)

European Dairy Restaurant 20th and Sansom Streets, 568-1298. If you're kosher, or won't have anything to do with meat, this no frills restaurant is a must. You can get borscht, noodle kugel, kreplach, latkes, pirogen, blintzas, gefilte fish, kasha, omelets, or fresh fish in season. Hours are Sunday to Thursday, 11 to 9, Friday till 3. BYO. (AE)

Falls Catfish Cafe 4007 Ridge Avenue, 229-9999. A fun and friendly wining and dining place just above the Schuylkill River in the East Falls neighborhood. There's a great old-fashioned bar area with piano, a dining room that seats 40, and outdoor garden dining for a lucky few when weather permits. The menu changes with the season, but always features fresh soups daily, fanciful salads and popular entrees like pasta, stir-fries, ke-bobs, steak and the house specialty, pan-fried or blackened catfish. Dinner daily from 4:30 till very late; lunch weekdays and Sunday brunch, except in July and August. (MC, V)

Famous Delicatessen 700 S. 4th Street, 922-3274. Your parents and grandparents have been going to the Famous for years. It's a Philadelphia institution for a fun, delicious bagel and lox brunch, hearty sandwiches, scrambled egg concoctions, knishes and kugels. It's the "in" place on Sunday to see celebrities, politicos and friends. David, your host, is equally famous for his Famous 4th Street chocolate chip cookies which he just happens to sell on the premises (and at Reading Terminal Market). Daily 7 A.M. to 6 P.M.; Sunday till 3. If you're seated upstairs, you can see the action that's happening downstairs on a TV. (No cards)

Fish & Company 207 Chestnut Street, 625-8605. Philadelphia's first mesquite restaurant where fresh seafood is cooked slowly over an open fire using mesquite wood charcoal. There's also a raw bar, and chicken and steak for those who prefer. Dinner daily; lunch except Sunday. (AE, MC, V)

The Fish Market 18th and Sansom Streets, 567-3559. A gourmet seafood restaurant that serves fresh fish daily. The fruit and vegetable accompaniments are equally enticing. The drinks are hearty and the desserts are nothing less than spectacular. It's multi-level and there are several dining rooms, each with great artwork. A nice ambience. Reservations suggested for lunch weekdays and dinner daily. (All major cards)

Flying Fish 8142 Germantown Avenue, 247-0707. Don't let this fish get away. It's served fresh for lunch except Monday and dinner daily, in a warm and comfortable pale blue and yellow Chestnut Hill locale. And for those who prefer other than seafood, there are grilled burgers for lunch and chicken and steak for dinner. (No cards)

Fountain Restaurant One Logan Square in the Four Seasons Hotel, 963-1500. A truly elegant and leisurely dining experience for Continental and American cuisine. The menu changes daily. An equally beautiful view to the outside overlooking Logan Circle and the Swann Fountain. Popular for business breakfasts weekdays; lunch except Sunday when there's a magnificent brunch; dinner daily. Reservations recommended. (All major cards)

Frankie Bradley's Juniper and Chancellor Streets, 545-4350. The rib steak with garlic, seafood specialties and delicious Jewish-style cooking are what have made Frankie Bradley's a Philadelphia institution for over 50 years. It's a popular place with movers and shakers and theater-goers, both before and after shows. Movie stars traditionally come here when they're in town, and their pictures adorn the walls. (Henny Youngman says this is his "home away from home.") Lunch and dinner daily. Group arrangements for up to 200. (All major cards)

Frankie's Trattoria 274 S. 20th Street, 546-3247. First there was a fruit huckster (three generations ago), then a 20th Street fruit and produce store named Rago's, and now Frankie's a few doors away. This sophisticated little restaurant is in the middle of a sophisticated retailing block. Oak and green marble tables are set on a rich green carpet. It's light and cheery, the bar is cozy and the Northern Italian home-style cooking is presented with care. Lunch weekdays; dinner except Sunday. (AE, DC, MC, V)

Fratelli 1701 Spruce Street, 546-0513. Another ever-popular establishment of the Rago family (known by three generations of those in the know around Rittenhouse Square). Delicious home-style Italian cooking of good quality and value. Veal, pasta, chicken and seafood specialties followed by rich desserts and real gelati. Four dining areas for casual to more elegant lunch except Sunday and dinner daily. Reservations are suggested. (All major cards)

Friday, Saturday, Sunday 261 S. 21st Street, 546-4232. *Philadelphia Magazine* called this the city's "best tiny romantic restaurant." The ceiling is canopied in fabric, the food is creative and the Rittenhouse Square crowd is equally colorful. The menu on the blackboard changes daily. Reservations aren't taken, but cocktails in the intimate upstairs "Tank Bar" are worth the wait. You can dine upstairs, too. Lunch weekdays; dinner daily. (AE, DC, MC, V)

Frog 1524 Locust Street, 735-8882. Frog moved to its chic and completely renovated three-story home late in 1980 and has been popular ever since. One look, one taste and you'll see why. The menu, which changes with each season, is always expansive and has a flair for the Oriental and exotic. Reservations a must for lunch weekdays; dinner daily; Sunday brunch except in the summer. The downstairs piano bar is intimate and relaxed. There's also a dining room for non-smokers. (All major cards)

Gaetano 705 Walnut Street, 627-7575. Tom and Inez welcome you to their lovely restaurant as if it were their home. In fact, it's on the ground floor of a centuries-old townhouse, seats just 48, and is filled with period furnishings and antiques. The fixed price menu is very fine and mostly Italian with the same appetizer and pasta for every guest and a choice of entrees and desserts. Reservations are necessary; not recommended for youngsters. Dinner from 6 to 9, Tuesday to Saturday; lunch Tuesday to Friday except in summer. (AE, DC, MC, V)

The Gallery at Market East* There are no fewer than 20 ethnic and popular fast food eateries with common seating in The Gallery's lower level near 10th Street. It's like a mini-United Nations. Other restaurants in The Gallery include The Owl's Nest, Casey O'Tooles, Fanny Silks, J.B. Winchells, McDonald's and Roy Rogers.

The Garden 1617 Spruce Street, 546-4455. You can dine outdoors in warm weather in a lovely garden. The inside is a beautiful townhouse-restaurant with a charming, casual oyster bar, small intimate dining rooms and an elegant main dining room. The food is country French; the overall decor is Old English. Popular with sophisticated people who enjoy quality. Lunch weekdays; dinner Monday to

Saturday, but closed weekends in summer. Reservations recommended. (All major cards)

The Gold Standard 3601 Locust Walk, 387-3463. An inexpensive gourmet cafeteria on the University of Pennsylvania campus that operates in conjunction with the college calendar and its sibling restaurant Palladium (described later in the chapter). During the school year breakfast and lunch served daily of wholesome fresh foods and home-baked goodies. (MC, V, with $10 minimum)

Gourmet Restaurant 3520 Cottman Avenue, 331-7174. In the Mayfair section of Northeast Philadelphia. (Take I-95 to Cottman Avenue, then go a block east of Frankford Avenue.) The decor of this small dining room is simple, comfortable and charming with candlelight and fresh flowers. The owner-chef is very creative, and the service is friendly. Dinner, except Monday. BYO. Reservations suggested for weekends. (All major cards)

The Happy Rooster 16th and Sansom Streets, 563-1481. This stately and impressive little bar-restaurant probably has the best stocked liquor and brandy cabinet in the city. The food is excellent, and there are interesting specialties like Scotch salmon and pumpernickle. Popular with political and movie magnates and a regular clientele who like to kibbitz with "Doc," the proprietor. Lunch and dinner, except Sunday and two weeks in September. Reservations. Not recommended for youngsters. (All major cards)

Harry's Bar & Grill 22 S. 18th Street, 561-5757. Comfortable and clublike with rich mahogany walls and bar adorned with hunt prints; manly elegance for mature tastes. Two floors of dining featuring aged prime beef, fresh seafood and homemade pasta. Reservations suggested for lunch and dinner, weekdays only. Convenient to the Stock Exchange, Parkway and the new Commerce Square and Liberty Place. (All major cards)

Harvest 19th and Market Streets, 568-6767. In the Stock Exchange building, Harvest draws a business and center city crowd for breakfast, lunch and dinner, except Sunday. A unique-to-Philadelphia, European-style cafeteria that features the likes of venison, rabbit, game birds, lamb, beef and white steak (pork) prepared on a grill or rotisserie. Interesting salads, hearty soups and fresh baked breads and muffins. Reasonably priced and casually comfortable. (All major cards)

Heart Throb Cafe & Philadelphia Bandstand 5th and Ranstead Streets at The Bourse, 627-0778. A recreation in high tech of a 1950s soda shop and dance club. Choose from American Bandstandwiches, Soopy Sales, Eatie Gourmet Burgers, Hoagies Carmichael, Tossin' 'n Turnin', Quiche me Quick or The Platters. Follow at the Bandstand with The Temptations and catch your favorite '50s TV shows on the video screen. Then, "bop 'til you drop" to your favorite old tunes. Have fun...daily from 11:30 A.M. till late at night. (AE, MC, V)

Head House Inn 2nd and Pine Streets, 925-6718. A colonial pub that serves lunch and dinner daily, except Tuesday, as well as brunch on Sunday. The hearty dinner menu includes seafood, chicken, lamb and beef entrees. Popular with the Society Hill crowd and convenient if you're on a walking tour of the neighborhood. (All major cards)

Hikaru 607 South 2nd Street, 627-7110. Authentic Japanese dining in the heart of Queen Village, with Tatami Room decor reminiscent of the homeland. (You'll be asked to remove your shoes.) Traditional sushi and sashimi for lunch weekdays and dinner daily, as well as several chef's specialties. Experiment and have fun! (All major cards)

Hoffman House 1214 Sansom Street, 925-2772. The atmosphere, food and service are authentic Old World German. Native specialties like veal sausage, rabbit, venison, steak tartare, sauerbratten and schnitzel are available for dinner every day except Sunday. Lunch is served weekdays and includes more traditional sandwiches. (AE, MC, V)

Horizons 17th and Race Streets (Wyndham Franklin Plaza), 448-2000. The view is spectacular from the 30th floor dining room and lounge; the Continental dinners are equally good. There's piano music during the cocktail hour starting at 4:30 and dancing to the live sounds of the big band era from 9 P.M. Dinner except Sunday. Reservations are a must. (All major cards)

Houlihan's Old Place 225 S. 18th Street, 546-5940. Houlihan's formula is a raging success throughout the country, and Philadelphia is no exception. Fun, food and spirits are offered in colorful surroundings of arts, antiques, stained glass, bright fabrics, wood panelling and plants. The menu has something for everyone: finger foods for starters, heaping salads, gourmet burgers, exotic sandwiches, eggs and omelets, pastas, fowl, seafood and steak. There are all-time favorite desserts, popular beverages and specialty drinks. The bar is usually jumping. Open daily for lunch and dinner till late; also a Sunday brunch. (AE, DC, MC, V)

Hu-Nan 1721 Chestnut Street, 567-5757. An atypical Chinese restaurant that's won gourmet awards. It's large and plush with a roomy bar. The name comes from a city in southeast China that's known for its peppery cooking style. Only fresh foods are used at Hu-Nan and the choices include beef, shrimp, lobster, pork, duck, chicken and lamb. Ask for suggestions if you prefer your meal not so fiery hot! Pritikin specials are also available. Lunch and dinner, except Sunday; occasional banquet festivals. (All major cards)

Il Gallo Nero 15th and Latimer Streets, 546-8065. The three dining rooms are each small, pleasant and cosmopolitan. There's a cozy piano bar, and the food is Northern Italian. Popular with sophisticated artists, musicians and media people who appreciate fine details. Convenient to the Academy of Music. Lunch weekdays; dinner except Sunday. Reservations. Not recommended for youngsters. (All major cards)

Irish Pub 1123 Walnut Street, 925-3311 and 2007 Walnut Street, 568-5603. They live up to their name with an Irish-American menu that features Irish stew, ham and cabbage, short ribs and pork chops. There are sandwiches and hamburgers at lunchtime and light snacks for late in the evening. Hours are daily from 11:30 A.M. to 1 A.M. Hardwood floors, a huge bar, high ceilings, oak beams and a balladeer make for a casual, fun time. (AE)

Jack Kramer's 2401 Pennsylvania Avenue, 232-2060. In the Philadelphian Apartments and across from the Philadelphia Museum of Art. Reasonable priced, traditional menu for breakfast, lunch and dinner daily; brunch on weekends. Popular outdoor cafe in warm weather. (AE)

Jamey's 4417 Main Street, 483-5354. Manayunk* is becoming "in," and Jamey's is a contributing factor. A delightful, warm and friendly restaurant opened in 1986 by young, creative, enthusiastic people. Fresh food; refreshing prices and presentation. A small bar. Lunch weekdays; dinner daily. Reservations recommended. (MC, V)

Jimmy's on Front 757 S. Front Street, 389-3855. A relaxed, glassed-in garden restaurant overlooking the Delaware from Queen Village for California-style ambiance and menu. A friendly bar and congenial host who returned to Philadelphia in 1986 from years of L.A. restaurant and acting experience. Dinner, except Monday, and Sunday brunch. (AE, MC, V)

Jimmy's Milan 39 S. 19th Street, 563-2499. One of Philadelphia's busiest bars also serves some of Philadelphia's best food. Specialties are the house salad, veal, chicken and the steak "Milan." There's never a dull moment at the bar. Lunch weekdays; dinner except Sunday. Reservations. Not suggested for youngsters. (AE)

Jim's Steak's 4th and South Streets, 928-1911. An art-deco steak shop in the heart of South Street. Take-out, stand-up or sit down to enjoy super steak sandwiches and hoagies. Monday to Thursday from 10 A.M. to 1 A.M.; till 3 A.M. on Friday and Saturday; noon to 10 P.M. on Sunday. Closed Thanksgiving and Christmas. (No cards)

Judy's Cafe 3rd and Bainbridge Streets, 928-1968. A funky Queen Village bar and restaurant with exotic food, drinks and music. Don't let the exterior fool you. It's good. Come casual for dinner daily. (AE, CB, MC, V)

Kanpai NewMarket in Society Hill, 925-1532. The name means "Cheers." It's a touch of the Orient with gardens, traditional dress, traditional cooking and a traditional presentation. A Japanese chef will conduct lunch (Tuesday to Friday) and dinner daily before your eyes at a table for eight. Fun for the whole family. (All major cards)

Kelly's 1500 Chestnut Street (lower level), 567-4333. A Philadelphia institution since 1901 (you might remember the previous Mole Street and Ludlow Street locations) known for fresh seafood at reasonable prices. Prime ribs and chicken are also available. Popular with business people, politicians and shoppers for lunch and dinner except Sunday. (AE, CB, MC, V)

Khyber Pass Pub 56 S. 2nd Street, 922-0763. This longtime Old City drinking establishment features dozens of beers, accompanied by local performers at the piano, playing folk rock or jazz. Upstairs, you'll fine **Miss Headley's Wine Bar** for dinner or a late supper (except Sunday) of cheeseboards, salads, entrees and curries. It's intimate and interesting. Popular for tete-a-tetes or a change from the everyday. (All major cards)

Knave of Hearts 230 South Street, 922-3956. Another cozy, adventurous, storefront restaurant along South Street. The menu and decor are eclectic. The dishes won't

417

match, the food varies from traditional to exotic, and you might have to sit and wait on an outside bench. But it's part of the fun, and it's worth it. Dinner daily; weekend brunch. (AE, CB, DC)

L'Americaine 135 S. 24th Street, 977-8918. American cuisine with a French flair, including a few choices of cuisine minceur, is the specialty at this intimate little restaurant down near the Schuylkill River. All fresh, original food for lunch Tuesday to Friday and dinner except Sunday. Reservations suggested. (AE, DC, MC, V)

La Buca 711 Locust Street, 928-0556. The cuisine is Florentine with several veal specialties and green gnocci. But if your favorite Italian dish isn't on the menu, ask, and maybe the chef will prepare it for you. Large and popular for business and family gatherings. Lunch weekdays; dinner daily. (All major cards)

La Camargue 1119 Walnut Street, 922-3148. La Camargue is the "Texas" section of France, and you'll see a hint of cowboy motif. The decor is a blend of casual, yet formal, country French. The Provincial cuisine and service are exquisite, the atmosphere is comfortable and the people are friendly. Across from the Forrest Theater. Lunch weekdays; dinner except Sunday. Reservations. (All major cards)

La Chaumiere 2040 Samsom Street, 567-8455. The granddaddy of French restaurants in Philadelphia. Intimate, not too formal, and classic French cuisine. Dinner from 5:30, Tuesday to Saturday. Reservations requested. (AE, DC, MC, V)

La Famiglia 8 S. Front Street, 922-2803. The Sena family came from Italy to Philadelphia to bring us their fine Northern Italian cooking. The bi-level room has colorful tile, exposed brick and unusual mirrors. It's comfortable and sophisticated. Lunch weekdays; dinner except Monday and when the family returns to Italy in August for new recipes. Reservations. (AE, DC, MC, V)

La Grolla 782 S. 2nd Street, 627-7701. Tucked into Queen Village, this sophisticated, cheerful little bar and restaurant seats only 30 in two attractive rooms. The menu combines French and Northern Italian for dinner except Monday. The name means "cup of joy" and you'll know why after you finish your meal with Coffee La Grolla. Reservations. (All major cards)

La Terrasse 3432 Sansom Street, 387-3778. You'll maneuver past the long lively and sophisticated bar to the indoor, terrace and upstairs dining rooms. La Terrasse was once four rowhouses on a block that's in the heart of the University of Pennsylvania campus, and where three other restaurants have followed. The Steinway grand is heard throughout the restaurant. Trees grow right through the porch roof, the windows come out in the summer and the staff is fun, i.e., they wear their pajamas to serve brunch on New Year's Day. The country French menu changes each season and daily specials are on the blackboard. Lunch weekdays; dinner daily; Sunday brunch. Popular with professors, authors and other intellectuals. Convenient to Annenberg Center. Group arrangements for up to 60. (All major cards)

La Truffe 10 S. Front Street, 925-5062. An intimate, fine French restaurant facing Penn's Landing. Classic cuisine or cuisine minceur in an elegant but country-flavored atmosphere. Popular with Main Liners and Philadelphia's movers and shakers, but not recommended for children. Lunch Tuesday to Friday; dinner except Sunday. Reservations. (All major cards)

Lautrec 408 S. 2nd Street, 923-6660. Elegant and intimate classic French dining at Head House Square and surrounded by the art of Toulouse Lautrec. Reservations suggested for dinner Tuesday to Saturday and fixed price Sunday brunch. Not recommended for youngsters. **The Borgia Cafe** is downstairs. (AE, MC, V)

Le Beau Lieu East Rittenhouse Square (Barclay Hotel), 545-0300. Atypical of a hotel dining room, Le Beau Lieu (as its name says) is a beautiful place for breakfast, lunch or dinner daily, or for an elegant Sunday brunch. The clientele is an interesting mixture of the building's residents and guests, business people, occasionally some movie stars and Philadelphians able to afford a well-priced, well-prepared meal. (All major cards)

Le Bec Fin 1523 Walnut Street, 567-1000. Craig Claiborne called it the "finest French restaurant in the East." If you don't know who Claiborne is, you wouldn't appreciate Le Bec Fin or its internationally acclaimed owner and French master chef, Georges Perrier. Everything here is exquisite, from the rich fabric walls, crystal chandeliers, tapestry chairs, colorful fresh flowers and French china, silver and glassware to the formal service and, of course, the magnificent meal. Lunch (fixed price or a la carte) weekdays; dinner (fixed price and five courses) in two seatings, except Sunday, at 6 and 9. Not suggested for youngsters. Reservations a must. This is one of only eight restaurants in the country to receive Mobil Travel Guide's five-star rating. (AE, DC)

Le Bus 3402 Sansom Street, 387-3800. A bustling, crowded, contemporary cafeteria on the University of Pennsylvania campus for innovative salads, homemade soups, quiche, pasta, stirfry, pizza, specials of the day and wonderful fresh-baked breads and pastries. Ample portions, reasonably priced. Breakfast, lunch and dinner daily from 8 A.M. to 11 P.M. (weekdays only in summer, till 10 P.M.) (No cards)

Le Champignon 122 Lombard Street, 925-1106. This charming French restaurant has been in Society Hill since 1968. You can have a superb French meal here while you enjoy the countryside ambiance. Lunch weekdays; dinner except Sunday. Reservations. (All major cards)

Levis 507 S. 6th Street, 627-2354. Levis has been continually serving delicious hot dogs, fishcakes and cherry cokes at their earthy 6th Street location since the turn of the century. Casual and fun, daily from 10:30 A.M. to 9 P.M., and 11 P.M. on weekends. Bring the kids. (No cards)

Le Wine Bar & All that Jazz 119 S. 18th Street, 568-5247. Chic and comfy for lunch, a light dinner and a wide choice of imported and domestic wines that are served by the glass. It's nice to experiment with untried vintages. Monday to Saturday, 11 A.M. to 2 A.M. Live jazz is upstairs nightly from 9 P.M. (All major cards)

Liberties 705 N. 2nd Street, 238-0660. A striking addition to the up-and-coming Northern Liberties neighborhood, this casual restaurant and bar was built and opened in 1986 by the distributor of restored furnishings and interiors whose business is down the block. Its tin ceiling and walls, oak and tile floors, marble washrooms, mahogany bar and wood booths for two and four make it a showplace. The menu is reasonably priced and offers popular salads, sandwiches, burgers and entrees for lunch and dinner daily from 11 A.M. to 1 A.M. Fixed price Sunday brunch is noon to 4. If you enjoy country rock, jazz, vocal or classical music, call ahead (scheduled a month in advance) to find out what entertainment is on tap for Sunday and Tuesday to Thursday evenings. (AE)

Lickety Split 401 South Street, 922-1173. This is the first, well practically the first, of the avant-garde South Street restaurants. The decor is snazzy with hundreds of ceiling lights reflecting in mirror-topped tables. A fun theatrical staff, creative good food, super drinks and lively music. Popular with the lively arts crowd. Dinner daily from 6 P.M. till late. Reservations. Not for youngsters. (All major cards)

Linoleum 22nd and South Streets, 545-5555. A neighborhood 1950ish eating and drinking place opened in 1984 with an enormous bar room and another room that seats around 35 for dining. Both rooms are as high as they are long and wide and have enormous pieces of funky artwork and 1950s collectibles. The floor lives up to its name. The food is reasonably priced popular choices for dinner daily from 6 to 11. (AE, DC, MC, V)

Locust Street Oyster House 815 Locust Street, 925-6175. As soon as they opened in 1981, the Oyster House (formerly called Dockside) became known for fresh and often char-grilled, affordably-priced fresh seafood. Modern, pleasant decor for lunch weekdays; dinner daily. Their capuccino ice cream is unique in this area. A sibling of the Sansom Street Oyster House with more elaborate decor. Reservations. (All major cards)

London 2301 Fairmount Avenue, 978-4545. A friendly little restaurant and lively neighborhood pub in the shadow of the Art Museum occupy what was once a corner bar. Good drinks, comfortable atmosphere, Continental cuisine and live music for the Wednesday to Friday evening crowd. Lunch and dinner, except Sunday. (All major cards)

Los Amigos 50 S. 2nd Street, 922-7061. All of your Mexican favorites are here: tacos, enchiladas, tostatas, guacamole and refried beans. Margaritas are the popular drink to accompany. Lively and fun. Lunch except Sunday and dinner daily. Buenos dias! (All major cards)

Mace's Crossing 1714 Cherry Street, 854-9592. A tastefully restored carriage house that survived high-rise encroachment on the Parkway. Popular at lunch weekdays for hamburgers and sandwiches; brunch weekends from 11 to 3; steak, veal or chicken for dinner daily. Also popular with young executives for drinks after work. (All major cards)

Magyar 2048 Sansom Street, 564-2492. This 26-seat informal storefront restaurant started out as a pastry shop, but now it has a hearty Hungarian cuisine featuring chicken, beef, cabbage, noodles and unusual game dishes. They'll roast a suckling pig for you if you give them a week's notice. Paprika is as common here as salt and pepper. BYO. Reservations suggested for dinner, Friday and Saturday only. Tea and pastries Monday to Thursday, noon to 4. Closed July and August. (AE, MC, V)

Mandana 18 S. 20th Street, 569-4050. Classic cuisine in a comfortable townhouse atmosphere with lace curtains, fresh flowers and old-world charm. Special seasonal soups and salads followed by a choice of seven or eight entrees featuring veal, pasta, chicken, fresh seafood or filet. Busy for lunch weekdays; quiet and pleasant for dinner except Sunday. (All major cards)

Marabella's 1420 Locust Street, 545-1845. Colorful, contemporary and casual decor for fresh, festive, reasonably-priced Italian-style fare. A big-screen TV over the bar and two levels of dining. Popular and fun after work, before or after a concert or show, with the same menu at all hours. Lunch except Sunday; dinner daily. (AE, CB, MC, V)

Marrakesh 517 S. Leithgow Street, 925-5929. Dinner at Marrakesh is a Moroccan ceremony that begins with a kettle of warm water and terry towels to wash your hands. Why do your hands have to be clean? Because there are no utensils here. Additional towels are provided for your lap. A salad plate is first, followed by bastilla (stuffed pastry), a whole chicken, lamb, couscous, fresh fruit, baklava and mint tea or Turkish coffee. Dress casually, and be prepared to relax on cushions around a low, hammered brass table. Bring good friends. Daily 5:30 to 11 P.M. Fixed price. Reservations. (No cards)

Marra's 1734 E. Passyunk Avenue, 463-9249. This is South Philadelphia's oldest Italian restaurant. The third generation of Marra's carries on the family tradition of making their own pasta and specialties like veal marsala, stuffed veal, mussels, fisherman's delight and fettucini pesto genovese. The bar is famous for its variety of imported wine and beer. The ambience is casual and friendly. Lunch Tuesday to Saturday; dinner till late, except Monday. (No cards)

Maxwell's 17th and Locust Streets (Warwick Hotel), 545-4655. An upscale Parisian-style cafe for breakfast, lunch, dinner and late snacks served daily. Two cocktail areas and a piano bar in trendy, comfortable decor. Lively and fun. (All major cards)

Melrose Diner 1501 Snyder Avenue, 467-6644. A South Philadelphia landmark that's open 24 hours, seven days a week with menus that are appropriate to the time of day or night. Good food, good people, counter seating and large booths to share. (No cards; no liquor)

Middle East 126 Chestnut Street, 922-1003. One of the best places in the East for Middle Eastern cuisine (with a few American favorites tossed in) and exotic belly dancers who entertain every night. Dinner daily till very late, and there's never a dull moment. Especially if the boss is around. The Comedy Works is upstairs. (All major cards)

Mirabelle 1836 Callowhill Street, 557-9793. A former union hall in the up-and-coming Franklintown neighborhood that has been converted into an intimate and well-designed bi-level restaurant-cafe for lunch weekdays and dinner except Sunday. Freshly prepared Continental cuisine. Sophisticated but casual. (All major cards)

Monte Carlo Living Room 2nd and South Streets, 925-2220. Finely prepared Italian cuisine goes just right in the elaborate mirrored, candlelit dining room, lavished with plush furnishings and crystal chandeliers. Men are requested to wear a jacket and tie. Dinner only, except Sunday. Reservations suggested. Not recommended for youngsters. Cocktails and dancing in the upstairs club. (AE, MC, V)

Morton's One Logan Square (19th Street, south of Parkway), 557-0724. Philadelphia now boasts the steak house made famous in Chicago. Man-sized portions of aged prime beef, veal, chicken and seafood shown to you tableside before it's prepared to your liking. Over-sized, beautiful fresh vegetables, too. Everything is a la carte. Reservations suggested for lunch weekdays and dinner, except Sunday, but accepted only for seating before 7 P.M. Proper dress required. Bustling and businesslike with a glamorous following. (AE, DC, MC, V)

More Than Just Ice Cream 1141 Pine Street, 574-0586. Charming Victorian atmosphere for homemade soups, salads, sandwiches, platters and desserts. Small and convenient to Antique Row. Breakfast, lunch, dinner and late snacks daily from 8 A.M. to 11:45 P.M. (No cards; no liquor)

The Moshulu Penn's Landing at Chestnut Street, 925-3237. The largest steel sailing ship afloat is now a restaurant and cocktail lounge. The restoration is Victoriana and there are great views of the Delaware River. An eclectic menu for lunch (except Sunday) and dinner daily till late. Fun for the whole family or a romantic evening. Welcome aboard! (All major cards)

Natural Foods Eatery 1345 Locust Street (second floor), 546-1350. If you want only all natural, fresh and healthy food in a casual, friendly atmosphere, stop by for lunch or dinner, Monday to Saturday; and Sunday brunch, except in summer. Live Jazz is on Friday and Saturday nights from 10 P.M. till 2 A.M. (MC, V)

New Deck Tavern 3408 Sansom Street, 386-4600. An expansive and expensive renovation of two old rowhouses of this newly restored block on the University of Pennsylvania campus. (Penn alumni from my class will remember the original Deck Tavern on Walnut Street.) Wood panelling and old brick decor with a lengthy bar and several dining areas. Burgers, hot and cold sandwiches, pasta, seafood and daily specials. Breakfast, lunch and dinner daily from 8 A.M. to 2 A.M., except in summer when dinner only on Saturday and closed Sunday. (AE, MC, V)

New London 114 S. 12th Street, 922-5875. A mahogany panelled 19th century florist shop enjoys new life as this chic marble-topped bar and multi-level American restaurant. Convenient for shoppers, business people and Forrest Theater-goers. Lunch weekdays; dinner except Sunday. (AE, DC, MC, V)

New Wave Food Co. 205 S. 18th Street, 985-9199. Stop by weekdays from 7 A.M. to 7:30 P.M. or Saturday from 10 to 6 for "healthy food for people on the go." Fresh salads, baked goods and daily specials can be eaten at the nine little round tables or at three stools by the window counter facing Rittenhouse Square. Or package a meal to go for home, the office or a picnic in the Square. Very casual but frequented by very chic people. (AE, MC, V, with $10 minimum)

94th Aero Squadron 2750 Red Lion Road, 671-9400. A jeep and an airplane are stationed on the lawn and that's just the beginning of the attention to detail that went into building the "division headquarters" for the 94th Aero Squadron. It's on the edge of the Northeast Philadelphia Airport, and part of the fun while dining is watching the runway activity and tuning in to the control tower. Lunch and dinner daily. Also a cocktail lounge and dance floor. Prime ribs, steaks, lemon veal, duck and chicken are specialties. Reservations suggested. (All major cards)

North Star Bar 2639 W. Poplar Street, 235-7827. Stop by this friendly and casual bar and restaurant in Fairmount that serves dinner daily from 5 P.M. till late. The menu is reasonable and fun as the crowd with burgers, sandwiches, pasta, stir fry, salads and the like. There's live entertainment most Wednesday to Saturday nights. (AE, MC, V)

Norm & Lou's 3301 S. Galloway Street, 336-4848. If you're looking for something really off-beat, here's an institution in the midst of the Food Distribution Center*. You can be sure everything is fresh for breakfast and lunch weekdays from 1 A.M. to 2 P.M. or Sunday "brunch" from 9 to 5. A huge counter and several tables for very casual, good eating from an extensive menu. Have fun! (No cards; no liquor)

Not Quite Cricket 17th and Walnut Streets (Latham Hotel), 563-9444. Everything's cricket here on weekdays for a cozy or business lunch of soups, salads, hot carved roast beef or ham sandwiches. Happy Hour buffet followed by cocktails and a piano bar from 8 P.M. till the early A.M. (All major cards)

October 26 S. Front Street, 925-4447. Contemporary black and white interior in a converted Old City warehouse overlooking Penn's Landing by the Delaware. Lunch weekdays; dinner except Sunday. Also a piano bar for cocktails. Menu features regional American cuisine and changes with the season. (All major cards)

Osteria Romana 935 Ellsworth Street, 271-9191. The main dining room is bright, white and simple with an old tin ceiling and tile floor. A balcony with additional seating overlooks it. The cuisine is authentic Roman-Italian with several choices of meats, fishes, and pastas cooked al dente. If you have a party of six or more, and if you give them 72 hours notice, they'll prepare an ancient Roman specialty, roast suckling pig. Dinner, except Monday, in the heart of the Italian Market area. (AE, MC, V)

Out To Lunch 1621 Sansom Street, 864-0777. A daily soup and quiche, endless varieties of gourmet and cold-cut sandwiches, salads, brownies, macaroons and several beverages are to eat here (for 40), for box lunches or delivered in center city. Clean and contemporary gray and white high tech design. Lunch weekdays, 11 to 3. (No cards)

Palladium 3601 Locust Walk, 387–3463. This is the more sophisticated, formal and refined sibling of The Gold Standard. At street level of a building that personifies Ivy League on the Penn campus, with an outdoor cafe for lunch and outdoor terrace bistro for light dinner in summer. During the school year lunch and dinner are served daily, except Saturday lunch, from 11:30 A.M. to 9 P.M. The menu is international. Everything is made fresh, from the bread and the pasta to the ice cream. (MC, V)

Palumbo's Nostalgia 807 S. 9th Street, 574–9091. The celebrities who've appeared at the adjoining **Palumbo's** adorn the walls of this popular Italian restaurant in the Italian Market area. The portions are large, the prices are reasonable, and you might see some famous people. Lunch and dinner daily. (All major cards)

Pat's King of Steaks 1237 E. Passyunk Avenue, 339–9872. Many have tried, but none have duplicated the aura of Pat's. It's almost as famous as the Liberty Bell. Drive by anytime, day or night, for a steak sandwich to go. Or, stand outside to eat with the other aficionados. Dress formal or casual. (No cards; no liquor)

PhilaDeli 410 South Street, 923–1986. True South Street aficionados might find PhilaDeli too pure and functional. It's neat and comfortable with booths or tables for Jewish-style sandwiches, platters, beer and Haagen-dazs ice cream. Daily from 7:30 A.M. to 10 P.M.; Friday and Saturday till 1 A.M. (No cards)

Philip's 1145 S. Broad Street, 334–0882. The atmosphere is home-like and the service is family-like for Italian cuisine at lunch and dinner from noon to 11 P.M., except Monday. Favorites include the veal scalloppine, several pasta dishes and, yes, calves brains. It's convenient to center city by bus or subway train south on Broad Street. Appropriate for the family, business people or private parties. Enjoy the owner's art and antiques collection as well. (AE, DC)

Pikkles Plus 113 S. 16th Street, 561–0990. Country-tiles with oak tables, booths and counter seating and Gucci colors. Informal and belly-filling from 7:30 A.M. to 3:30 P.M. except Sunday (and Saturday in summer). Bagels, fish and eggs for breakfast; Jewish-style deli-sandwiches and platters for lunch. (No cards; no liquor)

Pizzeria Uno 509 S. 2nd Street, 592-0400. Pizzeria Uno brings Chicago's legendary deep dish pizza to Society Hill. The pizza comes in 10 varieties in portions for one to four. You can eat it here or take it home partially baked, fully baked or frozen. There are also salads, soup, pizza-style beverages, hot coffee drinks, beers, wines and booze. Sit at the bar, a barber's chair, a shoeshine stand or a table. There's dark panelling, lots of brass and lots of fun. Sunday to Thursday, 11:30 A.M. to midnight; Friday and Saturday till 1:30 A.M. (AE)

Primavera 146 South Street, 925-7832. A sibling of its neighbor, the Monte Carlo Living Room, Primavera seats 40 and serves basic Italian cuisine and daily seafood specials for dinner except Monday. You might have to wait, but it's worth it. No reservations are taken. (No cards)

Priori's 10th and Wolf Streets, 339-9358. The third generation of South Philadelphia's Priori family chefs now presides over the kitchen making home-style, reasonably priced, Italian dishes including calamari, mussels, meat-balls and veal specialties. Small and earthy, seating only 20, for dinner except Monday. Buon Appetito. (No cards)

Pyrennes 2nd and Bainbridge Streets, 925-9117. An interesting brick, brass and leaded glass multi-level interior with a fireplace makes this an unusual and romantic spot for dinner daily. The menu features French, Spanish and Portuguese cuisine with specialties like paella, cioppino, duck and rack of lamb. Reservations suggested; not recommended for youngsters. (All major cards)

Ralph's 760 S. 9th Street, 627-6011. A family-managed and family-oriented restaurant that's been a landmark for almost a century. Chicken Sorrento, veal rollatini, linguini pescatore and mussels are some of the specialties. Homemade Italian cooking from the same menu for lunch and dinner daily. (No cards)

Raymond Haldeman, Restaurant 110 S. Front Street, 925-9888. An elegant dining experience overlooking Penn's Landing in a huge restaurant made intimate by several well-appointed rooms and warm weather dining outdoors in the herb garden. American, French and Italian cuisine. Local party-goers and party-givers knew Ray Haldeman's gastronomy talents prior to his restaurant from his catering business. Nice for a special occasion. Reservations suggested. (All major cards)

Reading Terminal* Market 12th and Arch Streets, 922-2317. The market is famous for its bakeries, butchers, fish stalls, fruit and produce stands. But there's also a variety of informal restaurants in the terminal. You can choose international specialties for a moderately priced lunch from among: Basic Four Vegetarian Snack Bar, Bassett's Ice Cream, Bassett's Turkey Sandwiches, The Beer Garden, Cafe Ole, Coastal Cave, Delilah's, Dinic's, Edibles, Famous 4th Street Cookies, Fireworks, Franks-a-Lot, The Glass House, The Golden Bowl, Middle Eastern Cuisine, Moveable Feast, Olivieri Prince of Steaks, Olympic Gyro, Pasta Natale, Pearl's Oyster Bar, Primarily Pasta, Spataro, 12th Street Cantina, Vorspeise, Wok's Cooking and Your Bagel Place. The Reading Terminal Market is a fun place to visit and it's unique. The eateries are open for lunch Tuesday to Saturday. (Some are open Monday, too.) Most have their own seating, and there's a central seating area with live musical entertainment at lunchtime. Try one course at each.

The Restaurant 2129 Walnut Street, 561-3649. The main floor of this elegant old brownstone has been converted into a distinguished dining room and kitchen. The Restaurant is a classroom for students of "The Restaurant School." Your waiter or waitress is a student who is learning the art of fine serving. His or her clasmates have planned the fixed-price menu, bought and prepared the food. They'll be pleased if you leave the children at home. Come for dinner Tuesday to Saturday from 5:30 to 10. Reservations a must. (All major cards) **Note:** Several of Philadelphia's creative and successful restaurants of the past decade are owned and operated by graduates of The Restaurant School.

Rib-It 52 S. 2nd Street, 923-5511 and 1709 Walnut Street, 568-1555. Try Paul Rimmeir's gracious oasis for an eating experience. Your placemat is the menu for terrific baby back ribs and chicken. You'll love getting barbeque sauce all over your hands and face. Rib-It serves wet-naps, but for the squeamish there's steak, cornish hen, seafood and salads. Sandwiches join the list of choices for lunch and after 10 P.M. More fun foods include wonder wings, the hot potato and the unique funion loaf. Rib-It is casual for lunch and dinner daily. The whole family will love it. (AE, MC, V)

Rindelaub's 128 S. 18th Street, 563-3993. The cakes and pastries from Rindelaub's Bakery are known to every sweet tooth in town. A counter and tables accommodate a regular following for breakfast from 6:30 A.M. (7 on Saturday), lunch, tea or coffee breaks. There are also eggs, sandwiches and hot and cold platters. It's a rare person who doesn't take some goodies home. Closed Sunday. (No cards)

Roller's 8705 Germantown Avenue, 242-1771. Come to the top of the hill in Chestnut Hill for a delightful lunch, Tuesday to Saturday; Sunday brunch, except in summer; and dinner, except Monday. The menu and presentation are fresh and creative, the ambience is bright and friendly, the kitchen is in view as are the outdoors through mostly glass walls. Reservations recommended for dinner. (No cards)

Rosemary's 8919 Ridge Avenue, 483-5556. If you're near Roxborough, Rosemary's is a fun and friendly family-style restaurant for lunch Tuesday to Friday; dinner except Monday; Sunday brunch except in summer. Dine in booths or at tables, all with fresh white linens and red roses. The cuisine is all-American, too. Ask for John and Rosemary, and tell them Julie says hello. Reservations suggested. (AE, MC, V)

Rose Tattoo Cafe 19th and Callowhill Streets, 569-8939. A premiere eatery in the Fairmount* neighborhood redevelopment. The first floor is a casual and lively neighborhood bar. Upstairs is a friendly little dining room for popular American and original International cuisine. Lunch weekdays; dinner except Sunday. Reservations requested; not recommended for youngsters. (AE, MC, V)

Russell's 609 E. Passyunk Avenue, 922-3959. Head just south of 5th and South Streets for a lovely dinner (except Monday) where everything is cooked to order and presented with care. Each of the three rooms is comfortable and different. Order fixed price or a la carte, but be sure to leave room for dessert. Reservations are a good idea. (MC, V)

Rusty Scupper Front and Pine Streets in NewMarket, 923-0291. Two floors of indoor and outdoor informal dining and cocktails surrounded by California redwood, exposed but colorful air conditioning ducts and plants. You'll get into a nice, nautical mood as you overlook Penn's Landing. Lunch (except Sunday) and dinner with a salad bar daily. "The Scup" has fresh seafood, prime ribs, steak, daily specials and a deli-bar. It's fun for the whole family. Reservations suggested, or you can explore

NewMarket while waiting. (All major cards)

Saigon 935 Washington Avenue, 925-9656. Philadelphia's Vietnamese community now provides restaurants in the Italian Market area. Their native clientele often stop by in conjunction with shopping on 9th Street for fresh fruits and vegetables. The Saigon is plain, simple and friendly in the downstairs of a typical rowhouse. The cuisine is a combination of authentic Chinese-style stir-fry and Vietnamese broiled and deep-fry. The charbroiled meat, chicken, pork and seafood are usually skewered. Beverages and desserts are Oriental, too. Lunch and dinner, 11 A.M. to 10 P.M., except Tuesday. (No cards)

Saladalley 1720 Sansom Street, 564-0767; 4040 Locust Street, 349-7644; The Bourse, 627-2406; Welsh Road and Roosevelt Boulevard, 969-5969; Suburban Square in Ardmore, 642-0602; also in Willow Grove and Cherry Hill Mall. Casual dining with a bottomless salad bar, fresh breads, gourmet soups from around the world and a few hot vegetarian, pasta, beef, chicken and seafood entrees. Hours vary at different locations for lunch, dinner and Sunday brunch that includes omelets. Wine by the glass. (MC, V, at some locations)

Salloum's 1029 S. 10th Street, 922-2445. This South Philadelphia family-owned Middle Eastern dining oasis is in two small rooms over the kitchen and take-out shop. Zitoon, tabouli, kibbee, mamool and felafel are a few of the traditional dishes. Many include lamb and beef, but vegetarians will be satisfied as well. You'll have fun here at dinner from 5:30 to 11, Wednesday to Saturday. BYO. (No cards)

The Saloon 750 S. 7th Street, 627-1811. Splendid Victorian decor with magnificent woodwork in the heart of South Philadelphia. Outstanding Italian dishes and prime steaks. Interesting bars upstairs and downstairs. Lunch Tuesday to Friday; dinner except Sunday. Popular with an arty, business and political crowd. Reservations. (No cards)

Sansom Street Oyster House 1516 Sansom Street, 567-7683. Simple, panelled decor, a 25-foot oyster bar and good quality seafood at reasonable prices. All of the fish is bought fresh daily. Come casual for lunch or dinner, except Sunday. (All major cards)

Sassafras 48 S. 2nd Street, 925–2317. An Old City restoration with turn-of-the-century oak, brass, tile, mirrors and a working marble fireplace. Sassafras attracts a sophisticated and often artistic crowd for drinks, omelets, quiche, salads, burgers and steak. Limited seating. From 11:30 A.M. till late, except Sunday. (MC, V)

Sechuan Garden 1322 Walnut Street, 735–1833. Hot and spicy Chinese food with several items unique to Philadelphia restaurants. Comfortable surroundings with a friendly staff who gladly describe the menu and are happy to make suggestions. The center city location is convenient to Forrest Theater and the Academy of Music. Lunch weekdays; dinner daily. (All major cards)

Shackamaxon Commissary 1080 N. Delaware Avenue, 425–1008. Stop by weekdays for breakfast, lunch or early dinner in a refurbished waterfront warehouse facing the Delaware River. Casual, friendly and reasonably priced for home-cooked food and baked goods to eat in or take out. While you're here, ask about the name. Frequented by truckers and businesspeople alike. That would please William Penn. (No cards; no liquor)

Silveri's 315 S. 13th Street, 545–5115. A casual bar and restaurant with stark contemporary design and friendly people. Fun foods like pasta, salads, burgers and buffalo-style chicken wings, supplemented by "neighborhood specials" of what's fresh at the market each day. Lunch weekdays; dinner daily. (MC, V)

Siva's 34 S. Front Street, 925–2700. An elegant white and wicker interior on multi-levels with a view of the tandoori oven. Plush booths or table dining for Northern Indian cuisine that features marvelous breads, chutneys, tandoori specials and lots of spices, if you so desire. Lunch weekdays; dinner daily. (All major cards)

16th Street Bar & Grill 264 S. 16th Street, 735–3316. A neighborhood bar and restaurant for informal dining and drinking and a light menu that offers omelets, salads, soup, sandwiches, hamburgers, deep dish pizza, pasta and fish of the day. Popular with center city sophisticates. Lunch except Sunday; dinner daily. (All major cards)

Smart Alex 36th and Chestnut Streets (Sheraton University City), 386–5556. Their ads say they're "an eating and drinking emporium for wild lunches, outrageous dinners, decadent drinks and smalltime entertainment," and it's true. Bizarre breakfasts, too. The bar is huge and there's plenty of seating. 7 A.M. to 2 A.M. daily. (All major cards)

Snockey's 1020 S. 2nd Street, 339-9578. A Philadelphia institution since 1912 for oysters, clams, shrimp and other fresh seafood. Across from the Mummers Museum and popular with folks from all over the city. Informal and friendly. Bring the kids. Dinner daily; lunch except Sunday. (No cards)

Society Hill Hotel 3rd and Chestnut Streets, 925-1919. A small, fun, airy, cheerful restaurant, piano bar and sidewalk cafe that's open daily from 11 A.M. to 2 A.M. (the kitchen closes an hour earlier). Creative hamburgers, cheesesteaks, cold sandwiches, omelets, salads and daily specials. Sunday brunch menu from 11 to 2. Popular with architects and Old City developers. (Upstairs is Philadelphia's first bed and breakfast hotel.) (All major cards)

Spaghetti Factory 530 South Street, 627-5595. Austere but whimsical decor in the heart of South Street. You'll find spaghetti in more ways than you can imagine, plus other Italian dishes. Drinks or wine by the glass or bottle. Lunch weekdays (except in summer) and dinner daily. (All major cards)

Spirit of Philadelphia Penn's Landing, 923-1419. Come aboard for Philadelphia's only dining while you cruise the Delaware. There are daily two-hour lunch cruises and three-hour dinner cruises. Meals are buffet-style and plentiful. Fun for the whole family. Reservations necessary. (MC, V)

S.P.Q.R. 2029 Walnut Street, 496-0177. Nestled in one room of a former brownstone townhouse, S.P.Q.R. is pleasant for a Roman lunch weekdays and dinner except Sunday. The menu features made-to-order Italian-style veal, chicken, pasta, seafood and steak entrees. While you're here, ask what the name means. Reservations suggested. (AE, DC)

Strolli's 1528 Dickinson Street, 336-3390. A South Philadelphia hideaway that's relatively small, serves good food at reasonable prices and is fun when the crowd around the bar starts to sing. Italian home-style cooking for lunch weekdays; dinner daily. A great neighborhood restaurant. (No cards)

Tacconelli's Pizzeria 2604 Somerset Street, 425-4983. Head to the Port Richmond section of lower Northeast Philadelphia for white pizza like you've never had before.

The ingredients are all fresh, but the real secret is the 20-foot by 20-foot brick oven built in 1928 by proprietor Vince Tacconnelli's grandfather. Very casual and open Wednesday to Sunday from 6 till the day's dough is used up. If you're stopping by after 10, call ahead and they'll reserve a pizza for you. Bring the family. (No cards)

Tang's 429 South Street, 928-0188. Oriental decor on two floors and Chinese cuisine with an imaginative menu that changes each season. There's fresh fish of the day, fresh vegetables and fresh flowers on the tables. Dinner daily; reservations suggested on the weekend. (All major cards)

Tavern on Green 21st and Green Streets, 235-6767. An informal bar and restaurant in the Art Museum neighborhood. Casual decor with hardwood floors, colorful exposed ductwork, poster art and plants. Lunch and dinner daily from 11:30 till late includes soups, pita sandwiches, omelets, burgers, chili, quiche, ribs, chicken and specials of the day. They also have a Sunday brunch. (All major cards)

Taylor's Country Store 1609 Sansom Street, 563-7627. Delightful and informal for homemade soups, gourmet made-to-order deli-sandwiches and hoagies, platter specials, chili and desserts. Your lunch is prepared before your eyes, and you'll sit in the midst of the store, outdoors when weather permits, or in any of the tiered dining rooms. Some describe the ambience as "organized clutter." Popular with the legal set. Weekdays, 11 to 3, and Saturdays from September to April. (No cards; no liquor)

Tea Garden of Independence National Historical Park Chestnut Street between 3rd and 4th Streets, 597-7919. Each summer day, from May (11 A.M. to 5 P.M.) through August (11 A.M. to 6 P.M.), the Friends of I.N.H.P. operate an outdoor cafe for light refreshments such as 18th century "squash punch," iced tea and ice cream. The garden is adjacent to the Second Bank of the United States.

T.G.I.Friday's 4000 City Line Avenue, 878-7070. A big and fun place for the whole family for any day of the week from 11 A.M. till 1 A.M., and for cocktails at the huge bar till 2. Order from the 22-page "Dictionary of Food and Drink" that's guaranteed to please any appetite and make you smile. See why they call it a "New York style restaurant-bar with large portions and good values," and see why New Yorkers made their T.G.I.Friday's so successful. (All major cards)

Thai Royal Barge 23rd and Sansom Streets, 567–2542. Authentic and exotic Thai cuisine is available right here in center city Philadelphia. If you're not familiar with Thai food, your waiter will help you. Thai dinner in an almost native atmosphere is every night from 5 P.M. Thai it, you'll like it. (All major cards)

Three Threes 333 S. Smedley Street, 545–9603. A charming little restaurant on a charming little street. Lunch and dinner daily and Sunday brunch are pleasant and relaxed in this converted townhouse that might remind you of college days. A Continental menu, reasonably priced. Not recommended for youngsters. (DC, MC, V)

Top of Centre Square 1500 Market Street, 563–9494. A modern restaurant and cocktail lounge that's eye-level with next-door neighbor Billy Penn. Marvelous views of the city and City Hall. Lunch (except Sunday) and dinner daily for traditional American food. A Stouffer's operation (as in Top of the 666s at Rockefeller Plaza, New York). Reservations. (All major cards)

Torano's 901 S. 11th Street, 925–2282. A large South Philadelphia restaurant with home-style ambience and cooking, some of it at tableside. Veal specialties, homemade pasta and gelato. Live entertainment from Wednesday to Sunday. Dinner except Monday from 5 P.M. (AE, DC, MC, V)

Triangle Tavern 10th and Reed Streets, 467–8683. Another of South Philadelphia's famous neighborhood bar-restaurants. The no frills decor makes it a popular background for movie people. Specialties are mussels, pasta and pizza. Lunch weekdays; dinner daily from 4 P.M. to 1 A.M.; local entertainment on Friday and Saturday from 9 P.M. till closing. (No cards)

Tuly's 603 S. 4th Street, 922–3553. Stop by any day from 11 A.M. to midnight for Middle Eastern food to eat in or take out. It's just south of South Street, very casual and moderately priced. (No cards; no liquor)

21 West 21 W. Highland Avenue, 242–8005. Mary Fretz is your hostess at this lovely Chestnut Hill restaurant. Lunch except Sunday and Continental dinner daily. Live piano music in the evening. Reservations. A relaxing retreat from Chestnut Hill shopping and worth the trip from center city. (AE, DC, MC, V)

Two Quails 1312 Spruce Street, 546–8777. Sophisticated, contemporary decor in a center city townhouse around the corner from the Academy of Music. Order fixed price or a la carte for out-of-the-ordinary creative dining on specialties like rabbit, sweetbreads, pheasant and two quails with cornbread stuffing. Dinner 5:30 to 9:30 Tuesday to Saturday. Reservations suggested; not recommended for youngsters. (All major cards)

Ulana's 205 Bainbridge Street, 922–4152. Ulana and her architect husband created a unique multi-story Queen Village restaurant, bar and club that features a Continental cuisine with a few Ukrainian specialties, dancing and a romantic below-ground dining room. Dinner Wednesday to Saturday and available for private parties. Not recommended for youngsters. Reservations. (All major cards)

Under the Blue Moon 8042 Germantown Avenue, 247–1100. A superb, refreshing and imaginative eatery in Chestnut Hill. The international home-cooking menu changes often for dinner from 6 P.M. Tuesday to Saturday. Everything is good, and save room for dessert. Reservations are a must. Try to meet the owner. He's as much fun as the meal. (No cards)

United States Hotel Bar & Grill 4439 Main Street, 483–9222. Another welcome addition in 1986 to the revival of Manayunk*. A huge old mahogany bar with raw bar, white tile floor, and just nine tables with as many dinner entrees. It's a fun place for drinking and dining. Lunch except Sunday; dinner daily. Look for the proprietor, former Philadelphia Mayor Bill Green, and tell him we said hello. (AE)

Valley Green Inn Valley Green Road and Wissahickon Creek, 247–3450. A quaint, picturesque, 19th century inn, in one of the most beautiful settings in Philadelphia. Have breakfast or lunch here (starting at 11:30 A.M. Tuesday to Friday and 10:30 on weekends) before or after a walk in the woods. Enjoy Sunday brunch, or come for a delightful dinner. Closed Mondays. Dine on the porch when weather permits. A lovely place for private parties, family gatherings and romanticists. Reservations for large groups. (AE, DC, MC, V)

Victor Cafe 1303 Dickinson Street, 468–3040. If you like opera, you'll love the Victor Cafe in the heart of South Philadelphia, because opera is served with every course. The record library has 25,000 selections, give or take a few. Italian dinners are served Tuesday to Sunday, from 5 to 10:30 or 11:30. (AE, CB, DC)

Villa di Roma 936 S. 9th Street, 592-1295. This informal and famous family restaurant-bar is smack-dab in the Italian Market. The menu covers the entire back wall, and everything is recommended. Popular with professional athletes. Lunch on Saturday; dinner daily from 5 to midnight, and you can be sure it will be busy, especially on Sunday. (No cards)

Vinh Hoa Vietnam Restaurant 746 Christian Street, 925-0307. The owners made several stops on their way to Philadelphia from the Far East, so the menu presents an exotic assortment of Chinese, Japanese, Korean and Vietnamese cuisine. Everything is cooked to order. "Happy pancakes" are a specialty; everything is interesting. Daily from 11 A.M. to 10 P.M.; till 11 on Friday and Saturday. (All major cards)

Waldorf Cafe & Charcuterie 20th and Lombard Streets, 985-1836. A center city neighborhood eatery with a popular small bar that serves moderately priced dishes, and a casual small dining room that seats no more than 40. Everything is prepared fresh and presented attractively. Leave room for homemade ice creams and Waldorf Hysteria for dessert. Okay for sophisticated youngsters, but nicer for a date or special occasion. (AE, MC)

Walt's King of Crabs 804 S. 2nd Street, 339-9124. Philadelphia's seafood lovers have made an institution of this casual, moderately priced restaurant and bar. Hardshell crabs, clams, mussels, shrimp and lobsters are served to order. Daily 11 A.M. to midnight; Sunday 2 to 10. (No cards)

Warsaw Cafe 306 S. 16th Street, 546-0204. This casual and chic restaurant resembles a small European cafe. The menu features Eastern European cuisine (Hungarian, Polish, Russian and German) and changes regularly. Lunch weekdays; dinner except Sunday. Reservations. (AE, DC)

White Dog Cafe 3420 Sansom Street, 386-9224. Popular with the University of Pennsylvania crowd and folks from all over who enjoy the casual funky decor, popular menu and prices. Fills the downstairs of two old row houses, plus a contemporary, airy addition. Large lively bar. Fun food for children like peanut butter and jelly sandwiches. Don't miss the legend of the White Dog as you read the

menu. Weekdays 7:30 A.M. to 2 A.M.; weekends from
11:30 A.M. Live music late in the evening and frequent
fun dining "events." Ask for the proprietress, Judy, and
tell her we said hello. (AE, MC, V)

J.B.Winberie 120 Lombard Street (Society Hill), 923–6112
and 8229 Germantown Avenue (Chestnut Hill), 247–6710.
An attractive place that's as nice for the family as for a
friendly date. Reasonably priced menu with popular foods
like pastas, fondues, pizzas, burgers, salads and fancy
sandwiches. Also traditional entrees and under-400 calories
choices. Top any of them off with a fanciful ice cream
dessert or drink. Lunch and dinner daily in Chestnut Hill;
lunch Friday and Saturday, dinner daily in Society Hill;
Sunday brunch at both locales. (All major cards)

Family Fun

These restaurants range from very casual to more
sophisticated. They're all appropriate for family outings
for a variety of occasions.

Any Thyme. The Bourse. Chinatown. City Tavern. City
Bites. Daniel's Riverfront. Eden. The Gallery at Market
East. Heart Throb Cafe. Houlihan's. Irish Pub. Jim's
Steaks. Kanpai. Levis. Marra's. The Moshulu. 94th Aero
Squadron. Pizzeria Uno. Reading Terminal. Rib-It.
Rosemary's. Rusty Scupper. Snockey's. Spirit of Philadel-
phia. Tacconelli's. T.G.I.Friday's. White Dog Cafe.
J.B.Winberie.

I Scream. You Scream.
We All Scream for Ice Cream.

Here are a few ice creameries. Many of them are described earlier in this chapter.

Any Thyme. Bassett's at Reading Terminal. **Ben &
Jerry's** (Vermont's finest all natural ice cream at 640
South Street). **Butterby's** (featuring frozen yogurt at 236
South Street). **Gelato Fresco** (creamy Italian sherbert at
309 South Street). **Haagen–Dazs Ice Cream Shoppe** (30th
Street Station and 242 South Street for the renowned ice
cream, sorbets, cream floats, sundaes and other delectable
treats). **Hillary's Gourmet Ice Cream** (1929 Chestnut
Street, 4040 Locust Street, 437 South Street, 200 Lom-

bard Street, 1207 Walnut Street and several other locations for dozens of exotic and traditional flavors, with a myriad of toppings, to eat in or take out). **Lots a Licks** at the Bourse. **Lick It** (featuring Bassett's, Tofutti and frozen yogurt at 1218 Spruce Street). **More Than Just Ice Cream. Scoop de Ville** (at Maron Candies, 107 S. 18th Street, where you can create your own ice cream or frozen yogurt flavor). **Steve's Ice Cream** (at 3919 Walnut Street where your choice of sinful toppings are mixed into the ice cream).

Sunday Brunch

Philadelphians as well as visitors can be found having Sunday brunch at the following restaurants. They range from casual to elegant. Keep in mind that Pennsylvania law prevents drinks from being served before 1 P.M. on Sundays. Some of these restaurants are closed on Sundays in the summer.

Astral Plane. Bread & Company. Bogart's. Bridget Foy's. Cafe Nola. Cafe Royal. Cantina del Dios. Carolina's. Chart House. Chautauqua. The Depot. Downey's. ECCO. elan. Falls Catfish Cafe. Famous. Fountain Restaurant. Frog. Head House Inn. Houlihan's. Jack Kramer's. Jimmy's on Front. Knave of Hearts. La Grolla. La Terrasse. Lautrec. Le Beau Lieu. Liberties. Mace's Crossing. Maxwell's. Melrose Diner. More Than Just Ice Cream. Natural Foods Eatery. Norm & Lou's.

Also: Roller's. Rosemary's. Russell's. Saladalley. Smart Alex. Society Hill Hotel. Tavern on Green. T.G.I.Friday's. Three Three's. Valley Green Inn. Waldorf Cafe. White Dog Cafe. J.B.Winberie.

Outdoor Dining

The following restaurants have outdoors or outdoorsy settings. For more details, read their descriptions in the preceding restaurant listing.

Apropos. Bridget Foy's. Cafe de Costa. City Lights. City Tavern. Downey's. Eden at International House. Falls Catfish Cafe. Fish & Company. The Garden. Jack Kramer's. La Terrasse. Palladium. Ray Haldeman. Rollers. Society Hill Hotel. Tavern on Green. Taylor's

Country Store. Tea Garden at I.N.H.P. Valley Green Inn.
J.B.Winberie in Chestnut Hill.

These restaurants serve cocktails outdoors.

Kanpai. Mace's Crossing. The Moshulu. Rusty Scupper.
Smart Alex.

Rooms With A View

The best rooftop views of Philadelphia are from
Horizons and Top of Centre Square.

The best waterfront views of the Delaware River and
Penn's Landing are at the Chart House, Daniel's Riverfront, The Moshulu, Rusty Scupper and the Spirit of
Philadelphia. The best view of the Wissahickon Creek is
from the porch of Valley Green Inn.

The best view of the Benjamin Franklin Parkway and
Logan Circle is at the Fountain Restaurant.

The most unusual view of an airfield is at the 94th Aero
Squadron.

Dinner Theaters

These dinner theaters are within an hour's drive of
center city Philadelphia. They offer a hearty meal and
popular shows at a reasonable price. Call for a schedule of
performances, reservations and directions.

Huntingdon Valley Dinner Theater 2633 Philmont
Avenue, Huntingdon Valley, Pa. (947-6000)

Lily Langtry's Sheraton Valley Forge Hotel, King of
Prussia, Pa. (337-LILY)

Peddler's Village Dinner Theater Cock 'n' Bull
Restaurant, Route 263, Lahaska, Pa. (794-3460) July
through September and January through March seasons.

Riverfront Dinner Theater Delaware River at Poplar
Street, Old City Philadelphia. (925-7000)

Tara Supper Club Brandywine Hotel and Resort, Route
30, Downingtown, Pa. (269-2000)

Cabaret and Cafe Theaters. Night Clubs.

Cafe Theater of Allens Lane See Chapter 10.

Chestnut Cabaret 38th and Chestnut Streets (382–1201). Seating for at least 400 for live entertainment a few nights a week. Some big names come here.

Comedy Factory Outlet 31 S. Bank Street (FUNNY–11). New York and L.A. headliners, local clowns, talent searches and midnight madness shows add up to quality entertainment at low prices.

The Comedy Works 126 Chestnut Street atop the Middle East Restaurant (WACKY–97). Stop in for laughs any Wednesday to Saturday night. The talent varies from talented locals to the greats.

Going Bananas 613 S. 2nd Street, off NewMarket (BANANA–1). The city's third comedy night club, with two shows nightly on Friday and Saturday.

Grendel's Lair Theater 500 South Street (923–5559). A 200-seat cabaret theater for off-Broadway revues. It's famous for its long run of "Let My People Come." They also have occasional dance nights.

Palumbo's 824 Catharine Street (627–7272). The South Philadelphia night club where many well-known entertainers got their start. Frankie Avalon, Joey Bishop and David Brenner will confirm this.

The Peak Theater at Montserrat 623 South Street (238–0458). Thursday and Saturday night comedy productions.

Jazz. Piano Bars.

The following restaurants and night spots have live musical entertainment. Some are ongoing gigs; others change nightly or weekly.

Apropos. Arthur's. Barclay Hotel. Borgia Cafe. Cafe Royal at the Palace Hotel. Chautauqua. Commissary Piano Bar. Downey's. Frog. Irish Pub. Khyber Pass Pub. Liberties. Maxwell's. Upstairs Jazz Club at the Natural Foods Eatery. White Dog Cafe. The Wine Bar & All That Jazz.

More Nightlife. And Some Dancing.

Adam's Mark Hotel. City Bites. Ciao! (upstairs at DiLullo in Fox Chase). elan (in the Warwick). Four Seasons Hotel. Grendel's Lair (500 South Street, 923-5560). Heart Throb Cafe. Horizons (in the Wyndham Franklin Plaza). Monte Carlo Living Room. North Star Bar. Not Quite Cricket. Penguin Club (714 South Street, 627-7333). P.T.'s (6 S. Front Street, 922-5676). Spirit of Philadelphia. The Trocadero (10th and Arch Streets, 627-8034).

This is by no means an exclusive list of the night club scene in Philadelphia. Restaurants all over town have jumped on the bandwagon with singers and musicians performing one or several nights a week.

New Restaurants. And Restaurants I've Missed.

Make your own listing on these two pages.

More Restaurants.

Chapter 19.
Calendar of Annual Events.

There are hundreds, maybe even thousands, of great events that take place in Philadelphia every year. After all, we've had over 300 years of experience at making things happen.

It's impossible to list all of them, so a few are highlighted in this chapter.

If your favorite event isn't here, write to me and we'll try to include it in the next edition of "A Guide's Guide to Philadelphia."

When you see an asterisk (*), that place or event is described elsewhere in the book. Look in the Index for the exact pages so you can get additional information.

Keep this guide handy, and refer to it as often as possible so you won't miss something special and have to wait a year for it to come around again.

New Year's Day is January 1.

There's at least one parade a month in Philadelphia, but Philadelphia is best known for its all-day, world-famous **New Year's Day Mummers Parade***. The magnificently costumed string bands, comics and fancy division perform the famous Mummers strut for two-and-a-half miles along Broad Street from Snyder Avenue to City Hall. Wear warm clothing. (The rain date is the following Saturday.)

City and state tributes are held around January 15 to honor the late **Dr. Martin Luther King, Jr.** The third Monday of the month is a holiday to commemorate the date.

Benjamin Franklin's Birthday is celebrated the weekend closest to January 17 with events at Franklin Court (597-8974) and "Ben's Birthday Bash" festivities at the Franklin Institute (448-1200). Call them or the Visitors Center (568-6599) for information.

Edgar Allan Poe's 1809 birthdate is celebrated at the National Historic Site* on the weekend closest to January 19. Call 597-8780 for the schedule.

The men's **U.S. Pro Indoor Tennis Championships*** are also at the Spectrum in late January or the first week of February. Call 947-2530 or 389-5000 for dates and details.

The annual **Philadelphia Auto Show** exhibits hundreds of new imported and American cars at the Philadelphia Civic Center along with family entertainment and guest celebrities.

The annual **Philadelphia Sportsmen's and Recreational Vehicle Show** is also at the Civic Center. It's your chance to see the latest in sports and equipment, camping, vacation and travel gear. For dates and details, call 823-7400.

February

Look for announcements of special activities to commemorate **Black History Month**. Or call the Afro-American Historical and Cultural Museum (574-0380) for a schedule of lectures, tours, visual and performing arts.

Don't forget your sweetheart on **St. Valentine's Day,** February 14.

It's suddenly summer when you're at the annual **Boat Show** at the Civic Center. This is a one-week exhibit of the latest in boats and boating accessories. More than 400 boats are displayed, making this one of the country's biggest boat shows. Call 823-7400 or 823-7327 for dates and details.

Presidents' Day is celebrated the third Monday of the month, honoring the birthdays of **Abraham Lincoln** (February 12) and **George Washington** (February 22).

If you missed the Mummers Parade in January, you have a chance to see and hear the string bands this month at the **Mummers String Bands "Show of Shows."** More than a dozen bands don their New Year's finery for evening and matinee performances at the Civic Center. All seats are reserved. Tickets are sold by the local string bands or at the Civic Center box office prior to each performance. Call 568-6599 for dates and details.

The **Ice Capades** dazzles viewers of all ages at the Spectrum in a week of afternoon and evening shows. Call 389-5000 for time and price details.

The **Chinese New Year** brings crowds to Chinatown* for parades and special events that herald the start of the new year this month or next. You can also celebrate with a 10-course fixed-price Chinese New Year's Banquet served at the Chinese Cultural Center and several Chinese restaurants. Call 923-6767 for details.

March

The Civic Center becomes a miraculous indoor garden wonderland for one week in March. Don't miss the thousands of flowers, plants and shrubs that are part of the **Philadelphia Flower Show**. Tickets can be purchased in advance at the Pennsylvania Horticultural Society* or at the door of the Civic Center.

Ash Wednesday is March 4, 1987.

One of Philadelphia's favorite parades honor **St. Patrick's Day**, on the Sunday closest to St. Patrick's Day (March 17).

Women's History Week is a national event honoring women at home and at work. Citywide celebrations occur, highlighted by a day-long annual Women's Festival at the Bourse, 5th and Market Streets. Call the Mayor's Commission for Women (686-8656) for details.

Poetry Week is observed at various locations and literary events under the auspices of the American Poetry Center. Call 800-ALL-MUSE for information.

World-renowned chefs, sommeliers and cookbook writers visit Philadelphia for a few days this month to meet, lecture, demonstrate and prepare meals for lucky local folks. It's called **The Book and the Cook**. If you would like to watch, have your favorite cookbook signed by its author, or partake in a gastronomic experience, call 568-6599 for details.

April

Good Friday is April 17, 1987; April 1, 1988. **Easter Sunday** is April 19, 1987; April 3, 1988.

SEPTA Bus Rambles* take one-day trips to nearby attractions in spring and summer.

The annual Hospital of the University of Pennsylvania **Antiques Show and Sale** has a one-week run this month. It's reputed to be the best show of its kind in the country. The HUP Show is at the 103rd Engineers Armory, 33rd and Market Streets. For details, call 687-6441, or 387-3500 during the show.

The **Phillies*** begin their season at Veterans Stadium this month, and play continues till October.

The **Penn Relays*** are traditionally the last weekend of the month. The world's oldest and largest scholastic, collegiate and amateur track meet is at Franklin Field, 33rd and Spruce Streets. For information, call 898-6151.

Dogwoods are usually in bloom at Valley Forge National Historical Park* by the end of the month. Feast your eyes on 50,000 of the flowering trees. The first weekend of Friends Hospital Garden Days (831-4772) is the last weekend of April. Feast your eyes on brilliant **azaleas** in more than 40 varieties. If you miss nature's show in April, you can catch it in May.

The **Philadelphia Festival Theater for New Plays** opens at the Harold Prince Theater at Annenberg and continues into June. Read more about it in Chapter 10 and try to attend at least one of the performances.

The **St. Walpurgis Night Festival** ushers in spring the last Saturday night of April at the American–Swedish Historical Museum*. There's a bonfire, folk dancing, refreshments and lots of fun.

Daylight Saving Time arrives the first Sunday in April. Spring forward, fall back; lose an hour's sleep.

May

Law Day is May 1. The local Bar Association has special programs. Naturalization ceremonies take place at the United States Courthouse*.

There's a Sunday parade in May on the Parkway. This one celebrates **Israel's Independence Day.** The route leads to Independence Mall where there's a day-long bazaar and festivities.

Mother's Day is the second Sunday in May.

An **Azalea Day Festival** ushers in spring the first Sunday of May at the four-acre Azalea Garden* in Fairmount Park just west of the Art Museum. Over 2,000 multi-colored azalea plants, rhododendrons, dogwoods, and spring bulbs bloom. **Friends Hospital* Garden Days** continue the first two weekends of May. Scores of varieties of azaleas cover more than 15 acres of the hospital's 99-acre grounds in Northeast Philadelphia. Call 831-4772 for the hours and group tour reservations.

Later this month, on a Wednesday and Thursday, thousands of Philadelphians will flock to the **Rittenhouse Square Flower Market** to buy plants, flowers, lemon sticks, pizza, egg rolls and other goodies.

While some of us are doing spring cleaning, others are holding open house.

Philadelphia Open House is 18 days of tours by bus, by boat or walking to neighborhoods, houses, gardens, museums, historic and contemporary sites sponsored by the Friends of Independence National Historical Park. Call 928-1188 for details and don't miss this once-a-year opportunity to visit attractions that aren't usually open to the public.

The Germantown Historical Society* (844-0514) along with Philadelphia Open House holds the annual **Germantown Open House Tours** in May.

Armed Forces Weekend is the third Saturday and Sunday in May at Penn's Landing. The Air Force, Army, Coast Guard, Marines, National Guard and Navy are represented with exhibits, demonstrations, aircraft and ships. Call 923-4992 for details.

Police Week festivities include open house at the Police Administration Building*. **Fire Recognition Day** features open house at your neighborhood firehouse*.

Art Week is when galleries hold open houses, artists open their studios for special tours and unusual Art Week happenings involve the public in once-a-year art events. Watch for newspaper announcements or call the Art Week "hotline" (636-9605) to discover what might interest you.

Manayunk Canal Day includes a parade and all-day festival in the section of Philadelphia that resembles San Francisco. Watch for newspaper announcements, or call 483-7530.

May is for music. **Mozart on the Square** is a three-week festival that pays tribute to Wolfgang Amadeus Mozart. There are noontime and evening concerts, recitals, films, lectures and opera at various locations surrounding Rittenhouse Square. Several of them are free. Call 988-9830 for details.

The **Devon Horse Show** opens at the end of the month at the Devon Fair Grounds on Lancaster Pike in Devon, Pennsylvania. More than 1,200 horses and riders appear in one of the country's largest and finest outdoor horse shows. The nine-day event also includes an enormous country fair. Call 964-0550 for dates and details.

Memorial Day is the last Monday in May (May 25, 1987; May 30, 1988; May 29, 1989). Old City* restaurants celebrate on Sunday and Monday of the holiday weekend with outdoor food vendors, string bands, belly dancers and street entertainers along Chestnut Street from Front to 3rd Street, and along 2nd Street from Market to Walnut Street. Be there to join the festivities to welcome summer.

Look for announcements about local fairs and festivals.

Elfreth's Alley Day* is celebrated the first Sunday in June when dwellers on the nation's oldest continuously occupied residential street hold Open House.

The **Head House Crafts Fair*** opens at 2nd and Pine Streets and continues on Saturdays from noon to midnight and Sundays from noon to 6 P.M. through August. Forty craftsmen demonstrate their skills in pottery, jewelry, batik, glassware, photography, prints, metal sculpture, leatherware, candles and woven goods.

The annual mid-summer Colonial Fair is a Saturday or Sunday in June at **Old Swedes' Church** and the **American-Swedish Historical Museum.** A festival complete with maypole, folk dancing and an authentic Swedish smorgasbord celebrates Sweden's mid-summer day when the sun shines for 24 hours.

The **Rittenhouse Square Fine Arts Annual** is where over a hundred local artists display thousands of works on Wednesday to Sunday, 10 A.M. to 6 P.M., the first week of June.

Stop by the **Visitors Center** at 16th and Kennedy Boulevard and pick up a schedule of free entertainment planned for popular locations during the summer. **Phillyfest** is hour-long noontime live entertainment weekdays June through August adjacent to the Visitors Center at John F. Kennedy Plaza. Be there to enjoy jazz, big band and popular music, dance, sports celebrities and competitions and more. Call 568–6599 for a schedule.

Flag Day (June 14) is celebrated with a parade, special observances and ceremonies at the Betsy Ross House*.

Old Newsboys' Day brings celebrities and bands together on center city corners to raise funds for handicapped children.

Father's Day is the third Sunday in June.

KYW-TV sponsors the **Annual Health Fair 3** each Saturday in June at locations in and around Philadelphia. So check out which locale is most convenient for you (238-4677) and check up on your health.

Mann Music Center* invites you outdoors for the summer season with the Philadelphia Orchestra. **Concerts by Candlelight*** open their season at **Laurel Hill** in East Fairmount Park. You're also invited to popular Dockside Concerts and Big Bands Live at **Penn's Landing***, and string band concerts at the **Mummers Museum***.

The **Philadelphia International Children's Festival*** presents indoor and outdoor performances for several days at the beginning of June at or near the Annenberg Center. See Chapter 15 for additional information and be sure to take advantage of this great opportunity for youngsters.

The week-long **Mellon Jazz Festival** brings jazz performers of world renown to Philadelphia for concerts at popular center city locales. Some of the events are free; others require tickets available from Ticketron outlets. Watch the local newspapers for dates and details.

The **Department of Recreation*** gears up for another full summer. Day camps are open, swimming pools are filled, play streets are closed to traffic and tennis lessons are underway.

Down in historic Philadelphia, afternoon and evening **Candlelight Tours** of Society Hill have resumed after the winter hiatus. See Chapter 1 for details.

The circus comes to town! Don't miss the **Ringling Bros. and Barnum & Bailey Circus** when they appear at the Spectrum in the greatest show on earth.

Visit the majestic ships and partake in the lively and free annual **Harbor Festival** at **Penn's Landing** the last Thursday to Sunday of the month. Don't miss the summertime fun down by the riverside.

July

Philadelphia's **Freedom Festival** celebrates America's independence in the city where it all began. Daytime and evening events in the days surrounding July 4 include a Great Philadelphia Hot-Air Balloon Race, a Summer Mummers Parade, food festivals, concerts, an Independence Day Parade and, of course, fireworks. The traditional **Fourth of July** ceremony and pageantry gets underway at 10 A.M. at Independence Hall. The newspapers and the Visitors Center will keep you abreast of the schedules.

Philadelphia's French restaurants have their celebrations on **Bastille Day**, July 14. The one at La Terrasse is our favorite.

Free and almost-free entertainment is in full swing for the entire summer. **Pop concerts** are at neighborhood parks and squares. **Big Band Live concerts** are at Penn's Landing. **Robin Hood Dell East*** joins the outdoor concert season. International **Folk Dancing*** is on Tuesday evenings at the Art Museum Terrace. The **Phillyfest** of free entertainment continues weekdays at noon at John F. Kennedy Plaza, 16th Street and Kennedy Boulevard.

Watch the Schuylkill **Regattas*** from the river's edge as college teams and crews compete in the summer.

You haven't been to Veterans Stadium to see the **Phillies** yet? Shame on you. Fireworks light up the sky following the game closest to July 4th. It's one of the season's most popular games.

August

Have you ridden a Fairmount Park Trolley-bus? Have you been to the Robin Hood Dell East or Mann Music Center? Did you rent a bike? Or a sailboat? Have you been to the Head House Crafts Fair? Who says there isn't much to do in the summer in Philadelphia?

The annual **Philadelphia Folk Festival** is held rain or shine the weekend before Labor Day weekend. Call the Philadelphia Folksong Society* (242-0150; 800-422-FOLK in Pennsylvania; or 800-556-FOLK outside Pennsylvania, from Connecticut to Washington, D.C.) for dates and details.

The Fairmount Park Commission sponsors an annual **"Pictures in the Park"** photography contest. Amateur shutterbugs of all ages can submit their favorite snapshots. (The judges are partial to those that relate to Fairmount Park.) Winners are exhibited next month during the Fairmount Fall Festival and several prizes are awarded. Call the Fairmount Park Commission (686-0052) for details, or pick up an entry form at the Visitors Center, 16th and Kennedy Boulevard.

September

Labor Day is the first Monday of the month (September 1, 1986; September 7, 1987; September 5, 1988).

The Old City Restaurant Association sponsors another **Old City Happening** on Labor Day and the Sunday before. Come down to Chestnut Street between Front and 3rd for international foods, entertainment and flea markets. For information, call 925-6999.

September 17, 1987 is the date of a major national celebration commemorating the adoption of the United States Constitution 200 years ago. It marks the culmination of events being reenacted since May 25 (opening date of the Constitutional Convention in 1787) that led to the historic occasion. What better place to celebrate than where it all happened?

The annual **Fairmount Fall Festival** features a few weeks of recreational and cultural activities in Fairmount Park and along the Benjamin Franklin Parkway.
The festival welcomes fall with the Pennsylvania Horticultural Society's annual weekend **Harvest Show** at the Horticultural Center*.
Memorial Hall, 42nd Street and Parkside Avenue, is the showplace for the winning entries in the **"Pictures in the Park"** photography contest, which was held in August.

The **Jewish New Year** and **Day of Atonement** are observed (September 27 and October 3, 1987; September 12 and September 21, 1988).

The **In-Water Boat Show** returns to the 10-acre boat basin at Penn's Landing with all types of pleasure craft and the latest in marine equipment. Call 923-4992 for details.

The Germantown Hospital Equestrian Festival featuring the **American Gold Cup*** and Grand Prix Horse Jumping Competition is a three-day weekend this month at the Devon Horse Show Grounds. There's a Fall Flower Festival as well. Tickets are available at the gate, or call 438-8383 for details.

The **Hero Scholarship Thrill Show** is on a Friday night

at John F. Kennedy Stadium. Top stars perform, there are motorcycle and firefighting feats and musical entertainment. Tickets are available at Room 592 City Hall and at police stations and firehouses. Proceeds are for scholarships for children of police and firemen who were permanently injured or who lost their lives in the line of duty. For information, call 686-3400 or 686-1776.

The **Von Steuben Day Parade** in center city on the last Saturday of the month honors the German General who trained American patriots at Valley Forge. The **Puerto Rican Day Parade** the following day honors Philadelphia's Puerto Rican residents. It's part of week-long festivities.

Football season gets underway with the **Eagles*** at Veterans Stadium and local college games.

October

The **Jewish New Year** and **Day of Atonement** are observed (October 4 and October 13, 1986).

Columbus Day is celebrated the second Monday of the month. There's always a parade on South Broad Street on the closest Sunday and a Columbus Day Festival at Marconi Plaza on South Broad Street at Oregon Avenue. The **Pulaski Day** Parade on the Parkway and Chestnut Street in center city pays tribute to a Polish patriot's contributions to America.

The **Fairmount Fall Festival** continues (see September). **Fall foliage** is magnificent this month at Morris Arboretum's* Fall Festival, in Fairmount Park, Valley Forge, Bucks County and anywhere you travel in the region.

Super Sunday is the second Sunday of the month. It's the original of the super block parties, started in 1970 and sponsored by the cultural institutions along the Benjamin Franklin Parkway. Exhibits, games, rides, crafts, entertainment, food and a flea market line the Parkway from Logan Circle to the Art Museum Terrace from noon to 6 P.M. See you there.

Chester County Day features two tours that cover some 45 historic homes and landmarks (see Chapter 17).

The 1777 **Battle of Germantown** is re-enacted, along with a country fair, crafts and flea market, on the grounds of historic Cliveden*.

The ice hockey season opens with the **Flyers*** at the Spectrum. The basketball season opens with the **76ers*** at the Spectrum. (The basketball floor is placed on top of the ice.) The Schuylkill and its shores are crammed on the Saturday of the annual **Thomas Eakins Regatta**. More than a thousand students participate from colleges across the country.

William Penn's Birthday is October 24. Philadelphia's founder is honored with special events and programs. There's a party at Pennsbury Manor*. Call the Visitors

Center (568-6599) or watch the newspapers for details.

City firehouses hold Open House during **Fire Prevention Week**. It's also the time to plan a fire drill at home and at the office.

Witches and goblins appear later this month (October 31) to celebrate **Halloween**. This is a fun time to visit the Italian Markets* and pick out a giant pumpkin to carve. There are hundreds of them at 9th Street and Washington Avenue. **Haunted houses** are open to daring visitors. Watch for newspaper announcements. Don't get spooked!

The last Sunday night in October is when we return to **Eastern Standard Time**. Pick up that hour's sleep you lost in April.

November

Election Day is the first Tuesday after the first Monday of the month (November 4, 1986; November 3, 1987; November 8, 1988).

Veterans Day is November 11.

Old Fort Mifflin* is under siege again as 400 "soldiers" in Revolutionary War dress re-enact the battle and spend a weekend demonstrating colonial military games and camp life.

The annual **Philadelphia Craft Show** draws thousands to the 103rd Engineers' Armory, at 33rd Street just north of Market, over three days to see the ceramics, jewelry, quilts, woodwork, clothing and weaving of 100 juried craftspeople from around the country. Call the Visitors Center or Philadelphia Museum of Art for details.

This is also a special month for dog lovers. The Kennel Club of Philadelphia holds its annual **Dog Show** at the Civic Center. It's one of the few benched dog shows in the country where the participants can be admired close-up, and more than 3,000 animals will be there. Call 823–7327 or 823–7400 for the date and ticket information.

The Nationalities Service Center* sponsors three days of singing, dancing, arts, crafts, exhibits and foods from around the world at the biennial **Philadelphia Folk Fair**. No less than 50 nationalities and all of Philadelphia's ethnic groups are represented under one roof at the Civic Center. For information, call 563–5363.

Thanksgiving Day is the fourth Thursday of the month. Thousands of marchers parade down the Benjamin Franklin Parkway for the annual **Thanksgiving Day Parade**. There are bands, colorful floats and famous personalities. It's always fun to see Santa Claus arrive in Philadelphia for the holiday season. And it's more fun to be at the parade than to watch it on television.

And if it's Thanksgiving, it's **Tinkertoy Time** at the Franklin Institute. Join the extravaganza for three days after Thanksgiving when the Benjamin Franklin National Memorial is the site of some major tinkering.

The **Greater Philadelphia Independence Marathon** the Sunday after Thanksgiving begins in Fort Washington, Pennsylvania and goes 26 miles to Independence Hall. Sign up to run along with a few thousand others, or be along the route to cheer the participants on. The Visitors Center, Department of Recreation and newspapers will provide details.

December

The midshipmen and cadets are in Philadelphia on the first Saturday of December for the **Army-Navy Football Classic** held each year at Veterans Stadium. The game is billed as college football's greatest spectacle.

For basketball* fans, the **Big Five** (LaSalle, St. Joseph's, Temple, University of Pennsylvania, Villanova) season starts with games at the Palestra.

Disney's Magic Kingdom on Ice makes its appearance at the Spectrum the last week of the year. This fabulous spectacle on ice is fun for the whole family. Call 336–3600 for dates and details.

The **Pennsylvania Ballet*** returns to the Academy of Music every year during the winter vacation with the ever-popular "**Nutcracker.**"

A 25-foot Menorah glows with a new light for each of the eight nights of **Hanukah**. It's at Independence Mall on Market Street across from the Liberty Bell Pavilion. The first night (December 26, 1986; December 15, 1987; December 3, 1988) is celebrated with music and latkes at sundown.

Christmas is a big thing in Philadelphia. The holiday season starts early in the month with tree-lighting ceremonies and choral singing at City Hall, Rittenhouse Square and several other well-publicized locations.

The annual **Lucia Fest** takes place at Old Swedes' Church* and the American-Swedish Historical Museum*. A candlelight procession on the first or second Saturday of the month calls for participants dressed as a queen, page boys, elves, fairies and star boys. Booths display and sell Swedish crafts and foods following the traditional holiday season welcome. This colorful Swedish event is something you should see.

The **Fairmount Park Houses** are splendid with their holiday finery. Special Fairmount Park Trolley-bus tours are scheduled the first weekend of the month. Call the Art Museum (763–8100) for details. The following weekend, the **Germantown Historical Society** (848–1777) also offers Christmas Tours of outstanding colonial homes decked with holiday lights and boughs of holly.

Longwood Gardens* is resplendent with lighted and decorated outdoor trees and thousands of poinsettias and Christmas flowers. The **Pennsylvania Horticultural Society*** exhibits ideas for your walls, door, table and mantle.

A live nativity scene is in the yard at Old First Reformed Church*.

Philadelphia's major **department stores** go all out with entertainment. Strawbridge and Clothier is splendid with holiday decor and festivities at every level. A Christmas Show with dancing fountains, animated characters and a "tree with a million lights" draws hundreds of wide-eyed spectators to the grand court of John Wanamaker every day from mid-November through December. And last but not least, Mr. and Mrs. Claus are available at the stores for personal consultation.

General George Washington and his troops crossed the Delaware river on December 25, 1776 to defeat the British at Trenton. The historic trip is re-enacted on Christmas Day at **Washington Crossing Historic Park***.

Kwanzaa is a week-long festival starting the day after Christmas and celebrated by many black Americans. There's a parade and a variety of cultural happenings. Call the Afro-American Historical and Cultural Museum* (574–0380) for a schedule.

Merry Christmas! Happy New Year!

Chapter 20.
Hotels and Camping Out.

Philadelphia's hotels provide almost 7,000 first class rooms for overnight visitors.

The following list includes features that are unique to each of these hotels. They are categorized according to their location.

If you're planning a convention or a class trip, most of Philadelphia's hotels will provide group rates. Many have Vacation Packages and Weekend Plans. If you're traveling with youngsters, most hotels have special plans for you, too.

For more information, visit or write to the Philadelphia Convention and Visitors Bureau*, 1525 John F. Kennedy Boulevard, Phila., Pa. 19102. Or see your travel agent.

Center City

These hotels are in the heart of Philadelphia. They're close to the historic and cultural attractions. They're approximately three miles north of the sports complex and six miles from Philadelphia International Airport.

THE BARCLAY 18th Street and Rittenhouse Square East, Philadelphia, Pa. 19103 (545-0300 or 800-421-6662). 235 rooms and suites (all with a refrigerator and some with 4-poster and canopied beds) in elegant early American style. Posh but low key; facing Rittenhouse Square, galleries and fine shops. Le Beau Lieu Restaurant and a cozy cocktail lounge. Valet parking.

BELLEVUE STRATFORD Broad and Walnut Streets, Phila., Pa. 19102 (893-1776). Landmark 18-story hotel closed in 1986 for total renovation around two new atriums. Reopening late in 1988 with 180 European-style suites and luxury rooms on top seven floors. Operated by The Continental Companies (Ciga Hotels). Lower floors will be an office, retail and restaurant complex. A short walk to theaters, the Academy of Music, City Hall, business and shopping.

FOUR SEASONS HOTEL One Logan Square, 18th Street and Benjamin Franklin Parkway, Phila., Pa. 19103 (963-1500 or 800-268-6282). Opened in 1983. 375 luxury rooms and suites; 8-story world-class hotel with fine dining at the Fountain Restaurant and Swan Cafe overlooking Logan Circle. Careful attention to personal service, a concierge, spa and indoor pool. No conventions here. Awarded Mobile Travel Guide's 4-star rating.

HERSHEY PHILADELPHIA HOTEL Broad and Locust Streets, Phila., Pa. 19107 (893-1600 or 800-533-3131). Opened in 1983. 450 rooms; 25-story transient and convention hotel with ballrooms, meeting rooms, a 5-story atrium lobby, indoor pool, racquetball and health spa. Sarah's and Cafe Academie for dining, and the Hershey Bar. Sarah's and Cafe Academie for dining and the Hershey Bar. Operated by Hershey Resort Company.

HOLIDAY INN—CENTER CITY 18th and Market Streets, Phila., Pa. 19103 (561-7500 or 800-HOLIDAY). 450 contemporary rooms, indoor parking, outdoor pool, Reflections Restaurant, Coffey's and lobby lounge. A good location if you plan to be west of Broad Street or visiting the Philadelphia Stock Exchange, Commerce Square or Liberty Place.

HOLIDAY INN—INDEPENDENCE MALL 4th and Arch Streets, Phila., Pa. 19106 (923-8660 or 800-HOLIDAY). 364 rooms in historic Old City Philadelphia. Free indoor parking, outdoor pool, restaurant and coffee shop. A convenient hotel to the historic attractions.

HOLIDAY INN—MIDTOWN 1311 Walnut Street, Phila., Pa. 19107 (735-9300 or 800-HOLIDAY). 160 rooms, indoor parking, outdoor pool, restaurant and cocktail lounge. In the heart of the business, shopping and theater district.

HOTEL INTER-CONTINENTAL Rittenhouse Square West. Opening in 1988. 360 luxury rooms and suites. A "saw-tooth" design gives every room a commanding view.

INN AT OLD CITY HARBOR Delaware and Vine Streets, Phila., Pa. 19106. Opening in 1987. A bed-and-breakfast hotel with 53 suites, all with a kitchen, across from the Philadelphia Marine Center. It's in a restored four-story complex of waterfront shops and warehouses dating from 1875 and originally designed by City Hall architect, John McArthur, Jr. A National Historic Site. Indoor and outdoor dining at Dr. Jayne's Bar and Restaurant.

LATHAM 17th and Walnut Streets, Phila., Pa. 19103 (563–7474 or 800–LATHAM-1). A Lincoln Hotel. 150 rooms, tailored for executives. Bogart's and Not Quite Cricket for dining and drinking, and a "private" bar in every room. A quiet, fashionable hotel surrounded by fine shops. One block from Rittenhouse Square.

PALACE HOTEL OF PHILADELPHIA 18th Street and Benjamin Franklin Parkway, Phila., Pa. 19103 (963–1800 or 800–223–5672). 285 luxury suites, each with a parlor, wet bar and terrace. A concierge, European-style service and managed by Trusthouse Forte Hotels. Indoor parking, outdoor pool and elegant Cafe Royale restaurant, all in a circular white tower facing Logan Circle and convenient to Parkway museums and Penn Center.

PENN CENTER INN 20th and Market Streets, Phila., Pa. 19103 (569–3000 or 800–523–0909). 300 comfortable rooms, free indoor self-parking, huge outdoor pool, The Cafe for dining and cocktails. A comfortable, convenient place to stay that's near the Parkway museums, Penn Center offices and the Philadelphia Stock Exchange.

PHILADELPHIA CENTRE HOTEL 1725 John F. Kennedy Boulevard, Phila., Pa. 19103 (568–3300 or 800–523–4300). 865 rooms; Crossroads Restaurant, Poncho 'n Richies (for Mexican fare) and Amelia's Lounge. Operated by Tollman–Hundley Hotels.

QUALITY INN—CENTER CITY 501 N. 22nd Street, Phila., Pa. 19130 (568–8300 or 800–228–5151). 250 rooms, free outdoor parking on premises, outdoor pool, Hemingway's Restaurant. A short walk to the Parkway museums.

QUALITY INN—DOWNTOWN SUITES 1010 Race Street, Phila., Pa. 19107 (922–1730 or 800–228–5151). 96 suites, all with a kitchen, and furnished with top-of-the-line Tai–Ming decor. Unique hotel interiors and locale. In the heart of Chinatown*, convenient to City Hall, Market East* and the Federal buildings. Meeting rooms and a moderately-priced Chinese-American restaurant.

SHERATON SOCIETY HILL One Dock Street (2nd and Walnut Streets), Phila., Pa. 19106 (238–6000 or 800–235–3535). Opened in 1986. Four-story red brick architecture designed to blend with the neighborhood. 365

rooms, underground parking, meeting rooms, indoor pool and health club, 24-hour room service and concierge. Americus restaurant and Spectacles bar. Convenient to Penn's Landing, Independence National Historical Park, South Street and historic attractions.

SOCIETY HILL HOTEL 3rd and Chestnut Streets, Phila., Pa. 19106 (925-1394). Philadelphia's smallest hotel has 6 single rooms and 6 suites, all with brass beds, dark wood furnishings and private bath. It was built in 1832 to house longshoremen from around the world who were in port in Philadelphia. Totally renovated, it reopened in 1979 as an historic "bed and breakfast." The restaurant is described in Chapter 18. In the heart of Independence National Historical Park.

THE WARWICK 17th and Locust Streets, Phila., Pa. 19103 (735-6000 or 800-523-4210). 190 rooms in a luxury apartment building one block from Rittenhouse Square. The Brasserie and elan for dining, dancing and entertainment. Awarded Mobil Travel Guide's 4-star rating.

WYNDHAM FRANKLIN PLAZA Two Franklin Plaza, 16th and Race Streets, Phila., Pa. 19103 (448-2000 or 800-822-4200). 800 rooms; 26-story modern and airy convention hotel opened in 1980. An underground garage; racquet, swim and health club with nautilus, outdoor running track, squash and glass-enclosed pool. Between Friends, Horizons, Terrace Restaurants and two lounges. Convenient to Parkway museums and Penn Center.

A 176-room **COMFORT INN** is planned for 136-148 N. Delaware Avenue, just north of Penn's Landing. A 140-room luxury **OMNI CLASSIC HOTEL** is scheduled to open in late 1988 at the northwest corner of 4th and Chestnut Streets in the heart of Independence National Historical Park.

University City

These hotels are convenient to the Civic Center, University City Science Center, major Philadelphia hospitals and the attractions of University City*. They're two miles or 10 minutes from center city. Or less.

HILTON HOTEL OF PHILADELPHIA 34th Street and Civic Center Boulevard, Phila., Pa. 19104 (387-8333 or 800-HILTONS). 320 modern rooms, adjacent to the University Museum*, Philadelphia Civic Center*, Children's Hospital, the Hospital of the University of Pennsylvania and the university campus. Indoor self-parking, year-round indoor swimming, Christopher's Restaurant, Networks Video Lounge and ample convention facilities.

SHERATON UNIVERSITY CITY 36th and Chestnut Streets, Phila., Pa. 19104 (387-8000 or 800-325-3535). 377 rooms, outdoor pool, indoor self-parking, Smart Alex restaurant. Convenient to the Philadelphia Civic Center, University of Pennsylvania, Drexel University and the University City Science Center.

South Philadelphia

These hotels are close to the sports complex* and Philadelphia International Airport. They're about 15 minutes from center city.

AIRPORT RAMADA INN 76 Industrial Highway, Route 291, Essington, Pa. 19029 (521-9600 or 800-228-2828). 290 rooms, free parking on premises, outdoor pool, restaurant, disco, 24-hour coffee shop and 24-hour van service to the airport. Four miles west of the airport.

AIRPORT QUALITY INN 20th Street and Penrose Avenue, Phila., Pa. 19145 (755-6500 or 800-228-5151). 240 rooms in a round high-rise. Charley's for dining and dancing, heated outdoor pool, free parking on premises and conference facilities.

BEST WESTERN-AIRPORT INN Industrial Highway, Route 291, Phila., Pa. 19153 (365-7000 or 800-528-1234). 224 rooms, restaurant and lounge, free parking on premises and free van service to and from the airport.

DAYS INN Two Gateway Center, 4101 Island Avenue, Phila., Pa. 19153 (492-0400 or 325-2525). Opened in 1985. 175 rooms, four-story contemporary decor with a restaurant. Free parking; free van service to and from the airport.

EMBASSY SUITES One Gateway Center, 4101 Island Avenue, Phila., Pa. 19153 (365-6600 or 800-EMBASSY). Opened in 1985. 250 two-room suites on eight floors designed around an atrium. Indoor pool and health club, restaurant and lounge, complimentary breakfast and a cocktail reception. Free parking; free van service to and from the airport.

HOLIDAY INN-AIRPORT SOUTH 45 Industrial Highway, Essington, Pa. 19029 (521-2400 or 800-HOLIDAY). 307 rooms, restaurant and a lounge with entertainment, outdoor pool and free parking on premises. Three miles south of the airport.

PHILADELPHIA AIRPORT HILTON INN 10th Street and Packer Avenue, Phila., Pa. 19148 (755-9500 or 800-HILTONS). 238 rooms, outdoor pool, free parking on premises and free van service to and from the airport. Cinnamon's Restaurant and bar; Cahoot's for cocktails and dancing. Popular with ball players and sports fans because of its adjacency to the stadiums.

PHILADELPHIA AIRPORT MARRIOTT HOTEL 4509 Island Avenue, Phila., Pa. 19153 (365-4150 or 800-228-9290). 330 rooms, free parking on premises, indoor pool (in the lobby), 2 restaurants and a cocktail lounge with entertainment. Contemporary design and only a block from the overseas terminal. Van service to and from the airport.

City Line Suburbs

These hotels are 15 minutes from center city Philadelphia. They're convenient to the shopping on City Line Avenue. They border on Montgomery County* and they're a step closer to Valley Forge and the nation's largest shopping mall complex at King of Prussia.

ADAM'S MARK City Line and Monument Road, Phila., Pa. 19131 (581-5000 or 800-231-5858). 515 luxury rooms, free parking, indoor pool, outdoor pool, saunas, health club. Family dining in Appleby's, gourmet at The Marker, Quincey's for dancing to live music, Pierre's jazz lounge and the Sports Bar. Complete banquet, meeting and convention facilities.

DUNFEY CITY LINE City Line and Monument Road, Phila., Pa. 19131 (667-0200 or 800-438-6339). 705 rooms, free parking on premises, indoor and 2 outdoor pools, row of shops, game rooms, convention and banquet facilities, King's Wharf, Kona Kai, Coriander's, Tingles Lounge, Dunfey Tavern with live entertainment and a 24-hour Coffee Store.

PHILADELPHIA BEST WESTERN City Line and Presidential Boulevard, Phila., 19131 (477-0200 or 800-528-1234). 350 rooms; 8-story contemporary design that was prefabricated in modules and assembled at the site. Moderate rates for junior executives and families. Free parking on premises, indoor pool, restaurant and cocktail lounge.

Northeast Philadelphia

The following hotels and inns are within a half-hour drive of center city Philadelphia on either the Roosevelt Boulevard (Route 1) or the Delaware Expressway (I-95). They're convenient to Northeast Philadelphia Airport, the Greater Northeast shopping centers, Philadelphia Park Race Track and the Bucks County* attractions.

HOWARD JOHNSON'S MOTOR LODGE 11580 Roosevelt Boulevard, Phila., Pa. 19116 (464-9500 or 800-654-2000). 110 rooms (some with jacuzzi), free parking on premises, adjacent restaurant, outdoor pool.

SHERATON NORTHEAST 9461 Roosevelt Boulevard, Phila., Pa. 19114 (671-9600 or 800-325-3535). 188 rooms, free parking on premises, year-round indoor–outdoor pool, saunas, Plum Tree restaurant and lounge.

TREADWAY MOHAWK INN 4200 Roosevelt Boulevard, Phila., Pa. 19124 (289-9200 or 800-631-0182). 116 rooms, free parking on premises, outdoor pool.

Other Accommodations

BED & BREAKFAST/CENTER CITY 1804 Pine Street, Phila., Pa. 19103 (735-1137). This reservation service arranges at-home personalized accommodations in unique, charming, historic and contemporary center city homes. It gives you the opportunity to be part of a Philadelphia family when you visit Philadelphia. Call or write for reservations at least two weeks in advance.

BED & BREAKFAST OF PHILADELPHIA P.O. Box 680, Devon, Pa. 19333 (688-1633). This reservations service arranges accommodations for business people and tourists in private homes in Philadelphia and the suburbs. Bed & Breakfast is a longtime European custom that provides comfortable, moderately priced, personalized lodgings in a private home. Now you can enjoy the same tradition in Philadelphia. Visa and MasterCard accepted for deposit.

CHAMOUNIX MANSION INTERNATIONAL YOUTH HOSTEL West Fairmount Park, Phila., Pa. 19131 (878-3676). Built in 1802 as an elegant country home, Chamounix is just 10 minutes by car from center city. Cooking facilities, bunks, mattresses and blankets are available, but bring your own linens. Sign in from 4:30 to 8 P.M. and out by 9:30 A.M. Room for 60 in summer and 40 the rest of the year (closed December); groups and families accepted; reservations advised. Chamounix is chartered by **American Youth Hostels**, 35 S. 3rd Street, Phila., Pa. 19106 (925-6004). Membership is required of international visitors, but non-members can purchase a special guest card from A.Y.H. or at Chamounix and stay for two nights. They'll also provide information on biking, hiking, canoeing, sailing and skiing in the area.

CHESTNUT HILL HOTEL 8229 Germantown Avenue, Phila., Pa. 19118 (242–5905). A four-story colonial-style country inn at the top of quaint Chestnut Hill*. 24 rooms, including three two-rooms suites, all with 18th century reproduction furnishings and breakfast included. A meeting room and two restaurants (see Chapter 18), Chautauqua and J.B. Winberie.

INTERNATIONAL HOUSE* 3701 Chestnut Street, Phila., Pa. 19104 (387–5125). This super-structure residence is for the area's foreign and American graduate students, but a limited number of accommodations for transients are available by reservation.

OLD FIRST REFORMED CHURCH* 4th and Race Streets, Phila., Pa. 19106 (922–4566). This restored church in historic Philadelphia provides mattresses and a light breakfast for up to 21 visitors per night (ages 18 to 26) in July and August. There's a three-night limit. Sign in from 5 to 10 P.M.; closes at midnight.

STATE CAMPGROUNDS INFORMATION Write or call the Bureau of State Parks, Regional Office 4, P.O. Box 197, Perkasie, Pa. 18944 (1–257–3646). Specify if you're interested in all of Pennsylvania or the region east of the Susquehanna River in Eastern Pennsylvania.

Elsewhere

Many other hotels and motels are within an hour's drive of center city Philadelphia. Many of them feature resort facilities, weekend get-aways, fine restaurants, discotheques and top quality accommodations. Some are less extravagant. A few of them are listed here.

Just to get your bearings, refer to Chapter 17 on Philadelphia's neighboring counties.

In Bucks County:

George Washington Motor Lodge Pa. Turnpike Exit 28, Trevose, Pa. 19047 (357-9100).

Hilton Inn Northeast 2400 Old Lincoln Highway and Route 1, Trevose, Pa. 19047 (638-8300).

Holiday Inn Route 13 and Pa. Turnpike Exit 26, Bristol, Pa. 19057 (946-1100).

Holiday Inn-New Hope Route 202, New Hope, Pa. 18939 (862-5221).

Holiday Inn Northeast 3499 Street Road, Bensalem, Pa. 19020 (638-1500).

In Delaware County:

Chadds Ford Ramada Inn 1110 Baltimore Pike (Routes 202 and 1), Glen Mills, Pa. 19342 (358-1700).

Hotel Regency 1124 W. Baltimore Pike, Media, Pa. 19063 (566-9600).

Media Inn Providence Road and Baltimore Pike, Media, Pa. 19063 (566-8460).

St. David's Inn Route 30 (Lancaster Pike) and Radnor-Chester Pike, St. Davids, Pa. 19087 (688-5800).

Also the **Holiday Inn-Airport South** and the **Airport Ramada Inn** described under "South Philadelphia."

In Montgomery County:

Budget Motor Lodge 815 DeKalb Pike, King of Prussia, Pa. 19406 (265-7200).

Embassy Suites Hotel/Valley Forge 888 Chesterbrook Boulevard, Wayne, Pa. 19087 (647-6700).

George Washington Motor Lodge Pa. Turnpike Exit 24, King of Prussia, Pa. 19406 (365–6100); Pa. Turnpike Exit 25, Plymouth Meeting, Pa. 19462 (825–1980); and Pa. Turnpike Exit 27, Willow Grove, Pa. 19090 (659–7200).

Holiday Inn Valley Forge 260 Goddard Boulevard, King of Prussia, Pa. 19406 (265–7500).

Howard Johnson's Motor Lodge Route 202 North and Gulph Road, King of Prussia, Pa. 19406 (265–4500).

Ramada Inn and Coach Inn Restaurant Commerce Drive, Fort Washington, Pa. 19034 (542–7930).

Sheraton Executive Tower 530 Pennsylvania Avenue, Fort Washington, Pa. 19034 (643–1111).

Sheraton Valley Forge Route 363 (North Gulph Road) and First Avenue, King of Prussia, Pa. 19406 (337–2000).

Stouffer's Valley Forge Route 363 (480 North Gulph Road), King of Prussia, Pa. 19406 (337–1800).

Valley Forge Hilton 251 West DeKalb Pike, King of Prussia, Pa. 19406 (337–1200).

Crossing the Delaware River into New Jersey (area code 609), there's a **Cherry Hill Hyatt** (662–1234), a **Cherry Hill Inn** Radisson Hotel and Conference Center (662–7200), a **Cherry Hill Sheraton Poste Inn** (428–2300) and a **Garden Park Hotel** (665–6900), **Colonial Motor Lodge** (663–0100) and **Best Western Tudor Inn** (665–1100), all in Cherry Hill. The closest **Holiday Inns** are in Cherry Hill, Gloucester, Maple Shade, Moorestown and Mt. Laurel.

Chapter 21.
Useful Information.

Philadelphia Glossary. Shopping Tips. Architectural Notes.

In addition to all of the distinctive Philadelphia neighborhoods, customs and traditions you've already come to know, there are other terms and expressions you'll probably come upon. Here they are:

Antique Row includes some two dozen or more antique shops between 9th and 12th Streets on Pine Street. It's mecca for collectors, dealers and plain folks interested in things that are old and collectible.

Avenue of the Arts refers to the six blocks south of Broad Street from City Hall. It packs in several cultural institutions you've read about including the Historical Society of Pennsylvania, Library Company of Philadelphia, Opera Company of Philadelphia, Pennsylvania Ballet, Philadelphia College of Art, the Shubert Theater, the Academy of Music and the Philadelphia Orchestra.

The Bourse was built as a merchants exchange in 1893 to 1895. Its grand scale and elaborate design were copied from the commercial exchanges of Europe where goods, commodities and services were bought and sold.

Some 1,500 members were allowed on the trading floor, a two-level balcony provided for spectators, a skylight provided bright daylight over the central core, and six floors of offices looked down on it all. The Bourse continued as a trading center till the Depression.

After two years of total restoration to its turn-of-the-century splendor, the Bourse reopened in 1981 as a one-of-a-kind office, shopping and dining complex. Overlooking Independence Mall, The Great Hall of The Bourse houses some of Philadelphia's unique boutiques and elegant European shops. The restaurants at The Bourse are described in Chapter 18.

Center City is Philadelphia's term for downtown. You can easily determine north, east, south and west from the compass in the center of the City Hall Courtyard.

The Chestnut Street Transitway is the mile on Chestnut Street between 6th and 18th Streets. It's off-limits during the day to all traffic except buses. Motorists can use the transitway from 7 P.M. to 6 A.M. for one lane of traffic in each direction. This is a major shopping district of Philadelphia with department stores, boutiques, specialty shops, restaurants and fast food services (see Chapter 18).

The tree-lined pedestrian walkway has extra-wide brick seating areas and protected bus stops. It's also an occasional outdoor stage for musicians, musical groups, mimes and street performers providing free entertainment.

The **Philadelphia Civic Center,** just 10 minutes from center city in West Philadelphia, is a multi-building, multi-function complex for sports events, conferences, conventions, exhibitions and trade shows. It's been the site of Presidential nominating conventions, high school and college commencements and shows for boats, dogs, flowers and just about everything imaginable.

The Civic Center includes Convention Hall, the exhibition halls, underground parking garages and Pennsylvania Hall.

A new Convention Center is on the drawing boards for the area north of Market Street and surrounding the old Reading Railroad Terminal between 11th and 12th Streets at Arch.

Commerce Square is two 41-story towers rising between Market Street and John F. Kennedy Boulevard, 20th and 21st Streets. In addition to offices, they'll have restaurants and retail space. The first tower is scheduled for completion in 1987. IBM is the major tenant. The architect is I.M. Pei & Partners.

Fabric Row is the 600 to 700 blocks of South 4th Street in Queen Village*. This is where you'll find shop after shop of fabrics with selections as good as the values.

Jeweler's Row is the 700 block of Sansom Street and its adjoining streets. This is a place to go for super selections and prices on diamonds, gold, silver and other beautiful things.

Liberty Place, under construction at 17th and Market Streets, is 60 stories tall. It's also the first building in Philadelphia's history that tops William Penn's statue on City Hall*. Completion is scheduled for late in 1987. Helmut Jann is the architect.

Independence Mellon Center opens in 1987 on the north side of Market Street, between 7th and 8th Streets (Market East), as an office and retail complex surrounding a huge atrium. Its magnificent cast iron facade dates from the late 19th century. Secretary of State Thomas Jefferson's office occupied part of the site in 1793. J.B. Lippincott Publishers was on part of the block from 1863 to 1899. Lit Brothers Department Store bought the block between 1893 and 1907 and built their original store here. It closed in the early 1980s and has remained vacant till the current monumental restoration.

Market East stretches east along Market Street from City Hall towards Independence Mall. With major department stores, office buildings, a commuter tunnel and good design, it will be the largest office and shopping center within a city in the country.

A major street and sidewalk renovation is underway and scheduled for completion in 1988, giving Market East a dramatically new boulevard look.

The Gallery at Market East brings an enormous new shopping mall to center city at 9th and Market Streets. It's a four-story, glass-roofed, suburban-style mall of 100 shops anchored on either side by the major department stores of **Stern's** and **Strawbridge and Clothier.** You can shop under and over 10th Street while traffic flows across it. **Gallery 2,** including a **J.C. Penney,** 125 more shops and eating places, bright courtyards and fountains, extends the mall a block further west to 11th Street.

SEPTA's Market–Frankford Subway–Elevated trains stop at The Gallery, as well as the PATCO High Speed Line and bus routes running on Market Street. Parking garages also connect directly with the shopping complex from Filbert Street.

The Gallery's lower level towards 10th Street houses dozens of fast food restaurants serving specialties from around the world. They circle a common seating area. (Additional restaurants occupy other sites in The Gallery.) The Gallery Market houses specialty food shops in the lower level near the 8th and Market Streets subway stop.

Shopping hours at most of The Gallery are Monday to Saturday, 10 A.M. to 6 P.M., Wednesday till 9, and Sunday, 12 to 5.

John Wanamaker, at 13th and Market Streets, is center city's other major department store. Its bronze eagle in the splendid Grand Court has been a meeting place for generations of shoppers. Don't miss the Philadelphia tradition. Wanamaker's is open Monday to Saturday, 10 to 6, Wednesday night till 9, and Sunday 12 to 5.

Wednesday night is the night most stores remain open late in Philadelphia, and most are open late for holiday shoppers from Thanksgiving till Christmas.

Other major shops are in the area of **Bonwit Teller** at 17th and Chestnut Streets. Dozens of boutiques and specialty shops line Chestnut and Walnut Streets, especially in the streets near Rittenhouse Square. Fine European specialty stores surround **Nan Duskin** on the 1700 block of Walnut Street. ("When you walk into Nan Duskin, you're walking into another world.") And don't forget the shops at **NewMarket** in Society Hill and **The Bourse.**

The Marketplace Design Center at 2400 Market Street houses showrooms catering to designers and decorators. It's the place to go for ideas on the latest in home and office decor, but unless you're a qualified professional buyer, you'll be welcome to browse only. There's also a pleasant cafe for light dining.

The National Register of Historic Places is published by the U.S. Department of the Interior. It currently lists almost 45,000 sites and structures in the United States that are of architectural, cultural or historical importance.

A more selective list issued by the Department of the Interior specifies **National Historic Landmarks.** They come from the National Register, but are deemed more important because of their national significance.

There are almost 325 Philadelphia sites in the National Register and at least 240 local attractions are National Landmarks. Many of them are described in this book: the Academy of Music, John Bartram's House, Carpenters' Hall, City Hall, Cliveden, Elfreth's Alley, Founder's Hall at Girard College, NewMarket, Old Fort Mifflin, Pennsylvania Hospital, the U.S.S. Olympia and the Walnut Street Theater, to name a few.

Penn Center is west on Market Street from City Hall to 19th Street. What is now a complex of skyscraper buildings was once the Pennsylvania Railroad's Chinese Wall.

Penn Center Concourse is the underground complex of shops, banks and restaurants with access from Richardson Dilworth Plaza of City Hall, the Philadelphia Center Hotel, office buildings, Greyhound and SEPTA train and bus routes, and connecting by SEPTA commuter trains to the Market East station.

Penn Treaty Park, East Columbia Avenue and Beach Street, is where William Penn is believed to have signed his treaty with the Indians.

Philadelphia Scrapple. Get it fresh and spicy at Reading Terminal Market*.

The **Philadelphia soft pretzel.** Have some before you leave town. There's no other like them.

Richardson Dilworth Plaza is the wide-open, two-level vista with fountains, benches, trees and shrubs on City Hall's west side between the Municipal Services Building and Kennedy Boulevard, 15th Street and Penn Center, and the Girard Plaza Building on South Penn Square. It's another link to the Penn Center Concourse. The Plaza honors the late Mayor Richardson Dilworth, who led Philadelphia from 1956 to 1962.

Schuylkill River Park will encompass 44 acres along the east bank of the Schuylkill River from the Museum of Art south to South Street. Markward Playground at Taney and Pine Streets at the southern end of the park marks completion of the park's first stage. Work continues to the north of it.

Handy Phone Numbers.
Handy Addresses.

Philadelphia telephone area code: 215
Philadelphia ZIP code: 191 plus 2 digits

CHAMBER OF COMMERCE
Avenue of the Arts Building
1346 Chestnut Street, Phila., Pa. 19107
545-1234

CITY HALL
Broad and Market Streets, Phila., Pa. 19107
686-1776
Mayor's Office for Information
121 City Hall, 686-2250
Mayor's Action Center
143 City Hall, 686-3000

EDUCATION
School District of Philadelphia
Public Schools, 299-7000
Archdiocese of Philadelphia
Superintendent of Schools, 587-3700

EMERGENCIES
Police, Fire and Rescue
in life-and-death situation, 911
Police Assistance, 231-3131
Poison, 922-5523
Suicide, 686-4420
See the Blue Pages "Guide to Human Services" in the
back of the Bell of Pennsylvania Philadelphia phonebook.

FEDERAL INFORMATION CENTER
600 Arch Street, Phila., Pa. 19106
597-7042

FREE LIBRARY OF PHILADELPHIA
Central Library—Logan Square, Phila., Pa. 19103
686-5322

HEALTH
Handicapped (see Chapter 16)
Tel-Med, 829-5500
See the Blue Pages "Guide to Human Services" in the
back of the Bell of Pennsylvania Philadelphia phonebook.

**INDEPENDENCE NATIONAL
HISTORICAL PARK**
Independence Hall
6th and Chestnut Streets, 627-1776
Visitor Center
3rd and Chestnut Streets, 597-8974 or 597-8975

LEGAL INFORMATION
Philadelphia Bar Association
Dial-Law, 586-5900

**PHILADELPHIA CONVENTION
AND VISITORS BUREAU**
Visitors Center
1525 John F. Kennedy Boulevard, Phila., Pa. 19102
568-6599; Philly Fun Phone, 568-7255

PUBLIC TRANSPORTATION
Amtrak—intercity rail service, 824-1600
Greyhound Bus Lines, 568-4800
SEPTA, 574-7800
Trailways Bus System, 569-3100

SPORTS
Daily News and WIP Dial Sports, 976-1313 (toll call)
Philadelphia Inquirer Dial-A-Score, 563-2842
The Spectrum, 389-5000

TICKETS FOR SPORTS AND THEATER
Instant Charge, All Star-Forum, 735-5266
Teletron (charge sales), 627-0532
Ticketron, 885-2515

TRAVEL ASSISTANCE
International Visitors Center
Foreign Language Bank, 879-5248
Keystone Automobile Club
2040 Market Street, Phila., Pa. 19103
864-5000
Traveler's Aid Society
310 S. Juniper Street, Phila., Pa. 19107 (and branches)
546-0571

TIME	**WEATHER**
TIme 6-1212	WEather 6-1212

INDEX

486

491

493

Notes.

Notes.

Notes.